Lecture Notes in Computer Science   **14112**

The series Lecture Notes in Computer Science (LNCS), including its subseries Lecture Notes in Artificial Intelligence (LNAI) and Lecture Notes in Bioinformatics (LNBI), has established itself as a medium for the publication of new developments in computer science and information technology research, teaching, and education.

LNCS enjoys close cooperation with the computer science R & D community, the series counts many renowned academics among its volume editors and paper authors, and collaborates with prestigious societies. Its mission is to serve this international community by providing an invaluable service, mainly focused on the publication of conference and workshop proceedings and postproceedings. LNCS commenced publication in 1973.

Osvaldo Gervasi · Beniamino Murgante ·
Ana Maria A. C. Rocha · Chiara Garau ·
Francesco Scorza · Yeliz Karaca ·
Carmelo M. Torre
Editors

Computational Science and Its Applications – ICCSA 2023 Workshops

Athens, Greece, July 3–6, 2023
Proceedings, Part IX

Springer

Editors
Osvaldo Gervasi ⓘ
University of Perugia
Perugia, Italy

Ana Maria A. C. Rocha ⓘ
University of Minho
Braga, Portugal

Francesco Scorza ⓘ
University of Basilicata
Potenza, Italy

Carmelo M. Torre ⓘ
Polytechnic University of Bari
Bari, Italy

Beniamino Murgante ⓘ
University of Basilicata
Potenza, Italy

Chiara Garau ⓘ
University of Cagliari
Cagliari, Italy

Yeliz Karaca ⓘ
University of Massachusetts Medical School
Worcester, MA, USA

ISSN 0302-9743 ISSN 1611-3349 (electronic)
Lecture Notes in Computer Science
ISBN 978-3-031-37128-8 ISBN 978-3-031-37129-5 (eBook)
https://doi.org/10.1007/978-3-031-37129-5

This Springer imprint is published by the registered company Springer Nature Switzerland AG
The registered company address is: Gewerbestrasse 11, 6330 Cham, Switzerland

Preface

These 9 volumes (LNCS volumes 14104–14112) consist of the peer-reviewed papers from the 2023 International Conference on Computational Science and Its Applications (ICCSA 2023) which took place during July 3–6, 2023. The peer-reviewed papers of the main conference tracks were published in a separate set consisting of two volumes (LNCS 13956–13957).

The conference was finally held in person after the difficult period of the Covid-19 pandemic in the wonderful city of Athens, in the cosy facilities of the National Technical University. Our experience during the pandemic period allowed us to enable virtual participation also this year for those who were unable to attend the event, due to logistical, political and economic problems, by adopting a technological infrastructure based on open source software (jitsi + riot), and a commercial cloud infrastructure.

ICCSA 2023 was another successful event in the International Conference on Computational Science and Its Applications (ICCSA) series, previously held as a hybrid event (with one third of registered authors attending in person) in Malaga, Spain (2022), Cagliari, Italy (hybrid with few participants in person in 2021 and completely online in 2020), whilst earlier editions took place in Saint Petersburg, Russia (2019), Melbourne, Australia (2018), Trieste, Italy (2017), Beijing, China (2016), Banff, Canada (2015), Guimaraes, Portugal (2014), Ho Chi Minh City, Vietnam (2013), Salvador, Brazil (2012), Santander, Spain (2011), Fukuoka, Japan (2010), Suwon, South Korea (2009), Perugia, Italy (2008), Kuala Lumpur, Malaysia (2007), Glasgow, UK (2006), Singapore (2005), Assisi, Italy (2004), Montreal, Canada (2003), and (as ICCS) Amsterdam, The Netherlands (2002) and San Francisco, USA (2001).

Computational Science is the main pillar of most of the present research, industrial and commercial applications, and plays a unique role in exploiting ICT innovative technologies, and the ICCSA series have been providing a venue to researchers and industry practitioners to discuss new ideas, to share complex problems and their solutions, and to shape new trends in Computational Science. As the conference mirrors society from a scientific point of view, this year's undoubtedly dominant theme was the machine learning and artificial intelligence and their applications in the most diverse economic and industrial fields.

The ICCSA 2023 conference is structured in 6 general tracks covering the fields of computational science and its applications: Computational Methods, Algorithms and Scientific Applications – High Performance Computing and Networks – Geometric Modeling, Graphics and Visualization – Advanced and Emerging Applications – Information Systems and Technologies – Urban and Regional Planning. In addition, the conference consisted of 61 workshops, focusing on very topical issues of importance to science, technology and society: from new mathematical approaches for solving complex computational systems, to information and knowledge in the Internet of Things, new statistical and optimization methods, several Artificial Intelligence approaches, sustainability issues, smart cities and related technologies.

In the workshop proceedings we accepted 350 full papers, 29 short papers and 2 PHD Showcase papers. In the main conference proceedings we accepted 67 full papers, 13 short papers and 6 PHD Showcase papers from 283 submissions to the General Tracks of the conference (acceptance rate 30%). We would like to express our appreciation to the workshops chairs and co-chairs for their hard work and dedication.

The success of the ICCSA conference series in general, and of ICCSA 2023 in particular, vitally depends on the support of many people: authors, presenters, participants, keynote speakers, workshop chairs, session chairs, organizing committee members, student volunteers, Program Committee members, Advisory Committee members, International Liaison chairs, reviewers and others in various roles. We take this opportunity to wholehartedly thank them all.

We also wish to thank our publisher, Springer, for their acceptance to publish the proceedings, for sponsoring part of the best papers awards and for their kind assistance and cooperation during the editing process.

We cordially invite you to visit the ICCSA website https://iccsa.org where you can find all the relevant information about this interesting and exciting event.

July 2023

Osvaldo Gervasi
Beniamino Murgante
Chiara Garau

Welcome Message from Organizers

After the 2021 ICCSA in Cagliari, Italy and the 2022 ICCSA in Malaga, Spain, ICCSA continued its successful scientific endeavours in 2023, hosted again in the Mediterranean neighbourhood. This time, ICCSA 2023 moved a bit more to the east of the Mediterranean Region and was held in the metropolitan city of Athens, the capital of Greece and a vibrant urban environment endowed with a prominent cultural heritage that dates back to the ancient years. As a matter of fact, Athens is one of the oldest cities in the world, and the cradle of democracy. The city has a history of over 3,000 years and, according to the myth, it took its name from Athena, the Goddess of Wisdom and daughter of Zeus.

ICCSA 2023 took place in a secure environment, relieved from the immense stress of the COVID-19 pandemic. This gave us the chance to have a safe and vivid, in-person participation which, combined with the very active engagement of the ICCSA 2023 scientific community, set the ground for highly motivating discussions and interactions as to the latest developments of computer science and its applications in the real world for improving quality of life.

The National Technical University of Athens (NTUA), one of the most prestigious Greek academic institutions, had the honour of hosting ICCSA 2023. The Local Organizing Committee really feels the burden and responsibility of such a demanding task; and puts in all the necessary energy in order to meet participants' expectations and establish a friendly, creative and inspiring, scientific and social/cultural environment that allows for new ideas and perspectives to flourish.

Since all ICCSA participants, either informatics-oriented or application-driven, realize the tremendous steps and evolution of computer science during the last few decades and the huge potential these offer to cope with the enormous challenges of humanity in a globalized, 'wired' and highly competitive world, the expectations from ICCSA 2023 were set high in order for a successful matching between computer science progress and communities' aspirations to be attained, i.e., a progress that serves real, place- and people-based needs and can pave the way towards a visionary, smart, sustainable, resilient and inclusive future for both the current and the next generation.

On behalf of the Local Organizing Committee, I would like to sincerely thank all of you who have contributed to ICCSA 2023 and I cordially welcome you to my 'home', NTUA.

On behalf of the Local Organizing Committee.

Anastasia Stratigea

Organization

ICCSA 2023 was organized by the National Technical University of Athens (Greece), the University of the Aegean (Greece), the University of Perugia (Italy), the University of Basilicata (Italy), Monash University (Australia), Kyushu Sangyo University (Japan), the University of Minho (Portugal). The conference was supported by two NTUA Schools, namely the School of Rural, Surveying and Geoinformatics Engineering and the School of Electrical and Computer Engineering.

Honorary General Chairs

Norio Shiratori	Chuo University, Japan
Kenneth C. J. Tan	Sardina Systems, UK

General Chairs

Osvaldo Gervasi	University of Perugia, Italy
Anastasia Stratigea	National Technical University of Athens, Greece
Bernady O. Apduhan	Kyushu Sangyo University, Japan

Program Committee Chairs

Beniamino Murgante	University of Basilicata, Italy
Dimitris Kavroudakis	University of the Aegean, Greece
Ana Maria A. C. Rocha	University of Minho, Portugal
David Taniar	Monash University, Australia

International Advisory Committee

Jemal Abawajy	Deakin University, Australia
Dharma P. Agarwal	University of Cincinnati, USA
Rajkumar Buyya	Melbourne University, Australia
Claudia Bauzer Medeiros	University of Campinas, Brazil
Manfred M. Fisher	Vienna University of Economics and Business, Austria
Marina L. Gavrilova	University of Calgary, Canada

Sumi Helal   University of Florida, USA and University of
                                    Lancaster, UK
Yee Leung   Chinese University of Hong Kong, China

International Liaison Chairs

Ivan Blečić   University of Cagliari, Italy
Giuseppe Borruso   University of Trieste, Italy
Elise De Donker   Western Michigan University, USA
Maria Irene Falcão   University of Minho, Portugal
Inmaculada Garcia Fernandez   University of Malaga, Spain
Eligius Hendrix   University of Malaga, Spain
Robert C. H. Hsu   Chung Hua University, Taiwan
Tai-Hoon Kim   Beijing Jaotong University, China
Vladimir Korkhov   Saint Petersburg University, Russia
Takashi Naka   Kyushu Sangyo University, Japan
Rafael D. C. Santos   National Institute for Space Research, Brazil
Maribel Yasmina Santos   University of Minho, Portugal
Elena Stankova   Saint Petersburg University, Russia

Workshop and Session Organizing Chairs

Beniamino Murgante   University of Basilicata, Italy
Chiara Garau   University of Cagliari, Italy

Award Chair

Wenny Rahayu   La Trobe University, Australia

Publicity Committee Chairs

Elmer Dadios   De La Salle University, Philippines
Nataliia Kulabukhova   Saint Petersburg University, Russia
Daisuke Takahashi   Tsukuba University, Japan
Shangwang Wang   Beijing University of Posts and
                                    Telecommunications, China

Local Organizing Committee Chairs

Anastasia Stratigea	National Technical University of Athens, Greece
Dimitris Kavroudakis	University of the Aegean, Greece
Charalambos Ioannidis	National Technical University of Athens, Greece
Nectarios Koziris	National Technical University of Athens, Greece
Efthymios Bakogiannis	National Technical University of Athens, Greece
Yiota Theodora	National Technical University of Athens, Greece
Dimitris Fotakis	National Technical University of Athens, Greece
Apostolos Lagarias	National Technical University of Athens, Greece
Akrivi Leka	National Technical University of Athens, Greece
Dionisia Koutsi	National Technical University of Athens, Greece
Alkistis Dalkavouki	National Technical University of Athens, Greece
Maria Panagiotopoulou	National Technical University of Athens, Greece
Angeliki Papazoglou	National Technical University of Athens, Greece
Natalia Tsigarda	National Technical University of Athens, Greece
Konstantinos Athanasopoulos	National Technical University of Athens, Greece
Ioannis Xatziioannou	National Technical University of Athens, Greece
Vasiliki Krommyda	National Technical University of Athens, Greece
Panayiotis Patsilinakos	National Technical University of Athens, Greece
Sofia Kassiou	National Technical University of Athens, Greece

Technology Chair

Damiano Perri	University of Florence, Italy

Program Committee

Vera Afreixo	University of Aveiro, Portugal
Filipe Alvelos	University of Minho, Portugal
Hartmut Asche	University of Potsdam, Germany
Ginevra Balletto	University of Cagliari, Italy
Michela Bertolotto	University College Dublin, Ireland
Sandro Bimonte	CEMAGREF, TSCF, France
Rod Blais	University of Calgary, Canada
Ivan Blečić	University of Sassari, Italy
Giuseppe Borruso	University of Trieste, Italy
Ana Cristina Braga	University of Minho, Portugal
Massimo Cafaro	University of Salento, Italy
Yves Caniou	Lyon University, France

Ermanno Cardelli	University of Perugia, Italy
José A. Cardoso e Cunha	Universidade Nova de Lisboa, Portugal
Rui Cardoso	University of Beira Interior, Portugal
Leocadio G. Casado	University of Almeria, Spain
Carlo Cattani	University of Salerno, Italy
Mete Celik	Erciyes University, Turkey
Maria Cerreta	University of Naples "Federico II", Italy
Hyunseung Choo	Sungkyunkwan University, Korea
Rachel Chieng-Sing Lee	Sunway University, Malaysia
Min Young Chung	Sungkyunkwan University, Korea
Florbela Maria da Cruz Domingues Correia	Polytechnic Institute of Viana do Castelo, Portugal
Gilberto Corso Pereira	Federal University of Bahia, Brazil
Alessandro Costantini	INFN, Italy
Carla Dal Sasso Freitas	Universidade Federal do Rio Grande do Sul, Brazil
Pradesh Debba	The Council for Scientific and Industrial Research (CSIR), South Africa
Hendrik Decker	Instituto Tecnológico de Informática, Spain
Robertas Damaševičius	Kausan University of Technology, Lithuania
Frank Devai	London South Bank University, UK
Rodolphe Devillers	Memorial University of Newfoundland, Canada
Joana Matos Dias	University of Coimbra, Portugal
Paolino Di Felice	University of L'Aquila, Italy
Prabu Dorairaj	NetApp, India/USA
Noelia Faginas Lago	University of Perugia, Italy
M. Irene Falcao	University of Minho, Portugal
Cherry Liu Fang	U.S. DOE Ames Laboratory, USA
Florbela P. Fernandes	Polytechnic Institute of Bragança, Portugal
Jose-Jesus Fernandez	National Centre for Biotechnology, CSIS, Spain
Paula Odete Fernandes	Polytechnic Institute of Bragança, Portugal
Adelaide de Fátima Baptista Valente Freitas	University of Aveiro, Portugal
Manuel Carlos Figueiredo	University of Minho, Portugal
Maria Celia Furtado Rocha	PRODEB–PósCultura/UFBA, Brazil
Chiara Garau	University of Cagliari, Italy
Paulino Jose Garcia Nieto	University of Oviedo, Spain
Raffaele Garrisi	Polizia di Stato, Italy
Jerome Gensel	LSR-IMAG, France
Maria Giaoutzi	National Technical University, Athens, Greece
Arminda Manuela Andrade Pereira Gonçalves	University of Minho, Portugal

Andrzej M. Goscinski   Deakin University, Australia
Sevin Gümgüm   Izmir University of Economics, Turkey
Alex Hagen-Zanker   University of Cambridge, UK
Shanmugasundaram Hariharan   B.S. Abdur Rahman University, India
Eligius M. T. Hendrix   University of Malaga, Spain and Wageningen
                              University, The Netherlands
Hisamoto Hiyoshi   Gunma University, Japan
Mustafa Inceoglu   EGE University, Turkey
Peter Jimack   University of Leeds, UK
Qun Jin   Waseda University, Japan
Yeliz Karaca   University of Massachusetts Medical School,
                              Worcester, USA
Farid Karimipour   Vienna University of Technology, Austria
Baris Kazar   Oracle Corp., USA
Maulana Adhinugraha Kiki   Telkom University, Indonesia
DongSeong Kim   University of Canterbury, New Zealand
Taihoon Kim   Hannam University, Korea
Ivana Kolingerova   University of West Bohemia, Czech Republic
Nataliia Kulabukhova   St. Petersburg University, Russia
Vladimir Korkhov   St. Petersburg University, Russia
Rosa Lasaponara   National Research Council, Italy
Maurizio Lazzari   National Research Council, Italy
Cheng Siong Lee   Monash University, Australia
Sangyoun Lee   Yonsei University, Korea
Jongchan Lee   Kunsan National University, Korea
Chendong Li   University of Connecticut, USA
Gang Li   Deakin University, Australia
Fang Liu   AMES Laboratories, USA
Xin Liu   University of Calgary, Canada
Andrea Lombardi   University of Perugia, Italy
Savino Longo   University of Bari, Italy
Tinghuai Ma   Nanjing University of Information Science &
                              Technology, China
Ernesto Marcheggiani   Katholieke Universiteit Leuven, Belgium
Antonino Marvuglia   Research Centre Henri Tudor, Luxembourg
Nicola Masini   National Research Council, Italy
Ilaria Matteucci   National Research Council, Italy
Nirvana Meratnia   University of Twente, The Netherlands
Fernando Miranda   University of Minho, Portugal
Giuseppe Modica   University of Reggio Calabria, Italy
Josè Luis Montaña   University of Cantabria, Spain
Maria Filipa Mourão   Instituto Politécnico de Viana do Castelo, Portugal

Giuseppe A. Trunfio	University of Sassari, Italy
Pablo Vanegas	University of Cuenca, Equador
Marco Vizzari	University of Perugia, Italy
Varun Vohra	Merck Inc., USA
Koichi Wada	University of Tsukuba, Japan
Krzysztof Walkowiak	Wroclaw University of Technology, Poland
Zequn Wang	Intelligent Automation Inc, USA
Robert Weibel	University of Zurich, Switzerland
Frank Westad	Norwegian University of Science and Technology, Norway
Roland Wismüller	Universität Siegen, Germany
Mudasser Wyne	SOET National University, USA
Chung-Huang Yang	National Kaohsiung Normal University, Taiwan
Xin-She Yang	National Physical Laboratory, UK
Salim Zabir	France Telecom Japan Co., Japan
Haifeng Zhao	University of California, Davis, USA
Fabiana Zollo	University of Venice "Cà Foscari", Italy
Albert Y. Zomaya	University of Sydney, Australia

Workshop Organizers

Advanced Data Science Techniques with Applications in Industry and Environmental Sustainability (ATELIERS 2023)

Dario Torregrossa	Goodyear, Luxemburg
Antonino Marvuglia	Luxembourg Institute of Science and Technology, Luxemburg
Valeria Borodin	École des Mines de Saint-Étienne, Luxemburg
Mohamed Laib	Luxembourg Institute of Science and Technology, Luxemburg

Advances in Artificial Intelligence Learning Technologies: Blended Learning, STEM, Computational Thinking and Coding (AAILT 2023)

Alfredo Milani	University of Perugia, Italy
Valentina Franzoni	University of Perugia, Italy
Sergio Tasso	University of Perugia, Italy

Advanced Processes of Mathematics and Computing Models in Complex Computational Systems (ACMC 2023)

Yeliz Karaca	University of Massachusetts Chan Medical School and Massachusetts Institute of Technology, USA
Dumitru Baleanu	Cankaya University, Turkey
Osvaldo Gervasi	University of Perugia, Italy
Yudong Zhang	University of Leicester, UK
Majaz Moonis	University of Massachusetts Medical School, USA

Artificial Intelligence Supported Medical Data Examination (AIM 2023)

David Taniar	Monash University, Australia
Seifedine Kadry	Noroff University College, Norway
Venkatesan Rajinikanth	Saveetha School of Engineering, India

Advanced and Innovative Web Apps (AIWA 2023)

Damiano Perri	University of Perugia, Italy
Osvaldo Gervasi	University of Perugia, Italy

Assessing Urban Sustainability (ASUS 2023)

Elena Todella	Polytechnic of Turin, Italy
Marika Gaballo	Polytechnic of Turin, Italy
Beatrice Mecca	Polytechnic of Turin, Italy

Advances in Web Based Learning (AWBL 2023)

Birol Ciloglugil	Ege University, Turkey
Mustafa Inceoglu	Ege University, Turkey

Blockchain and Distributed Ledgers: Technologies and Applications (BDLTA 2023)

Vladimir Korkhov   Saint Petersburg State University, Russia
Elena Stankova   Saint Petersburg State University, Russia
Nataliia Kulabukhova   Saint Petersburg State University, Russia

Bio and Neuro Inspired Computing and Applications (BIONCA 2023)

Nadia Nedjah   State University of Rio De Janeiro, Brazil
Luiza De Macedo Mourelle   State University of Rio De Janeiro, Brazil

Choices and Actions for Human Scale Cities: Decision Support Systems (CAHSC–DSS 2023)

Giovanna Acampa   University of Florence and University of Enna Kore, Italy
Fabrizio Finucci   Roma Tre University, Italy
Luca S. Dacci   Polytechnic of Turin, Italy

Computational and Applied Mathematics (CAM 2023)

Maria Irene Falcao   University of Minho, Portugal
Fernando Miranda   University of Minho, Portugal

Computational and Applied Statistics (CAS 2023)

Ana Cristina Braga   University of Minho, Portugal

Cyber Intelligence and Applications (CIA 2023)

Gianni Dangelo   University of Salerno, Italy
Francesco Palmieri   University of Salerno, Italy
Massimo Ficco   University of Salerno, Italy

Conversations South-North on Climate Change Adaptation Towards Smarter and More Sustainable Cities (CLAPS 2023)

Chiara Garau	University of Cagliari, Italy
Cristina Trois	University of kwaZulu-Natal, South Africa
Claudia Loggia	University of kwaZulu-Natal, South Africa
John Östh	Faculty of Technology, Art and Design, Norway
Mauro Coni	University of Cagliari, Italy
Alessio Satta	MedSea Foundation, Italy

Computational Mathematics, Statistics and Information Management (CMSIM 2023)

Maria Filomena Teodoro	University of Lisbon and Portuguese Naval Academy, Portugal
Marina A. P. Andrade	University Institute of Lisbon, Portugal

Computational Optimization and Applications (COA 2023)

Ana Maria A. C. Rocha	University of Minho, Portugal
Humberto Rocha	University of Coimbra, Portugal

Computational Astrochemistry (CompAstro 2023)

Marzio Rosi	University of Perugia, Italy
Nadia Balucani	University of Perugia, Italy
Cecilia Ceccarelli	University of Grenoble Alpes and Institute for Planetary Sciences and Astrophysics, France
Stefano Falcinelli	University of Perugia, Italy

Computational Methods for Porous Geomaterials (CompPor 2023)

Vadim Lisitsa	Russian Academy of Science, Russia
Evgeniy Romenski	Russian Academy of Science, Russia

Workshop on Computational Science and HPC (CSHPC 2023)

Elise De Doncker	Western Michigan University, USA
Fukuko Yuasa	High Energy Accelerator Research Organization, Japan
Hideo Matsufuru	High Energy Accelerator Research Organization, Japan

Cities, Technologies and Planning (CTP 2023)

Giuseppe Borruso	University of Trieste, Italy
Beniamino Murgante	University of Basilicata, Italy
Malgorzata Hanzl	Lodz University of Technology, Poland
Anastasia Stratigea	National Technical University of Athens, Greece
Ljiljana Zivkovic	Republic Geodetic Authority, Serbia
Ginevra Balletto	University of Cagliari, Italy

Gender Equity/Equality in Transport and Mobility (DELIA 2023)

Tiziana Campisi	University of Enna Kore, Italy
Ines Charradi	Sousse University, Tunisia
Alexandros Nikitas	University of Huddersfield, UK
Kh Md Nahiduzzaman	University of British Columbia, Canada
Andreas Nikiforiadis	Aristotle University of Thessaloniki, Greece
Socrates Basbas	Aristotle University of Thessaloniki, Greece

International Workshop on Defense Technology and Security (DTS 2023)

Yeonseung Ryu	Myongji University, South Korea

Integrated Methods for the Ecosystem-Services Accounting in Urban Decision Process (Ecourbn 2023)

Maria Rosaria Guarini	Sapienza University of Rome, Italy
Francesco Sica	Sapienza University of Rome, Italy
Francesco Tajani	Sapienza University of Rome, Italy

Carmelo Maria Torre	Polytechnic University of Bari, Italy
Pierluigi Morano	Polytechnic University of Bari, Italy
Rossana Ranieri	Sapienza Università di Roma, Italy

Evaluating Inner Areas Potentials (EIAP 2023)

Diana Rolando	Politechnic of Turin, Italy
Manuela Rebaudengo	Politechnic of Turin, Italy
Alice Barreca	Politechnic of Turin, Italy
Giorgia Malavasi	Politechnic of Turin, Italy
Umberto Mecca	Politechnic of Turin, Italy

Sustainable Mobility Last Mile Logistic (ELLIOT 2023)

Tiziana Campisi	University of Enna Kore, Italy
Socrates Basbas	Aristotle University of Thessaloniki, Greece
Grigorios Fountas	Aristotle University of Thessaloniki, Greece
Paraskevas Nikolaou	University of Cyprus, Cyprus
Drazenko Glavic	University of Belgrade, Serbia
Antonio Russo	University of Enna Kore, Italy

Econometrics and Multidimensional Evaluation of Urban Environment (EMEUE 2023)

Maria Cerreta	University of Naples Federico II, Italy
Carmelo Maria Torre	Politechnic of Bari, Italy
Pierluigi Morano	Polytechnic of Bari, Italy
Debora Anelli	Polytechnic of Bari, Italy
Francesco Tajani	Sapienza University of Rome, Italy
Simona Panaro	University of Sussex, UK

Ecosystem Services in Spatial Planning for Resilient Urban and Rural Areas (ESSP 2023)

Sabrina Lai	University of Cagliari, Italy
Francesco Scorza	University of Basilicata, Italy
Corrado Zoppi	University of Cagliari, Italy

Gerardo Carpentieri   University of Naples Federico II, Italy
Floriana Zucaro   University of Naples Federico II, Italy
Ana Clara Mourão Moura   Federal University of Minas Gerais, Brazil

Ethical AI Applications for a Human-Centered Cyber Society (EthicAI 2023)

Valentina Franzoni   University of Perugia, Italy
Alfredo Milani   University of Perugia, Italy
Jordi Vallverdu   University Autonoma Barcelona, Spain
Roberto Capobianco   Sapienza University of Rome, Italy

13th International Workshop on Future Computing System Technologies and Applications (FiSTA 2023)

Bernady Apduhan   Kyushu Sangyo University, Japan
Rafael Santos   National Institute for Space Research, Brazil

Collaborative Planning and Designing for the Future with Geospatial Applications (GeoCollab 2023)

Alenka Poplin   Iowa State University, USA
Rosanna Rivero   University of Georgia, USA
Michele Campagna   University of Cagliari, Italy
Ana Clara Mourão Moura   Federal University of Minas Gerais, Brazil

Geomatics in Agriculture and Forestry: New Advances and Perspectives (GeoForAgr 2023)

Maurizio Pollino   Italian National Agency for New Technologies,
                                  Energy and Sustainable Economic
                                  Development, Italy
Giuseppe Modica   University of Reggio Calabria, Italy
Marco Vizzari   University of Perugia, Italy
Salvatore Praticò   University of Reggio Calabria, Italy

Geographical Analysis, Urban Modeling, Spatial Statistics (Geog-An-Mod 2023)

Giuseppe Borruso	University of Trieste, Italy
Beniamino Murgante	University of Basilicata, Italy
Harmut Asche	Hasso-Plattner-Institut für Digital Engineering Ggmbh, Germany

Geomatics for Resource Monitoring and Management (GRMM 2023)

Alessandra Capolupo	Polytechnic of Bari, Italy
Eufemia Tarantino	Polytechnic of Bari, Italy
Enrico Borgogno Mondino	University of Turin, Italy

International Workshop on Information and Knowledge in the Internet of Things (IKIT 2023)

Teresa Guarda	Peninsula State University of Santa Elena, Ecuador
Modestos Stavrakis	University of the Aegean, Greece

International Workshop on Collective, Massive and Evolutionary Systems (IWCES 2023)

Alfredo Milani	University of Perugia, Italy
Rajdeep Niyogi	Indian Institute of Technology, India
Valentina Franzoni	University of Perugia, Italy

Multidimensional Evolutionary Evaluations for Transformative Approaches (MEETA 2023)

Maria Cerreta	University of Naples Federico II, Italy
Giuliano Poli	University of Naples Federico II, Italy
Ludovica Larocca	University of Naples Federico II, Italy
Chiara Mazzarella	University of Naples Federico II, Italy

Stefania Regalbuto — University of Naples Federico II, Italy
Maria Somma — University of Naples Federico II, Italy

Building Multi-dimensional Models for Assessing Complex Environmental Systems (MES 2023)

Marta Dell'Ovo — Politechnic of Milan, Italy
Vanessa Assumma — University of Bologna, Italy
Caterina Caprioli — Politechnic of Turin, Italy
Giulia Datola — Politechnic of Turin, Italy
Federico Dellanna — Politechnic of Turin, Italy
Marco Rossitti — Politechnic of Milan, Italy

Metropolitan City Lab (Metro_City_Lab 2023)

Ginevra Balletto — University of Cagliari, Italy
Luigi Mundula — University for Foreigners of Perugia, Italy
Giuseppe Borruso — University of Trieste, Italy
Jacopo Torriti — University of Reading, UK
Isabella Ligia — Metropolitan City of Cagliari, Italy

Mathematical Methods for Image Processing and Understanding (MMIPU 2023)

Ivan Gerace — University of Perugia, Italy
Gianluca Vinti — University of Perugia, Italy
Arianna Travaglini — University of Florence, Italy

Models and Indicators for Assessing and Measuring the Urban Settlement Development in the View of ZERO Net Land Take by 2050 (MOVEto0 2023)

Lucia Saganeiti — University of L'Aquila, Italy
Lorena Fiorini — University of L'Aquila, Italy
Angela Pilogallo — University of L'Aquila, Italy
Alessandro Marucci — University of L'Aquila, Italy
Francesco Zullo — University of L'Aquila, Italy

Modelling Post-Covid Cities (MPCC 2023)

Giuseppe Borruso	University of Trieste, Italy
Beniamino Murgante	University of Basilicata, Italy
Ginevra Balletto	University of Cagliari, Italy
Lucia Saganeiti	University of L'Aquila, Italy
Marco Dettori	University of Sassari, Italy

3rd Workshop on Privacy in the Cloud/Edge/IoT World (PCEIoT 2023)

Michele Mastroianni	University of Salerno, Italy
Lelio Campanile	University of Campania Luigi Vanvitelli, Italy
Mauro Iacono	University of Campania Luigi Vanvitelli, Italy

Port City Interface: Land Use, Logistic and Rear Port Area Planning (PORTUNO 2023)

Tiziana Campisi	University of Enna Kore, Italy
Socrates Basbas	Aristotle University of Thessaloniki, Greece
Efstathios Bouhouras	Aristotle University of Thessaloniki, Greece
Giovanni Tesoriere	University of Enna Kore, Italy
Elena Cocuzza	University of Catania, Italy
Gianfranco Fancello	University of Cagliari, Italy

Scientific Computing Infrastructure (SCI 2023)

| Elena Stankova | St. Petersburg State University, Russia |
| Vladimir Korkhov | St. Petersburg University, Russia |

Supply Chains, IoT, and Smart Technologies (SCIS 2023)

Ha Jin Hwang	Sunway University, South Korea
Hangkon Kim	Daegu Catholic University, South Korea
Jan Seruga	Australian Catholic University, Australia

Spatial Cognition in Urban and Regional Planning Under Risk (SCOPUR23)

Domenico Camarda	Polytechnic of Bari, Italy
Giulia Mastrodonato	Polytechnic of Bari, Italy
Stefania Santoro	Polytechnic of Bari, Italy
Maria Rosaria Stufano Melone	Polytechnic of Bari, Italy
Mauro Patano	Polytechnic of Bari, Italy

Socio-Economic and Environmental Models for Land Use Management (SEMLUM 2023)

Debora Anelli	Polytechnic of Bari, Italy
Pierluigi Morano	Polytechnic of Bari, Italy
Benedetto Manganelli	University of Basilicata, Italy
Francesco Tajani	Sapienza University of Rome, Italy
Marco Locurcio	Polytechnic of Bari, Italy
Felicia Di Liddo	Polytechnic of Bari, Italy

Ports of the Future - Smartness and Sustainability (SmartPorts 2023)

Ginevra Balletto	University of Cagliari, Italy
Gianfranco Fancello	University of Cagliari, Italy
Patrizia Serra	University of Cagliari, Italy
Agostino Bruzzone	University of Genoa, Italy
Alberto Camarero	Politechnic of Madrid, Spain
Thierry Vanelslander	University of Antwerp, Belgium

Smart Transport and Logistics - Smart Supply Chains (SmarTransLog 2023)

Giuseppe Borruso	University of Trieste, Italy
Marco Mazzarino	University of Venice, Italy
Marcello Tadini	University of Eastern Piedmont, Italy
Luigi Mundula	University for Foreigners of Perugia, Italy
Mara Ladu	University of Cagliari, Italy
Maria del Mar Munoz Leonisio	University of Cadiz, Spain

Smart Tourism (SmartTourism 2023)

Giuseppe Borruso	University of Trieste, Italy
Silvia Battino	University of Sassari, Italy
Ainhoa Amaro Garcia	University of Alcala and University of Las Palmas, Spain
Francesca Krasna	University of Trieste, Italy
Ginevra Balletto	University of Cagliari, Italy
Maria del Mar Munoz Leonisio	University of Cadiz, Spain

Sustainability Performance Assessment: Models, Approaches, and Applications Toward Interdisciplinary and Integrated Solutions (SPA 2023)

Sabrina Lai	University of Cagliari, Italy
Francesco Scorza	University of Basilicata, Italy
Jolanta Dvarioniene	Kaunas University of Technology, Lithuania
Valentin Grecu	Lucian Blaga University of Sibiu, Romania
Georgia Pozoukidou	Aristotle University of Thessaloniki, Greece

Spatial Energy Planning, City and Urban Heritage (Spatial_Energy_City 2023)

Ginevra Balletto	University of Cagliari, Italy
Mara Ladu	University of Cagliari, Italy
Emilio Ghiani	University of Cagliari, Italy
Roberto De Lotto	University of Pavia, Italy
Roberto Gerundo	University of Salerno, Italy

Specifics of Smart Cities Development in Europe (SPEED 2023)

Chiara Garau	University of Cagliari, Italy
Katarína Vitálišová	Matej Bel University, Slovakia
Paolo Nesi	University of Florence, Italy
Anna Vaňová	Matej Bel University, Slovakia
Kamila Borsekova	Matej Bel University, Slovakia
Paola Zamperlin	University of Pisa, Italy

Smart, Safe and Health Cities (SSHC 2023)

Chiara Garau	University of Cagliari, Italy
Gerardo Carpentieri	University of Naples Federico II, Italy
Floriana Zucaro	University of Naples Federico II, Italy
Aynaz Lotfata	Chicago State University, USA
Alfonso Annunziata	University of Basilicata, Italy
Diego Altafini	University of Pisa, Italy

Smart and Sustainable Island Communities (SSIC_2023)

Chiara Garau	University of Cagliari, Italy
Anastasia Stratigea	National Technical University of Athens, Greece
Yiota Theodora	National Technical University of Athens, Greece
Giulia Desogus	University of Cagliari, Italy

Theoretical and Computational Chemistry and Its Applications (TCCMA 2023)

Noelia Faginas-Lago	University of Perugia, Italy
Andrea Lombardi	University of Perugia, Italy

Transport Infrastructures for Smart Cities (TISC 2023)

Francesca Maltinti	University of Cagliari, Italy
Mauro Coni	University of Cagliari, Italy
Francesco Pinna	University of Cagliari, Italy
Chiara Garau	University of Cagliari, Italy
Nicoletta Rassu	University of Cagliari, Italy
James Rombi	University of Cagliari, Italy

Urban Regeneration: Innovative Tools and Evaluation Model (URITEM 2023)

Fabrizio Battisti	University of Florence, Italy
Giovanna Acampa	University of Florence and University of Enna Kore, Italy
Orazio Campo	La Sapienza University of Rome, Italy

Urban Space Accessibility and Mobilities (USAM 2023)

Chiara Garau   University of Cagliari, Italy
Matteo Ignaccolo   University of Catania, Italy
Michela Tiboni   University of Brescia, Italy
Francesco Pinna   University of Cagliari, Italy
Silvia Rossetti   University of Parma, Italy
Vincenza Torrisi   University of Catania, Italy
Ilaria Delponte   University of Genoa, Italy

Virtual Reality and Augmented Reality and Applications (VRA 2023)

Osvaldo Gervasi   University of Perugia, Italy
Damiano Perri   University of Florence, Italy
Marco Simonetti   University of Florence, Italy
Sergio Tasso   University of Perugia, Italy

Workshop on Advanced and Computational Methods for Earth Science Applications (WACM4ES 2023)

Luca Piroddi   University of Malta, Malta
Sebastiano Damico   University of Malta, Malta
Marilena Cozzolino   Università del Molise, Italy
Adam Gauci   University of Malta, Italy
Giuseppina Vacca   University of Cagliari, Italy
Chiara Garau   University of Cagliari, Italy

Sponsoring Organizations

ICCSA 2023 would not have been possible without the tremendous support of many organizations and institutions, for which all organizers and participants of ICCSA 2023 express their sincere gratitude:

 Springer Nature Switzerland AG, Switzerland
(https://www.springer.com)

computers Computers Open Access Journal
(https://www.mdpi.com/journal/computers)

 National Technical University of Athens, Greece
(https://www.ntua.gr/)

 University of the Aegean, Greece
(https://www.aegean.edu/)

 University of Perugia, Italy
(https://www.unipg.it)

 University of Basilicata, Italy
(http://www.unibas.it)

 MONASH University

Monash University, Australia
(https://www.monash.edu/)

 **K U**
九州産業大学
KYUSHU SANGYO UNIVERSITY

Kyushu Sangyo University, Japan
(https://www.kyusan-u.ac.jp/)

Universidade do Minho
Escola de Engenharia

University of Minho, Portugal
(https://www.uminho.pt/)

Referees

Francesca Abastante	Turin Polytechnic, Italy
Giovanna Acampa	University of Enna Kore, Italy
Adewole Adewumi	Algonquin College, Canada
Vera Afreixo	University of Aveiro, Portugal
Riad Aggoune	Luxembourg Institute of Science and Technology, Luxembourg
Akshat Agrawal	Amity University Haryana, India
Waseem Ahmad	National Institute of Technology Karnataka, India
Oylum Alatlı	Ege University, Turkey
Abraham Alfa	Federal University of Technology Minna, Nigeria
Diego Altafini	University of Pisa, Italy
Filipe Alvelos	University of Minho, Portugal
Marina Alexandra Pedro Andrade	University Institute of Lisbon, Portugal
Debora Anelli	Polytechnic University of Bari, Italy
Mariarosaria Angrisano	Pegaso University, Italy
Alfonso Annunziata	University of Cagliari, Italy
Magarò Antonio	Sapienza University of Rome, Italy
Bernady Apduhan	Kyushu Sangyo University, Japan
Jonathan Apeh	Covenant University, Nigeria
Daniela Ascenzi	University of Trento, Italy
Vanessa Assumma	University of Bologna, Italy
Maria Fernanda Augusto	Bitrum Research Center, Spain
Marco Baioletti	University of Perugia, Italy

Ginevra Balletto	University of Cagliari, Italy
Carlos Balsa	Polytechnic Institute of Bragança, Portugal
Benedetto Barabino	University of Brescia, Italy
Simona Barbaro	University of Palermo, Italy
Sebastiano Barbieri	Turin Polytechnic, Italy
Kousik Barik	University of Alcala, Spain
Alice Barreca	Turin Polytechnic, Italy
Socrates Basbas	Aristotle University of Thessaloniki, Greece
Rosaria Battarra	National Research Council, Italy
Silvia Battino	University of Sassari, Italy
Fabrizio Battisti	University of Florence, Italy
Yaroslav Bazaikin	Jan Evangelista Purkyne University, Czech Republic
Ranjan Kumar Behera	Indian Institute of Information Technology, India
Simone Belli	Complutense University of Madrid, Spain
Oscar Bellini	Polytechnic University of Milan, Italy
Giulio Biondi	University of Perugia, Italy
Adriano Bisello	Eurac Research, Italy
Semen Bochkov	Ulyanovsk State Technical University, Russia
Alexander Bogdanov	St. Petersburg State University, Russia
Letizia Bollini	Free University of Bozen, Italy
Giuseppe Borruso	University of Trieste, Italy
Marilisa Botte	University of Naples Federico II, Italy
Ana Cristina Braga	University of Minho, Portugal
Frederico Branco	University of Trás-os-Montes and Alto Douro, Portugal
Jorge Buele	Indoamérica Technological University, Ecuador
Datzania Lizeth Burgos	Peninsula State University of Santa Elena, Ecuador
Isabel Cacao	University of Aveiro, Portugal
Francesco Calabrò	Mediterranea University of Reggio Calabria, Italy
Rogerio Calazan	Institute of Sea Studies Almirante Paulo Moreira, Brazil
Lelio Campanile	University of Campania Luigi Vanvitelli, Italy
Tiziana Campisi	University of Enna Kore, Italy
Orazio Campo	University of Rome La Sapienza, Italy
Caterina Caprioli	Turin Polytechnic, Italy
Gerardo Carpentieri	University of Naples Federico II, Italy
Martina Carra	University of Brescia, Italy
Barbara Caselli	University of Parma, Italy
Danny Casprini	Politechnic of Milan, Italy

Omar Fernando Castellanos Balleteros	Peninsula State University of Santa Elena, Ecuador
Arcangelo Castiglione	University of Salerno, Italy
Giulio Cavana	Turin Polytechnic, Italy
Maria Cerreta	University of Naples Federico II, Italy
Sabarathinam Chockalingam	Institute for Energy Technology, Norway
Luis Enrique Chuquimarca Jimenez	Peninsula State University of Santa Elena, Ecuador
Birol Ciloglugil	Ege University, Turkey
Elena Cocuzza	Univesity of Catania, Italy
Emanuele Colica	University of Malta, Malta
Mauro Coni	University of Cagliari, Italy
Simone Corrado	University of Basilicata, Italy
Elisete Correia	University of Trás-os-Montes and Alto Douro, Portugal
Florbela Correia	Polytechnic Institute Viana do Castelo, Portugal
Paulo Cortez	University of Minho, Portugal
Martina Corti	Politechnic of Milan, Italy
Lino Costa	Universidade do Minho, Portugal
Cecília Maria Vasconcelos Costa e Castro	University of Minho, Portugal
Alfredo Cuzzocrea	University of Calabria, Italy
Sebastiano D'amico	University of Malta, Malta
Maria Danese	National Research Council, Italy
Gianni Dangelo	University of Salerno, Italy
Ana Daniel	Aveiro University, Portugal
Giulia Datola	Politechnic of Milan, Italy
Regina De Almeida	University of Trás-os-Montes and Alto Douro, Portugal
Maria Stella De Biase	University of Campania Luigi Vanvitelli, Italy
Elise De Doncker	Western Michigan University, USA
Luiza De Macedo Mourelle	State University of Rio de Janeiro, Brazil
Itamir De Morais Barroca Filho	Federal University of Rio Grande do Norte, Brazil
Pierfrancesco De Paola	University of Naples Federico II, Italy
Francesco De Pascale	University of Turin, Italy
Manuela De Ruggiero	University of Calabria, Italy
Alexander Degtyarev	St. Petersburg State University, Russia
Federico Dellanna	Turin Polytechnic, Italy
Marta Dellovo	Politechnic of Milan, Italy
Bashir Derradji	Sfax University, Tunisia
Giulia Desogus	University of Cagliari, Italy
Frank Devai	London South Bank University, UK

Piero Di Bonito	University of Campania Luigi Vanvitelli, Italy
Chiara Di Dato	University of L'Aquila, Italy
Michele Di Giovanni	University of Campania Luigi Vanvitelli, Italy
Felicia Di Liddo	Polytechnic University of Bari, Italy
Joana Dias	University of Coimbra, Portugal
Luigi Dolores	University of Salerno, Italy
Marco Donatelli	University of Insubria, Italy
Aziz Dursun	Virginia Tech University, USA
Jaroslav Dvořak	Klaipeda University, Lithuania
Wolfgang Erb	University of Padova, Italy
Maurizio Francesco Errigo	University of Enna Kore, Italy
Noelia Faginas-Lago	University of Perugia, Italy
Maria Irene Falcao	University of Minho, Portugal
Stefano Falcinelli	University of Perugia, Italy
Grazia Fattoruso	Italian National Agency for New Technologies, Energy and Sustainable Economic Development, Italy
Sara Favargiotti	University of Trento, Italy
Marcin Feltynowski	University of Lodz, Poland
António Fernandes	Polytechnic Institute of Bragança, Portugal
Florbela P. Fernandes	Polytechnic Institute of Bragança, Portugal
Paula Odete Fernandes	Polytechnic Institute of Bragança, Portugal
Luis Fernandez-Sanz	University of Alcala, Spain
Maria Eugenia Ferrao	University of Beira Interior and University of Lisbon, Portugal
Luís Ferrás	University of Minho, Portugal
Angela Ferreira	Polytechnic Institute of Bragança, Portugal
Maddalena Ferretti	Politechnic of Marche, Italy
Manuel Carlos Figueiredo	University of Minho, Portugal
Fabrizio Finucci	Roma Tre University, Italy
Ugo Fiore	University Pathenope of Naples, Italy
Lorena Fiorini	University of L'Aquila, Italy
Valentina Franzoni	Perugia University, Italy
Adelaide Freitas	University of Aveiro, Portugal
Kirill Gadylshin	Russian Academy of Sciences, Russia
Andrea Gallo	University of Trieste, Italy
Luciano Galone	University of Malta, Malta
Chiara Garau	University of Cagliari, Italy
Ernesto Garcia Para	Universidad del País Vasco, Spain
Rachele Vanessa Gatto	Università della Basilicata, Italy
Marina Gavrilova	University of Calgary, Canada
Georgios Georgiadis	Aristotle University of Thessaloniki, Greece

Ivan Gerace	University of Perugia, Italy
Osvaldo Gervasi	University of Perugia, Italy
Alfonso Giancotti	Sapienza University of Rome, Italy
Andrea Gioia	Politechnic of Bari, Italy
Giacomo Giorgi	University of Perugia, Italy
Salvatore Giuffrida	Università di Catania, Italy
A. Manuela Gonçalves	University of Minho, Portugal
Angela Gorgoglione	University of the Republic, Uruguay
Yusuke Gotoh	Okayama University, Japan
Mariolina Grasso	University of Enna Kore, Italy
Silvana Grillo	University of Cagliari, Italy
Teresa Guarda	Universidad Estatal Peninsula de Santa Elena, Ecuador
Eduardo Guerra	Free University of Bozen-Bolzano, Italy
Carmen Guida	University of Napoli Federico II, Italy
Kemal Güven Gülen	Namık Kemal University, Turkey
Malgorzata Hanzl	Technical University of Lodz, Poland
Peter Hegedus	University of Szeged, Hungary
Syeda Sumbul Hossain	Daffodil International University, Bangladesh
Mustafa Inceoglu	Ege University, Turkey
Federica Isola	University of Cagliari, Italy
Seifedine Kadry	Noroff University College, Norway
Yeliz Karaca	University of Massachusetts Chan Medical School and Massachusetts Institute of Technology, USA
Harun Karsli	Bolu Abant Izzet Baysal University, Turkey
Tayana Khachkova	Russian Academy of Sciences, Russia
Manju Khari	Jawaharlal Nehru University, India
Vladimir Korkhov	Saint Petersburg State University, Russia
Dionisia Koutsi	National Technical University of Athens, Greece
Tomonori Kouya	Shizuoka Institute of Science and Technology, Japan
Nataliia Kulabukhova	Saint Petersburg State University, Russia
Anisha Kumari	National Institute of Technology, India
Ludovica La Rocca	University of Napoli Federico II, Italy
Mara Ladu	University of Cagliari, Italy
Sabrina Lai	University of Cagliari, Italy
Mohamed Laib	Luxembourg Institute of Science and Technology, Luxembourg
Giuseppe Francesco Cesare Lama	University of Napoli Federico II, Italy
Isabella Maria Lami	Turin Polytechnic, Italy
Chien Sing Lee	Sunway University, Malaysia

Marcelo Leon	Ecotec University, Ecuador
Federica Leone	University of Cagliari, Italy
Barbara Lino	University of Palermo, Italy
Vadim Lisitsa	Russian Academy of Sciences, Russia
Carla Lobo	Portucalense University, Portugal
Marco Locurcio	Polytechnic University of Bari, Italy
Claudia Loggia	University of KwaZulu-Natal, South Africa
Andrea Lombardi	University of Perugia, Italy
Isabel Lopes	Polytechnic Institut of Bragança, Portugal
Immacolata Lorè	Mediterranean University of Reggio Calabria, Italy
Vanda Lourenco	Nova University of Lisbon, Portugal
Giorgia Malavasi	Turin Polytechnic, Italy
Francesca Maltinti	University of Cagliari, Italy
Luca Mancini	University of Perugia, Italy
Marcos Mandado	University of Vigo, Spain
Benedetto Manganelli	University of Basilicata, Italy
Krassimir Markov	Institute of Electric Engineering and Informatics, Bulgaria
Enzo Martinelli	University of Salerno, Italy
Fiammetta Marulli	University of Campania Luigi Vanvitelli, Italy
Antonino Marvuglia	Luxembourg Institute of Science and Technology, Luxembourg
Rytis Maskeliunas	Kaunas University of Technology, Lithuania
Michele Mastroianni	University of Salerno, Italy
Hideo Matsufuru	High Energy Accelerator Research Organization, Japan
D'Apuzzo Mauro	University of Cassino and Southern Lazio, Italy
Luis Mazon	Bitrum Research Group, Spain
Chiara Mazzarella	University Federico II, Naples, Italy
Beatrice Mecca	Turin Polytechnic, Italy
Umberto Mecca	Turin Polytechnic, Italy
Paolo Mengoni	Hong Kong Baptist University, China
Gaetano Messina	Mediterranean University of Reggio Calabria, Italy
Alfredo Milani	University of Perugia, Italy
Alessandra Milesi	University of Cagliari, Italy
Richard Millham	Durban University of Technology, South Africa
Fernando Miranda	Universidade do Minho, Portugal
Biswajeeban Mishra	University of Szeged, Hungary
Giuseppe Modica	University of Reggio Calabria, Italy
Pierluigi Morano	Polytechnic University of Bari, Italy

Filipe Mota Pinto	Polytechnic Institute of Leiria, Portugal
Maria Mourao	Polytechnic Institute of Viana do Castelo, Portugal
Eugenio Muccio	University of Naples Federico II, Italy
Beniamino Murgante	University of Basilicata, Italy
Rocco Murro	Sapienza University of Rome, Italy
Giuseppe Musolino	Mediterranean University of Reggio Calabria, Italy
Nadia Nedjah	State University of Rio de Janeiro, Brazil
Juraj Nemec	Masaryk University, Czech Republic
Andreas Nikiforiadis	Aristotle University of Thessaloniki, Greece
Silvio Nocera	IUAV University of Venice, Italy
Roseline Ogundokun	Kaunas University of Technology, Lithuania
Emma Okewu	University of Alcala, Spain
Serena Olcuire	Sapienza University of Rome, Italy
Irene Oliveira	University Trás-os-Montes and Alto Douro, Portugal
Samson Oruma	Ostfold University College, Norway
Antonio Pala	University of Cagliari, Italy
Maria Panagiotopoulou	National Technical University of Athens, Greece
Simona Panaro	University of Sussex Business School, UK
Jay Pancham	Durban University of Technology, South Africa
Eric Pardede	La Trobe University, Australia
Hyun Kyoo Park	Ministry of National Defense, South Korea
Damiano Perri	University of Florence, Italy
Quoc Trung Pham	Ho Chi Minh City University of Technology, Vietnam
Claudio Piferi	University of Florence, Italy
Angela Pilogallo	University of L'Aquila, Italy
Francesco Pinna	University of Cagliari, Italy
Telmo Pinto	University of Coimbra, Portugal
Luca Piroddi	University of Malta, Malta
Francesco Pittau	Politechnic of Milan, Italy
Giuliano Poli	Università Federico II di Napoli, Italy
Maurizio Pollino	Italian National Agency for New Technologies, Energy and Sustainable Economic Development, Italy
Vijay Prakash	University of Malta, Malta
Salvatore Praticò	Mediterranean University of Reggio Calabria, Italy
Carlotta Quagliolo	Turin Polytechnic, Italy
Garrisi Raffaele	Operations Center for Cyber Security, Italy
Mariapia Raimondo	Università della Campania Luigi Vanvitelli, Italy

Maria Somma	University of Naples Federico II, Italy
Changgeun Son	Ministry of National Defense, South Korea
Alberico Sonnessa	Polytechnic of Bari, Italy
Inês Sousa	University of Minho, Portugal
Lisete Sousa	University of Lisbon, Portugal
Elena Stankova	Saint-Petersburg State University, Russia
Modestos Stavrakis	University of the Aegean, Greece
Flavio Stochino	University of Cagliari, Italy
Anastasia Stratigea	National Technical University of Athens, Greece
Yue Sun	European XFEL GmbH, Germany
Anthony Suppa	Turin Polytechnic, Italy
David Taniar	Monash University, Australia
Rodrigo Tapia McClung	Centre for Research in Geospatial Information Sciences, Mexico
Tarek Teba	University of Portsmouth, UK
Ana Paula Teixeira	University of Trás-os-Montes and Alto Douro, Portugal
Tengku Adil Tengku Izhar	Technological University MARA, Malaysia
Maria Filomena Teodoro	University of Lisbon and Portuguese Naval Academy, Portugal
Yiota Theodora	National Technical University of Athens, Greece
Elena Todella	Turin Polytechnic, Italy
Graça Tomaz	Polytechnic Institut of Guarda, Portugal
Anna Tonazzini	National Research Council, Italy
Dario Torregrossa	Goodyear, Luxembourg
Francesca Torrieri	University of Naples Federico II, Italy
Vincenza Torrisi	University of Catania, Italy
Nikola Tosic	Polytechnic University of Catalonia, Spain
Vincenzo Totaro	Polytechnic University of Bari, Italy
Arianna Travaglini	University of Florence, Italy
António Trigo	Polytechnic of Coimbra, Portugal
Giuseppe A. Trunfio	University of Sassari, Italy
Toshihiro Uchibayashi	Kyushu University, Japan
Piero Ugliengo	University of Torino, Italy
Jordi Vallverdu	University Autonoma Barcelona, Spain
Gianmarco Vanuzzo	University of Perugia, Italy
Dmitry Vasyunin	T-Systems, Russia
Laura Verde	University of Campania Luigi Vanvitelli, Italy
Giulio Vignoli	University of Cagliari, Italy
Gianluca Vinti	University of Perugia, Italy
Katarína Vitálišová	Matej Bel University, Slovak Republic
Daniel Mark Vitiello	University of Cagliari

Marco Vizzari	University of Perugia, Italy
Manuel Yañez	Autonomous University of Madrid, Spain
Fenghui Yao	Tennessee State University, USA
Fukuko Yuasa	High Energy Accelerator Research Organization, Japan
Milliam Maxime Zekeng Ndadji	University of Dschang, Cameroon
Ljiljana Zivkovic	Republic Geodetic Authority, Serbia
Camila Zyngier	IBMEC-BH, Brazil

Plenary Lectures

A Multiscale Planning Concept for Sustainable Metropolitan Development

Pierre Frankhauser

Théma, Université de Franche-Comté, 32, rue Mégevand, 20030 Besançon, France
pierre.frankhauser@univ-fcomte.fr

Keywords: Sustainable metropolitan development · Multiscale approach · Urban modelling

Urban sprawl has often been pointed out as having an important negative impact on environment and climate. Residential zones have grown up in what were initially rural areas, located far from employment areas and often lacking shopping opportunities, public services and public transportation. Hence urban sprawl increased car-traffic flows, generating pollution and increasing energy consumption. New road axes consume considerable space and weaken biodiversity by reducing and cutting natural areas. A return to "compact cities" or "dense cities" has often been contemplated as the most efficient way to limit urban sprawl. However, the real impact of density on car use is less clear-cut (Daneshpour and Shakibamanesh 2011). Let us emphasize that moreover climate change will increase the risk of heat islands on an intra-urban scale. This prompts a more nuanced reflection on how urban fabrics should be structured.

Moreover, urban planning cannot ignore social demand. Lower land prices in rural areas, often put forward by economists, is not the only reason of urban sprawl. The quality of the residential environment comes into play, too, through features like noise, pollution, landscape quality, density etc. Schwanen et al. (2004) observe for the Netherlands that households preferring a quiet residential environment and individual housing with a garden will not accept densification, which might even lead them to move to lower-density rural areas even farther away from jobs and shopping amenities. Many scholars emphasize the importance of green amenities for residential environments and report the importance of easy access to leisure areas (Guo and Bhat 2002). Vegetation in the residential environment has an important impact on health and well-being (Lafortezza et al. 2009).

We present here the Fractalopolis concept which we developed in the frame of several research projects and which aims reconciling environmental and social issues (Bonin et al., 2020; Frankhauser 2021; Frankhauser et al. 2018). This concept introduces a multiscale approach based on multifractal geometry for conceiving spatial development for metropolitan areas. For taking into account social demand we refer to the fundamental work of Max-Neef et al. (1991) based on Maslow's work about basic human needs. He introduces the concept of satisfiers assigned to meet the basic needs of "Subsistence, Protection, Affection, Understanding, Participation, Idleness, Creation, Identity and Freedom". Satisfiers thus become the link between the needs of everyone and society and may depend on the cultural context. We consider their importance, their location and their accessibility and we rank the needs according to their importance for individuals or households. In order to enjoy a good quality of life and to shorten trips and to reduce automobile use, it seems important for satisfiers of daily needs to be easily accessible. Hence, we consider the purchase rate when reflecting on the implementation of shops which is reminiscent of central place theory.

The second important feature is taking care of environment and biodiversity by avoiding fragmentation of green space (Ekren and Arslan 2022) which must benefit, moreover, of a good accessibility, as pointed out. These areas must, too, ply the role of cooling areas ensuring ventilation of urbanized areas (Kuttler et al. 1998).

For integrating these different objectives, we propose a concept for developing spatial configurations of metropolitan areas designed which is based on multifractal geometry. It allows combining different issues across a large range of scales in a coherent way. These issues include:

- providing easy access to a large array of amenities to meet social demand;
- promoting the use of public transportation and soft modes instead of automobile use;
- preserving biodiversity and improving the local climate.

The concept distinguishes development zones localized in the vicinity of a nested and hierarchized system of public transport axes. The highest ranked center offers all types of amenities, whereas lower ranked centers lack the highest ranked amenities. The lowest ranked centers just offer the amenities for daily needs. A coding system allows distinguishing the centers according to their rank.

Each subset of central places is in some sense autonomous, since they are not linked by transportation axes to subcenters of the same order. This allows to preserve a linked system of green corridors penetrating the development zones across scales avoiding the fragmentation of green areas and ensuring a good accessibility to recreational areas.

The spatial model is completed by a population distribution model which globally follows the same hierarchical logic. However, we weakened the strong fractal order what allows to conceive a more or less polycentric spatial system.

We can adapt the theoretical concept easily to real world situation without changing the underlying multiscale logic. A decision support system has been developed allowing to simulate development scenarios and to evaluate them. The evaluation procedure is based on fuzzy evaluation of distance acceptance for accessing to the different types of amenities according to the ranking of needs. We used for evaluation data issued from a great set of French planning documents like Master plans. We show an example how the software package can be used concretely.

References

Bonin, O., et al.: Projet SOFT sobriété énergétique par les formes urbaines et le transport (Research Report No. 1717C0003; p. 214). ADEME (2020)

Daneshpour, A., Shakibamanesh, A.: Compact city; dose it create an obligatory context for urban sustainability? Int. J. Archit. Eng. Urban Plann. **21**(2), 110–118 (2011)

Ekren, E., Arslan, M.: Functions of greenways as an ecologically-based planning strategy. In: Çakır, M., Tuğluer, M., Fırat Örs, P.: Architectural Sciences and Ecology, pp. 134–156. Iksad Publications (2022)

Frankhauser, P.: Fractalopolis—a fractal concept for the sustainable development of metropolitan areas. In: Sajous, P., Bertelle, C. (eds.) Complex Systems, Smart Territories and Mobility, pp. 15–50. Springer, Cham (2021). https://doi.org/10.1007/978-3-030-59302-5_2

Frankhauser, P., Tannier, C., Vuidel, G., Houot, H.: An integrated multifractal modelling to urban and regional planning. Comput. Environ. Urban Syst. **67**(1), 132–146 (2018). https://doi.org/10.1016/j.compenvurbsys.2017.09.011

Guo, J., Bhat, C.: Residential location modeling: accommodating sociodemographic, school quality and accessibility effects. University of Texas, Austin (2002)

Kuttler, W., Dütemeyer, D., Barlag, A.-B.: Influence of regional and local winds on urban ventilation in Cologne, Germany. Meteorologische Zeitschrift, 77–87 (1998) https://doi.org/10.1127/metz/7/1998/77

Lafortezza, R., Carrus, G., Sanesi, G., Davies, C.: Benefits and well-being perceived by people visiting green spaces in periods of heat stress. Urban For. Urban Green. **8**(2), 97–108 (2009)

Max-Neef, M. A., Elizalde, A., Hopenhayn, M.: Human scale development: conception, application and further reflections. The Apex Press (1991)

Schwanen, T., Dijst, M., Dieleman, F. M.: Policies for urban form and their impact on travel: The Netherlands experience. Urban Stud. **41**(3), 579–603 (2004)

Graph Drawing and Network Visualization – An Overview – (Keynote Speech)

Giuseppe Liotta

Dipartimento di Ingegneria, Università degli Studi di Perugia, Italy
giuseppe.liotta@unipg.it

Abstract. Graph Drawing and Network visualization supports the exploration, analysis, and communication of relational data arising in a variety of application domains: from bioinformatics to software engineering, from social media to cyber-security, from data bases to powergrid systems. Aim of this keynote speech is to introduce this thriving research area, highlighting some of its basic approaches and pointing to some promising research directions.

1 Introduction

Graph Drawing and Network Visualization is at the intersection of different disciplines and it combines topics that traditionally belong to theoretical computer science with methods and approaches that characterize more applied disciplines. Namely, it can be related to Graph Algorithms, Geometric Graph Theory and Geometric computing, Combinatorial Optimization, Experimental Analysis, User Studies, System Design and Development, and Human Computer Interaction. This combination of theory and practice is well reflected in the flagship conference of the area, the *International Symposium on Graph Drawing and Network Visualization*, that has two tracks, one focusing on combinatorial and algorithmic aspects and the other on the design of network visualization systems and interfaces. The conference is now at its 31st edition; a full list of the symposia and their proceedings, published by Springer in the LNCS series can be found at the URL: http://www.graphdrawing.org/.

Aim of this short paper is to outline the content of my Keynote Speech at ICCSA 2023, which will be referred to as the "Talk" in the rest of the paper. The talk will introduce the field of Graph Drawing and Network Visualization to a broad audience, with the goal to not only present some key methodological and technological aspects, but also point to some unexplored or partially explored research directions. The rest of this short paper briefly outlines the content of the talk and provides some references that can be a starting point for researchers interested in working on Graph Drawing and Network Visualization.

2 Why Visualize Networks?

Back in 1973 the famous statistician Francis Anscombe, gave a convincing example of why visualization is fundamental component of data analysis. The example is known as the *Anscombe's quartet* [3] and it consists of four sets of 11 points each that are almost identical in terms of the basic statistic properties of their $x-$ and $y-$ coordinates. Namely the mean values and the variance of x and y are exactly the same in the four sets, while the correlation of x and y and the linear regression are the same up to the second decimal. In spite of this statistical similarity, the data look very different when displayed in the Euclidean plane which leads to the conclusion that they correspond to significantly different phenomena. Figure 1 reports the four sets of Anscombe's quartet. After fifty years, with the arrival of AI-based technologies and the need of explaining and interpreting machine-driven suggestions before making strategic decision, the lesson of Anscombe's quartet has not just kept but even increased its relevance.

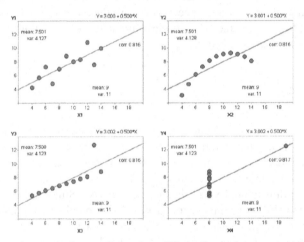

Fig. 1. The four point sets in Anscombe's quartet [3]; the figure also reports statistical values of the x and y variables.

As a matter of fact, nowadays the need of visualization systems goes beyond the verification of the accuracy of some statistical analysis on a set of scattered data. Recent technological advances have generated torrents of data that area relational in nature and typically modeled as networks: the nodes of the networks store the features of the data and the edges of the networks describe the semantic relationships between the data features. Such networked data sets (whose algebraic underlying structure is a called graph in discrete mathematics) arise in a variety of application domains including, for example, Systems Biology, Social Network Analysis, Software Engineering, Networking, Data Bases, Homeland Security, and Business Intelligence. In these (and many other) contexts, systems that support the visual analysis of networks and graphs play a central role in critical decision making processes. These are human-in-the-loop processes where the

continuous interaction between humans (decision makers) and data mining or optimization algorithms (AI/ML components) supports the data exploration, the development of
verifiable theories about the data, and the extraction of new knowledge that is used to
make strategic choices. A seminal book by Keim et al. [33] schematically represents the
human-in-the-loop approach to making sense of networked data sets as in Fig. 2. See
also [46–49].

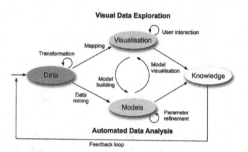

Fig. 2. Sense-making/knowledge generation loop. This conceptual interaction model between
human analysts and network visualization system is at the basis of network visual analytics system
design [33].

To make a concrete application example of the analysis of a network by interact-
ing with its visualization, consider the problem of contrasting financial crimes such
as money laundering or tax evasion. These crimes are based on relevant volumes of
financial transactions to conceal the identity, the source, or the destination of illegally
gained money. Also, the adopted patterns to pursue the illegal goals continuously change
to conceal the crimes. Therefore, contrasting them requires special investigation units
which must analyze very large and highly dynamic data sets and discover relationships
between different subjects to untangle complex fraudulent plots. The investigative cycle
begins with data collection and filtering; it is then followed by modeling the data as a
social network (also called *financial activity network* in this context) to which different
data mining and data analytic methods are applied, including graph pattern matching,
social network analysis, machine learning, and information diffusion. By the network
visualization system detectives can interactively explore the data, gain insight and make
new hypotheses about possible criminal activities, verify the hypotheses by asking the
system to provide more details about specific portions of the network, refine previous
outputs, and eventually gain new knowledge. Figure 3 illustrates a small financial activity network where, by means of the interaction between an officer of the Italian Revenue
Agency and the MALDIVE system described in [10] a fraudulent pattern has been identified. Precisely, the tax officer has encoded a risky relational scheme among taxpayers
into a suspicious graph pattern; in response, the system has made a search in the taxpayer
network and it has returned one such pattern. See, e.g., [9, 11, 14, 18, 38] for more papers
and references about visual analytic applications to contrasting financial crimes.

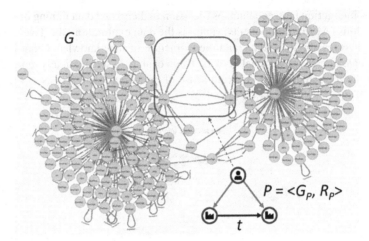

Fig. 3. A financial activity network from [10]. The pattern in the figure represents a Sup-pliesFromAssociated scheme, consisting of an economic transaction and two shareholding relationships.

3 Facets of Graph Drawing and Network Visualization

The Talk overviews some of the fundamental facets that characterize the research in Graph Drawing and Network Visualization. Namely:

- Graph drawing metaphors: Depending on the application context, different metaphors can be used to represent a relational data set modeled as a graph. The talk will briefly recall the matrix representation, the space filling representation, the contact representation, and the node-link representation which is, by far, the most commonly used (see, e.g., [43]).
- Interaction paradigms: Different interaction paradigms have different impacts on the sense-making process of the user about the visualized network. The Talk will go through the full-view, top-down, bottom-up, incremental, and narrative paradigms. Pros and cons will be highlighted for each approach, also by means of examples and applications. The discussion of the top-down interaction paradigm will also consider the hybrid visualization models (see, e.g., [2, 24, 26, 28, 39]) while the discussion about the incremental paradigm will focus on research about graph storyplans (see, e.g., [4, 6, 7]).
- Graph drawing algorithms: Three main algorithmic approaches will be reviewed, namely the force-directed, the layered), and the planarization-based approach; see, e.g., [5]. We shall also make some remarks about FPT algorithms for graph drawing (see, e.g., [8, 19, 20, 25, 27, 40, 53]) and about how the optimization challenges vary when it is assumed that the input has or does not have a fixed combinatorial embedding (see, e.g., [12, 13, 16, 17, 23]).
- Experimental analysis and user-studies: The Talk will mostly compare two models to define and experimentally validate those optimization goals that define a "readable"

network visualization, i.e. a visualization that in a given application context can easily convey the structure of a relational data set so to guarantee efficiency both in its visual exploration and in the elaboration of new knowledge. Special focus will be given to a set emerging optimization goals related to edge crossings that are currently investigated in the graph drawing and network visualization community unedr the name of "graph drawing beyond planarity" (see, e.g., [1, 15, 29, 35]).

The talk shall also point to some promising research directions, including: (i) Extend the body of papers devoted to user-studies that compare the impact of different graph drawing metaphors on the user perception. (ii) Extend the study of interaction paradigms to extended reality environments (see, e.g., [21, 30, 36, 37]); (iii) Engineer the FPT algorithms for graph drawing and experimentally compare their performances with exact or approximate solutions; and (iv) Develop new algorithmic fameworks in the context of graph drawing beyond planarity.

We conclude this short paper with pointers to publication venues and key references that can be browsed by researchers interested in the fascinating field of Graph Drawing and Network Visualization.

4 Pointers to Publication venues and Key References

A limited list of conferences where Graph Drawing and Network Visualization papers are regularly part of the program includes *IEEE VIS, EuroVis, SoCG, ISAAC, ACM-SIAM SODA, WADS,* and *WG.* Among the many journals where several Graph Drawing and Network Visualization papers have appeared during the last three decades we recall *IEEE Transactions on Visualization and Computer Graphs, SIAM Jounal of Computing, Computer Graphics Forum, Journal of Computer and System Sciences, Algorithmica, Journal of Graph Algorithms and Applications, Theoretical Computer Science, Information Sciences, Discrete and Computational Geometry, Computational Geometry: Theory and Applications, ACM Computing Surveys,* and *Computer Science Review.* A limited list of books, surveys, or papers that contain interesting algorithmic challenges on Graph Drawing and Network Visualization include [5, 15, 22, 29, 31–35, 41–45, 50–52].

References

1. Angelini, P., et al.: Simple k-planar graphs are simple (k+1)-quasiplanar. J. Comb. Theory, Ser. B, **142**, 1–35 (2020)
2. Angori, L., Didimo, W., Montecchiani, F., Pagliuca, D., Tappini, A.: Hybrid graph visualizations with chordlink: Algorithms, experiments, and applications. IEEE Trans. Vis. Comput. Graph. **28**(2), 1288–1300 (2022)
3. Anscombe, F.J.: Graphs in statistical analysis. Am. Stat. **27**(1), 17–21 (1973)
4. Di Battista, G., et al.: Small point-sets supporting graph stories. In: Angelini, P., von Hanxleden, R. (eds.) Graph Drawing and Network Visualization. GD 2022, LNCS, vol. 13764, pp. 289–303. Springer, Cham (2022). https://doi.org/10.1007/978-3-031-22203-0_21

5. Battista, G.D., Eades, P., Tamassia, R., Tollis, I.G.: Graph Drawing: Algorithms for the Visualization of Graphs. Prentice-Hall, Hoboken (1999)

6. Binucci, C., et al.: On the complexity of the storyplan problem. In: Angelini, P., von Hanxleden, R. (eds.) Graph Drawing and Network Visualization. GD 2022. LNCS, vol. 13764, pp. 304–318. Springer, Cham (2023). https://doi.org/10.1007/978-3-031-22203-0_22

7. Borrazzo, M., Lozzo, G.D., Battista, G.D., Frati, F., Patrignani, M.: Graph stories in small area. J. Graph Algorithms Appl. **24**(3), 269–292 (2020)

8. Chaplick, S., Giacomo, E.D., Frati, F., Ganian, R., Raftopoulou, C.N., Simonov, K.: Parameterized algorithms for upward planarity. In: Goaoc, X., Kerber, M. (eds.) 38th International Symposium on Computational Geometry, SoCG 2022, June 7–10, 2022, Berlin, Germany, LIPIcs, vol. 224, pp. 26:1–26:16. Schloss Dagstuhl - Leibniz-Zentrum für Informatik (2022)

9. Didimo, W., Giamminonni, L., Liotta, G., Montecchiani, F., Pagliuca, D.: A visual analytics system to support tax evasion discovery. Decis. Support Syst. **110**, 71–83 (2018)

10. Didimo, W., Grilli, L., Liotta, G., Menconi, L., Montecchiani, F., Pagliuca, D.: Combining network visualization and data mining for tax risk assessment. IEEE Access **8**, 16073–16086 (2020)

11. Didimo, W., Grilli, L., Liotta, G., Montecchiani, F., Pagliuca, D.: Visual querying and analysis of temporal fiscal networks. Inf. Sci. **505**, 406–421 (2019)

12. W. Didimo, M. Kaufmann, G. Liotta, and G. Ortali. Didimo, W., Kaufmann, M., Liotta, G., Ortali, G.: Rectilinear planarity testing of plane series-parallel graphs in linear time. In: Auber, D., Valtr, P. (eds.) Graph Drawing and Network Visualization. GD 2020. LNCS, vol. 12590, pp. 436–449. Springer, Cham (2020). https://doi.org/10.1007/978-3-030-68766-3_34

13. Didimo, W., Kaufmann, M., Liotta, G., Ortali, G.: Rectilinear planarity of partial 2-trees. In: Angelini, P., von Hanxleden, R. (eds.) Graph Drawing and Network Visualization. GD 2022. LNCS, vol. 13764, pp. 157–172. Springer, Cham (2023). https://doi.org/10.1007/978-3-031-22203-0_12

14. Didimo, W., Liotta, G., Montecchiani, F.: Network visualization for financial crime detection. J. Vis. Lang. Comput. **25**(4), 433–451 (2014)

15. Didimo, W., Liotta, G., Montecchiani, F.: A survey on graph drawing beyond planarity. ACM Comput. Surv. **52**(1), 4:1–4:37 (2019)

16. Didimo, W., Liotta, G., Ortali, G., Patrignani, M.: Optimal orthogonal drawings of planar 3-graphs in linear time. In: Chawla, S. (ed.) Proceedings of the 2020 ACM-SIAM Symposium on Discrete Algorithms, SODA 2020, Salt Lake City, UT, USA, January 5–8, 2020, pp. 806–825. SIAM (2020)

17. Didimo, W., Liotta, G., Patrignani, M.: HV-planarity: algorithms and complexity. J. Comput. Syst. Sci. **99**, 72–90 (2019)

18. Dilla, W.N., Raschke, R.L.: Data visualization for fraud detection: practice implications and a call for future research. Int. J. Acc. Inf. Syst. **16**, 1–22 (2015)

19. Dujmovic, V., et al.: A fixed-parameter approach to 2-layer planarization. Algorithmica **45**(2), 159–182 (2006)

20. Dujmovic, V., et al.: On the parameterized complexity of layered graph drawing. Algorithmica **52**(2), 267–292 (2008)

21. Dwyer, T., et al.: Immersive analytics: an introduction. In: Marriott, K., et al. (eds.) Immersive Analytics, LNCS, vol. 11190, pp. 1–23. Springer, Cham (2018)

22. Filipov, V., Arleo, A., Miksch, S.: Are we there yet? a roadmap of network visualization from surveys to task taxonomies. Computer Graphics Forum (2023, on print)

23. Garg, A., Tamassia, R.: On the computational complexity of upward and rectilinear planarity testing. SIAM J. Comput. **31**(2), 601–625 (2001)

24. Di Giacomo, E., Didimo, W., Montecchiani, F., Tappini, A.: A user study on hybrid graph visualizations. In: Purchase, H.C., Rutter, I. (eds.) Graph Drawing and Network Visualization. GD 2021. LNCS, vol. 12868, pp. 21–38. Springer, Cham (2021). https://doi.org/10.1007/978-3-030-92931-2_2

25. Giacomo, E.D., Giordano, F., Liotta, G.: Upward topological book embeddings of dags. SIAM J. Discret. Math. **25**(2), 479–489 (2011)

26. Giacomo, E.D., Lenhart, W.J., Liotta, G., Randolph, T.W., Tappini, A.: (k, p)-planarity: a relaxation of hybrid planarity. Theor. Comput. Sci. **896**, 19–30 (2021)

27. Giacomo, E.D., Liotta, G., Montecchiani, F.: Orthogonal planarity testing of bounded treewidth graphs. J. Comput. Syst. Sci. **125**, 129–148 (2022)

28. Giacomo, E.D., Liotta, G., Patrignani, M., Rutter, I., Tappini, A.: Nodetrix planarity testing with small clusters. Algorithmica **81**(9), 3464–3493 (2019)

29. Hong, S., Tokuyama, T. (eds.) Beyond Planar Graphs. Springer, Singapore (2020). https://doi.org/10.1007/978-981-15-6533-5

30. Joos, L., Jaeger-Honz, S., Schreiber, F., Keim, D.A., Klein, K.: Visual comparison of networks in VR. IEEE Trans. Vis. Comput. Graph. **28**(11), 3651–3661 (2022)

31. Jünger, M., Mutzel, P. (eds.) Graph Drawing Software. Springer, Berlin (2004). https://doi.org/10.1007/978-3-642-18638-7

32. Kaufmann, M., Wagner, D. (eds.): Drawing Graphs, Methods and Models (the book grow out of a Dagstuhl Seminar, April 1999), LNCS, vol. 2025. Springer, Berlin (2001). https://doi.org/10.1007/3-540-44969-8

33. Keim, D.A., Kohlhammer, J., Ellis, G.P., Mansmann, F.: Mastering the Information Age - Solving Problems with Visual Analytics. Eurographics Association, Saarbrücken (2010)

34. Keim, D.A., Mansmann, F., Stoffel, A., Ziegler, H.: Visual analytics. In: Liu, L., Özsu, M.T. (eds.) Encyclopedia of Database Systems, 2nd edn. Springer, Berlin (2018)

35. Kobourov, S.G., Liotta, G., Montecchiani, F.: An annotated bibliography on 1-planarity. Comput. Sci. Rev. **25**, 49–67 (2017)

36. Kraus, M., et al.: Immersive analytics with abstract 3D visualizations: a survey. Comput. Graph. Forum **41**(1), 201–229 (2022)

37. Kwon, O., Muelder, C., Lee, K., Ma, K.: A study of layout, rendering, and interaction methods for immersive graph visualization. IEEE Trans. Vis. Comput. Graph. **22**(7), 1802–1815 (2016)

38. Leite, R.A., Gschwandtner, T., Miksch, S., Gstrein, E., Kuntner, J.: NEVA: visual analytics to identify fraudulent networks. Comput. Graph. Forum **39**(6), 344–359 (2020)

39. Liotta, G., Rutter, I., Tappini, A.: Simultaneous FPQ-ordering and hybrid planarity testing. Theor. Comput. Sci. **874**, 59–79 (2021)

40. Liotta, G., Rutter, I., Tappini, A.: Parameterized complexity of graph planarity with restricted cyclic orders. J. Comput. Syst. Sci. **135**, 125–144 (2023)

41. Ma, K.: Pushing visualization research frontiers: essential topics not addressed by machine learning. IEEE Comput. Graphics Appl. **43**(1), 97–102 (2023)

42. McGee, F., et al.: Visual Analysis of Multilayer Networks. Synthesis Lectures on Visualization. Morgan & Claypool Publishers, San Rafael (2021)

43. Munzner, T.: Visualization Analysis and Design. A.K. Peters visualization series. A K Peters (2014)

44. Nishizeki, T., Rahman, M.S.: Planar Graph Drawing, vol. 12. World Scientific, Singapore (2004)

45. Nobre, C., Meyer, M.D., Streit, M., Lex, A.: The state of the art in visualizing multivariate networks. Comput. Graph. Forum **38**(3), 807–832 (2019)

46. Sacha, D.: Knowledge generation in visual analytics: Integrating human and machine intelligence for exploration of big data. In: Apel, S., et al. (eds.) Ausgezeichnete Informatikdissertationen 2018, LNI, vol. D-19, pp. 211–220. GI (2018)

47. Sacha, D., et al.: What you see is what you can change: human-centered machine learning by interactive visualization. Neurocomputing **268**, 164–175 (2017)

48. Sacha, D., Senaratne, H., Kwon, B.C., Ellis, G.P., Keim, D.A.: The role of uncertainty, awareness, and trust in visual analytics. IEEE Trans. Vis. Comput. Graph. **22**(1), 240–249 (2016)

49. Sacha, D., Stoffel, A., Stoffel, F., Kwon, B.C., Ellis, G.P., Keim, D.A.: Knowledge generation model for visual analytics. IEEE Trans. Vis. Comput. Graph. **20**(12), 1604–1613 (2014)

50. Tamassia, R.: Graph drawing. In: Sack, J., Urrutia, J. (eds.) Handbook of Computational Geometry, pp. 937–971. North Holland/Elsevier, Amsterdam (2000)

51. Tamassia, R. (ed.) Handbook on Graph Drawing and Visualization. Chapman and Hall/CRC, Boca Raton (2013)

52. Tamassia, R., Liotta, G.: Graph drawing. In: Goodman, J.E., O'Rourke, J. (eds.) Handbook of Discrete and Computational Geometry, 2nd edn., pp. 1163–1185. Chapman and Hall/CRC, Boca Raton (2004)

53. Zehavi, M.: Parameterized analysis and crossing minimization problems. Comput. Sci. Rev. **45**, 100490 (2022)

Understanding Non-Covalent Interactions in Biological Processes through QM/MM-EDA Dynamic Simulations

Marcos Mandado

Department of Physical Chemistry, University of Vigo, Lagoas-Marcosende s/n, 36310 Vigo, Spain

mandado@uvigo.es

Molecular dynamic simulations in biological environments such as proteins, DNA or lipids involves a large number of atoms, so classical models based on widely parametrized force fields are employed instead of more accurate quantum methods, whose high computational requirements preclude their application. The parametrization of appropriate force fields for classical molecular dynamics relies on the precise knowledge of the non-covalent inter and intramolecular interactions responsible for very important aspects, such as macromolecular arrangements, cell membrane permeation, ion solvation, etc. This implies, among other things, knowledge of the nature of the interaction, which may be governed by electrostatic, repulsion or dispersion forces. In order to know the balance between different forces, quantum calculations are frequently performed on simplified molecular models and the data obtained from these calculations are used to parametrize the force fields employed in classical simulations. These parameters are, among others, atomic charges, permanent electric dipole moments and atomic polarizabilities. However, it sometimes happens that the molecular models used for the quantum calculations are too simple and the results obtained can differ greatly from those of the extended system. As an alternative to classical and quantum methods, hybrid quantum/classical schemes (QM/MM) can be introduced, where the extended system is neither truncated nor simplified, but only the most important region is treated quantum mechanically.

In this presentation, molecular dynamic simulations and calculations with hybrid schemes are first introduced in a simple way for a broad and multidisciplinary audience. Then, a method developed in our group to investigate intermolecular interactions using hybrid quantum/classical schemes (QM/MM-EDA) is presented and some applications to the study of dynamic processes of ion solvation and membrane permeation are discussed [1–3]. Special attention is paid to the implementation details of the method in the EDA-NCI software [4].

References

1. Cárdenas, G., Pérez-Barcia, A., Mandado, M., Nogueira, J.J.: Phys. Chem. Chem. Phys. **23**, 20533 (2021)
2. Pérez-Barcia, A., Cárdenas, G., Nogueira, J.J., Mandado, M.: J. Chem. Inf. Model. **63**, 882 (2023)

3. Alvarado, R., Cárdenas, G., Nogueira, J.J., Ramos-Berdullas, N., Mandado, M.: Membranes **13**, 28 (2023)
4. Mandado, M., Van Alsenoy, C.: EDA-NCI: A program to perform energy decomposition analysis of non-covalent interactions. https://github.com/marcos-mandado/ EDA-NCI

Contents – Part IX

Short Paper (VRA 2023)

Short Paper (AIWA 2023)

PHD Showcase Paper (SSIC 2023)

"The Most Deafening Silence You Can Hear": The International Comparison of Landscape Value Mapping on Linguistic Expressions of Islands

Yuyao Mei[(⊠)] [iD], Frans Sijtsma [iD], Dimitris Ballas [iD], Daan Vegter, and Yfke Ongena

University of Groningen, Landleven 1, 9747 AD Groningen, The Netherlands
yuyao.mei@rug.nl

Abstract. This paper presents a research framework aimed at enhancing our understanding of how people value natural places, focusing on islands. In particular, the paper presents a conceptual basis for a protocol to systematically analyze the information richness of the open answer valuation questions qualitative data in the Greenmapper dataset in people's native language, with an application on islands with specific case study examples. This protocol can be used for spatial planning purposes since it provides valuable insights into how people value landscapes. The paper presents a theoretical framework underpinned by the concepts of landscape perception, Public Participation Geographical Information Systems (PPGIS). It also considers the role of language in order to frame the scientific context of mapping landscape values research. The paper also explores the empirical application of the framework conducting an international comparative case study of a small set of landscape appreciation statements in three countries, focusing on islands.

Keywords: Land Value Mapping · Landscape Perception · PPGIS · Greenmapper

1 Introduction

Many studies have been conducted on the interactions between humans and landscape [1–5]. Scientific work on landscape value mapping becomes an increasing body of empirical work within landscape research field, for their significance in well-formed decision-making in both landscape management and spatial planning [6, 7]. Both quantitative and qualitative methods in can support an increased understanding of how people value nature, but the qualitative use of language can serve to better capture landscape representations for its advantages in identifying value that people attribute to landscapes [8].

Furthermore, in an international context, qualitative methods are hampered by language barriers, preventing in-depth comparisons. In order to fill the gap of international comparisons, data from islands of three countries will be collected using an online survey

O. Gervasi et al. (Eds.): ICCSA 2023 Workshops, LNCS 14112, pp. 3–14, 2023.
https://doi.org/10.1007/978-3-031-37129-5_1

based on Public Participatory Geographical Information System (called Greenmapper), and analyzed by a modified landscape perception model.

The PPGIS method refers to "a set of methods for integrating public knowledge of places to inform land use planning and decision-making" [9]. "Public" and "participation" are its crucial features: Public may involve decision-makers, implementer, and affected individuals; participation, on the other hand, refers to the gradual involvement of the public in decision-making processes [10]. Therefore, the combination of value mapping and PPGIS is fruitful in various studies enhancing knowledge about the valuation of natural places in a participatory manner.

In line with Wartmann et al.'s argument [5, 8], this paper empirically explore qualitative, semantic descriptions of landscapes. We attempt to develop and analyze a protocol capable of grasping the information richness in landscape value mapping both in a qualitative and quantitative manner. Various indicators are developed based on data of a cluster of markers retrieved from three different islands: Sylt (Germany), Sicily (Italy) and Jeju (South-Korea). Several clusters of markers have been selected from islands by means of comparability.

The scientific contribution of this paper lies in providing a conceptual basis for a protocol to systematically analyze the information richness of the open answer valuation questions qualitative data in the Greenmapper dataset in people's native language. This protocol can be used for spatial planning purposes since it provides valuable insights into how people value landscapes.

In the next section, a theoretical framework introducing the concepts of landscape perception, Public Participation Geographical Information Systems (PPGIS), and the role of language will be developed and discussed in order to frame the scientific context of mapping landscape values research. Subsequently, we will explore the empirical application of the framework conducting an international comparative case study of a small set of landscape appreciation statements in three countries. Furthermore, we will describe details of the employed method, followed by a discussion of the results, describing the study. Afterwards, the outcomes will be considered with regard to existing scientific literature. This concluding section presents a research agenda to identify several steps that can be developed in order to progress along the preliminary lines of this paper. In turn, this ultimately enhances our understanding of how people value natural places.

2   Theoretical Framework

2.1   Landscape Perception

To capture the intangible landscape perception, Zube et al. [11] identifies three elements of the model [see Fig. 1], and concluded four paradigms relating to human-landscape interactions.

The human concept includes the nature of humanity that interacts with the landscape and reflects on the interaction itself. The landscape includes tangible and intangible properties, for instance, physical features as scales, perceived complexity, and gestalts, etc., or relations in the landscape that are important to the interaction. The interaction then leads to outcomes, which must be viewed in its interactional context, and in turn feedback to both human and landscape inputs.

In this research, the human element refers to tourists or fans who experience and express their attachment to the landscape. The landscape is ambiguous as it varies in our three research sites. To include both tangible and intangible features of landscapes, analyses of physical characteristics and discourses from interviewers must be combined. The interaction outcomes are illustrated by analyzing data collected by Greenmapper survey.

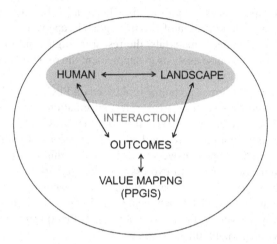

Fig. 1. Modified landscape perception model by the author from the model of Zube et al., 1982.

The four emergent landscape paradigms concluded by Zube are: (1) *the expert paradigm*, featured by evaluation of landscape quality by skilled and trained observers from interdisciplinary perspective; (2) *the psychophysical paradigm*, in which the objectives of assessments are general public or selected populations, and a correlational or stimulus-response relation is expected between observer evaluations and behavior; (3) *the cognitive paradigm*, emphasizing the sociocultural meaning associated with landscapes or landscape properties; (4) *the experiential paradigm*, which considers the experience of the human-landscape interaction as the basis of landscape values.

The four paradigms provide perspectives to deeper understand the mechanism, but however, do not conflict with each other. This research does not fall into the scope of a single paradigm but a fusion of the latter two. The objectives are not categorized by their profession or based on other selection criteria, and the cognitive and experiential paradigm provide insights on how people value the landscape.

2.2 Value Mapping, PPGIS, and Greenmapper

The concept of PPGIS has increasingly been applied in various contexts. For instance, Brown and Brabyn extrapolate social landscape values to a national level in New Zealand using a landscape character classification and PPGIS [3]. Their results indicate that extrapolating land use values can assist impact assessment for land use change but that it should be kept simple for decision support. Additionally, Brown and Brabyn analyze the relationships between multiple values and physical landscapes at a regional scale using PPGIS and landscape character [4]. In this case, landscape values appear to be largely associated with urban areas, water features, indigenous land cover, and mountains. In his later work, Brown and Kyttä identify over forty empirical studies practicing with PPGIS and its implications for land use planning and management [13].

The field of PPGIS has progressed over the last decade aiming to enhance the knowledge of social and cultural landscapes. The mainstream of value mapping using PPGIS is to quantify landscapes values in terms of classification [3, 12, 13]. However, despite the strong advantage in identification of classifying landscape values, when translating and grouping massive linguistic materials, the research might confront with information losses. Therefore, discourse analysis to supplement the rough PPGIS analysis is of importance.

The Greenmapper platform is an online tool based on PPGIS, which allows participants to map their appreciated natural areas. Basic information of the land, participants, and human-landscape interactions will be collected by answers to close-ended questions regarding activities they enjoyed at research sites. Expressions of their landscape perception will be gathered by open answers to "what makes this specific place attractive to you" [14]. Participants are free to express appreciations in their own language or choose between their native language and others. The Greenmapper survey, therefore, is able to obtain abundant linguistic materials. Combining with discourse analysis, the Greenmapper survey answers to the information losses that quantitative PPGIS might face when roughly categorizing linguistic data.

Drawing on Wartman et al., we argue that language should be considered a starting point to analyze people's notions and reflections of landscapes [8]. Wartmann and Purves, use free listing tasks on landscape terms and interviews with visitors [5]. They compare and analyse descriptions of five different landscape types both quantitatively and qualitatively using an index which combines frequency and mean rank of terms. They *"elicit landscape terms that distinguish different landscapes and identify features to which cultural ecosystem services can be attached"* [8]. In doing so, they made a first step towards obtaining semantically rich descriptions of landscape.

Qualitative and extensive texts provide a wide variety of information contributing to information rich data. But the openness of this question challenges comparability due to the diverse nature of the data.

A quantitative approach appears to deliver the opposite; less information rich data but increased comparability. In order to cope with this dilemma, this study will develop a protocol consisting of both quantitative and qualitative indicators grasping the information richness present in the open question of the Greenmapper survey, an online PPGIS tool requesting people about their most attractive natural areas.

3 Methods

3.1 The Greenmapper Survey

The Greenmapper survey has been used for various research purposes with a central theme of landscape values [14–18]. Other than mapping function, which allows users to mark their favorite natural spaces, the survey include several multi-choice questions, one scaling question, and one open question where participants freely type their expressions. An overview of the survey portal is shown in Fig. 2.

The data has been standardized and stored. The standardized characteristics of the Greenmapper survey allow an international comparison between natural places [16]. In this international comparative study, the standardization process is guaranteed by native translators. Such characteristics of the Greenmapper survey can be highly beneficial in this study.

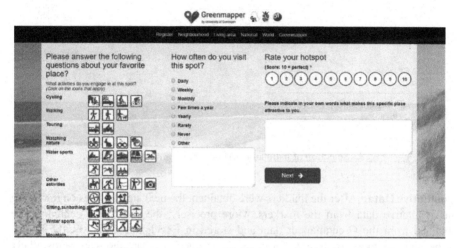

Fig. 2. An overview of the Greenmapper survey.

3.2 Data Selection: Clusters and Qualitative Data

Cluster of Markers. From the Greenmapper database (data.greenmapper.org), clusters of markers can be retrieved from places worldwide. This can be accomplished through a box that can be drawn around a certain cluster of markers. The markers can be categorized in four spatial levels: local, regional, national, and worldwide [16].

In this paper, the following procedures have been followed. Using ArcGIS, the national markers were selected from clusters from three islands: Sylt, Germany (N = 32), Sicily, Italy (N = 255) and Jeju, South-Korea (N = 303).

Example of selected national markers at the island of Sicily is shows in Fig. 3. The islands have been chosen because the collection of markers is relatively simple due to well-defined boundaries.

Furthermore, the relative similarity between the islands allows for an excellent comparison. The national level of markers was selected because on the one hand it includes as many participants as possible, from inhabitants of the islands, to internal tourists/visitors, and on the other hand because it ensures that participants are from the country the islands belong to. This means that it is likely that they answered the survey questions in the same language which allows for a comparison and analysis of three different languages.

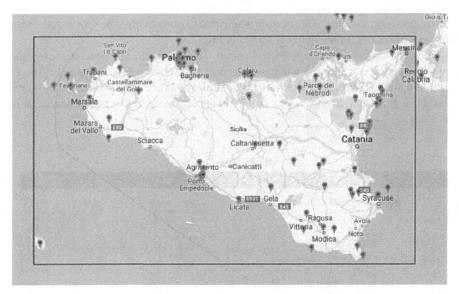

Fig. 3. Selection of national markers at the island of Sicily, Italy.

Qualitative Data. After the markers were obtained, the next step focuses on retrieving the qualitative data from the markers. More precisely, the words and sentences are obtained from the Greenmapper data and stored in Excel. Subsequently, the nouns, verbs, and adjectives are filtered for the analysis since those are the words most likely possessing information about the appreciation of natural lands. The linguistic data are categorized using Excel, and then processed into quantitative and qualitative indicators of landscape perception.

3.3 Indicators of Landscape Perception

Quantitative Indicators. In order to illustrate the information richness of the data per island, three quantitative measures have been developed. First of all, the average characters used per person per island. The average number of characters being used might potentially be a proxy of how extensively people value landscapes at islands.

A second indicator is the number of different words (words here refer to adjectives, nouns and verbs) that is being used to describe the islands thereby providing an overview of the diversity. Overcoming the challenge of difference in language, required all words and sentences used in the analysis to be translated to English with Google translate. The South-Korean data has been double checked with a native speaker. The translated data has been used to compare both the number of characters used averagely and the number of different words. To account for the differences in sample size per island, this indicator has been based on the first 33 cases in each sample thereby incorporating the fact that Sylt has the lowest number of cases, namely 33.

The third indicator is the Sutrop's index. This indicator calculates a word rank based on the frequency and the mean position of a term using the formula $S = F/(NR)$ where

F is term frequency, N the number of participants, and R the mean rank [19]. The idea is that incorporating the number of participants multiplied by the mean rank allows for a relative comparison between different countries.

Qualitative Indicators. Besides the three quantitative indicators of information richness, four qualitative indicators have been developed. Firstly, the most often used words have been identified. This provided an overview of what people often say about a particular place. This might be useful in order to understand the qualities of a particular place.

A second qualitative indicator considers the rarely mentioned but content rich words. The rareness lies in word frequency, which is the opposite to the first indicator; and the richness lies in its psychological sphere. For instance, "affections", "freeing" and "world" are mentioned only once but relate to extraordinary feelings people might have at a certain natural place. This indicator has been included because it presents the remarkable and rich words. These statements often start with more commonplace notions and end with words with more character, richness, and personal meaning. For instance, "The island is very beautiful, the sea, the dunes and the island atmosphere." Or, "The island and the sea are fantastic. We used to come here with my grandfather". Thus, it appears to be the combination of both common and rare linguistic expressions that can provide useful insights into how and why people value natural places. The first and second qualitative indicators of Sicily are presented in Fig. 4 as an example.

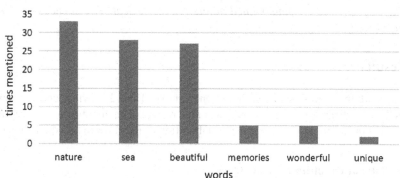

Fig. 4. Word frequency analysis of the island of Sicily, Italy.

A third indicator deals with the context of the often mentioned words. Since the meaning is often not exact, the context might provide more information around one word. The following table [see Table 1] provides an overview of the context of the word "sea".

The fourth and final indicator considers three of the longest quotes. This indicator was developed in order to gain a "sense of place" of the place under investigation and

Table 1. The word 'Sea' and its context on the island of Sicily.

Marker No	Example
4	"Nature includes North African landscapes such as sandy dunes. The **sea** is transparent. If you are lucky you could also find a rare human specimen to which everyone hunts and help make the world better by freeing it from the mafia."
6	"The **sea** of Sicily."
7	"**sea** and beautiful landscapes."
8	"There is a beautiful **sea**."
12	"Near the **sea**."
14	"**Sea**, places and people."

to make maximum use of the context of words in their natural linguistic setting. In the case of Sicily, Italy, the following three quotes belong among the longest:

> "A visit to the Nebrodi Park is recommended for several reasons. I was there once and it hit me. Meanwhile, because there are still few tourists. Then because the nature here is still very intact, both in the cultivated areas and in the forest."

> "Sicily, the place where I was born and grew up. I lived near the Etna and then immersed in nature. What to say we had everything: sea, sun, mountain, snow, everything!"

> "The true Sicilian uncontaminated nature, the most deafening silence you can hear in Sicily."

4 Results

Together with the sample indicators mentioned above, Table 2 provides an overview of the results of indicators in three islands. Detailed results of each indicator are presented in the following sections. Comprehensive elaborations will follow in the conclusion part.

4.1 Results of Quantitative Indicators

The Average Used Words Per Person. The first quantitative indicator describes the average used characters per person. As can be seen in Table 2, Italians included in this dataset tend to describe most extensively why they appreciate certain parts of Sicily with an average of 33,4 English characters per person. Koreans involved in this study used 33,4 characters as well whereas Germans only use 17,3 characters on average.

Most Used Words Per Island. A second quantitative indicator copes with the number of different words that is being used to describe the different islands. Here, we only considered the first 33 markers due to reasons of comparability. Italians describing Sicily

Table 2. Main results from the pilot study.

	Jeju (South Korea)	Sylt (Germany)	Sicily (Italy)
Averagely used characters per person	33,41	17,25	33,39
Number of different words used in first 33 cases	71	43	84
Sutrop's Index of five most used words	1. Scenery (0,13) 2. Beautiful (0,06) 3. Good (0,04) 4. Natural (0,03) 5. Island (0,02)	1. Sea (0,24) 2. Beach (0,08) 3. Vacation (0,05) 4. Beautiful (0,04) 5. North (0,02)	1. Nature (0,13) 2. Sea (0,05) 3. Beautiful (0,04) 4. Place (0,02) 5. Relaxing (0,01)
Three of the most frequent words	Nature, scenery, good	Sea, beach, vacation	Nature, sea, beautiful
Three of the most rare words	Heaven, charms, memories	Homeland, peace, loneliness	Memories, wonderful, unique
Three of the longest sentences	1. "Jeju Island, the largest island in the Republic of Korea, is a beautiful scenic spot and a place for foreigners to visit. Especially, Halla Mountain is very scenic and is a very good place for walking and hiking." 2. "The scenery is very beautiful and the charm of each season is different. Where there is a tiring charm enough to try to visit every year." 3. "Jeju is a rejuvenating heaven. It's a place to visit once or twice a year. It's a very attractive place that does not need explanation."	1. "Beach, vacation, Sylt - that must be enough:)." 2. "Sylt is the most beautiful island in Germany." 3. "Wad and sandy beach is available."	1. "A visit to the Nebrodi park is recommended for several reasons. I was there once and it hit me. Meanwhile, because there are still few tourists. Then because the nature here is still very intact, both in the cultivated areas and in the forest." 2. "Sicily, the place where I was born and grew up. I lived near the Etna and then immersed in nature. What to say we had everything: sea, sun, mountain, snow, everything!" 3. "The true Sicilian uncontaminated nature, the most deafening silence you can hear in Sicily."

used the most different words with a total number of 84 words. Koreans use 71 different words to describe the attractiveness of the island of Jeju. Germans used 43 words.

Sutrop's Index. The third quantitative indicator considers the Sutrop's index. With regard to the outcomes in Table 2, it can be seen that the word "Sea" at Sylt scores particularly strong (Sutrop's index = 0,24), especially compared to the word "Sea" at Sicily. Remarkably, the first two quantitative indicators appear to follow a consistent pattern. Italian and Korean people in this sample seem to explain and describe most extensively why they value a particular natural place, followed by German people.

4.2 Results of Qualitative Indicators

The first qualitative indicator considers the three most often used words. In the case of Jeju (South-Korea), these are "natural", "scenery" and "good". Furthermore, the words "sea", "beach" and "vacation" were most often used when Germans described "Sylt". Lastly, the words "nature", "sea" and "beautiful" were most often used in the case of Sicily. From the results, it appears that the physical characteristics of the natural place are often mentioned.

The second qualitative indicator relates to the words that are remarkable and rarely mentioned but still might be of interest. Remarkable words that are not that often mentioned with regard to Jeju are "heaven", "fly" and "resort". In the case of Sylt, "relaxation", "peace" and "loneliness" were found. Finally, when looking at Sicily, the words "wonderful", "memories" and "unique", among others, appear. These words appear to be less directly related to the natural place but rather describe a certain "sphere" that is present at a particular natural place.

The third qualitative indicator copes with the context of certain often mentioned words. Considering the example, this indicator seems useful in describing linguistic connections of words. For instance, "sea" is mentioned twice in one sentence with "beautiful". Embedding frequently mentioned words in a certain context provides more information about what is exactly meant when a particular word is mentioned.

Therefore, when working with more cases, a more standardized account of word combinations could be developed. In doing so, the context of words can be further explored ultimately leading to a further understanding of how people value natural places.

A fourth qualitative indicator copes with some of the three longest sentences per island. The Italian sentences are the longest. This is mainly because the sentences consist of many adjectives. The Korean sentences seem to align with the Italian regarding the amount of adjectives being used. The German sentences seem to be more direct and to the point, using less adjectives. True language richness can be found in the following longest sentences:

Jeju: "Jeju Island ...a rejuvenating heaven".

Sylt: "Pure relaxation, the peace, the environment".

Sicily: "The true Sicilian uncontaminated nature, the most deafening silence you can hear".

5 Discussion

This study aims to enhance the understanding of how people value natural places, focusing on islands. In particular, the paper presents a conceptual basis for protocol to systematically analyze the information richness of the open answer to valuation questions.

The paper presents a theoretical framework underpinned by the concepts of landscape perception, Public Participation Geographical Information Systems (PPGIS). It also considers the role of language in order to frame the scientific context of mapping landscape values research. Linguistic data in the Greenmapper dataset is stored in participants' chosen language, mainly their native language, and translated for further standardized studies.

The paper also explores the empirical application of the framework conducting an international comparative case study of a small set of landscape appreciation statements in three countries, focusing on islands. With specific samples of Jeju, Sylt, and Sicily islands, this protocol has proved to be suitable for spatial planning purposes since it provides valuable insights into how people value landscapes. The supplementary linguistic expressions add to its characteristic of "participatory", and the open access regarding registration and downloading dataset add to the characteristic of "pubic".

From a methodological point of view, four quantitative indicators and three qualitative ones are proposed. The selection of indicators are based on word frequency and information richness, as well as its context. The results provide insight both quantitatively and qualitatively into language being used to value landscapes at three islands.

With specific samples in three countries, this method allows for an international comparison, but also leads to information missing. This inevitable cost in translation process might cause inaccuracy in indicator calculation. All responses to the open question were translated from German, Italian and South-Korean to English in order to assure comparability. Translation often fail to capture the full and exact meaning of the original language. Therefore, a further discussion about how to deal with such translation issues is therefore desirable. Key sentence analysis is essential but is dependent on the researcher's judgement.

Therefore, a priority in our research agenda is to develop relevant algorithms and apply the Greenmapper methodologies more extensively in other contexts.

References

1. Kaplan, R., Kaplan, S.: The Experience of Nature: A Psychological Perspective. Cambridge University Press, New York, NY, US (1989)
2. Howard, P.: An Introduction to Landscape. Routledge, Farnham, Surrey, England (2011)
3. Brown, G., Brabyn, L.: The extrapolation of social landscape values to a national level in New Zealand using landscape character classifications. Appl. Geogr. **35**, 84–94 (2012)
4. Brown, G., Brabyn, L.: An analysis of the relationships between multiple values and physical landscapes at a regional scale using public participation GIS and landscape character classification. Landsc. Urban Plan. **107**, 317–331 (2012)
5. Wartmann, M.F., Purves, R.S.: Investigating sense of place as a cultural ecosystem service in different landscapes through the lens of language. Landsc. Urban Plan. **175**, 169–183 (2018)

6. Garcia-Martin, M., et al.: Participatory mapping of landscape values in a Pan-European perspective. Landscape Ecol. **32**(11), 2133–2150 (2017). https://doi.org/10.1007/s10980-017-0531-x
7. Kühne, O.: Landscape Theories: A Brief Introduction. Springer (2019). https://doi.org/10.1007/978-3-658-25491-9
8. Wartman, M.F., Acheson, E., Purves, R.S.: Describing and comparing landscapes using tags, texts, and free lists: an interdisciplinary approach. Int. J. Inf. Sci. **32**(8), 1572–1592 (2018)
9. Brown, G.: An empirical evaluation of the spatial accuracy of public participation GIS (PPGIS) data. Appl. Geogr. **34**, 289–294 (2012)
10. Schlossberg, M., Shuford, E.: Delineating 'public' and 'participation' in PPGIS. J. Urban Reg. Inf. Syst. Assoc. **16**, 15–26 (2005)
11. Zube, E.H., Sell, J.L., Taylor, J.G.: Landscape perception: research, application and theory. Landscape Planning **9**, 1–33 (1982)
12. Brown, G., Strickland-Munro, J., Kobryn, H., Moore, S.: Mixed methods participatory GIS: an evaluation of the validity of qualitative and quantitative mapping methods. Appl. Geogr. **79**, 153–166 (2017)
13. Brown, G., Kyttä, M.: Key issues and research priorities for public participation GIS (PPGIS): a synthesis based on empirical research. Appl. Geogr. **46**, 122–136 (2014)
14. Sijtsma, F.J., Daams, M.N., Farjon, H., Buijs, A.E.: Deep feelings around a shallow coast. A spatial analysis of tourism jobs and the attractivity of nature in the Dutch Wadden area. Ocean Coast. Manag. **68**, 138–148 (2012)
15. de Vries, S., Buijs, A.E., Langers, F., Farjon, H., van Hinsberg, A., Sijtsma, F.J.: Measuring the attractiveness of Dutch landscapes: identifying national hotspots of highly valued places using Google Maps. Appl. Geogr. **45**, 220–229 (2013). https://doi.org/10.1016/j.apgeog.2013.09.017
16. Bijker, R.A., Sijtsma, F.J.: A portfolio of natural places: using a participatory GIS tool to compare the appreciation and use of green spaces inside and outside urban areas by urban residents. Landsc. Urban Plan. **158**, 155–165 (2017). https://doi.org/10.1016/j.landurbplan.2016.10.004
17. Daams, M.N., Sijtsma, F.J., van der Vlist, A.J.: The effect of natural space on nearby property prices: accounting for perceived attractiveness. Land Econ. **92**(3), 389–410 (2016)
18. Daams, M.N., Veneri, P.: Living near to attractive nature? a well-being indicator for ranking Dutch, Danish, and German functional urban areas. Soc. Indic. Res. **133**(2), 501–526 (2016). https://doi.org/10.1007/s11205-016-1375-5
19. Sutrop, U.: List task and a cognitive salience index. Field Methods **13**(3), 263–276 (2001)
20. Davis, N., Daams, M.N., Van Hinsberg, A., Sijtsma, F.J.: How deep is your love – of nature? A psychological and spatial analysis of the depth of feeling towards Dutch nature areas. Appl. Geogr. **77**, 36–48 (2016)

PHD Showcase Paper (EIAP 2023)

Multiscale Digital Landscape Reconstructions for Resilient Mountain Inner Areas

Chiara Chioni[✉] [ID]

Department of Civil, Environmental and Mechanical Engineering (DICAM), University of
Trento, 38123 Trento, Italy
chiara.chioni@unitn.it

Abstract. Lacking, declining, marginal, inner areas overlap worldwide with intermediate, rural and mountain territories where climate change and inherent social-
spatial vulnerabilities inhibit a smart, sustainable, and inclusive development.
Within this framework, the present contribution addresses the lack of methodologies for engaging and empowering community resilience in the case of Italian
mountain inner areas by investigating the integrated application of digital tools,
technologies and techniques for their planning, design, and management.

In a landscape-scale perspective, this work adopts an interdisciplinary and
multiscale approach towards the development of rapid and low-cost workflows
for 3D reconstructions to support information management activities. Connecting
a wide range of methods and tools (i.e., GIS mapping, photogrammetry, point cloud
modeling), two research explorations conducted in the Autonomous Province of
Trento (Italy) are presented as complementary approaches towards the digital representation of fragile landscapes at different spatial scales of action: the territorial
scale of municipal planning in Val di Sole, where 2.5D visualizations of cartographic information in a GIS environment and 3D models relying on satellite data
are identified; and the tree scale of forest management in the Mesiano University
park, where low-cost alternatives for under-storey vegetation 3D mapping (i.e.,
Apple iPad Pro with LiDAR sensor and Ricoh Theta V 360° camera) are tested.

Keywords: Inner Areas · Community Resilience · Landscape Representation ·
Digital Modeling

1 Introduction

1.1 A 'Glocal' Framework: Areas Suffering from Territorial Imbalances

'Inner areas' is the Italian terminological declination [1] of the internationally debated
issue concerning territorial imbalances and spatial inequalities [2]. In the framework
of the current (2021–2027) European Cohesion Policy, the new season of the Italian
National Strategy for Inner Areas (SNAI) – which has also been funded by the 2021
National Recovery and Resilience Plan (PNRR) – aims to counteract the marginalization
and demographic decline of 114 'reservoirs of resilience' [3], corresponding to almost
4,000 municipalities covering the 58.8% of the national territory [4].

© The Author(s), under exclusive license to Springer Nature Switzerland AG 2023
O. Gervasi et al. (Eds.): ICCSA 2023 Workshops, LNCS 14112, pp. 17–26, 2023.
https://doi.org/10.1007/978-3-031-37129-5_2

Worldwide, lacking, declining, marginal, or 'peripheral' [5] areas – regardless of the various classification methodologies, if any – overlap with intermediate, rural and mountain territories where climate change and inherent social-spatial vulnerabilities inhibit a smart, sustainable, and inclusive development.

Trying to go beyond standardized definitions, the ongoing research project of national interest "B4R Branding4Resilience. Tourist infrastructure as a tool to enhance small villages by drawing resilient communities and new open habitats" (B4R) proposes an interdisciplinary and multiscale methodological approach which integrates different qualitative and quantitative tools (i.e., data analyses and mapping, territorial portraits, stakeholder analysis, a collaborative platform) to explore inner territories, interact with local actors (i.e., public and private institutions, and associations), and support them in designing future strategic scenarios [6]. Specifically, the B4R research unit of the University of Trento, focusing on the Val di Sole inner area in the Autonomous Province of Trento (Italy), aims to create a territorial branding strategy on the value of (thermal) water resources by promoting the enhancement of the natural capital through co-designed spatial transformations, also in response to the medium-high level of risk [7] (Fig. 1).

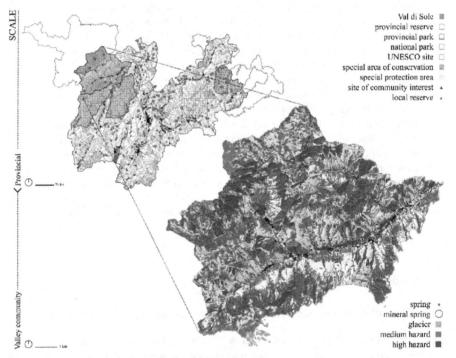

Fig. 1. Left: location of the Val di Sole in the Autonomous Province of Trento (Italy), and the protected natural sites. Right: medium-high multi-hazard risk (hydrogeological, avalanche, seismic and forest fire) and hydrological resources in the valley. Image from [8].

Within this 'glocal' (i.e., simultaneously 'global' and 'local') framework [9], the present contribution addresses the lack of methodologies for engaging and empowering resilience in society, focusing on the paradigmatic case of Italian mountain inner areas which are nodes of larger social, political, and economic frameworks [10]. Acknowledging that the term 'resilience' is used in different disciplinary fields, in the following the author will refer to 'community resilience', as embedded in the broader social-ecological resilience perspective (i.e., implying consideration of spatial aspects, environmental features of built and natural environments, and issues of equity, inclusion, and justice) [11]. Accordingly, in mountain areas, the existing gaps should be addressed by relying on local knowledge and co-creating solutions with communities [12].

1.2 A Landscape-Scale Perspective for Resilient Mountain Inner Areas

For the management, planning, and design of mountain inner areas, this study, as part of an ongoing PhD research, adopts a landscape-scale perspective: since landscape derives from the actions and the interrelationships of human and natural factors [13], encompassing multiscale ecosystems from the territory to the single tree (and beyond), it seems the suitable spatial unit to be addressed in order to meet both the global Sustainable Development Goals (i.e., Goal 9, 'Industry, innovation and infrastructure'; Goal 10, 'Reduced inequalities'; and Goal 11, 'Sustainable cities and communities') and the local SNAI objectives, and to achieve the 'twin' green and digital transitions in the long-term future [14].

However, focusing on digital tools, technologies and techniques, there is an enduring gap between the mainstream approaches in landscape management, planning, and design [15], and the industry-standard mapping and modeling for the architectural and urban scales (Fig. 2).

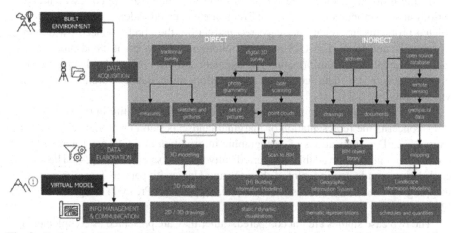

Fig. 2. Each scale of study privileges different data acquisition techniques and returns information in different shapes, which can be mixed, integrated, and adapted depending on the specific object of investigation, the purposes of the analysis, and the project. Image from [16].

Indeed, at the landscape scale, digital reconstructions are generally based on a Geographic Information System (GIS) approach, drawing data from cartography or remotely sensed images, but there is an increasing interest in adopting the Building Information Modeling (BIM) paradigm – as demonstrated by the relatively new term Landscape Information Modeling (LIM) [17, 18], that could be approached also as an integration of BIM and GIS – or the 'cloudism' methodology, where landscape design is driven by point cloud modeling [19].

Moving in this critical gap, exacerbated in 'infrastructurally' raw systems as inner areas (because of poor Internet connectivity, lack of sensors, etc.), the methodological and operational proposal of this contribution investigates the integrated application of digital tools, technologies and techniques (especially if rapid and low-cost) in the landscape management, planning, and design of resilient mountain inner areas to support information management activities and help democratize decision-making also towards the overcoming of digital divide and lack of digital literacy.

2 Materials and Methods

The research design adopts an inherently interdisciplinary and multiscale approach towards the development of rapid and low-cost workflows for digital landscape reconstructions; respectively, it integrates landscape planning and design with survey and digital modeling disciplines and investigates micro (single tree) and macro (territorial) spatial scales (translating into landscape the concept "From the Spoon to the City", lit. "Dal Cucchiaio alla Città", by Ernesto Nathan Rogers). In completion of the B4R methodological framework based on 'Research by Design' [6, 20], this research also adopts a 'Learning by Doing' approach [21] to further investigate the use of digital data acquisition and representation tools in landscape architecture.

In the following, selected results from two self-contained applied research explorations in the Autonomous Province of Trento are presented. Addressing different scale-related problems in digital landscape reconstruction, they both connect a wide range of methods and tools (i.e., GIS mapping, photogrammetry, point cloud modeling) to tackle different steps of information management activities oriented at landscape planning and design (i.e., data acquisition and transformation, data elaboration and results' visualization) [22, 23].

The first exploration, applied to a portion of Peio municipality in the upper Val di Sole, concerns the representation of marginal landscapes at a territorial scale: ranging from the 2.5D visualizations of cartographic information in a GIS environment to 3D models from globally available and periodically updated satellite data [24]. The second exploration, conducted in a plot of the Mesiano University park in Trento, regards 3D mapping of trees with low-cost sensors (i.e., Apple iPad Pro with integrated LiDAR [25], and Ricoh Theta V 360° camera [26]).

The two case studies are not compared, rather they are presented as complementary approaches (Table 1) towards the development of digital 'twins' of the landscape at different scales of action – from the territorial scale of municipal planning [27] to the tree scale of forest management [28] – in order to support the spatial decision-making, ultimately promoting stakeholder engagement and public empowerment from a community resilience perspective [8].

Table 1. Summary information about the workflows for 3D reconstructions in the two applied research explorations.

Case study	Peio municipality in the upper Val di Sole		Mesiano University park in Trento	
Workflow	'Automatic' image-based modeling from the web	Image-based modeling from Google Earth	Point cloud modeling from LiDAR sensor	Image-based modeling from a panoramic camera
Data input	Satellite image (from Jaxa)	Satellite image (from Landsat/Copernicus)	Point clouds	360° video
Method	-	Photogrammetry	Point cloud modeling	Spherical photogrammetry
Tool(s)	Dell Inspiron 16 Plus 7620 (personal laptop)	Dell Inspiron 16 Plus 7620 (personal laptop)	Apple iPad Pro WI-FI 12.9", Dell Inspiron 16 Plus 7620 (personal laptop)	Ricoh Theta V 360° camera, Dell Inspiron 16 Plus 7620 (personal laptop)
Software	Lands Design plugin for Rhinoceros	Google Earth Pro, Autodesk ReCap Photo	3D Scanner App, CloudCompare	Agisoft Metashape
Data output	Textured mesh surface with 3D buildings	Textured mesh surface	Textured point cloud	Textured point cloud

3   Results

3.1   Territorial Scale: Digital Reconstructions from 'Indirect' Data

In the case of Val di Sole, the B4R research unit of the University of Trento conducted a preliminary quali-quantitative exploration to gather and reorganize the existing distributed information resources in thematic maps, diagrams, and plots of cross-cutting indicators [7]. Among the open data retrieved from the Autonomous Province of Trento, the Digital Terrain Model (DTM) acquired with airborne LiDAR technologies in 2014 (and integrated in 2018), and the digital orthophoto (i.e., a 4-band RGBI orthophotomosaic) acquired through an aero-photogrammetric survey between 2014 and 2016, were used in this study to produce textured 2.5D visualizations of portions of Peio municipality in a GIS environment with the Qgis2threejs plugin for QGIS software.

Without conducting new extensive and resource-consuming survey campaigns to acquire more updated data, 'agile' (i.e., expeditious and inexpensive – both in terms of economic resources and computational power) 3D geometric digital modeling workflows, relying on current available online satellite data, have been tested for virtually reconstructing portions of Peio municipality [24]. A textured mesh surface with 3D buildings is obtained with an 'automatic' geometric modeling from the cloud by importing elevation data of the selected location through the Lands Design plugin for Rhinoceros software; similarly, but without elevation data for buildings, a textured mesh surface is generated with an image-based geometric modeling from Google Earth data by acquiring a video tour of the selected location through Google Earth Pro software and processing frames in cloud with Autodesk ReCap Photo software (Fig. 3).

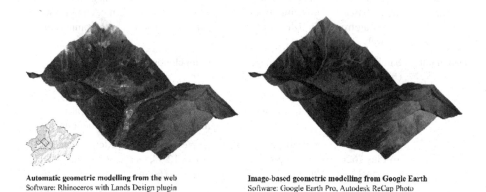

Automatic geometric modelling from the web
Software: Rhinoceros with Lands Design plugin
Output: textured mesh surface with 3D buildings

Image-based geometric modelling from Google Earth
Software: Google Earth Pro, Autodesk ReCap Photo
Output: textured mesh surface

Fig. 3. 3D textured mesh surfaces of the same portion of Peio municipality (pink-colored, in the upper Val di Sole) from rapid satellite image processing. Left: result from the 'automatic' geometric modeling workflow (~ ten minutes); right: result from the image-based geometric modeling workflow (~ one hour). Image from [24].

3.2   Tree Scale: Digital Reconstructions from 'Direct' Data

In the case of a plot of the Mesiano University park in Trento, two low-cost sensors (i.e., the Apple iPad Pro WI-FI 12.9" with LiDAR sensor, and the Ricoh Theta V 360° camera) are explored and compared (in terms of data acquisition time, processing and modeling, and the overall visual fidelity of the results) to close-range photogrammetry (conducted with the Canon EOS600D 18 mm camera) and terrestrial laser scanning (conducted with the Leica ScanStation 2 scanner) which currently is the gold standard for 3D reconstructions in forestry [29]. The description of workflows for the point clouds generation by means of classical photogrammetry and terrestrial laser scanning are overlooked in the following because belong to an established practice.

Following the current best practices to scan with iPad [30] and aware that the range of its sensor is approximately 5 m, the data acquisition was conducted by the author using the 3D Scanner App (between the most suitable for this application), slowly circling each tree in the plot and trying not to scan the same area twice (~ half an hour). After the first processing of the scans directly in the app, the generated point clouds were exported in a XYZ file format and imported into CloudCompare software for the alignment through the targets (~ one hour) (Fig. 4).

With regards to spherical video acquisitions with the Ricoh Theta V, they were acquired by the author again walking around the study plot, circling each tree slowly (~

Fig. 4. 3D textured point cloud of the study plot in the Mesiano University park acquired with the Apple iPad Pro with LiDAR sensor.

fifteen minutes). With the software Agisoft Metashape, first the frames (i.e., panoramic images) were split and oriented using the spherical camera model, then the point cloud was obtained via dense matching. Unlike the point clouds generated with the iPad, the textured 3D model derived from spherical photogrammetry needed to be scaled (through the targets) and oriented in space (~ two hours) (Fig. 5).

Fig. 5. 3D textured point cloud of the study plot in the Mesiano University park generated from the acquisition with the Ricoh Theta V 360° camera.

4 Discussion and Conclusion

The presented range of methods and tools (i.e., GIS mapping, photogrammetry, point cloud modeling) have been investigated to evaluate their capacity to support rapid and inexpensive 3D digital reconstructions of landscapes at different scales of action, from municipal planning and design to forest management.

Both the research explorations aim to make the acquisition, elaboration, and/or fruition of technical information more intuitive and interactive: in the case of a portion of Peio municipality in the upper Val di Sole, mapping and modeling processes based on cartography and remotely sensed images are oriented at improving accessibility of scattered geospatial data towards the management and design of territorial transformations; in the case of a plot of the Mesiano University park in Trento, because the crown canopy hinders the above-measurements of the below-foliage stem part, a direct 3D mapping of the under-storey vegetation is oriented to support the low-cost monitoring, analysis and visualization of forest development.

While the geometric accuracy of the results may be challenged, the overall visual outputs of these 3D digital reconstructions are satisfactory for their purposes, given the limited time and expense required to generate them.

The long-term goal of this PhD research is to outline a process that connects and operationalizes existing distributed information resources by enabling real-time/regularly updated data integration into Territorial Digital Twins – of which Forest Digital Twins would be essential components – as 3D virtual copies of that landscape to ultimately promote stakeholder engagement and public empowerment.

Indeed, because of the global availability of smartphones and the increasing popularity of cameras and drones even among non-professionals, the actualization of information technologies' affordances for landscape planning and design in mountain inner areas could rely also on citizens as prosumers (i.e., both consumers and producers) of data. While combining crowdsourced street-level and/or aerial imagery with other data sources requires further research on integrating citizen science inputs into data collection and elaboration processes, low-cost sensors promise to significantly reduce the future costs of 3D digital documentation campaigns. The research still needs to verify how and whether, through the presented workflows, the citizens can be placed at the center of the project, sharing criticalities and results with them.

Acknowledgments. This work is part of an ongoing PhD research financially supported by the Department of Civil, Environmental and Mechanical Engineering (DICAM) of the University of Trento and by the Italian Ministry of University and Research (MUR) in the frame of "B4R–Branding4Resilience. Tourist Infrastructure as a Tool to Enhance Small Villages by Drawing Resilient Communities and New Open Habitats" (Project number: 201735N7HP). The latter is a research project of relevant national interest (PRIN 2017—Youth Line) coordinated by the Università Politecnica delle Marche (Principal Investigator Prof. Maddalena Ferretti) and involves as partners the Università degli Studi di Palermo (Local Coordinator Prof. Barbara Lino), the Università degli Studi di Trento (Local Coordinator Prof. Sara Favargiotti), and the Politecnico di Torino (Local Coordinator Prof. Diana Rolando).

The author acknowledges her supervisors, Prof. Sara Favargiotti and Prof. Giovanna A. Massari (University of Trento), for their essential contribution to the development and the outcome of the overall research.

With regard to the acquisition of data in the Mesiano University park, the author also acknowledges Prof. Giovanna A. Massari and Prof. Alfonso Vitti (University of Trento) for the free loan of the instrumentation used in the survey campaigns, and Prof. Marco Ciolli, PhD candidates Chiara Frungillo, Anna Maragno, Angelica Pianegonda, Research fellow Andrea Biotti (Univerisity of Trento) for their operative contributions during the acquisitions.

References

1. Barca, F., Casavola, P., Lucatelli, S.: A strategy for inner areas in Italy: definition, objectives, tools and governance. Mater. UVAL **31** (2014)
2. Oppido, S., Ragozino, S., De Vita, G.E.: Exploring territorial imbalances: a systematic literature review of meanings and terms. In: Bevilacqua, C., Calabrò, F., Della Spina, L. (eds.) NMP 2020. SIST, vol. 177, pp. 90–100. Springer, Cham (2020). https://doi.org/10.1007/978-3-030-52869-0_8
3. Dipartimento per lo Sviluppo e la Coesione Economica: Strategia Nazionale per le Aree Interne: Definizione, Obiettivi, Strumenti e Governance; Accordo di Partenariato 2014–2020. Rome (2013)
4. Dipartimento per le Politiche di Coesione: Aggiornamento 2020 della mappa delle Aree Interne. Nota tecnica NUVAP. 14 febbraio 2022 (2022)
5. ESPON: PROFECY – Processes, Features and Cycles of Inner Peripheries in Europe. Applied Research. Final report. Version 07/12/2017 (2017)
6. Ferretti, M., Favargiotti, S., Lino, B., Rolando, D.: Branding4Resilience: explorative and collaborative approaches for inner territories. Sustainability **14**(8), 11235 (2022)
7. Favargiotti, S., Pasquali, M., Chioni, C., Pianegonda, A.: Water resources and health tourism in Val di Sole: key elements for innovating with nature in the Italian inner territories. Sustainability **14**(8), 11294 (2022)
8. Chioni, C., Pezzica, C., Favargiotti, S.: Territorial digital twins: a key for increasing the community resilience of fragile mountain inner territories? Sustainable Development (2023). (in Press)
9. Robertson, R.: Globalization: Social Theory and Global Culture. Sage, London (1992)
10. Carrer, F., Walsh, K., Mocci, F.: Ecology, economy, and upland landscapes: socio-ecological dynamics in the alps during the transition to modernity. Hum. Ecol. **48**(1), 69–84 (2020). https://doi.org/10.1007/s10745-020-00130-y
11. Imperiale, A.J., Vanclay, F.: Conceptualizing community resilience and the social dimensions of risk to overcome barriers to disaster risk reduction and sustainable development. Sustain. Dev. **29**(5), 891–905 (2021)
12. Wyss, R., et al.: Mountain resilience: a systematic literature review and paths to the future. Mt. Res. Dev. **42**(2), A23–A36 (2022)
13. Council of Europe: European Landscape Convention. Florence (2000)
14. Muench, S., Stoermer, E., Jensen, K., Asikainen, T., Salvi, M., Scapolo, F.: Towards a Green and Digital Future. Publications Office of the European Union, Luxembourg (2022)
15. Edler, D., Jenal, C., Kühne, O. (eds.): Modern Approaches to the Visualization of Landscapes. RSRL, Springer, Wiesbaden (2020). https://doi.org/10.1007/978-3-658-30956-5
16. Barbini, A., Chioni, C.: Reality vs virtual modeling. from building to landscape heritage representation. In: Proceedings of the 26th Conference on Cultural Heritage and New Technologies (2023). (in Press)
17. Nessel, A.: The place for information models in landscape architecture, or a place for landscape architects in information models. In: Buhmann, E., Ervin, S.M., Pietsch, M. (eds.) Peer Review Proceedings of Digital Landscape Architecture 2013 at Anhalt University of Applied Sciences (2013)
18. Zhang, Z.: Application of LIM technology in landscape design. In: Abawajy, J., Xu, Z., Atiquzzaman, M., Zhang, X. (eds.) ATCI 2021. LNDECT, vol. 81, pp. 916–921. Springer, Cham (2021). https://doi.org/10.1007/978-3-030-79197-1_138
19. Girot, C.: Cloudism. In: An, M., Hovestadt, L., Bühlmann, V. (eds.) Architecture and Naturing Affairs, pp. 96–101. Birkhäuser, Berlin, Boston (2020)

20. Roggema, R.: Research by design: proposition for a methodological approach. Urban Sci. **1**, 2 (2016)
21. Freire, P.: Creating alternative research methods: learning to do it by doing it. In: Hall, B., Gillette, A., Tandon, R. (eds.) Creating Knowledge: A Monopoly?, pp. 29–37. International Council for Adult Education, Toronto (1982)
22. Hadar, L., et al.: Envisioning future landscapes: a data-based visualization model for ecosystems under alternative management scenarios. Landsc. Urban Plan. **215**, 104214 (2021)
23. Huang, J., Lucash, M.S., Scheller, R.M., Klippel, A.: Walking through the forests of the future: using data-driven virtual reality to visualize forests under climate change. Int. J. Geogr. Inf. Sci. **35**(6), 1155–1178 (2020)
24. Chioni, C., Favargiotti, S.: Digital representation of marginal landscapes: 'agile' 3D modeling workflows for an Italian inner valley. J. Digit. Landscape Architect. **8**, 134–141 (2023). (in Press)
25. Gollob, C., Ritter, T., Kraßnitzer, R., Tockner, A., Nothdurft, A.: Measurement of forest inventory parameters with Apple iPad Pro and integrated LiDAR technology. Remote Sens. **13**, 3129 (2021)
26. Murtiyoso, A., Hristova, H., Rehush, N., Griess, V.C.: Low-cost mapping of forest understorey vegetation using spherical photogrammetry. Int. Arch. Photogram. Remote Sens. Spatial Inf. Sci., XLVIII-2/W1-2022 **48**, 185–190 (2022)
27. Dembski, F., Linzer, H., Voigt, A., Wieshofer, I.: Green, digital, inclusive: new directions in urban and regional planning. In: AESOP Annual Congress Space for Species: Redefining Spatial Justice – Book of Abstracts, pp. 432–433 (2022)
28. Buonocore, L., Yates, J., Valentini, R.: A proposal for a forest digital twin framework and its perspectives. Forests **13**, 498 (2022)
29. Mokroš, M., et al.: Novel low-cost mobile mapping systems for forest inventories as terrestrial laser scanning alternatives. Int. J. Appl. Earth Obs. Geoinf. **104**, 102512 (2021)
30. Bobrowski, R., Winczek, M., Zięba-Kulawik, K., Wężyk, P.: Best practices to use the iPad Pro LiDAR for some procedures of data acquisition in the urban forest. Urban Forestry & Urban Greening **79**, 127815 (2023)

Short Paper (AAILT 2023)

An Approach to Decentralized Hybrid Question Answering Systems

Dilan Bakır[ID] and Mehmet S. Aktas[(✉)][ID]

Yildiz Technical University, Istanbul, Turkey
dilan.bakir@std.yildiz.edu.tr, aktas@yildiz.edu.tr

Abstract. Question answering (QA) systems are sequence-to-sequence model based programs that find the most accurate answer to a query by using given texts. In today's world, QA system software is run on different platforms by various institutions. This means that users have to use different QA system software, developed with different technologies on various platforms, to find the most accurate answer to their queries. However, there is a lack of systems that allow these types of systems to be used in a hybrid manner on a single interface. To address this issue, this research investigates a software architecture that will enable QA systems trained with different datasets on various platforms to be used with a single programming interface. To demonstrate the feasibility and usefulness of the proposed hybrid question answering system framework software architecture, a prototype software has been developed. The performance of the developed prototype software has been compared with standalone QA system software based on the execution time performance metric. The obtained results demonstrate that the proposed framework software architecture has negligible processing overheads.

Keywords: Hybrid System · Question answering · Artificial intelligence · Transformer · Sequence-to-Sequence Models

1 Introduction

In today's world, the vast amount of information available on the internet has made it increasingly difficult to find accurate answers to queries. To address this challenge, researchers have developed question answering systems that are capable of understanding natural language queries and providing relevant answers. However, these systems are often developed by different institutions and run on different platforms, making it difficult for users to access accurate answers in a timely manner.

In this context, the development of a hybrid question answering systems has emerged as a potential solution. The hybrid question and answer systems will enable users to access multiple question answering systems that have been trained on different data sets and run on different platforms through a single interface. This approach has the potential to significantly improve the efficiency and accuracy of finding information from large amounts of text data.

© The Author(s), under exclusive license to Springer Nature Switzerland AG 2023
O. Gervasi et al. (Eds.): ICCSA 2023 Workshops, LNCS 14112, pp. 29–38, 2023.
https://doi.org/10.1007/978-3-031-37129-5_3

This paper presents a study that investigates the feasibility of developing a hybrid question answering system framework. The proposed software architecture enables question answering systems to be used in a transparent manner by allowing systems trained on different data sets and run on different platforms to be accessed through a single interface. The authors developed a prototype software to demonstrate the usability of the proposed framework software architecture, and found that it is useful and feasible.

Overall, the results of this study have important implications for the future of hybrid question answering systems, as the development of hybrid systems could significantly improve the accessibility and accuracy of information retrieval from large amounts of text data.

In this study, we compare the results of T5 and BERT models in hybrid question answering systems. By integrating hybrid question answering systems, we aim to advance the field and improve the accuracy of natural language processing models.

In Sect. 1, provides an introduction to the study, highlighting the importance of hybrid question answering system. In Sect. 2, outlines the research questions we sought to answer through our study. In Sect. 3, provides a literature review of question answering systems fields, discussing the challenges and recent advancements in these areas. In Sect. 4, we give information about the methodology we propose. In Sect. 5, we cover the details of our prototype implementation and experimental work. In Sect. 6 describes the result of our work and how we should work for the future.

2   Research Questions

The aim of this research is to explore the feasibility of developing a hybrid question answering system framework that allows for the efficient and accurate retrieval of information from large amounts of text data. To achieve this aim, the study will focus on addressing the following research questions:

RQ1: What are the technical requirements and software architecture for developing a hybrid question answering system framework that can access multiple systems trained on different datasets and run on different platforms through a single interface?

RQ2: How can a hybrid question answering system framework be developed to enable multiple question answering systems to be accessed through a single interface?

RQ3: What are the key considerations for integrating question answering systems trained on different data sets and run on different platforms within a hybrid framework?

RQ4: How can we evaluate the performance of the hybrid Question Answering Systems from the execution time performance metric perspective?

By addressing these research questions, this study aims to provide insights into the development of hybrid question answering systems and their potential to improve the accessibility and accuracy of information retrieval. The findings of this study could have important implications for the future development and application of question answering systems.

3 Question Answering Literature Review

Studies in the field of Question Answering first started as Knowledge Bases (KB). However, it has been observed that there are certain difficulties in extracting the answer from the raw text. With these difficulties, the need to be read and understood by a machine and the answer to be produced by the machine has increased. These need studies have led to Deep learning techniques. And with the development of deep learning, studies in the field of QA have increased.

Studies in the field of question Answering systems are increasing day by day. We have done a literature review [12] about Question Answering systems in our previous studies. When we examine the literature, the first studies were done on dynamic attention mechanisms [13], and context is updated with query weights [14]. Following this work, the memoryless Bidirectional+attention model (Bidaf) attention mechanism was developed [15]. Bidaf, one of the question Answering systems, is an extractive reader system that estimates the start and end position from the context and accepts that the answer is in the context. Transformer models such as BART, and T5 are generative systems that produce the answer randomly, not from within the context. Extractive readers have been found to produce more consistent and logical answers than generative readers.

All of these studies focus on improving machine comprehension reader performance using different approaches. However, more work is still needed in this area, and better models are expected to be developed in the future. Transformer models have become very popular in the field of machine-understanding readers in recent years. These models give successful results in solving many problems, especially in the field of natural language processing. Below are some machine-understanding reader exercises using transformer models:

BERT (Bidirectional Encoder Representations from Transformers) [16]: This work is an important example of the use of transformer models in the field of machine understanding readers. BERT is a set of models that are trained on an unformatted text corpus and then fine-tuned for different tasks. BERT has achieved high accuracy rates on datasets such as SQuAD.

RoBERTa (Robustly Optimized BERT Pretraining Approach) [17]: RoBERTa is a model that extends BERT's core pretraining methodology. RoBERTa is trained longer on a larger text corpus and then fine-tuned on datasets such as SQuAD. This model outperformed BERT.

ALBERT (A Lite BERT for Self-supervised Learning of Language Representations) [18]: ALBERT is a lightened version of BERT. ALBERT uses a number of innovative methods that keep BERT's encodings smaller while maintaining its performance. This model outperformed BERT on datasets such as SQuAD.

ELECTRA (Efficiently Learning an Encoder that Classifies Token Replacements Accurately) [19]: This model offers a more efficient learning method by changing the learning process of BERT. ELECTRA misleadingly changes some words in the input text and then learns that the model must detect these misleading changes. This model achieved high accuracy rates on datasets such as SQuAD.

These studies show that transformer models can be used successfully in the field of machine understanding readers. It is envisaged that these models will be used in the future to further improve machine comprehension reader performance.

The T5 (Text-to-Text Transfer Transformer) [20] transformer model has made a significant contribution to the field of machine understanding readers. T5 is a model developed by Google that provides better performance by combining various natural language processing tasks into a single model.

In the machine understanding reader area, the T5 model is pre-trained for several different tasks. For example, the T5 model was trained on the SQuAD and Natural Questions (NQ) datasets and was among the best-performing models in both datasets.

The T5 is also a large model that enables fast and efficient learning. Therefore, large transformer models such as the T5 model may become even more common in the machine understanding reader field in the future and can be used to provide better performance. The BART (Bidirectional and Auto-Regressive Transformer) [21] transformer model has made a significant contribution to the field of machine understanding readers. BART is a model developed by Facebook and is a machine-understanding reader model that is both pre-trained and task-specific.

BART is a large model that successfully performs a variety of natural language processing tasks. In the machine understanding reader field, the BART model has achieved good results in experiments on the SQuAD, Natural Questions (NQ), and TriviaQA datasets.

The BART model is especially useful when there are data constraints. As a pre-trained language model, the model performs well on many datasets and achieves good results even when trained with a limited dataset.

The contribution of the BART model is especially important for researchers and application developers who want to achieve better results with less data in the machine-understanding reader area.

Federated Learning for Mobile Keyboard Prediction [9], In this study, Google used federated learning in mobile keyboard prediction to prevent learning data from being collected on a central server. In this way, the confidentiality of the data collected from users was preserved.

Federated Learning with Non-IID Data [10], In this study, Google demonstrated how the federated learning model can deal with different distributions of data (non-IID). This study showed that differences in data distribution were not a barrier during the data collection phase of federative learning.

Towards Federated Learning at Scale [11], In this study, Google presented a set of recommendations on systems design to enable large-scale federated learning applications.

In this study, we focus on an hybrid question answering system that can work on different sub systems. There exists examples of such hybrid systems in the literature for web services domain [23,24]. We observe studies in web services based systems with variety of focus area such as [25–30,32,38,39,41]. In this study, we utilize restful based web services for question and answering systems. There exits studies for data representation in different domains such as web usage mining [33,36,37]. In this study, we focus on the hybrid and federated question and answering systems. We leave the representation of the questions and answers as out-of-focus. We also observe studies that focus on quality of software systems [34,35].In this study, we mainly focus on building the question and answering system and leave out the analysis of software quality aspect for future work. There are studies focusing on misinformation and privacy policy violation in social networks [22,40]. Different from these studies, we focus on providing the right answer to the given questions. And we focus on transformer models trained based on the data available on the Web domain.

4   Proposed Methodology

In this study, we propose a hybrid questions and answering system as it is illustrated in Fig. 1. The proposed architecture enables users to utilize multiple question and answer systems in a transparent way via a single user interface. The proposed architecture also has a federation capability. The architecture includes modules that are responsible for merging the results coming from multiple sub-question and answer systems.

The proposed module has various modules: Distributor Module, Data Post Processing Module, Federator Module. We explain the details of each module below.

Distributor Module: This module is responsible for relaying incoming requests to corresponding question and answer subsystems. To do this, this module utilizes a mapping rule file. The mapping rule file maps the path for the subsystems with their description. It also includes the class names and the function names for the prediction functions of corresponding sub question answering systems. The distributed module also utilizes a properties file, which includes the configuration details of the proposed hybrid question and answering system. The distributed module is not dependent on the technology used in the subsystems. It is one layer above the subsystems. Hence, if the subsystems' implementations change, this will not affect the functioning of the Distributed Module. To archive this property, we utilize Facade Design pattern.

Data-Post Processing Module: The proposed framework will not only enable the hybrid prediction functions but also federated prediction functions. In case, the federation based prediction capability is requested by the end-user, then the post-processing module will process the results of each question and answering subsystem for federation capability. Here, the results will be processed for tasks like stop word removal, stemming etc.

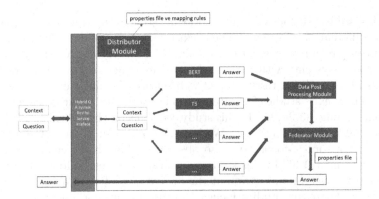

Fig. 1. Our approach on hybrid question answering architecture

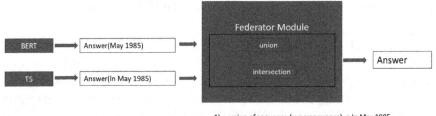

1) union of sequence (supersequence). = In May 1985
2) intersection of sequences (subsequence) = May 1985

Fig. 2. Federator Module

Federator Module: This module is responsible federating the results coming from more than one question and answer systems. This module is illustrated in Fig. 2. It includes two sub modules, each is responsible for a federation method. Here, we only implemented union and intersection based result federation. We discuss the details of these methods below.

We denote a sequence s by $< a_1, a_2 \ldots, a_r >$, where a_i is an wordset, which is also called an element of s. We denote an element (or an itemset) of a sequence by $x_1, x_2, \ldots, x_k$, where x_i is an item. A sequence of length k is called a k-sequence.

If we depict the question-answering system as a sequence, we can show it as s sequence <hello world, explore the world>.
$a_1 =$ hello world, $a_2 =$ explore the world
$a_1 = \{$hello, world$\}$ $a_2 = \{$explore, the, world$\}$

Union: The union of two sequences contains all elements in either sequence, without duplicates. For example, if sequence A = [hello, world] and sequence B = [explore, the, world], then their union A ∪ B = [hello, explore, the, world].

Intersection: The intersection of two sequences contains only the elements that appear in both sequences. For example, if sequence A = [hello, world] and sequence B = [explore, the, world], then their intersection A ∩ B = [world].

5   Prototype Application and Experimental Study

Prototype: We implemented the proposed software architecture using Pytorch library (version 1.13.1) by using Python programming language. We used T5 and BERT models as transformer model, T5tokenizer and BertTokenizer as tokenizer.

Dataset: In this study, a hybrid question answering systems study was performed using BERT and T5 transformer models. The TQUAD dataset was used in this study. TQUAD (Turkish Question Answering Dataset) is a question-answer dataset created for use in the field of Turkish natural language processing. This dataset has been prepared by researchers at Bilkent University for use in the field of Turkish natural language processing. TQUAD contains a total of 27,503 question-answer pairs, and these pairs were automatically extracted from the Turkish Wikipedia pages. This dataset can contribute to the advancement of research in Turkish natural language processing.

Experimental Study and Discussion on the Results: This study, by designing a hybrid question-answering system, We observed measure the execute time of the hybrid system by taking the results from many transformer models and hybrid system. The results from Transformer models, T5 and Bert, are obtained from sequence operations such as union and intersect, and the results according to execute time and standard deviation are shared in Table 1.

By sending a request thirty times in a row, we calculate the execute time and standard deviation of each response we obtained from Bert, t5 and the hybrid response, and show them in Table 1. Table 1 shows that the hybrid system offers negligible runtime by comparing the execution times by giving an additional load to the system. Our goal here is to integrate many transformer models into the hybrid system and to establish a more effective, useful system without losing time and we have examined the success of the hybrid system. The results indicate that the hybrid question and answering system has negligible processing overheads. Hence, it provides the hybrid question and answer system capability by providing a competitive execution performance.

Table 1. Execution Performance for Hybrid Question and Answering

	Hybrid T5 (ms)	T5 (ms)	Hybrid BERT (ms)	BERT (ms)
avg	699.58	692.64	92.19	86.71
std	24.45	17.84	7.89	5.44

6   Conclusion and Future Works

The study presented in this paper aims to address the challenges associated with using different question answering (QA) systems developed by various institutions and run on different platforms. The proposed software architecture enables QA systems to be used in a hybrid manner, allowing systems trained on different data sets and run on different platforms to be accessed through a single interface. The results of the study demonstrate the feasibility and usefulness of the proposed hybrid QA system framework software architecture, which can help improve the efficiency and accuracy of finding information from large amounts of text data. In addition, the study compares the effectiveness of T5 and BERT models in hybrid question answering systems. The results of the experimental study on the prototype application indicates that the proposed architecture has negligible processing overheads while providing the hybrid functionality.

Overall, the study highlights the importance of hybrid question answering systems and the potential of hybrid system to improve the accuracy of natural language processing models. The proposed framework software architecture can help address the current challenges associated with running QA systems on different platforms and using various technologies.

In the future, we plan on conducting experimental studies on federation capability of the proposed system architecture. We also plan on conducting further experimental studies to investigate the system performance as the size of the simultaneous users, using the system for question answer capabilities, increase.

References

1. McMahan, B., Ramage, D.: Google Ai Blog. Communication-Efficient Learning with Federated Learning: An Overview (2020). https://ai.googleblog.com/2020/05/communication-efficient-learning-with.html
2. Tensorflow Federated: Machine Learning on Decentralized Data (2020). https://www.tensorflow.org/federated/. Accessed 16 Apr 2023
3. Federated AI Ecosystem-Collaborative Learning and Knowledge Transfer With Data Protection (2020). https://www.fedai.org/. Accessed 16 Apr 2023
4. PySyft: A Library for Encrypted, Privacy Preserving Machine Learning (2020). https://github.com/OpenMined/PySyft. Accessed 16 Apr 2023
5. PaddleFL: Federated Deep Learning in PaddlePaddle (2020). https://github.com/PaddlePaddle/PaddleFL. Accessed 16 Apr 2023
6. Nvidia Developer Blog: Federated Learning Powered by Nvidia Clara (2020). https://developer.nvidia.com/blog/federated-learning-clara/. Accessed 16 Apr 2023
7. McMahan, B., Moore, E., Ramage, D., Hampson, S., Arcas, B.: Communication efficient learning of deep networks from decentralized data. In: Proceedings of the 20th International Conference on Artificial Intelligence and Statistics (AISTATS) (2017)
8. Ekmefjord, M., et al.: Scalable federated machine learning with FEDN. In: 22nd IEEE International Symposium on Cluster, Cloud and Internet Computing (CCGrid) (2022). https://doi.org/10.1109/CCGrid54584.2022.00065

9. Hard, A., et al.: Federated learning for mobile keyboard prediction (2019). ArXiv:1811.03604
10. Zhao, Y., Li, M., Lai, L., Suda, N., Civin, D., Chandra, V.: Federated learning with non-IID data. ArXiv:1806.00582 (2018)
11. Bonawitz, K., et al.: Towards federated learning at scale: System design. ArXiv: 1902.01046 (2019)
12. Bakir, D., Aktas, M.: A systematic literature review of question answering: research trends, datasets, methods and frameworks. In: The 22nd International Conference on Computational Science and Its Applications (ICCSA), Malaga, Spain, 4–07 July 2022, pp. 1–16 (2022)
13. Bahdanau, D., Cho, K., Bengio, Y.: Neural machine translation by jointly learning to align and translate. arXiv:1409.0473 (2014)
14. Chen, D., Bolton, J., Manning, C.D.: A thorough examination of the CNN/daily mail reading comprehension task. In: Proceedings of the 54th Annual Meeting of the Association for Computational Linguistics (Volume 1: Long Papers), In ACL, pp. 2358–2367 (2016)
15. Seo, M.J., et al.: Bidirectional attention flow for machine comprehension. ICLR. arxiv:1611.01603 (2017)
16. Devlin, J., Chang, M.W., Lee, K., Toutanova, K.: Bidirectional encoder representations from transformers. In: Proceedings of the 2019 Conference of the North American Chapter of the Association for Computational Linguistics: Human Language Technologies, Volume 1 (Long and Short Papers), pp. 4171–4186. Association for Computational Linguistics (2019)
17. Liu, Y., Liu, D., Li, D., Lv, Y.: Robustly Optimized BERT Pretraining Approach. arXiv preprint arXiv:1907.11692 (2019)
18. Qi, Y., Wang, W., Zhang, B., Dauphin, Y.: A Lite BERT for Self-supervised Learning of Language Representations. arXiv preprint arXiv:2004.10948 (2020)
19. Xu, K., Zhu, W., Yang, Z., Bai, X.: Efficiently Learning an Encoder that Classifies Token Replacements Accurately. arXiv preprint arXiv:2009.13258 (2020)
20. Raffel, C., et al.: Exploring the limits of transfer learning with a unified text-to-text transformer. arXiv preprint arXiv:1910.10683 (2019)
21. Ghazvininejad, M., Levy, O., Liu, Y., Zettlemoyer, L.: A Knowledge-Grounded Autoencoder for Commonsense Inference. In: Proceedings of the 57th Conference of the Association for Computational Linguistics, pp. 5669–5674
22. Baeth, M.J., Aktas, M.S.: An approach to custom privacy policy violation detection problems using big social provenance data. Concurr. Comput. Pract. Exp. **30**(21) (2018)
23. Aktas, M.S., Fox, G.C., Pierce, M., Oh, S.: XML metadata services. Concurr. Comput. Pract. Exp. **20**(7), 801–823 (2008)
24. Aktas, M.S., Pierce, M.: High-performance hybrid information service architecture. Concurr. Comput. Pract. Exp. **22**(15), 2095–2123 (2010)
25. Fox, G.C., et al.: Real time streaming data grid applications. In: Davoli, F., Palazzo, S., Zappatore, S. (eds.) Distributed Cooperative Laboratories: Networking, Instrumentation, and Measurements. Signals and Communication Technology, pp. 253–267. Springer, Boston, MA (2006). https://doi.org/10.1007/0-387-30394-4_17
26. Tufek, A., Gurbuz, A., Ekuklu, O.F., Aktas, M.S.: provenance collection platform for the weather research and forecasting model. In: 2018 14th International Conference on Semantics, Knowledge and Grids (2018)
27. Aktas, M.S., Fox, G.C., Pierce, M.: Fault tolerant high performance information services for dynamic collections of grid and web services. Futur. Gener. Comput. Syst. **23**(3), 317–337 (2007)

28. Aydin, G., et al.: Building and applying geographical information system Grids. Concurr. Comput. Pract. Exp. **20**(14), 1653–1695 (2008)

29. Fox, G.C., et al.: Algorithms and the Grid. Comput. Vis. Sci. **12**, 115–124 (2009)

30. Aktas, M., et al.: ISERVO: implementing the international solid earth research virtual observatory by integrating computational grid and geographical information Web Services. Comput. Earthq. Phys. Simul. Anal. Infrastruct. Part **II**, 2281–2296 (2007)

31. Aydin, G., Aktas, M.S., Fox, G.C., Gadgil, H., Pierce, M., Sayar, A.: SERVOGrid complexity computational environments CCE integrated performance analysis. In: The 6th IEEE/ACM International Workshop on Grid Computing (2005)

32. Pierce, M.E., et al.: The QuakeSim project: Web services for managing geophysical data and applications. Earthq. Simul. Sourc. Tsunamis. 635–651 (2008)

33. Uygun, Y., Oguz, R.F., Olmezogullari, E., Aktas, M.S.: On the large-scale graph data processing for user interface testing in big data science projects. In: 2020 IEEE International Conference on Big Data (Big Data), pp. 2049–2056 (2020)

34. Sahinoglu, M., Incki, K., Aktas, M.S.: Mobile application verification: a systematic mapping study. In: Computational Science and Its Applications-ICCSA: 15th International Conference, Banff, AB, Canada, June 22–25, 2015, Proceedings. Part V, vol. 15(2015)

35. Kapdan, M., Aktas, M., Yigit, M.: On the structural code clone detection problem: a survey and software metric based approach. In: Computational Science and Its Applications-ICCSA,: 14th International Conference, Guimarães, Portugal, June 30-July 3, 2014, Proceedings. Part V, vol. 14 (2014)

36. Olmezogullari, E., Aktas, M.S.: Pattern2Vec: representation of clickstream data sequences for learning user navigational behavior. Concurr. Comput. Pract. Exp. **34**(9) (2022)

37. Olmezogullari, E., Aktas, M.S.: Representation of click-stream datasequences for learning user navigational behavior by using embeddings. In: 2020 IEEE International Conference on Big Data (Big Data), pp. 3173–3179 (2020)

38. Nacar, M.A.et al.: VLab: collaborative Grid services and portals to support computational material science. Concurr. Comput. Pract. Exp. **19**(12), 1717–1728 (2007)

39. Dundar, B., Astekin, M., Aktas, M.S.: A big data processing framework for self-healing internet of things applications. In: 2021 IEEE International Conference on Big Data (Big Data), pp. 2353–2361 (2021)

40. Baeth, M.J., Aktas, M.S.: Detecting misinformation in social networks using provenance data. In: 2017 13th International Conference on Semantics, Knowledge and Grids (2017)

41. Aktas, M., et al.: Implementing geographical information system grid services to support computational geophysics in a service-oriented environment. NASA Earth-Sun System Technology Conference, University of Maryland, Adelphi, Maryland (2005)

Short Paper (ACMC 2023)

Studying Arrhythmic Risk with In-Silico Programmed Ventricular Stimulation and Patient-Specific Computational Models

Thaís de Jesus Soares[1], João Pedro Banhato Pereira[1(✉)] [iD],
Yan Barbosa Werneck[1], Yuri Rhios Araújo Santos[1], Tiago Dutra Franco[1],
Joventino de Oliveira Campos[1] [iD], Rafael Sachetto Oliveira[2] [iD],
Thaiz Ruberti Schmal[1] [iD], Thiago Gonçalves Schroder e. Souza[1] [iD],
Bernardo Martins Rocha[1,2] [iD], and Rodrigo Weber dos Santos[1] [iD]

[1] Federal University of Juiz de Fora, Juiz de Fora, MG, Brazil
jpbbanhato@gmail.com
[2] Federal University of São João del Rei, São João del Rei, MG, Brazil

Abstract. Cardiac arrhythmias can be life-threatening, and early identification of patients at high risk of developing arrhythmias is crucial
to implementing preventive measures. Programmed ventricular stimulation (PVS) is a clinical tool to assess arrhythmic risk. In this study,
we developed patient-specific computational models using magnetic resonance imaging (MRI) data to evaluate arrhythmic risk through virtual PVS simulations. We applied virtual PVS on a patient with dilated
cardiomyopathy and a history of non-sustained ventricular tachycardia.
The simulation results revealed the presence of cardiac arrhythmias in
the form of spiral waves circulating a fibrotic scar in the patient's heart.
These findings, consistent with the patient's medical history, indicate
that patient-specific computational models hold great promise as a tool
for assessing cardiac arrhythmic risk. The patient-specific computational
models have the potential to assist clinicians in identifying high-risk
patients and developing personalized treatment plans. By incorporating
patient-specific information and simulating various scenarios, computational models can provide valuable insights into the underlying mechanisms of arrhythmia and guide clinical decision-making.

Keywords: Computational Modeling of the Heart · Cardiac
Arrhythmia

1 Introduction

Dilated cardiomyopathy (DCM) is characterized by the ventricular chambers
enlargement, often accompanied by impaired myocardial contractile function [7].
Although DCM is typically observed in adults and can be caused by various factors, including infections, myocarditis, autoimmune disorders, and certain medications, it also has a genetic component and may be associated with specific
hereditary syndromes [11].

© The Author(s), under exclusive license to Springer Nature Switzerland AG 2023
O. Gervasi et al. (Eds.): ICCSA 2023 Workshops, LNCS 14112, pp. 41–51, 2023.
https://doi.org/10.1007/978-3-031-37129-5_4

In addition to symptoms of heart failure, including reduced ejection fraction, patients with DCM may also present atrial and ventricular arrhythmias and sudden cardiac death (SCD), which can occur at any stage of the disease [7]. As such, it is crucial to identify the etiology and any potential risk factors after a diagnosis of DCM is made.

Currently, implantable cardioverter-defibrillators (ICDs) are recommended for patients with DCM who are at risk of sudden death. However, the decision to use an ICD involves performing complementary tests, some of which may be invasive, such as an electrophysiological study called programmed ventricular stimulation (PVS). This procedure involves the insertion of electrodes into the heart's cavities, which are used to electrically stimulate the heart for varying periods to evaluate the electrical propagation in the cardiac tissue and the induction of arrhythmias.

In this context, virtual models of the heart have emerged as an innovative and increasingly important technology for the non-invasive stratification of SCD risk. Indeed, early research suggests that cardiac computational models are more accurate in predicting SCD risk in patients than classical biomarkers [5].

However, there is still a need for more studies in the literature on non-ischemic patient groups and their correlation with potentially fatal arrhythmias. Thus, the study presented here aimed to create personalized computational models for patients with non-ischemic dilated cardiomyopathy (DCM) and a medical history of non-sustained ventricular tachycardia.

To this end, it is worth noting that magnetic resonance imaging (MRI) data were used to evaluate the patient's arrhythmia risk, and virtual simulations of programmed ventricular stimulation (PVS) were performed.

The results of the implemented simulations revealed the presence of cardiac arrhythmias in the form of spiral waves circulating a fibrotic scar in the patient's heart. Finally, compared to the patient's medical history, these findings were considered consistent.

Finally, it is important to note that the results presented in this work are the first step in an ongoing research project, which aims to help stratify the risk of patients with DCM using computational models. In this sense, the initially obtained results demonstrate the potential of personalized patient computational models to improve risk assessment.

2   Materials and Methods

In this section, a clinical description of the patient and the methods used to construct the patient-specific computational model were presented. More specifically, the electrophysiological protocol employed to verify the potential for induction of arrhythmias using a virtual heart of a patient with DCM was presented.

2.1   Patient Report

A 61-year-old Caucasian male who smokes presented with symptoms of fatigue, orthopnea, dyspnea NYHA III, and paroxysmal nocturnal dyspnea during his initial visit to the cardiology outpatient clinic at the Federal University of Juiz de Fora's university hospital in January 2023.

The electrocardiogram showed: a heart rate (HR) of 98 bpm, first-degree atrioventricular block, left bundle branch block (LBBB), left atrial enlargement, and left ventricular hypertrophy (LVH). A Doppler echocardiogram revealed dilated cardiomyopathy with an ejection fraction of 19%. The 24-hour Holter evidenced non-sustained ventricular tachycardia. Magnetic resonance imaging showed dilated cardiomyopathy with severe biventricular dysfunction. The exam also showed a left ventricle with greatly increased diameters and cavity volume. Likewise, the right ventricle had increased diameters and cavity volumes. The left atrium was greatly enlarged, and significant mitral regurgitation was also found.

Specific sequences for delayed enhancement showed small regions of linear mesocardial anteroseptal and inferoseptal basal fibrosis and subepicardial fibrosis and inferolateral medial septal fibrosis. This pattern of fibrosis is seen in non-ischemic heart disease.

To treat the symptoms and reduce disease progression Sarcubitril/Valsartan 200mg, Spironolactone 25mg, Bisoprolol 5mg and Dapaglifozin 10mg were prescribed.

Two months after starting the medications, he reports improvement of dyspnea, denies orthopnea, and presents NYHA II. A new ECG showed a positive response to the treatment, with a reduced heart rate of 52 bpm, sinus rhythm, prolonged PR interval, and LBBB.

2.2   Magnetic Resonance Imaging (MRI)

Cardiac MRI protocols are designed to evaluate the morphology, functional status, and the presence of myocardial fibrosis in cardiac structures, which may be associated with changes in the cardiac conduction system and possible arrhythmias [1].

Figure 1 presents the image used in the present work, which was acquired using a 1.5 T machine (Avanto, Siemens, Germany) equipped with a dedicated cardiac coil. ECG-gated cine images were obtained in both short-axis and long-axis views, followed by late-enhancement (LGE) imaging 10 min after the injection of a Gadolinium-based contrast agent at a dose of 0.2 mmol/kg, using an inversion recovery T1-weighted gradient-echo sequence. T1-scout was used to determine the appropriate inversion time to null the signal from normal myocardium and regions with LGE were identified and manually segmented.

2.3   Computational Mesh

In order to construct a computational mesh for the simulations, the medical image (Fig. 1) was segmented using Seg3D software [2]. Figure 2a presents the

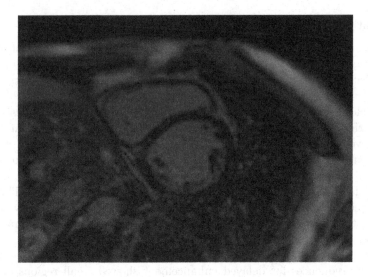

Fig. 1. Cardiac MRI image from the patient used to generate the computational domain for the simulations of the present study.

segmentation process, where the epicardium and endocardium borders of the ventricles are marked with green lines. The regions with fibrosis are also marked in red on the image.

The segmented regions were exported, and the Gmsh software [4] was used to generate a discretization for the domain, resulting in the mesh presented in Fig. 2b. In addition, each element was marked to indicate the presence or absence of fibrosis.

Finally, a script was used to convert the Gmsh mesh to the format used in MonoAlg3D [8], which was the chosen software to carry out the computational simulations.

2.4   Mathematical Model

To model the electrical activity of the patient's heart, the monodomain equation [9] was used. The monodomain equation describes the propagation of action potential in cardiac tissue via a rection-diffusion partial differential equation. To describe the action potential generation at the myocyte level, the ten-Tusscher cell model [10] was used, which consists of 19 ordinary differential equations. A complete description of the ten-Tusscher model is available in [10].

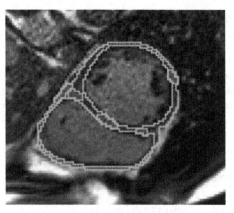
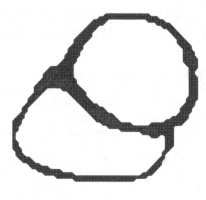

(a) Segmented region.   (b) Computational mesh.

Fig. 2. Image processing to generate the computational mesh for the simulations. (a) the segmented region from a short-axis MRI image of the patient's heart including healthy tissue (in green) and fibrotic regions (in red); (b) computational mesh representation of the segmented domain. (Color figure online)

The model consists of a reaction-diffusion partial differential equation coupled to a system of ordinary differential equations, which is given by:

$$\chi \left(C_m \frac{\partial V}{\partial t} \right) + (I_{ion} + I_s) = \nabla \cdot (\sigma \nabla V), \tag{1}$$

$$I_{ion} = g(V, \eta, t), \tag{2}$$

$$\frac{\partial \eta}{\partial t} = f(V, \eta, t), \tag{3}$$

where χ is the surface-to-volume ratio of cells (mm^{-1}), C_m is the specific membrane capacitance per unit area (μF mm^{-2}), V is the transmembrane potential (mV), η is a vector of state variables, I_{ion} is the transmembrane current density (μA mm^{-2}) representing the sum of all transmembrane ionic currents and I_s is the density of an imposed stimulus current, while σ is the electrical conductivity (mS mm^{-1}).

The electrical conductivity was considered isotropic and heterogeneous, with a reduced conductivity value used in fibrotic regions. Besides, the no-flux boundary condition is applied in the entire boundary to represent that the tissue is electrically insulated.

The mathematical model was solved using the finite volume method on the discretized domain, which consists of approximately 70000 volumes of the same size ($0.2 \times 0.2 \times 0.2$ mm^3). To obtain the transmembrane potential for each computational cell, the simulation of the monodomain equation requires the solution of a system of linear equations for each time step, which is solved using the conjugate gradient iterative method. This numerical solution is implemented in the MonoALG3d simulator [8], used in the present work.

Table 1. Results of the simulated study protocol. The first column identifies the stimulus, and the second column shows the number of applications of each stimulus. The third and fourth columns show the start and end times at which it was analyzed. The fifth column shows the interval between the current stimulus and the previous one. The last three columns show the classification for each simulation.

Stimulus (S)	Applications	Start time	End time	Interval	Reentry	Block	Normal
1	8	0	4200	600			X
2	1	4580	6000	380		X	
2	1	4590	6000	390	X		
3	1	4970	7000	380			X
3	1	4960	7000	370			X
3	1	4950	7000	360			X
3	1	4940	7000	350			X
3	1	4930	7000	340			X
3	1	4920	7000	330			X
3	1	4910	7000	320			X
3	1	4900	7000	310			X
3	1	4890	7000	300	X		
3	1	4880	7000	290	X		
3	1	4870	7000	280	X		
3	1	4860	7000	270		X	
4	1	5250	7000	380	X		
4	1	5240	7000	370	X		
4	1	5230	7000	360	X		
4	1	5220	7000	350	X		
4	1	5210	7000	340	X		
4	1	5200	7000	330		X	

2.5   Simulating Programmed Ventricular Stimulation

Programmed ventricular stimulation was performed in-silico using a simple sequential protocol, as previously described [3]. The protocol consists of the extra stimulus mode, using an 8-beat drive train at the outflow tract at the ventricular-paced cycle length of 600 ms. The first extra stimulus (S2) is delivered initially with an S1-S2 interval of 380 ms and decremented in 10 ms steps until the effective refractory period (ERP) or when 200 ms is reached. S2 is then moved out 10 ms, and S3 is introduced with an initial S2-S3 interval of 380 ms, decremented in a similar fashion. S4 was delivered in a similar pattern.

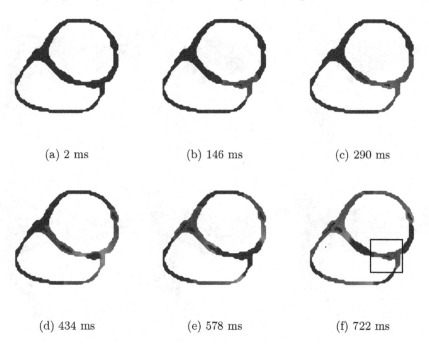

(a) 2 ms   (b) 146 ms   (c) 290 ms

(d) 434 ms   (e) 578 ms   (f) 722 ms

Fig. 3. Electrical propagation of Stimulus 1 (S1) at different time steps, showing a normal propagation. (a) the stimulus has been applied, (b) the stimulus propagates regularly in all directions. In (c), (d), and (e), the wave continues to propagate stimulating the whole tissue. In (f) we have the beginning of the propagation of the second stimulus in the S1 protocol. Transmembrane potential ranges from -80 mV (blue color) to 40 mV (red color). The black square shows the region around the stimulus in which we'll focus our analysis. (Color figure online)

2.6   Computational Experiment

Computational simulations were performed to reproduce the Programmed Ventricular Stimulation protocol using the mesh presented in Fig. 2b. The conductivity is considered isotropic with $\sigma = 0.00002$ mS mm^{-1} at healthy volumes and $\sigma = 2.5 \cdot 10^{-7}$ mS mm^{-1} for volume with fibrosis. Furthermore, to simulate the use of a catheter during the electrophysiological study protocol, a stimulus with a duration of 2 ms and amplitude of -38 μA/μm^2 was used. The stimulated region was a 2 mm square near the right ventricular outflow tract (RVOT). This region was chosen because, according to literature studies [6], it is the most pro-arrhythmic ectopic location.

During the protocol simulation, it is worth noting that three possible outcomes were considered: normal propagation, block, or arrhythmia. In normal propagation, the stimulus is able to electrically activate neighboring cells in the

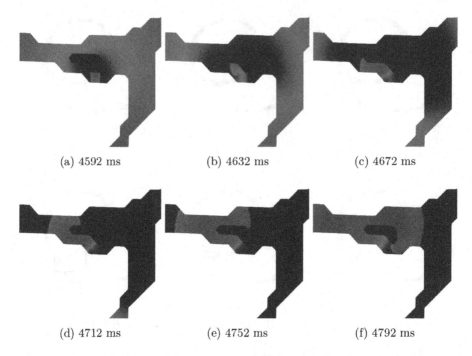

(a) 4592 ms   (b) 4632 ms   (c) 4672 ms

(d) 4712 ms   (e) 4752 ms   (f) 4792 ms

Fig. 4. Propagation of the (S2) stimulus with an interval of 390 ms at different time steps. (a) the beginning of propagation right after a stimulus. (b) and (c) after 40–80ms, the wave propagates to the right but not the left, causing the beginning of the spiral formation. (d) 120 ms after the stimulus, the wave now starts propagating to the left. (e) and (f) generation of a reentry spiral in the zoomed region. Transmembrane potential ranges from -80 mV (blue color) to 40 mV (red color).

region where it was applied. Moreover, the stimulated cells return to their initial conditions after surpassing their refractory periods.

On the other hand, in block, the stimulus is applied to a region that is still in its refractory period and therefore becomes unable to stimulate the cells in its vicinity.

Finally, in arrhythmia or reentry, the cells within a region are able to self-stimulate, either sustainably or unsustainably. In the computational model, this condition is represented by the generation of a spiral wave of electrical excitation.

3   Results

This section presents the results obtained with the simulation of the electrophysiological study protocol. With a fixed initial stimulus (S1) at the start, various simulations were run for each subsequent stimulus (S2, S3, S4), in order to find

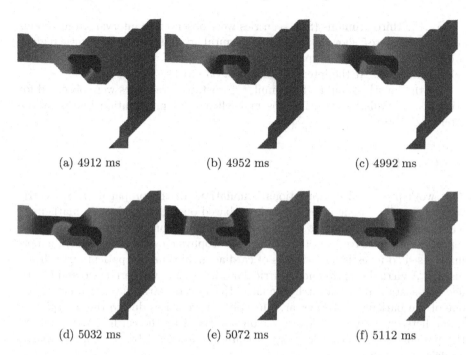

(a) 4912 ms   (b) 4952 ms   (c) 4992 ms

(d) 5032 ms   (e) 5072 ms   (f) 5112 ms

Fig. 5. Propagation of Stimulus S3 with an interval of 300 ms at different time steps, showing a spiral formation. (a) 2 ms after the stimulus shows that right after it, the region around the stimulus is still depolarized, with a small portion of repolarized tissue to the left. (b) the S3 wave propagating to this region of repolarized tissue. In (c) and (d) the regions to the right and above the fibrosis region start the repolarization while in (e) the wave starts propagating to the right. (f) Formation of a reentry spiral, which will cause 4 arrhythmia cycles. Transmembrane potential ranges from -80 mV (blue color) to 40 mV (red color). (Color figure online)

the blockage time for each stimulus and advance to the next step of the protocol. Each run was classified as block, normal propagation, or reentry and the results are summarized in Table 1.

As expected, it was observed that during the initial 8-beat drive train (S1) application, all stimuli resulted in normal propagation to the whole tissue without generating a spiral or block, as presented in Fig. 3.

Then, the second stimulus (S2) was applied. At this stage, it is important to highlight two different situations. S2 when applied with an interval of 380 ms blocks. However, when we moved to the S3 step, S2 is applied again with an interval of 10 ms greater than previously, which caused reentry. The observed reentry is in the pattern of a small spiral around one of the fibrotic regions, as presented in Fig. 4.

For the third stimulus (S3), reentries were observed in intervals from 300 ms to 280 ms. Figure 5 shows an unsustained spiral around one of the fibrotic regions after the S3 stimulus. The spiral re-excited the tissue four times (4 waves) before self-termination. At the interval of 270 ms, S3 blocks.

For the fourth stimulus (S4), similar unsustained reentries were observed for stimulus intervals between 380 ms and 340 ms S4 propagation blocks at the interval of 330 ms.

4 Conclusion

This work presented computational simulations of the propagation of electric waves in cardiac tissue using a simulator based on the Monodomain mathematical model. The simulations using patient-specific geometry were performed to reproduce an invasive procedure called electrophysiological study, which is normally used to investigate the risks of cardiac arrhythmia in patients with heart disease. A virtual programmed ventricular stimulation was performed and identified non-sustained cardiac arrhythmias in the form of spiral waves that circulated one of the patient's fibrotic scar. The spiral wave arises due to the interplay of tissue heterogeneity, i.e., fibrotic regions captured by the cardiac MRI exam of the patient, and electrophysiology features, reproduced by the computational models.

The cardiac arrhythmias found using the patient-specific model are consistent with the patient's history of non-sustained ventricular tachycardia, as described in Subsect. 2.1. It is crucial to emphasize that the modeling and results outlined in this work are just the first steps of a broader ongoing research project. The ultimate goal is to enhance our understanding of the physiopathological mechanisms responsible for generating cardiac arrhythmias in patients with heart diseases. This research will help us identify new therapeutic targets and enhance clinical practice in cardiology, thereby improving patient outcomes.

Acknowledgements. This work was supported by NVIDIA (project "Patient-specific models of the heart for precision medicine", NVIDIA Academic Hardware Grant Program), by the Federal University of Juiz de Fora (UFJF), through a scholarship from the "Coordenação de Aperfeiçoamento de Emprego de Ensino Superior" (CAPES) - Brazil - Finance Code 001, by the National Council for Scientific and Technological Development (CNPq), by the "Empresa Brasileira de Serviços Hospitalares" (Ebserh) grant numbers 423278/2021-5, 310722/2021-7, and 315267/2020-8, and by the Minas Gerais State Research Support Foundation (FAPEMIG) - Brazil TEC APQ 01340-18 and APQ 00748-18.

References

1. Balaban, G., et al.: Late-gadolinium enhancement interface area and electrophysiological simulations predict arrhythmic events in patients with nonischemic dilated cardiomyopathy. Clin. Electrophysiol. **7**(2), 238–249 (2021)
2. CIBC: seg3D: Volumetric Image Segmentation and Visualization. Scientific Computing and Imaging Institute (SCI) (2016). http://www.seg3d.org
3. Fisher, J.D., Kim, S.G., Ferrick, K.J., Roth, J.A.: Programmed ventricular stimulation using tandem versus simple sequential protocols. Pacing Clin. Electrophysiol. **17**(3), 286–294 (1994)
4. Geuzaine, C., Remacle, J.F.: GMSH: a 3-d finite element mesh generator with built-in pre-and post-processing facilities. Int. J. Numer. Meth. Eng. **79**(11), 1309–1331 (2009)
5. Huynh, K.: Arrhythmia risk stratification using virtual heart models. Nat. Rev. Cardiol. **13**(7), 381–381 (2016)
6. Martinez-Navarro, H., Zhou, X., Bueno-Orovio, A., Rodriguez, B.: Electrophysiological and anatomical factors determine arrhythmic risk in acute myocardial ischaemia and its modulation by sodium current availability. Interface Focus **11**(1), 20190124 (2021)
7. Report of the WHO/ISCF task force: On the definition and classification of cardiomyopathies. Br. Heart J. **44**, 672–673 (1980)
8. Sachetto Oliveira, R., et al.: Performance evaluation of GPU parallelization, space-time adaptive algorithms, and their combination for simulating cardiac electrophysiology. Int. J. Numer. Methods Biomed. Eng. **34**(2), e2913 (2018)
9. Sundnes, J., Lines, G.T., Cai, X., Nielsen, B.F., Mardal, K.A., Tveito, A.: Computing the Electrical Activity in the Heart, vol. 1. Springer Science & Business Media, Heidelberg (2007). https://doi.org/10.1007/3-540-33437-8
10. Ten Tusscher, K.H., Panfilov, A.V.: Alternans and spiral breakup in a human ventricular tissue model. Am. J. Physiol.-Heart Circ. Physiol. **291**(3), H1088–H1100 (2006)
11. Walter, H.A., Beverly, H.L.: The challenge of cardiomyopathy. J. Am. Coll. Cardiol. **13**(6), 1219–1239 (1989)

Short Paper (IONCA 2023)

PSO–FWA: A New Hybrid Algorithm
for Solving Nonlinear Equation Systems

Sérgio Ribeiro[1]([✉]) and Luiz Guerreiro Lopes[2][iD]

[1] Postgraduate Program in Informatics Engineering, University of Madeira, Funchal,
Madeira Is., Portugal
sergioribeiro_91@hotmail.com
[2] Faculty of Exact Sciences and Engineering, University of Madeira,
9020-105 Funchal, Madeira Is., Portugal
lopes@uma.pt

Abstract. Nature-inspired optimization algorithms have been proposed
for solving hard optimization problems, including the optimization-based
solution of difficult systems of nonlinear equations. While there is no
perfect optimization algorithm, the hybridization of such metaheuristic
optimization algorithms has produced positive results by enhancing their
capabilities and reducing their weaknesses. This paper presents a novel
hybridization of Particle Swarm Optimization and the Fireworks Algorithm for solving nonlinear equation systems. The experimental results
obtained indicate that the proposed hybrid algorithm outperforms both
Particle Swarm Optimization and the Fireworks Algorithm, as well as a
previously developed hybridization of these algorithms.

Keywords: Computational intelligence · Particle swarm
optimization · Fireworks Algorithm · Hybrid algorithms · Nonlinear
equation systems

1 Introduction

Nonlinear equation systems are recognized as challenging problems to solve using
traditional iterative numerical methods, whose effectiveness largely depends on
the characteristics of the problem considered and the quality of the initial approximations taken, with non-convergence occurring relatively frequently.

In contrast, the use of population-based metaheuristic algorithms, such as
Particle Swarm Optimization (PSO) and the Fireworks Algorithm (FWA), for
solving this important class of problems, which have an extensive importance in
fields such as chemistry, physics, engineering, and economics, has the advantage
of being problem-independent, derivative-free, and not dependent on good initial
estimates. However, there is no guarantee of convergence with these population-
based stochastic algorithms, and each of them has different advantages and
drawbacks, which motivates their hybridization to capitalize on their respective
strengths and mitigate their weaknesses.

With this in mind, this article proposes a novel hybrid metaheuristic algorithm for solving systems of nonlinear equations that is the result of the combination of Particle Swarm Optimization and the Fireworks Algorithm.

© The Author(s), under exclusive license to Springer Nature Switzerland AG 2023
O. Gervasi et al. (Eds.): ICCSA 2023 Workshops, LNCS 14112, pp. 55–65, 2023.
https://doi.org/10.1007/978-3-031-37129-5_5

Population-based approaches, such as the hybrid algorithm proposed in this paper, can solve a system of n nonlinear equations by converting it into an n-dimensional nonlinear optimization problem by minimizing the sum of squares of the residuals, $F(\mathbf{x}) = \sum [f_i(x_1, \ldots, x_n)]^2$, or the sum of absolute values of the residuals, $F(\mathbf{x}) = \sum |f_i(x_1, \ldots, x_n)|$. This optimization-based approach for solving nonlinear equation systems was adopted, and the performance of the proposed hybrid algorithm is here evaluated.

The structure of this paper is as follows. The next section describes the PSO and FWA algorithms, which served as basis for the proposed algorithm. Section 3 describes briefly some simple ways to combine PSO and FWA, as well as a previous hybridization of these two algorithms. Section 4 presents the proposed algorithm, and the experimental setup and test problems used in this study are described in Sect. 5. The main results obtained are presented and discussed in Sect. 6. Finally, the conclusion is given in Sect. 7.

2   Background

2.1   Particle Swarm Optimization

Particle Swarm Optimization (PSO), proposed by Eberhart and Kennedy [3], is a population-based stochastic algorithm, based on swarm intelligence, that draws inspiration from the cooperative behavior of groups of animals when searching for food. In PSO, each particle represents a candidate solution to the problem, and "remembers" the best solution it found, as well as the one by its group. At each iteration, the particles update their velocity and position as follows:

$$\mathbf{v}_i^{t+1} = w \cdot \mathbf{v}_i^t + r_{1i}^t \cdot c_1 \cdot (\mathbf{pbest}_i^t - \mathbf{x}_i^t) + r_{2i}^t \cdot c_2 \cdot (\mathbf{gbest}^t - \mathbf{x}_i^t), \qquad (1)$$

$$\mathbf{x}_i^{t+1} = \mathbf{x}_i^t + \mathbf{v}_i^{t+1}, \qquad (2)$$

where $\mathbf{v}$ is the velocity of the particle, $\mathbf{x}$ is its position, w is the inertia weight introduced by Shi and Eberhart [12], r_1 and r_2 are random numbers uniformly distributed in $[0, 1]$, and c_1 and c_2 are the cognitive and social factors, respectively. These affect how much the particle is drawn to their own previous experience, compared to the one found by their group, with **pbest** and **gbest** representing the particle's best position and the group's best position, respectively.

This sharing of information is at the core of the flexibility of PSO. It allows not only changes to the algorithm itself, but also different topologies for the group of particles that communicate between themselves. The initial topology is the gbest topology, where all particles communicate with each other. Premature convergence was observed as a result of this [8].

The pseudocode of the standard PSO is given in Algorithm 1.

Other topologies that reduce the degree of communication have been proposed. One of these topologies is the von Neumann topology [6], where every particle is connected with a small fixed number of particles, typically four. This topology was found to improve the performance of the algorithm by allowing a more efficient search space exploration [8].

Algorithm 1. Pseudocode for the standard PSO algorithm
1: Initialize a swarm of N particles randomly;
2: **while** $t < MaxIter$ and not terminate **do**
3:     **for** each particle position $\mathbf{x}_i$ in the swarm **do**
4:         Evaluate $f(\mathbf{x}_i)$
5:         **if** $f(\mathbf{x}_i) < f(\mathbf{pbest})$ **then**
6:             Update the particle **pbest**
7:             **if** $f(\mathbf{x}_i) < f(\mathbf{gbest})$ **then**
8:                 Update the particle **gbest**
9:             **end if**
10:         **end if**
11:     **end for**
12:     **for** i from 1 to N **do**
13:         Calculate $\mathbf{v}_i^{t+1}$ using Eq. 1;
14:         Calculate $\mathbf{x}_i^{t+1}$ using Eq. 2;
15:     **end for**
16: **end while**
17: Return the best particle found;

2.2 Fireworks Optimization

The Fireworks Algorithm (FWA) [13] is a population-based swarm intelligence algorithm inspired by the fireworks explosion, as each potential solution "explodes", creating a new sub-swarm. The amplitude of such explosion is dependent on the performance of the fireworks, where less-optimal solutions spread further apart, allowing for greater global exploration, whereas better performing fireworks spread much less, allowing for better local exploitation.

The amplitude of explosion for each firework can be calculated as follows:

$$A_i = \hat{A} \cdot \frac{f(\mathbf{x}_i) - y_{min} + \xi}{\sum_{i=1}^{N} (f(\mathbf{x}_i) - y_{min}) + \xi}, \tag{3}$$

where $\hat{A}$ is the maximum explosion amplitude, $f(\mathbf{x}_i)$ is the fitness value of the firework $\mathbf{x}_i$, $y_{min} = \min f(\mathbf{x}_i)\,(i = 1, \ldots, N)$ is the fitness value of the best firework, and ξ is an arbitrarily small number used to avoid division by 0.

The number of sparks produced by the exploding firework is given by:

$$S_i = m \cdot \frac{y_{max} - f(\mathbf{x}_i) + \xi}{\sum_{i=1}^{N} (y_{max} - f(\mathbf{x}_i)) + \xi}, \tag{4}$$

where m is a parameter that control the number of sparks, and y_{max} is as in (3).

Since the number of sparks must be an integer, there is an additional step that limits the number of sparks that can be generated as follows:

$$S_i = \begin{cases} round(a \cdot m) & \text{if } S_i < a \cdot m \\ round(b \cdot m) & \text{if } S_i > b \cdot m \quad (a < b < 1) \\ round(S_i) & \text{otherwise.} \end{cases} \tag{5}$$

Algorithm 2. Pseudocode for the FWA algorithm

1: Initialize a swarm of N fireworks randomly;
2: Evaluate fitness $f(\mathbf{x})$ of each firework;
3: **while** $t < MaxIter$ and not terminate **do**
4:     **for** each firework in the swarm **do**
5:         Calculate A_p according to Eq. 3;
6:         Calculate S_p according to Eq. 4 and Eq. 5;
7:         Generate and evaluate new sparks;
8:         **for** each spark **do**
9:             Evaluate the fitness of the spark;
10:             Select the best firework/sparks to be "Gaussian fireworks";
11:             Generate a few "Gaussian sparks" around the "Gaussian fireworks" based on a Gaussian distribution;
12:             Evaluate the fitness for each "Gaussian spark";
13:         **end for**
14:     **end for**
15:     Select the best points from the current fireworks and sparks to form the next generation of fireworks;
16: **end while**
17: Return the best firework found;

Algorithm 2 provides a pseudocode for the Fireworks Algorithm.

FWA has been proposed as a better alternative to PSO, and boasts a faster convergence. This is an advantage on some problems, but it can also lead to premature convergence, which was one of the reasons that motivated modifications to the PSO topology.

3   Related Work

PSO and FWA are population-based optimization approaches that can be combined to leverage their respective strengths. PSO is known for its simplicity and efficiency, while FWA is known for its ability to prevent local optima.

A simple way to combine these algorithms is to use FWA to initialize the particles in PSO, providing the swarm with a good starting point for exploration. Similarly, PSO can be used to influence the FWA explosion operation, directing the sparks to promising areas of the search space.

In the newly Dynamic Fireworks Algorithm with Particle Swarm Optimization (DFWPSO) [16], PSO was utilized in a new mechanism for update fireworks, aiming to accelerate the convergence of the FWA algorithm and reduce the computing time, thus improving the overall performance of the fireworks algorithm.

By appropriately combining the strong exploitation abilities of PSO with the strong exploration capabilities of FWA, it is possible to build more sophisticated hybrid algorithms that achieve a better balance between the exploration of the entire search space and exploitation, i.e., refinement of the best-known solutions.

In the PS–FW algorithm [2], modified FWA operators are incorporated into the PSO solution procedure. The concept behind this hybrid algorithm is that at the start of each iteration, the velocity and position of each particle are updated in the same way as in the PSO algorithm, and then the so-called abandonment and supplement mechanism is applied aiming to balance the exploration and exploitation ability of the PS–FW algorithm. These two operations follow the logic of FWA. A number of particles with the worst fit are discarded as a result of the abandonment operation, while a number of particles with better fitness fit are retained for the subsequent iteration in view of the supplement operation.

These best particles are used to implement a modified explosion operator, a new mutation operator, and a fitness-based selection operator, of which the first two were developed to accelerate global convergence and prevent premature convergence to local optima. The new particles obtained by the FWA operators are added to the original swarm in order to balance the number of particles and generate a new particle swarm for the next algorithm iteration.

4   Proposed PSO–FWA Algorithm

Although the PS–FW algorithm [2] combines PSO and FWA and uses the local exploitation of PSO and the global exploration of FWA to achieve better results, the new PSO and FWA hybrid proposed in this paper, PSO-FWA, does not follow the same principle.

In fact, the new hybrid approach here presented does in a way the opposite, as PSO is here used for global exploration and FWA for local exploitation. In PSO–FWA, the von Neumann topology [6] is assumed to be used, but every few iterations, the bp best particles multiply using the amplitude and number of new particles (i.e., sparks) randomly generated within the amplitude A_i in the new swarm from FWA.

The PSO–FWA algorithm pseudocode is shown in Algorithm 3.

Whenever creating new particles dynamically in PSO, these new particles need belong to a group or sub-swarm, which can create problems in recalculating a new group for every particle. To avoid this, as well as to utilize the exploitation capabilities of FWA, since only the best particles get to reproduce in this way, there is not a large concern with premature convergence, so these new groups form a gbest topology with each other, as well as with their "parent" particle.

For a newly created particle to be able to communicate, it must know which particles belong to its group and make every existing particle aware of its existence. To maintain the von Neumann topology, this would mean recalculating the configuration of the entire swarm. Every time a particle multiplies, each new particle is connected to its parent and the other particles in the same sub-swarm via a gbest topology, in order to avoid this computational effort. As only a small number of particles multiply, and those selected to do so are the ones exploring the most promising regions, all new particles originate from such regions.

The use of the gbest topology for the new particles does not affect the general capacity of the swarm for global exploration, since the new particle only share information directly with its parent. This iterative creation of new sub-swarms connected to a single particle has an impact on the topology of the swarm.

Algorithm 3. Pseudocode for the proposed PSO–FWA algorithm

1: Initialize N particles with von Neumann topology;
2: Evaluate the fitness value $f(\mathbf{x})$ of each particle;
3: **while** $t < maxIter$ and not terminate **do**
4:     **if** $t \% k = 0$ **then**
5:        Sort particles by fitness;
6:        $y_{min} \leftarrow$ particles[1];
7:        $y_{max} \leftarrow$ particles[$N/2$];
8:        $best\_particles \leftarrow particles[1 : bp]$;
9:        **for** p in bp **do**
10:           Calculate A_p according to Eq. 3;
11:           Calculate S_p according to Eq. 4 and Eq. 5;
12:           Generate new sub-swarm according to Algorithm 4;
13:        **end for**
14:     **end if**
15:     Calculate $\mathbf{v}_n^{t+1}$ for each particle according to Eq. 1;
16:     Calculate $\mathbf{x}_n^{t+1}$ for each particle according to Eq. 2;
17:     Evaluate fitness of each particle;
18: **end while**
19: Return the best particle found;

In the case of a problem with numerous local minima, where the particles are spread apart, the new sub-swarms will also be separated, allowing for a faster exploitation of the promising regions.

Algorithm 4. Pseudocode for the sub-swarm algorithm

1: **for** s in S_p **do**
2:     $new\_particles[s] \leftarrow p \cdot$ Gaussian() $\cdot A_p$;
3:     Connect all $new\_particles$ in same group;
4: **end for**
5: Return $new\_particles$;

This does not impede the global exploration capabilities of the algorithm, as the new particles only indirectly share information to the rest of the particles while locally searching promising regions. This successive generation of new particles connected to a single parent particle slowly morphs the overall topology of the swarm. If the best particles are spread apart, indicating an objective function with many local minima, the particles that multiply will quickly explore these promising regions and further multiplications will abandon the groups that got stuck in local minima. By opposition, if the particles that multiply are close to each other, this will result in an increase in the number of particles in the promising regions, allowing for a fast convergence.

5 Experimental Setup

5.1 Experimental Setting

To allow for a fair comparison, the standard PSO, FWA, PS–FW, and PSO–FWA algorithms were implemented and compared in the same experimental setting. All algorithms were run 51 times each, as suggested in [7], using the same control parameters. The maximum number of iterations allowed for each algorithm was set to 1,000, the inertia weight w was set to 0.7, and the acceleration coefficients c_1 and c_2 were both set to 1.8. In all experiments, a tolerance of 1e−12 was adopted.

Regarding algorithm-specific parameters, the number of best particles bp was set to 5 and a new sub-swarm was generated every 50 iterations.

The von Neumann topology was used in both the standard PSO and PSO–FWA, whereas the gbest topology was utilized for PS–FW, as it was used in the original algorithm [2].

The values used for the specific parameters in the FWA and PS–FW algorithms were the same as in [2,13], respectively.

The comparison also included the Enhanced Jaya (EJAYA) algorithm [15], a variant of the Jaya metaphor-less algorithm [10] that has recently been demonstrated to be quite effective in solving systems of nonlinear equations [11].

The implementation of the algorithms was done in Julia [1] using double-precision floating-point arithmetic. All experiments were run on a portable computer with an Intel® Core™ i7-4720HQ processor at 2.60 GHz and 8 GB RAM.

5.2 Test Problems

The following systems of nonlinear equations, which are difficult to solve using traditional iterative methods, were chosen as test problems for the comparison performed in this study:

Problem 1. ([4], Problem D1 – Modified Rosenbrock), $n = 12$.

$$f_{2i-1}(\mathbf{x}) = \frac{1}{1 + \exp(-x_{2i-1})} - 0.73$$
$$f_{2i}(\mathbf{x}) = 10(x_{2i} - x_{2i-1}^2), \quad i = 1, \ldots, \frac{n}{2}$$
$$D = ([-10, 10], \ldots, [-10, 10])^T$$

Problem 2. ([4], Problem D3 – Powell badly scaled), $n = 12$.

$$f_{2i-1}(\mathbf{x}) = 10^4 x_{2i-1} x_{2i} - 1$$
$$f_{2i}(\mathbf{x}) = \exp(-x_{2i-1}) + \exp(-x_{2i}) - 1.0001, \quad i = 1, \ldots, \frac{n}{2}$$
$$D = ([0, 100], \ldots, [0, 100])^T$$

Problem 3. ([4], Problem D6 – Shifted and augmented trigonometric function with an Euclidean sphere), $n = 12$.

$$f_i(\mathbf{x}) = n - 1 - \sum_{j=1}^{n-1} \cos(x_j - 1) + i(1 - \cos(x_i - 1)) - \sin(x_i - 1), \quad i = 1, \ldots, n-1$$

$$f_n(\mathbf{x}) = \sum_{j=1}^{n} x_j^2 - 10000$$

$$D = ([-200, 200], \ldots, [-200, 200])^T$$

Problem 4. ([14], Economics modeling application), $n = 12$.

$$f_i(\mathbf{x}) = \left(x_i + \sum_{k=1}^{n-i-1} x_k x_{i+k} \right) x_n - c_i, \quad i = 1, \ldots, n-1$$

$$f_n(\mathbf{x}) = \sum_{j=1}^{n-1} x_j + 1$$

where the constants c_i can be chosen arbitrarily; here $c_i = 0$, $i = 1, \ldots, n-1$
$$D = ([-100, 100], \ldots, [-100, 100])^T$$

Problem 5. ([5], Example 1 – The Bratu problem), $n = 12$.

$$f_1(\mathbf{x}) = -2x_1 + x_2 + \alpha h^2 \exp(x_1)$$
$$f_n(\mathbf{x}) = x_{n-1} - 2x_n + \alpha h^2 \exp(x_n)$$
$$f_i(\mathbf{x}) = x_{i-1} - 2x_i + x_{i+1} + \alpha h^2 \exp(x_i), \ i = 2, \ldots, n-1,$$

where $\alpha \geq 0$ is a parameter, assuming here $\alpha = 3.5$, and $h = \dfrac{1}{n+1}$.
$$D = ([-100, 100], \ldots, [-100, 100])^T$$

Problem 6. ([5], Example 2 – The beam problem), $n = 12$.

$$f_1(\mathbf{x}) = -2x_1 + x_2 + \alpha h^2 \sin(x_1)$$
$$f_n(\mathbf{x}) = x_{n-1} - 2x_n + \alpha h^2 \sin(x_n)$$
$$f_i(\mathbf{x}) = x_{i-1} - 2x_i + x_{i+1} + \alpha h^2 \exp(x_i), \ i = 2, \ldots, n-1,$$

where $h = \dfrac{1}{n+1}$ and $\alpha \geq 0$ is a parameter; here $\alpha = 11$.
$$D = ([-100, 100], \ldots, [-100, 100])^T$$

Problem 7. ([9], 21 – Extended Rosenbrock function), $n = 12$.

$$f_{2i-1}(\mathbf{x}) = 10(x_{2i} - x_{2i-1}^2)$$
$$f_{2i}(\mathbf{x}) = 1 - x_{2i-1}, \quad i = 1, \ldots, \frac{n}{2}$$
$$D = ([-100, 100], \ldots, [-100, 100])^T$$

Problem 8. ([9], 26 – Trigonometric function), $n = 12$.

$$f_i(\mathbf{x}) = n - \sum_{j=1}^{n} \cos x_j + i(1 - \cos x_i) - \sin x_i, \quad i = 1, \ldots, n$$

$$D = ([-100, 100], \ldots, [-100, 100])^T$$

Problem 9. ([9], 27 – Brown almost-linear function), $n = 12$.

$$f_i(\mathbf{x}) = x_i + \sum_{j=1}^{n} x_j - (n+1), \quad i = 1, \ldots, n-1$$

$$f_n(\mathbf{x}) = \left(\prod_{j=1}^{n} x_j \right) - 1$$

$$D = ([-10, 10], \ldots, [-10, 10])^T$$

Problem 10. ([9], 28 – Discrete boundary value function), $n = 12$.

$$f_1(\mathbf{x}) = 2x_1 - x_2 + h^2(x_1 + h + 1)^3/2$$
$$f_n(\mathbf{x}) = 2x_n - x_{n-1} + h^2(x_n + nh + 1)^3/2$$
$$f_i(\mathbf{x}) = 2x_i - x_{i-1} - x_{i+1} + h^2(x_i + t_i + 1)^3/2, \quad i = 2, \ldots, n-1,$$

where $h = \frac{1}{n+1}$ and $t_i = ih$.
$$D = ([0, 5], \ldots, [0, 5])^T$$

6   Results and Discussion

The average fitness value for each pair algorithm/problem was calculated and the results thus obtained are shown in Table 1. The best (i.e., minimum) fitness values found for each different algorithm and problem are shown in Table 2. The best result for each problem is bolded, while the second-best value is underlined.

Table 1. Average performance of each algorithm

Problem	PSO	FWA	PSO–FWA	PS–FW	EJAYA
01	0.093696602	8.231227429	**0.023829129**	2.688307333	0.786323905
02	**0.000611303**	10528.36554	0.053180425	4.929956145	5.845716462
03	**0.673563009**	17637.37896	0.813282593	7.37086e+15	24.94501395
04	7.68886e−13	121.161161	**3.50538e−13**	7.08888e+24	6.919e−13
05	2.472214572	405.3670455	**0.017626657**	0.180648169	18.40166643
06	**0.629464887**	449.2970073	0.708199283	0.554307947	16.3762457
07	**0.740239982**	1166.651425	1.946738341	4.30706e+11	11.87298727
08	**0.003830296**	0.032297347	0.03146428	0.025972228	4.244178222
09	3.08272e−05	27.63435204	**4.73538e−06**	4.77479e+66	0.019622826
10	0.001165984	0.156890307	**6.90023e−05**	7.32552e+14	0.237439165

Table 2. Best performance of each algorithm

Problem	PSO	FWA	PSO–FWA	PS–FW	EJAYA
01	**6.58917e−07**	0.214234267	2.67113E-05	0.616052907	0.005183943
02	0.0006113	837.2544034	**0.000413175**	2.278576919	5.000485975
03	0.00467257	3447.14932	**3.14072e−09**	3.68477048	11.79736641
04	1.64973e−13	1.93052557	2.79099e−13	**3.64338e−14**	1.2451e−13
05	2.469796642	45.3698909	**7.61427e−05**	0.061573931	1.01676417
06	0.517634554	80.45977863	**0.514741134**	0.518018226	1.212673401
07	4.71128E-07	60.61553916	**4.2838e−08**	3.047900675	2.048738198
08	0.003270911	0.021813477	**9.59711e−13**	6.0212E-05	1.282223168
09	9.7311e−13	1.41803206	**9.06386e−13**	0.29030721	3.5519e−06
10	**9.29977e−13**	0.111856778	9.8634e−13	0.045728666	0.237439165

From the results obtained, a few conclusions can be drawn. PSO–FWA achieved the best average result in half the problems, tied with PSO. While this may indicate a failure of the other algorithms, it should be noted that what these two algorithms have in common is the von Neumann topology, used to allow for a better exploration.

Due to their rapid convergence, the remaining algorithms do not perform well on challenging problems, such as nonlinear equation systems, for which exploration plays a crucial role.

Even though PSO on average performed similarly to the PSO–FWA algorithm, this approach has shown to have better convergence, as it achieved either the best result or a result quite close to the best in almost all problems.

7 Conclusion

PSO–FWA, a novel optimization algorithm based on a hybridization of PSO and FWA, was proposed to solve complex nonlinear equation systems. The performance of the proposed PSO–FWA hybrid algorithm was compared to PS–FW, another hybrid algorithm based on PSO and FWA, as well as to PSO and FWA.

The Enhanced Jaya (EJAYA) algorithm [15], which was recently shown quite effective at solving systems of nonlinear equations [11], was also included in the computational comparison carried out.

While the previous algorithms considered for comparison appear to perform better in simple optimization problems with few local minima, PSO–FWA was able to achieve better results in more difficult problems, as evidenced by the results obtained with the set of complex nonlinear equation systems chosen for this study.

References

1. Bezanson, J., Edelman, A., Karpinski, S., Shah, V.: Julia: a fresh approach to numerical computing. SIAM Rev. **59**(1), 65–98 (2017). https://doi.org/10.1137/141000671

2. Chen, S., Liu, Y., Wei, L., Guan, B.: PS-FW: a hybrid algorithm based on particle swarm and fireworks for global optimization. Comput. Intell. Neurosci. **2018**, 6094685 (2018). https://doi.org/10.1155/2018/6094685
3. Eberhart, R., Kennedy, J.: A new optimizer using particle swarm theory. In: 6th International Symposium on Micro Machine and Human Science, Nagoya, Japan, pp. 39–43. IEEE (1995). https://doi.org/10.1109/MHS.1995.494215
4. Friedlander, A., Gomes-Ruggiero, M., Kozakevich, D., Martínez, J., Santos, S.: Solving nonlinear systems of equations by means of quasi-Newton methods with a nonmonotone strategy. Optim. Methods Softw. **8**(1), 25–51 (1997). https://doi.org/10.1080/10556789708805664
5. Kelley, C., Qi, L., Tong, X., Yin, H.: Finding a stable solution of a system of nonlinear equations. J. Ind. Manag. Optim. **7**(2), 497–521 (2011). https://doi.org/10.3934/jimo.2011.7.497
6. Kennedy, J., Mendes, R.: Population structure and particle swarm performance. In: Proceedings of the 2002 Congress on Evolutionary Computation. CEC 2002 (Cat. No.02TH8600), vol. 2, pp. 1671–1676 (2002). https://doi.org/10.1109/CEC.2002.1004493
7. Liang, J., Qu, B., Suganthan, P., Hernández-Díaz, A.: Problem definitions and evaluation criteria for the CEC 2013 special session on real-parameter optimization. Technical report 201212, Computational Intelligence Laboratory, Zhengzhou University, Zhengzhou, China (2013)
8. Liu, Q., Wei, W., Yuan, H., Zhan, Z.H., Li, Y.: Topology selection for particle swarm optimization. Inf. Sci. **363**, 154–173 (2016). https://doi.org/10.1016/j.ins.2016.04.050
9. Moré, J., Garbow, B., Hillstrom, K.: Testing unconstrained optimization software. ACM Trans. Math. Softw. **7**(1), 17–41 (1981). https://doi.org/10.1145/355934.355936
10. Rao, R.: Jaya: a simple and new optimization algorithm for solving constrained and unconstrained optimization problems. Int. J. Ind. Eng. Comput. **7**, 19–34 (2016). https://doi.org/10.5267/j.ijiec.2015.8.004
11. Ribeiro, S., Silva, B., Lopes, L.G.: Solving systems of nonlinear equations using Jaya and Jaya-based algorithms: a computational comparison. In: Yadav, A., Nanda, S.J., Lim, M.H. (eds.) Proceedings of the International Conference on Paradigms of Communication, Computing and Data Analytics: PCCDA 2023. Springer, Singapore (to appear, 2023)
12. Shi, Y., Eberhart, R.: A modified particle swarm optimizer. In: 1998 IEEE International Conference on Evolutionary Computation Proceedings. IEEE World Congress on Computational Intelligence (Cat. No. 98TH8360), 1998, pp. 69–73. IEEE (1998). https://doi.org/10.1109/ICEC.1998.699146
13. Tan, Y., Zhu, Y.: Fireworks algorithm for optimization. In: International Conference on Swarm Intelligence, pp. 355–364 (2010). https://doi.org/10.1007/978-3-642-13495-1_44
14. van Hentenryck, P., McAllester, D., Kapur, D.: Solving polynomial systems using a branch and prune approach. SIAM J. Numer. Anal. **34**(2), 797–827 (1997). https://doi.org/10.1137/S0036142995281504
15. Zhang, Y., Chi, A., Mirjalili, S.: Enhanced Jaya algorithm: a simple but efficient optimization method for constrained engineering design problems. Knowl. Based Syst. **233**, 107555 (2021). https://doi.org/10.1016/j.knosys.2021.107555
16. Zhu, F., Chen, D., Zou, F.: A novel hybrid dynamic fireworks algorithm with particle swarm optimization. Soft. Comput. **25**(3), 2371–2398 (2020). https://doi.org/10.1007/s00500-020-05308-6

Short Papers (CAHSC DSS 2023)

Optimal Computing Budget Allocation for Urban Regeneration: An Unprecedented Match Between Economic/Extra-Economic Evaluations and Urban Planning

Giovanna Acampa$^{(\boxtimes)}$ ⓘ and Alessio Pino ⓘ

University of Enna "Kore", Enna Cittadella Universitaria, 94100 Enna, Italy
giovanna.acampa@unikore.it, alessio.pino@unikorestudent.it

Abstract. The path to creating livable cities passes through the transformation of underexploited urban areas and the revivification of neglected bits of urban fabrics within the contemporary and relevant theme of urban regeneration. However, this process is characterized by an operational misalignment between the urban administrative scale and the small scale of single neighborhoods. Due to their limited budget, public administrations refrain from attempting to perform capillary punctual regeneration interventions, as it would require higher economic investments. For this reason, local-scale actions often arise as bottom-up initiatives. These are sometimes effective, but their target context is hardly chosen by considering all the available possibilities through a higher-scale analysis.

A solution to this issue can be obtained by selecting the most suitable actions to implement according to a criterion of effectiveness and impact: this offers the ground for original contamination of OCBA (Optimal Computing Budget Allocation) methods and tools by using them in the field of urban planning. These methodologies are most frequently used in business management to determine the best use of limited resources: transferring them to urban planning involves finding criteria and parameters to quantify the impact of urban actions and compare alternatives. This paper describes the early reflections and articulations of this research work through a literature review of OCBA methods and their parameters and a tentative outline of suitable criteria for urban planning.

Keywords: urban regeneration · Optimal Computing Budget Allocation · livability · economic evaluation · green areas

1 Introduction

Most people reside in cities, which are the hub of global technical and economic progress [1]. Despite being temporary, the recent pandemic crises highlighted the urban environment's severe susceptibility [2]. Because of their rapid urbanization, fast population increase, and extensive use of transportation resources, cities have been to blame for the greatest COVID-19 transmission rate [3]. This temporary event has pushed urban

O. Gervasi et al. (Eds.): ICCSA 2023 Workshops, LNCS 14112, pp. 69–79, 2023.
https://doi.org/10.1007/978-3-031-37129-5_6

planners, designers, and the scientific community to perform a more careful examination of urban structures and their capability to fulfill health needs, both in emergency scenarios and in the daily improvement of their population's well-being, and especially concerning the importance of green areas [4, 5]. Indeed, it has revealed the need for a diffuse distribution of urban services, spaces for leisure, meeting, and a detailed design of interstitial areas as a response to a spontaneous human tendency [7].

In order to create new urban management models that are resilient to the current and upcoming pandemic occurrences, the scientific community has continuously worked to examine the social and environmental effects of COVID-19. Both consolidated and in-development cities should be predicated on resilient and smart planning and design [8].

Several urban models have been introduced – and had been introduced in previous years – to systematize the design of this transformation aimed at urban regeneration [9]. They are now gathered under the broad and popular concept of the "15-min city", a city where, in any neighborhood, essential human functions (living, working, commerce, healthcare, education, and entertainment) are available within 15 min by walking or riding a bicycle [10].

This concept has already been warmly welcomed in several European cities, among which Paris [11]; in Italy, as well, several towns have accepted the challenge to realize this model, among which Rome [12] and Milan [13]. This positive and encouraging reception is motivated by the multiple benefits in this perspective: on the one hand, the achievement of a softer-paced life [14]; on the other hand, higher environmental sustainability thanks to the decrease in transport-based emissions [15].

However, implementing urban regeneration according to this model is not an easy task. The size of the involved cities requires a significant budget for a capillary regeneration to achieve the 15-min city model, which is not entirely in the Municipalities' availability. A frequent solution is a partnership with private stakeholders for private/public cooperation; however, the benefit for private stakeholders lies in the economic benefit deriving from improving the areas' conditions, which increases their economic attractiveness. For this reason, these cooperations are more often carried out in areas with higher economic potential, possibly creating inequality between the various areas of the city: this contradicts the model's foundation. It has also been highlighted that the difficulty of simultaneously considering the whole urban fabric when establishing the intervention targets ends up overlooking various social groups' needs [16]. Some attempts have been made in this direction, especially with the Italian experimentations in Parma and Milan, where intervention planning has been preceded by a consistent mapping of the urban and social fabric [17]; however, this has been fully implemented only in the latter and mainly consisted of the realization of residential neighborhoods outside the central areas.

This paper proposes an alternative solution for intervening in urban areas to perform urban regeneration along the "15-min city" model principles through Optimal Computing Budget Allocation (OCBA) methods. These methods originate in computer science and are employed for optimization purposes to establish the best use of given resources among some available alternatives. In addition, they are commonly utilized in finance and business management as a tool for selecting items of economic expenditure.

The scenario of large-scale urban regeneration outlined above may be assumed as a set of investment alternatives with different outcomes and effectiveness. Hence, OCBA methodologies, if correctly fine-tuned to fit this context, could be a valid support to.

The following section presents an outline of OCBA methodologies, briefly illustrating their framework, typologies of application, and alternative possibilities following a literature review. Then, the third section proposes an example of OCBA structure for applying the methods to urban regeneration cases, with an indication of the parameters to consider and their assessment modalities.

2 Materials and Methods

2.1 Literature Review

This section analyzes the investigation of OCBA in the scientific literature since its introduction in 1997. It focuses on the evolution of the popularity of these methods in scientific research and on the main items of interest within this theme.

The literature review was conducted through the Scopus platform, and the results related to the time distribution of the scientific articles are reported in Fig. 1.

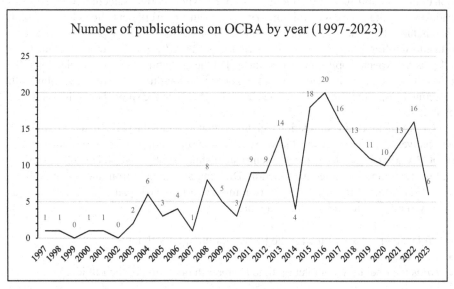

Fig. 1. Diagram reporting the number of scientific publications on OCBA methods found in the scientific literature from 1997 to 2023 (2023 data until April have been considered).

The review was only conducted using the Scopus platform, so it must be pointed out that it is not comprehensive of all the articles published on this theme; however, it allows inferring some trends concerning this topic. The diagram reports that these methods have received increasing interest from the scientific community in the last few years, with a peak in 2016. The total number of individuated articles is 195; 141 out of 195 have been published in the last 10 years (from 2013 to 2023), resulting in over 70% of the total.

One reason for this drastic increase is the expansion of the range of fields these methods encompass. While the pioneering articles by H.C. Chen focused on the field of manufacturing, hence proposing applications for industrial purposes [18], more recent articles expand the scope to broader aspects, such as infrastructural themes, with a proposal for a time-of-day pricing system for toll roads [19], and healthcare, with a study on the management of hospital inpatient beds by using OCBA techniques [20] and one on the resolution of health examination scheduling problems [21]. These and other applications also show their adaptability for public uses, where several parameters are involved, besides their native private-sector applications. Some examples are represented by experimentation with OCBA methods for joint car-sharing relocation based on modular simulations [22] and a stochastic simulation optimization for route selection according to flight delay [23].

2.2 Outline of Optimal Computing Budget Allocation Techniques

Single-Parameter OCBA. The Optimal Computing Budget Allocation (OCBA) was introduced by H.C. Chen [18, 24] as a technique for the maximization of an approximation of the probability of correct selection P{CS}, where correct selection (CS) indicates choosing the alternative with minimum mean, leading to an efficient allocation algorithm that includes both means and variances. Extensions of the OCBA approach include correlated sampling [25]; non-normal distributions [26, 27]; multiple objective functions [28]; using expected opportunity cost instead of the probability of correct selection [29]; minimizing variance instead of maximizing the probability of correct selection [30]; selecting an optimal subset of top-m solutions rather than the single best solution (Chen et al. 2008).

OCBA methods are simulation techniques that evaluate the performance of multiple alternatives to achieve a given objective to minimize or maximize. The preliminary phase of OCBA utilization is to set the problem: establishing an objective and its sub-objectives and then defining the objective function. Drawing an example from the scientific literature [31], considering the objective of minimizing the makespan of a vehicle in a car factory, the following terms can be adopted:

- P_{ij} is the processing time for the j-th operation of the i-th job;
- T_{ij} is the travel time for the j-th operation of the i-th job;
- O_{ij} is the operation completion time for the j-th operation of the i-th job.

The following relation results:

$$O_{ij} = T_{ij} + P_{ij} \tag{1}$$

Then, the summation of the completion time of the j operations for each i-th job can be considered:

$$C_i = \sum_{j=i}^{n} O_{ij} \tag{2}$$

The objective function is hence defined as:

$$Min\,makespan = E[Max(C_1, C_2, C_3, \ldots, C_n), \omega] \tag{3}$$

where ω represents randomness in this system.

Another aspect to consider in OCBA is noise; when it is too high, re-evaluation is needed to obtain a more precise function value. Its assessment is performed by assessing the means and variances of action performances. In the algorithmic structure of most OCBA methodologies, this is achieved through the allocation of an equal quantity of initial samples B_0 to each action. The following step is the allocation of an additional budget B_Δ that is sequentially based on the means and variances. Both are updated once after the reception of a response. The final step is the asymptotical maximization of the approximate probability of correct selection when the budget is used up according to the following equations:

$$\frac{N_i(t)}{N_j(t)} = \left(\frac{\frac{\sigma_i(t)}{(\delta_{i,m}(t))}}{\frac{\sigma_j(t)}{(\delta_{j,m}(t))}} \right)^2, \forall i, j \in IN_r \text{ and } i \neq j \neq m \tag{4}$$

$$N_m(t) = \sigma_m(t) \sqrt{\sum_{i=1, i \neq m}^{r} \frac{N_i^2(t)}{(\sigma_i(t))^2}} \tag{5}$$

where $N_i(t)$ refers to the total number of evaluations arranged to action i at allocation time t, $d_i(t)$ and $\sigma_i(t)$ store its sample mean and variance, respectively, and m stands for the best action with the lowest mean, $\delta_{i,m}(t) = d_i(t) - d_m(t)$.

Multiparametric Optimization. The traditional formulation of OCBA is based on the individuation of a single objective to optimize, which stands as the reference parameter of the objective function [32]. However, this does not often comply with decision-making situations: the presence of heterogeneous items involved in the effects of the alternatives can hardly be entirely neglected [33]. For this reason, OCBA can be integrated with multiparametric optimization techniques [34] to consider various needs and effects of the choices.

The formulation of a multi-parametric optimization problem must include the multi-objective function (minimization or maximization), constraints for each involved parameter, and coefficients to determine the weight of the characteristics in the overall evaluation. The following are some multi-parametric optimization methods that can be integrated into OCBA's formulation:

- Branch and Bound [35];
- Tabu Search [36];
- Multi-Parametric Programming [37];
- Benders decomposition [38];
- Penalty Function [39];
- Chvatal-Gomory cuts (cutting plane) [40];
- Evolutionary Algorithm [41];

- Multi-Parametric Quadratic Programming [42].

The latter will be used for the exemplification of an optimization problem, structured as follows [43]:

$$\begin{aligned} x(t+1) &= Ax(t) + Bu(t) \\ y(t) &= Cx(t) \end{aligned} \tag{6}$$

where $x(t)$ is the state variable, $u(t)$ is the input, and (A,B) is a controllable pair. For the current $x(t)$, the optimization problem can be solved by applying the Karush-Kuhn-Tucker (KKT) conditions, resulting in:

$$V_z(x(t)) = min_z \frac{1}{2} z^T Hz \tag{7}$$

$$s.t. \; Gz \le W + Sx(t) \tag{8}$$

where $z = U + H^{-1}F^T x(t)$, $U = \left[u_t^T, \ldots, u_{t+M-1}^T \right]$ and $x(t)$ is the current state, which can be treated as a vector of parameters.

Finally, the constraints are expressed as follows:

$$\begin{aligned} y_{min} &\le y_{t+k|t} \le y_{max}, k = 1, \ldots, N \\ u_{min} &\le u_{t+k} \le u_{max}, k = 0, \ldots, M-1 \\ u_{t+k} &= Kx_{t+k|t}, M \le k \le N-1 \\ x_{t|t} &= x(t) \\ x_{t+k+1|t} &= Ax_{t+k|t} + Bu_{t+k}, k \ge 0 \\ y_{t+k|t} &= Cx_{t+k|t}, k \ge 0 \end{aligned} \tag{9}$$

3 Elaborations on the Application for Urban Regeneration

As described above, OCBA single-parameter and multi-parameter methodologies require setting a problem by defining one or more objectives to be minimized or maximized by increasing the dependent variable to a given extent, determined by the budget.

Hence, exploring the possibilities for the application of these techniques to urban regeneration, it is first necessary to define the urban regeneration problem as a choice between discreet actions. For this reason, it is best to consider a case of punctual urban regeneration intervention (RI) occurring through:

- the redevelopment of a regeneration action on a public area to increase the quality of a neighborhood-scale public space;
- the reuse of an abandoned private location to realize a neighborhood-scale proximal service.

An intervention in one of these two categories produces a benefit for the neighborhood where it is performed, which can be associated with a Livability Benefit function in the form *LB(RI)*. It must be considered that, due to the form of the OCBA, *RI* represents a generic intervention; in this way, the *LB* can be used to determine the maximum benefit that can be attained through any intervention of the two typologies outlined above.

The following step is to hypothesize the independent variables associated with the *LB(RI)* function: a significant suggestion can be drawn from the 15-min city model, which solidly relates urban livability with the distance from a service belonging to one of the six macro-categories (living, working, commerce, healthcare, education, and entertainment). These can be used as a parameter to estimate the benefit deriving from the insertion of a service in the 15-min walking range, which can be calculated as:

$$LB(RI) = P_i \cdot f_U(d_{15+} - d_{RI}) \tag{10}$$

where P_i is the population involved in the action (depending on the size of the neighborhood where it is carried out), f_U is the frequency of use of the service realized (in terms of a number of expected weekly visits for the average population), d_{15+} is the distance from the closest location where the given service is provided (outside the 15-min walking range), and d_{RI} is the distance from the place where the regeneration intervention would be carried out.

Homogeneous neighborhood population groups must perform the analysis and quantification of the values of these parameters. This mainly affects the determination of the frequency of use, which closely depends on the demographic characteristics of the involved population, as the use of education facilities is more frequent for younger individuals and families with children. In contrast, the use of healthcare can be considered more relevant for the elderly population. In this sense, the frequency of use is adopted as a parameter to determine the relevance of a service for a given part of the population. Then, distance is not a homogeneous value in both d_{15+} and d_{RI}, as it changes for each building block, each with a different involved population. Hence, since a whole neighborhood is considered as the scope of the realization of an intervention, the expression (10) can be further elaborated into:

$$LB(RI) = \sum_{j=1}^{n} P_{i,j} \cdot f_{U,j}(d_{15+,j} - d_{RI,j}) \tag{11}$$

That is, the neighborhood is broken down into *j* areas, whose demographic and spatial features determine the specific assignment of the values of $P_{i,j}, f_{U,j}, d_{15+,j}$, and $d_{RI,j}$, and the single products are summated to obtain the estimate of total *LB*. $P_{i,j}$ serves as a ponderation coefficient, which allows relating the intrinsic goodness of the intervention to the real share of the population that will benefit from it.

Then, the objective function results to be:

$$\max LB = f(f_U, P_i, d_{15+} - d_{RI}) \tag{12}$$

By constructing a continuous function for the determination of the Livability Benefit, it is possible to run OCBA analyses on the whole urban fabric, subjecting the individuated opportunities to a segmentation of the involved residents. This application is intended as an exemplification of the possibilities to model the features of urban interventions for preliminary strategic planning. At the same time, it does not consider the detailed aspects related to the architectural, typological, and morphological characteristics of the interventions. If they were also evaluated through an OCBA-based methodology, their analysis should be more detailed and focused on multiple factors affecting urban livability. The results of this subsequent analysis could overturn the initial suggestions deriving from this preliminary application of the OCBA methodology, leading to a new full routine of the process.

4 Conclusions and Future Developments

In such a complex and interdisciplinary field as urban planning, the most successful and updated design approaches encourage thorough and direct knowledge acquisition on the involved urban fabric, up to the modern operations that actively include participatory design, and co-design labs [44]. In this typology of contexts, active discussion and understanding of territorial and local criticalities and needs are an essential pre-requirement to conceive and define urban interventions. This positive evolution of urban planning must be preserved and continued.

However, it must also be considered that the issues of urban congestion and high distance from the services for the fulfillment of basic human needs mostly affect large metropolises. There, it is difficult to ensure an overall knowledge of the whole urban space, and some valid opportunities for redevelopment might be neglected. This instance has been the starting point for the presented research work: algorithmic optimization processes, such as OCBA methods, can be used to perform a general mapping of the locations characterized by higher strategic convenience in the introduction of a new service in a specific underused area or in the requalification of a specific abandoned place.

Further developments in using this method could include the extension of OCBA to other phenomena that involve the whole urban fabric, considering the maximization of the economic benefits deriving from the regeneration interventions and the redevelopment of the areas where they are performed. In detail, while this exemplification of the methodology focuses on determining the point where the maximum walkability benefit can be achieved, it will also be interesting to outline critical factors for the increase of environmental sustainability in cities concerning various typologies and locations of areal regenerations involving the introduction of green spaces. However, in this case, the economic objective function would have to be paired with other objectives in a multi-parametric structure, such as the other components of sustainability, in addition to the benefits provided by reducing vehicular transport thanks to the enhancement of 15-min walking mobility.

Finally, using computational methods for urban strategic planning should not overshadow the reflection on the symbolic and natural values of the urban fabric: interventions on the urban form shape a broader common imagery beyond strategic convenience. This embodies complex characters of abstraction, genericity, and sociality, which require deeper comprehension before an intervention is finalized.

References

1. Derudder, B.: Network analysis of 'urban systems': potential, challenges, and pitfalls. Royal Dutch Geographical Society KNAG, 1–17 (2019)
2. Ahmed, N.O., El-Halafawy, A.M., Amin, A.M.: A critical review of urban livability. Eur. J. Sustain. Dev. 8(1), 165 (2019)
3. Truszkowska, A., et al.: Urban determinants of COVID-19 spread: a comparative study across three cities in New York State. J. Urban Health 99(5), 909–921 (2022). https://doi.org/10.1007/s11524-022-00623-9
4. Davies, C., Sanesi, G.: COVID-19 and the importance of urban green spaces. Urban for Urban Green 74, 127654 (2022). https://doi.org/10.1016/j.ufug.2022.127654
5. Korpilo, S., et al.: Coping with crisis: green space use in helsinki before and during the COVID-19 pandemic. Front. Sustain. Cities 3, 713977 (2021)
6. Burnett, H., Olsen, J.R., Mitchell, R.: Green space visits and barriers to visiting during the COVID-19 pandemic: a three-wave nationally representative cross-sectional study of UK adults. Land 11(4), 503 (2022). https://doi.org/10.3390/land11040503
7. Lee, K.O., Mai, K.M., Park, S.: Green space accessibility helps buffer declined mental health during the COVID-19 pandemic: evidence from big data in the United Kingdom. Nat. Ment. Health 1, 124–134 (2023)
8. Tiboni, M., Botticini, F., Sousa, S., Silva, N.J.: A systematic review for urban regeneration effects analysis in urban cores. Sustainability 12(21), 9296 (2020)
9. D'Acci, L.: Simulating future societies in isobenefit cities: social isobenefit scenarios. Futures 54, 3–18 (2013)
10. Moreno, C., et al.: Introducing the "15-Minute City": sustainability, resilience and place identity in future post-pandemic cities. Smart Cities 4(1), 93–111 (2021)
11. Paris, the 15-minute city. https://tomorrow.city/a/paris-the-15-minute-city. last accessed 2023/04/11
12. Website of the Municipality of Rome, "Città dei 15 minuti". https://www.comune.roma.it/web/it/dipartimento-decentramento-servizi-delegati-e-citta-in-15-minuti-citta-dei-15-min. page. last accessed 2023/04/11
13. The Plan, "The 15-minute city: Milan focuses on its suburbs for a polycentric future". https://www.theplan.it/eng/whats_on/the-15%E2%80%93minute-city-milan-focuses-on-its-suburbs-for-a-polycentric-future. last accessed 2023/04/11
14. Wu, H., Wang, L., Zhang, Z., Gao, J.: Analysis and optimization of 15-minute community life circle based on supply and demand matching: a case study of Shanghai. PLoS ONE 16(8), e0256904 (2021). https://doi.org/10.1371/journal.pone.0256904
15. Allam, Z., Moreno, C., Chabaud, D., Pratlong, F.: In: The Palgrave Handbook of Global Sustainability, Brinkmann, S. (ed.). Palgrave Macmillan (2020)
16. Khavarian-Garmsir, A.R., Sharifi, A., Sadeghi, A.: The 15-minute city: urban planning and design efforts toward creating sustainable neighborhoods. Cities 132, 104101 (2023)
17. Papas, T., Basbas, S., Campisi, T.: Urban mobility evolution and the 15-minute city model: from holistic to bottom-up approach. Transportation Research Procedia 69, 544–551 (2023)
18. Chen, H.C., Chen, C.H., Dai, L., Yucesan, E.: New development of optimal computing budget allocation for discrete event simulation. In: Proceedings of the 1997 Winter Simulation Conference, pp. 334–341. Piscataway, NJ (1997)
19. Zheng, L., et al.: Time-of-day pricing for toll roads under traffic demand uncertainties: a distributionally robust simulation-based optimization method. Transp. Res. Part C Emerg. Technol. 144, 103894 (2022)
20. Gong, X., Wang, X., Zhou, L., Geng, N.: Managing hospital inpatient beds under clustered overflow configuration. Comput. Oper. Res. 148, 1060 (2022)

21. Liu, D., Geng, N.: Stochastic health examination scheduling problem based on genetic algorithm and simulation optimization. In: Proceedings of the 7th International Conference on Industrial Engineering and Applications (ICIEA), pp. 620–624. Bangkok, Thailand (2020)

22. Jiang, Y., et al.: Optimization for joint relocation of carsharing based on modular simulation. J. Southwest Jiaotong Univ. **58**(1), 74–82 (2023)

23. Tian, Y., Ye, B., Estupiñá, M.S., Wan, L.: Stochastic simulation optimization for route selection strategy based on flight delay cost. Asia-Pacific J. Oper. Res. **35**(06), 1850045 (2018). https://doi.org/10.1142/S0217595918500458

24. Chen, C.H., Lin, J., Yucesan, E., Chick, S.E.: Simulation budget allocation for further enhancing the efficiency of ordinal optimization. Discrete Event Dyn. Syst. Theor. Appl. **10**, 251–270 (2000)

25. Fu, M.C., Hu, J.Q., Chen, C.H., Xiong, X.: Simulation allocation for determining the best design in the presence of correlated sampling. INFORMS J. Comput. **19**(1), 101–111 (2007)

26. Glynn, P., Juneja, S.: A large deviations perspective on ordinal optimization. In: Proceedings of the 2004 Winter Simulation Conference, pp. 577–585. Piscataway, NJ (2004)

27. Fu, M.C., Healy, K.J.: Techniques for simulation optimization: an experimental study on an (s, S) inventory system. IIE Trans. **29**(3), 191–199 (1997)

28. Lee, L.H., Chew, E.P., Teng, S.Y., Goldsman, D.: Optimal computing budget allocation for multi-objective simulation models. In: Proceedings of 2004 Winter Simulation Conference, pp. 586–594. Piscataway, NJ (2004)

29. Chick, S.E., Wu, Y.: Selection procedures with frequentist expected opportunity cost bounds. Oper. Res. **53**(5), 889 (2005)

30. Trailovic, L., Pao, L.Y.: Variance estimation and ranking of target tracking position errors modeled using Gaussian mixture distributions. Automatica **41**(8), 1433–1438 (2005)

31. Lin, J.T., Chiu, C.-C., Chang, Y.-H.: Simulation-based optimization approach for simultaneous scheduling of vehicles and machines with processing time uncertainty in FMS. Flex. Serv. Manuf. J. **31**(1), 104–141 (2019). https://doi.org/10.1007/s10696-017-9302-x

32. Ammeri, A., et al.: A comprehensive literature review of mono-objective simulation optimization methods. Adv. Prod. Eng. Manage. **6**(4), 291–302 (2011)

33. Chen, H.C.: Optimal computing budget allocation in selecting the best design via discrete event simulation. Dissertations available from ProQuest (1998)

34. Pappas, I., et al.: Multiparametric programming in process systems engineering: recent development and path forward. Front. Chem. Eng. **2**, 620168 (2020)

35. Moore, J.T., Bard, J.F.: The mixed integer linear bilevel programming problem. Oper. Res. **38**, 911–921 (1990)

36. Wen, U.P., Huang, A.D.: A simple tabu search method to solve the mixed755 integer linear bilevel programming problem. Eur. J. Oper. Res. **88**, 563–571 (1996)

37. Faisca, N.P., Dua, V., Rustem, B., Saraiva, P.M., Pistikopoulos, E.N.: Parametric global optimisation for bilevel programming. J. Global Optim. **38**, 609–623 (2007)

38. Caramia, M., Mari, R.: A decomposition approach to solve a bilevel capacitated facility location problem with equity constraints. Optim. Lett. **10**(5), 997–1019 (2016). https://doi.org/10.1007/s11590-015-0918-z

39. Vicente, L., Savard, G., Judice, J.: Discrete linear bilevel programming 750 problem. J. Optim. Theory Appl. **89**, 597–614 (1996)

40. Dempe, S., Kalashnikov, D.V., Rios-Mercado, R.: Discrete bilevel programming: application to a natural gas cash-out problem **166**, 469–488 (2005)

41. Handoko, S., Chuin, L., Gupta, A., Soon, O., Kim, H., Siew, T.: Solving multi-vehicle profitable tour problem via knowledge adoption in evolutionary bi-level programming. In: Proceedings of the 2015 IEEE Congress on Evolutionary Computation, pp. 2713–2720 (2015)

42. Bemporad, A., Morari, M., Dua, V., Pistikopoulos, E.: The explicit linear quadratic regulator for constrained systems. In: Proceedings of the American Control Conference, pp. 872–876. Chicago, IL (2000)
43. Tondel, P., Johansen, T.A., Bemporad, A.: An algorithm for multi-parametric quadratic programming and explicit MPC solutions. In: Proceedings of the 40th IEEE Conference on Decision and Control, pp. 1199–1205. Orlando, USA (2001)
44. Kunze, A., et al.: A conceptual participatory design framework for urban planning. In: Proceedings of the 29th eCAADe Conference "Respecting Fragile Places". Ljubljana, Slovenia (2011)

Crowdmapping: Inclusive Cities and Evaluation

Fabrizio Finucci$^{(\boxtimes)}$ ⒾⒹ and Antonella G. Masanotti ⒾⒹ

Roma Tre University, 00154 Roma, RM, Italy
{fabrizio.finucci,antonellagiulia.masanotti}@uniroma3.it

Abstract. Recent technological innovations are redefining some key steps in the disciplines dealing with urban changes and the evaluation processes connected to the decision-making support system. Moreover, the voluntary input of community stakeholders has, over time, become the procedural center of most decision-making nodes. In addition to traditional participatory techniques, technology is enabling a new phase of less wasteful citizenship practices, where the participatory contribution is the provision of knowledge-based local knowledge the return of data based on voluntary contribution. This is the case of crowdsourcing, a web model based on open and voluntary collaboration in investigation or research by an indefinite and large group of people, aimed at building an informational mapping.

The paper aims to return some of the recent applications of crowdmapping by highlighting the possible contributions that these processes can make to the implementation of information in the service of project evaluation tools.

Keywords: Crowdmapping · Crowdsourcing · Inclusive city · Participation process

1 Introduction

Recent technological developments impact on many disciplines, including those dealing with urban policy, planning, design, and management of urban transformation, and, in the end, support system approaches to decision-making. However, while new technologies had the power to revolutionize the financial sectors, health care or consumer and service delivery systems, in the field of urban planning the adjustments are much slower [1] including the assessment methods that affect and guide it. Among the most relevant (though no longer extremely recent) innovations are the ability to handle large amounts of data, decision support tools, and applications of geographic information systems (GIS) [2]. The recent scientific literature, moreover, shows evidence of a wide and growing application of artificial intelligence (AI) related techniques for planning, in various areas such as land use, zoning, environmental planification, and transportation [1] and for big data management, which is increasingly available and accessible. These new technologies approaches allow openings to innovative ways of collecting, managing, and returning the information needed to implement any assessment operation: among these, the concepts of crowdsourcing and crowdmapping stand out for innovativeness.

Crowdsourcing is a key element of research on open innovation and co-creation processes that addresses whether a large number of individuals, the "crowd," can actively participate in a company's innovation processes [3] enabling access to intelligence and knowledge that would otherwise be scattered among many users or stakeholders.

The concept of crowdsourcing consists of a web model based on open and voluntary collaboration to develop innovative solutions; this resolution first appeared in an article by Jeff Howe for Wired Magazine [4], as the act of outsourcing a job, investigation or research to an unfinished and large group of people, usually in the form of an open and anonymous call.

The methodology -framed as public and participatory- draws on diverse and multiple subjects through Web 2.0 technologies[1] easing the spatial and temporal constraints associated with data collection in public participation processes [5].

As early as 2010, in response to the Haiti earthquakes, the first examples of crowdsourcing were glimpsed: Yates and Paquette [6] use the action line of participatory research for community involvement in disaster management. In the management of the same disaster Starbird and Palen [7] highlight how a severe lack of map data has hampered aid organizations in understanding places in need of assistance.

There are multiple definitions, subcategories, and applications in the literature in crowdsourcing field[2], which differ in the type of application, in the characteristics of the participatory model, in the scope of use in different application fields, and in the complexity through which the so-called crowd, and thus the users, will contribute their knowledge. In this process, the crowdsourcer will benefit by resolving the proposed problem [8] by the demand for mapping. In addition, the proliferation of participative platforms has made it more accessible and easier for individuals to get involved in different types of crowdsourcing initiatives.

Considering what introduced crowdsourcing field, this paper considers the sub category of crowdmapping, whereby one can intend to aggregate crowd-generated inputs, and thus the crowd component such as text messages and social media accompanied by geographic data, and thus the mapping component, in order to provide real time interactive information [9].

Participatory type mapping is used in inclusive research and initiatives in planning and management of development activities at the local level, in planning and management of development activities at the local level. In its broadest sense, participatory mapping refers to the creation of maps by local communities often with the involvement of supporting organizations, comprehending governments, NGOs or other actors involved in development or land-use planning [10].

The paper aims to return some of the recent experiences in which the shared and bottom-up construction of maps has posed itself as a tool with a dual effect: on one hand, that of increasing the level of information, enriched by perceptual information, reconstructed through the user's experience; on the other hand, that of transforming the mapping process into an experience of engagement in which the construction of

---

[1] There is a tendency to refer to Web 2.0 as the set of all online applications that allow a high level of site-user interaction such as social media, forums etc.

[2] Some of the sub-categories in the literature are: crowdfunding (collective financing), crowdcreation (collective creativity), crowdvoting (collective voting), crowdwisdom (collective wisdom), crowd-shipping (collective shipping services), crowd-solving (col-lective problem-solving).

information becomes an act of participation and citizenship. Both land transformation processes and assessment methods are always looking for inclusive and participatory procedures to be implemented within their operational and procedural baggage [11].

2 Crowdmapping e Crowdsourcing: Definition and Principal Platforms

Crowdsourcing is helping to democratize the planning process by providing low-cost data for real time planning, and to mitigate the limitations of traditional data collection methods, such as, for example, census data [12]. In terms of urban planning, crowdmapping is extensively debated in the literature in relation to issues such as problem-solving, idea proposals, and collaborative mappings [13]. The goal is to provide cities with inclusive spaces, framed as spaces that equally value each user, are accessible, and in which the users themselves are self-representative, invested with a role in governance and planning processes [14].

Crowdmapping, therefore, can be interpreted as the collection and sharing process of geographic information through crowdsourcing, understanding them, in some cases, as tools as well as processes. Collaborative maps and the use of related platforms - such as Application Programming Interfaces (APIs) -and major cartographic datasets propose a democratic approach for topics very often related to issues of civic engagement and digital activism.

The first experiments in the crowdmapping arena take place in Kenya in 2008, with the aim of collecting citizen complaints and reports on post-election violence on a map [15]; In this context, an open-source platform was developed [16] in order to collect necessary information and data (via SMS, e-mail, or web) and then match it with geolocation data so that it can be displayed on a map.

Data collection, which is widely debated in the scientific literature, can be done first through social media with voluntary participation on social pages and second through skimming through other datasets (Table 1), such as: Ushahidi, which manages and visualizes data, collects georeferenced information from multiple sources through customized crowdsourced surveys developed by the crowdsourcer; OpenStreetMaps, whose initiative is to foster the growth, development and distribution of geospatial data, a team of volunteers manages the infrastructure and websites where collaborative projects are found for specific purposes, while users contribute data to the map; Google My Maps, where places can be indicated and selected in the form of different labels or layers; StreetBump, designed for the purpose of improving public streets; Crowdspot, designed to generate greater levels of participation, education and engagement. On one hand, the method is seen as a less costly approach to mapping the urban environment; on the other hand, it is seen as an exclusive method due to limited participation and, consequently, due to spatial coverage and dutiful specification of variables [17]. Several studies [18] integrate different platforms in order to make the participants familiar with the area of interest, through a street-level imagery, (Google Street view or mapillary) facilitating the participant in simulating the process of walking along the streets, thus providing detailed three-dimensional information of the visible spatial elements. Recent applications [17] associated 100 google street views images with the construction of a database through online theme data collection development and the construction of an algorithm based on three main steps: (1) Initialization; (2) Crowdmapping; and (3) Geolocalization. From the perspective of the geographic data management model, three classifications emerge [19] -for tools and datasets- based on the code used to make it (open source or closed) and the possibility of being able to re-access or reuse data collected by users or crowdmappers: open, open source platform collecting data produced by crowdmappers free and reusable by anyone; hybrid, open source system embedded within a proprietary platform and data are not reusable; closed, proprietary platform collecting data are not reusable.

The use of collaborative platforms not only can return a comprehensive picture of the state of affairs in relation to the problem but can become a potential tool for defining indicator [20] For the scope of smart cities and the assessment of urban sustainability goals and project quality assessment [21].

Table 1. Most widely used platforms for crowdmapping.

Name	Classification	Data Collection
Ushahidi www.ushahidi.com	Open source	Data can be managed and classified with filters and workflows according to a role-based security model that grants permission to each defined user. Data visualization can be done through a map, list, chart or table, setting the periods when specific variables need to be analyzed and confronted
OpenStreetMaps (OSM) www.wiki.openstreetmap.org	Open source	Data collection is based on two structures (elements and labels). Elements correspond to nodes (defined points), paths (linear features and boundary areas) and relationships. Labels, on the other hand, are used to describe the significance of elements
Google My Maps www.google.com/maps	Closed	Data collection and subsequent classification is done through user labels
Street Bump www.streetbump.org	Hybrid	Data collection occurs during users' use of devices connected to the platform while they are driving
CrowdSpot www.crowdspot.com.au	Hybrid	Collection of "spot" data can be done manually by user input or via Social Networks

3   Application Experiments

There are multiple applications in the literature declined in different areas of intervention and research, demonstrating the versatility of use of the tool.

The supporting platforms fall into the three classifications previously repurposed, and the most widely used ones are Google My Maps, OpenStreet Maps and Ushashidi. Below, we report more precisely on the projects summarized in Table 2.

Table 2. Summary of Crowdmapping projects displayed.

Name	Location	Year	Platform & Support
CrowdMapping Mira Fiori Su – MiraMap	Turin (Italy)	2013–2016	Ushahidi
Recostruction of Building interior	-	2015	IndoorCrowd2D
CIRCO	Rome (Italia)	2017–2023	Google My Maps
Free to Be Map	Sidney (Australia) Lima (Perù) Madrid (Spain) Kampala (Uganda) Delhi (India)	2018	CrowdSpot
Pedestrian street lengths around the world	992 cities around the world	2022	OpenStreetMaps

The paper aims to return some of the most interesting experiences encountered in crowdmapping projects.

3.1 The Project MiraMap

The CrowdMapping Mirafiori Sud project, conducted at the Politecnico di Torino [22, 23] aims to map and identify the barriers and obstacles that prevent vulnerable users from accessing and using public spaces, focusing on connections in the territory and of institutional relations between the community and the public administration, to propose active and participatory solutions in which citizens are active subjects. The information collected, processed, and classified is made available through an opensource platform. The project was developed in two phases: the first, as a preliminary phase of knowledge and translation of citizens' needs, through interviews, data collection, support in the use of smartphones, etc.; the second, as a phase that provides innovative solutions for citizens to interact with the public administration, with particular attention to the needs of the elderly. The collected data were addressed in three main categories: problem in case there was the presence of criticality; proposal, in case a potential solution could be identified; positive reality, in case the element to be detected was positive. Among the data extrapolated, as problems reported were the presence of architectural barriers, obstacles to the use of space, and the scarcity of street furniture. Among the positives reported was the area of green areas, whether public or pertaining to schools, and neighborhood commercial premises. In terms of contributing to project evaluation tools, it is stressed that such mapping can provide a very useful procedural basis for ex post evaluations, (or monitoring) of public space transformation projects. In that case, the evaluation would be based directly on the direct perceptions of users by returning an experiential and direct evaluation without the mediation of questionnaires or other techniques.

3.2 Reconstruction of Building Interior

The project proposes a smartphone supported crowdmapping system for indoor environment reconstruction [24]. The method consists of to formulate the aimed problem solved, and through the system developed by the project researchers, image information and sensory data are used in a coordinated manner. Evaluation results show that IndoorCrowd2D achieves 85% accuracy for reconstructing university buildings from 1,151 datasets uploaded by 25 users. It is, in fact a hybrid method of images and sensors here the result is an interactive panoramic map, which can be divided into two parts: the first part includes panoramic images of the interior, and the second part includes the structure of the building in which the environment of interest is contained.

3.3 CIRCO Laboratory: The Map of Urban Waste in Rome

Since 2017, a Teaching and Research Laboratory called CIRCO (an acronym in Italian for Irreplaceable Home for Civic Recreation and Hospitality) has been launched at the Department of Architecture of Roma Tre University[3]. The theme of the Design Studio is the transformation of disused heritage into a metropolitan network of intercultural condominiums based on hospitality and stems from the direct observation of the limits of hospitality policies, proposing a rethinking of hospitality by starting again from the many abandoned empty spaces in the city, reinserting them into an innovative process of reuse and management [25]. The research, which is still in progress, addresses both the urban and spatial aspect and the economic strategy; the latter refers to new modes of social regeneration based on the involvement of third sector actors, social enterprises, social managers, and a new generation of urban actors who frame their business vision by combining the use of fixed public territorial capital, the creation of social value, the ability to intercept public funding, and the use of innovative financing tools (such as ethical finance) in a new model of welfare [26]. In the economic-functional mixite CIRCO substantiates its strategy, with the idea of a context in which residents self-manage the delivery of services conjointly with social managers (legal counters, clinics, reading rooms, cultural exhibition spaces, etc.). The elements of feasibility (technical, economic, and social) become key aspects of project implementation. The first necessity of the CIRCO Laboratory was the reconnaissance of disused housing stock, especially of public property, as a fundamental and prodromal act for the formulation of systemic proposals for residences and services to residences. Over the years, as part of teaching activities, a student led mapping system has been implemented, which has engaged in the reconnaissance of different types of disused space. The mapping, which immediately took the form of crowdmapping, was based on a preliminary categorization of what were called discards, divided into: former health care facilities, abandoned sports facilities, disused military garrisons, large disused mobility storage and sorting spaces, former places dedicated to education and culture (schools, cinemas, theaters), decommissioned church heritage, and, finally, the many production-related properties such as factories

---

[3] The CIRCO project maps can be found at the following address: https://laboratoriocirco.wordpress.com/2018/04/07/mappe/; CIRCO is a research lead by proff. Francesco Careri e Fabrizio Finucci with Chiara Luchetti, Alberto Marzo, Sara Monaco, Serena Olcuire, Enrico Perini, Maria Rocco.

or warehouses, containers of activities that the city has expelled to its margins but has not yet replaced. Over the years, the project has continued to set up processes of map production and to develop specific thematic maps (Fig. 1).

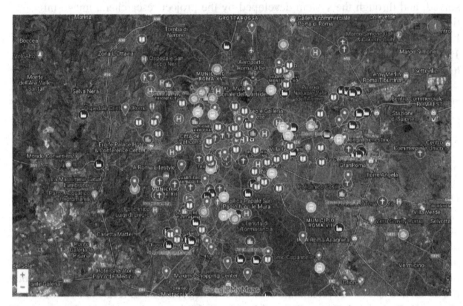

Fig. 1. CIRCO mapping: urban waste in the city of Rome. Source: *Laboratorio* (Laboratory) CIRCO, available on: https://laboratoriocirco.wordpress.com/2018/04/07/mappe/

In addition to the monitoring of the quantity and dispersion of abandoned properties, the crowdmapping process designed in CIRCO, from the assessment point of view stands as a useful tool for the possible identification of possible alternatives for intervention, based on the locations of the abandoned property and early construction and dimensional characteristics. In addition, the monitoring of unused property resources can be an excellent framework for urban-scale assessments of possible strategic reuses.

3.4   Free to Be Map

The map was developed by Plan International in collaboration with XYX Lab and CrowdSpot. Piloted in Melbourne in 2016 and spread to Sydney, Lima, Madrid, Kampala and Delhi in 2018 [27]. The purpose of the tool is the identification of so-called Safe and Unsafe Spots for women and young women through an interactive map that allows them to individuate "bad pins" within their city by answering a small number of closed and open-ended questions. In addition, given the risk of bias related to possible "bad pins," participants were asked to identify not only negative experiences in the city, but also positive ones through "good pins," and, in addition to adding their own pins, users can cast votes via social media. Methods of recruiting participants in order to collect as much data as possible include social media campaigns, media news, television and radio exposure. To collect data from those who otherwise would not have access to the necessary digital and online facilities, in Delhi and Kampala, and to a lesser extent in Lima and Madrid, women and young women were recruited directly from the streets. Survey results were evaluated by country and comments attached to the pins were translated into English and coded.

3.5   Pedestrian Street Lengths in 992 Cities Around the World

The goal of the project is to compensate for the poor quantification analysis of pedestrian streets around the world in order to ascertain the possible benefits in their implementation in terms of urban quality of life, sustainability and public health. In addition, the integration of comparable global indicators on the quantity of pedestrian streets is proposed as an objective [28]. The tool used for the project is OpenStreetMap (OSM) combining it with spatial analysis techniques (Fig. 2).

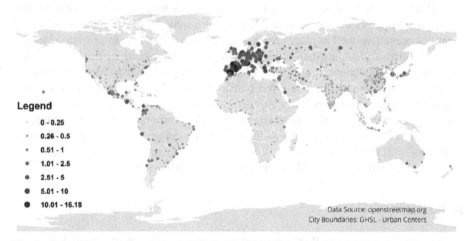

Fig. 2. Pedestrian street length (km) (OSM) per 100.000 inhabitants per city. Source: Bartzokas-Tsiompras, A. (2022)

The results show that European cities have the largest amount of pedestrian street networks, revealing, however, huge differences between southern and western European cities. In urban quality assessment processes, based on the reading of indicators, detailed knowledge of such data can stand as an excellent informative and in-depth knowledge tool of the urban contexts being addressed.

4   Conclusion

Although many crowdmapping applications are still in their beginning and need to be further implemented, the practices and experiences reported in this paper undoubtedly work on different issues and at different scales. In the background, the crowdmapping approaches presented assume a social point of view with respect to the urban issues they aim to address people with vulnerabilities, urban safety, returning abandoned heritage to the citizenry, etc. It is precisely the use of inclusive and participatory practice that may be the key to understanding this prevalent social valence of crowdmapping processes. Not surprisingly, these experiences, with the support of technological developments, are leading to increasingly participatory forms of communication, referred to as self and social mapping [29]. Access to the production and use of geographic information and, therefore, maps, through Web 2.0 cartographic applications, are challenging top-down narratives of territories, reflecting a renewed need for the social construction of knowledge expressed and articulated in the meshes of the participatory architecture of the social web [30]. The user who collaborates in the construction of knowledge simultaneously carries out an interpretive reading activity of the urban space in which he or she lives, a narrative and perceptual restitution activity, a self-representation and, last but not least, a participatory process.

The map produced by the community in a shared form can be considered an enabling factor of active and participatory citizenship, a map that allows for the representation through a non-technical description of the landscape, knowledge, products, stories, memories, favorite places to remember and where one meets, in which one recognizes or identifies oneself, as well as places characterized by social and environmental vulnerabilities, by critical elements such as those related to urban decay, a map that can become, therefore, an act of denunciation [19]. It should also be considered that decision-making processes related to new forms of urban transformation now postulate the involvement of communities in every aspect of enhancement projects, given the civic and inclusive nature of the commons involved in transformations [31]. Information produced by inhabitants with the help of digital technologies is shaping a citizenship made up of "citizens as sensors" [32] in reference to a new "citizen science" in which the role of the citizen in building a bottom-up vision of his or her territory and urban sphere becomes decisive.

References

1. Sanchez, T.W., Shumway, H., Gordner, T., Lim, T.: The prospects of artificial intelligence in urban planning. Int. J. Urban Sci. **26**, 1–16 (2022)
2. Kontokosta, C.E.: Urban informatics in the science and practice of planning. J. Plan. Educ. Res. **41**(4), 382–395 (2021)
3. Chui, M., et al.: The social economy: unlocking value and productivity through social technologies. J. Plann. Educ. Res. (2012)
4. Howe, J.: The Rise of Crowdsourcing. Wired Magazine **14**, 1–4 (2006). https://www.wired.com/2006/06/crowds/. last access 2023/04/03
5. Diop, E.B., Chenal, J., Tekouabou, S.C.K., Azmi, R.: Crowdsourcing public engagement for urban planning in the global south: methods, challenges and suggestions for future research. Sustainability **14**(18), 1–21 (2022)
6. Yates, D., Paquette, S.: Emergency knowledge management and social media technologies: a case study of the 2010 Haitian earthquake. Int. J. Inf. Manage. **31**, 6–13 (2011)
7. Starbird, K., Palen, L.: Voluntweeters: self-organizing by digital volunteers in times of crisis. In: SIGCHI Conference on Human Factors in Computing Systems, pp. 1071–1080 (2011)
8. Estellés-Arolas, E., González-Ladrón-De-Guevara, F.: Towards an integrated crowdsourcing definition. J. Inf. Sci. **38**(2), 189–200 (2012)

9. Quintance, K.: What is crowdmapping? https://kimoquaintance.com/2011/09/04/concepts-to-know-crowdmapping/. last access 2023/04/03

10. Participatory Mapping for Decision Making I SSWM - Find tools for sustainable sanitation and water management. https://sswm.info/planning-and-programming/decision-making/dec iding-community/participatory-mapping-for-decision-making. last access 2023/04/03

11. Miccoli, S., Finucci, F., Murro, R.: Integrating stated preference methods for property valuations in housing markets. Int. J. Hous. Markets Anal. **12**(3), 474–486 (2019)

12. Griffin, G.P., Jiao, J.: The geography and equity of crowdsourced public participation for active transportation planning. Transp. Res. Rec. **2673**(1), 460–468 (2019)

13. Schuurman, D., Baccarne, B., De Marez, L., Mechant, P.: Smart ideas for smart cities: investigating crowdsourcing for generating and selecting ideas for ICT innovation in a city context. J. Theor. Appl. Electron. Commer. Res. **7**(3), 49–62 (2012)

14. Douglas, R.: What We Mean By Inclusive Cities. https://nextcity.org/informalcity/entry/com mentary-what-we-mean-by-inclusive-cities#:~:text=An%20inclusive%20city%20is%20o ne,people%20and%20their%20needs%20equally. last access 2023/04/03

15. Larrota-Forero, R.A., González-Sanabria, J.S., Sarmiento-Rojas, J.A.: Proposal for the implementation of crowdmapping for the recognition of social housing in urban city councils. Revista Facultad de Ingeniería **31**(62), 1–17 (2022)

16. Ushahidi - Inform Decisions & Empower Communities. https://www.ushahidi.com/about/our-story/. last access 2023/04/03

17. Qiu, S., Bozzon, A., Psyllidis, A., Houben, G.J.: Crowd-mapping urban objects from street-level imagery. In: Conference 2019 - Proceedings of the World Wide Web Conference, WWW 2019, pp. 1521–1531 (2019)

18. Van Alphen, G.: A multi-platform crowd-mapping application for urban object mapping using street-level imagery. Delft University of Technology (2020)

19. Mezzacapo, U.: Crowdmap e Civic Engagement Nella Società Digitale. Università di Bologna, Alma Mater Studiorum (2017)

20. Shen, L.Y., Ochoa, J., Shah, M.N., Zhang, X.: The application of urban sustainability indicators - a comparison between various practices. Habitat Int. **35**(1), 17–29 (2011)

21. Miccoli, S., Finucci, F, Murro, R.: The evaluation of architectural design quality. In: SGEM 2014 Scientific Sub Conference on arts, performing arts, architecture and design, pp. 1023–1030 (2014)

22. De Filippi, F., Coscia, C., Cocina, G.: Piattaforme collaborative per progetti di innovazione sociale. Il caso Miramap a Torino. Techne **14**, 219–226 (2017)

23. Coscia, C., De Filippi, F.: The crowdmapping mirafiori sud experience (Torino, Italy): an educational methodology through a collaborative and inclusive process. J. Prob. Based Learn. High. Educ. **8**(1), 86–98 (2020)

24. Chen, S., Li, M., Ren, K., Fu, X., Qiao, C.: Rise of the indoor crowd: reconstruction of building interior view via mobile crowdsourcing. In: Proceedings of the 13th ACM Conference on Embedded Networked Sensor Systems SenSys 2015, pp. 59–71. Association for Computing Machinery, Inc. (2015)

25. C.I.R.C.O. Casa Irrinunciabile per la Ricreazione Civica e l'Ospitalità. https://laboratorioc irco.wordpress.com/2018/04/07/mappe/. last access 2023/04/03

26. Careri, F., Finucci, F., Lucchetti, C., Monaco, S., Olcuire, S., Perini, E. (a cura di): CIRCO. Un Immaginario Di Città Ospitale, Edizioni Bordeaux, Roma (2021)

27. Tanner, S., Kalms, N., Cull, H., Matthewson, G.: Aisenberg: A. Disruption and design: crowdmapping young women's experience in cities. IDS Bulletin **51**(2), 113-128 (2020)

28. Bartzokas-Tsiompras, A.: Utilizing OpenStreetMap data to measure and compare pedestrian street lengths in 992 cities around the world. Eur. J. Geogr. **13**(2), 127–141 (2022)

29. Mazzoli, L., Antonioni, S.: Self mapping e social mapping: per uno sguardo personale e condiviso sul territorio. Sociologia della comunicazione **44**, 9–24 (2013)

30. Boccia Artieri, G.: I media-mondo, Meltemi, Roma (2004)
31. Miccoli, S., Finucci, F., Murro, R.: Measuring shared social appreciation of community goods: an experiment for the east elevated expressway of Rome. Sustainability **7**(11), 15194–15218 (2015)
32. Goodchild, M.: Citizens as sensors: the world of volunteered geography. GeoJournal **69**, 211–221 (2007). https://doi.org/10.1007/s10708-007-9111-y

City of Proximity: A Participative Methodology to Evaluate and Regenerate Residual and Underused Urban Areas

Giovanna Acampa[1] , Luca S. D'Acci[2] , and Fabrizio Finucci[3]([⊠])

[1] University of Enna "Kore", 08544 Enna, NJ, Italy
giovanna.acampa@unikore.it
[2] Polytechnic University of Turin, Turin, Italy
luca.dacci@polito.it
[3] Department of Architecture, University of Roma Tre, Rome, Italy
fabrizio.finucci@uniroma3.it

Abstract. This paper returns the first stages of preliminary investigation for a research path that involved the Faculty of Engineering and Architecture of Kore University in Enna, the Interateneo Department of Science, Design and Territorial Policies of the Polytechnic University of Turin and the Department of Architecture of Roma Tre University.

The proposed research pathway, still in its early stages, is aimed at the definition and the application of a methodology to select the most suitable and effective locations to perform local urban transformations on abandoned, residual, unused, and underused places.

The purpose is to provide local communities with services that are not available on a small scale, to achieve the realization of the x-minute city model or the neighborhood city.

The realization of an x-minute city model accomplishes several Missions of Italian NRRP, especially in relation to Sustainable Mobility, Inclusion and Cohesion, and Health.

It encompasses the reduction of daily distances, the decongestion of main urban roads, which contribute to decarbonization, and the improvement of citizens' well-being by realizing a human-scale environment. The final result of the research project will be achieved through the application of logic, tools, and methods drawn from the field of appraisal. They will allow considering at the same time multiple and heterogeneous variables and endogenous/exogenous characteristics, synthesizing them into indicators for global evaluation.

After outlining the structure, path, objectives and expected results of the research, the paper tries to outline the outcomes of the preliminary investigations.

Keywords: urban walkability · city of proximity · evaluation tools · liveable city

1 Introduction

Underlying the proposed research project is the intention to combine some of the most recent input from theories and research on urban development issues, the city models most widely pursued by international urban policies, and the contribution of the

O. Gervasi et al. (Eds.): ICCSA 2023 Workshops, LNCS 14112, pp. 91–100, 2023.
https://doi.org/10.1007/978-3-031-37129-5_8

most advanced evaluation methods and techniques. To this end, it is deemed necessary to briefly introduce the main references guiding the research path, namely: the Network Analysis of Urban Systems, the Urban Model of the x-minute city, Multicriteria approaches and indices for urban analysis and, finally, the crowdmapping processes.

1.1 Urban Planning and x-Minute Cities

Concerning the evolution of urban planning, a first x-minute planning model for residential development in metropolitan areas is associated with Clarence Perry's proposal (1929): a pedestrian unit, where, within ¼ mile, one reaches shops, schools, parks, community institutions, rapid transit and arterial streets.

It has had a certain influence on the evolution of modern urban form, and at the same time has been the object of debates, which last until today (Mehaffy et al., 2015). This debate was followed by several x-minute city *or* x-minute neighborhood (they are two different things) idea, e.g. see the New Urbanism, the urban quarter, Traditional Neighborhood, Transit oriented development (Acampa et al, 2019), including the Isobenefit Urbanism concept (D'Acci, 2013, 2014, 2019) aimed at the development of a more walkable city. These models, suggest a way to guarantee the residents of urban areas access to residential functions within a walking distance – e.g. work, services, education, entertainment.

1.2 Multi-criteria and Indexes for Urban Analysis

In the context of the service-proximity evaluation, several recent attempts have been proposed to evaluate the quality of urban accessibility. For instance, Borghetti et al. (2021) develop an evaluation model which, through a set of indicators, considers the distance between service sand railway stations to evaluate their accessibility; Graells-Garrido et al. (2021) aim at measuring the correspondence of the city of Barcelona to the 15-min city concept by calculating the number and diversity of amenities within15-minutes walking distance from any specific neighborhood and analyzing different local patterns of human mobility in relation to urban amenities. In the context of urban transformations, a wider approach is the use of Multicriteria Analysis (MCA) methods to include different types of indicators simultaneously (qualitative and quantitative, as well as heterogeneous in nature), aiming at considering the complex interrelation among urban sustainability aspects (Bottero et al., 2019). Furthermore, these methods are characterized by a strong interaction between the Decision Makers and the stakeholders (citizens, investors) involved in the process, allowing for a higher level of participation (Munda, 2005).

1.3 Crowdmapping

In urban themes, crowdmapping has contributed to democratizing the planning process, thanks to citizens' contribution to providing real-time, low-cost data, which are useful for planning and mitigating the limits of traditional data collection methods, such as census data (Griffin and Jiao, 2019). In the field of urban planning, crowdmapping is vastly discussed in the scientific literature concerning themes such as problem-solving, idea proposal, and collaborative mapping, integrating different platforms to enhance participants' familiarity with the involved area, through an imaginary street level that facilitates participants in the simulation of the walking process along streets, hence providing detailed 3D information of the visible spatial elements.

2 Research Approach: Themes and Objectives

The contemporary cities are congested by a strong need for vehicular mobility due to the distance from services, and lack of diffuse public spaces for social aggregation. The contemporary scenario imposes a need for transformation and devehicularization of cities: the EU Missions in the framework of the Horizon Europe project, which are aimed at achieving tangible results by 2030, include the "Climate-Neutral and Smart Cities" mission. This Mission involves specific urban actions in European cities for the achievement of climate neutrality goals set by the European Green Deal, that is the reduction of emissions by 55% by 2030, and zeroing by 2050, as they play a major role in global decarbonization: despite covering just the 4% of Italian territory, they host 75% of citizens, and contribute to climate-altering emissions by 65–70%. Mobility has a decisive weight in this regard: low-emissive vehicles are still a very limited share (11.5%) of the total number of private cars in Italy (MIMS, 2022), while, concerning public transport, especially buses, a consistent quota (above 25%) is represented by vehicles of Euro 4 class or below (MIMS, 2022). Hence, the contribution of urban mobility to pollution is all but negligible, and actions to affect it involve changing regulations on emission thresholds, and increasing walkability, both by educating urban societies to perform different behaviors and operating on the material urban fabrics to allow performing daily functions in the proximity of residential households. In most areas, basic services and spaces (green areas, entertainment, education, work, social aggregation) are not immediately available. This leads to a majority of hard-mobility movements, with an impact on pollution, but also on the health and well-being of residents.

This spatial and functional problem has deeply rooted origins, dating back to the industrial revolution and the sprawl that affected urban centers while creating productive areas that lacked any kind of centrality, and has evolved through ages, leading to a strong complexity. In addition to that, its solution is often regarded as difficult to achieve for municipalities, due to the disproportion between the available budget and the economic expense required for an urban-scale plan. For this reason, a methodology for the individuation of the most impactive opportunities for the local achievement of this improvement can stand as the missing link to trigger the start of these urban regeneration processes, taking moves from residual, abandoned, underused, and unused areas to create walkable city areas.

Because of this problem the underlying assumption of the research lies in the fact that it becomes necessary to individuate and determine the most effective and suitable locations to perform punctual urban transformations, aiming to the achievement of local walkability, and hence fostering administrations to use economic resources for this purpose by demonstrating their optimal allocation.

The research, which in its early stages was named InTenTCity (Inclusive Networks to deliver the fifTeEn miNuTes City concept) aims at devising, applying, and validating an appraisal-based methodology to determine the most effective and suitable locations in an urban fabric to perform a transformation, aimed at providing residents of the involved area with walking-distance services, amenities, centralities, and spaces for social relationships.

The general goal of the research can be summarized as follow:

– To collect, analyze and systematize data on an x minutes city model, including its best practices and the factors underlying its goals, and on the useful methods and tools for the individuation and evaluation of its optimal opportunities (network analysis, multicriteria, crowdmapping).
– To achieve a taxonomic classification of residual, abandoned, unused, and underused places in urban areas through a crowdmapping methodology, and of the morphology of urban fabrics.
– To codify the transformations associated with the functions to implement for the local realization of x-minute cities, establishing and calibrating parameters for the evaluation of their impacts and benefits.
– To elaborate the methodology for the evaluation of the selection of the optimal locations and transformations, developed according to an Optimal Computing Budget Allocation (OCBA) structure.
– To validate the methodology and its databases through its application selected sites and the comparison with their specific contexts, engaging local communities and improving the methodology through internal and external feedback.

3   Methodology and First Understanding of the Investigation

From the early stages of preliminary investigation, it seems clear that research project encompasses several disciplinary aspects, among which sociology, ecology, urban planning, transportation, urban economics, and decision making. At the same time, it is considered useful that the guidance is strongly based on the techniques of economic evaluation drawn from the field of Real Estate Appraisal. The above can be considered reasonable for the following reasons:

– on the one hand, appraisal techniques now encompass a wide variety of methodologies to evaluate heterogeneous aspects through multi-criteria structures, allowing the combined consideration of social and environmental aspects, economic costs, and benefits.
– On the other hand, economic feasibility– or rather, the emphasis on the economic point – is deemed to be the key factor for the achievement of the goal. Indeed, the "x-minute city" is an increasingly discussed theme but defining programmatic and realistic steps for its progressive realization is now the task to accomplish to fill the gap with the current situation.

3.1   Urban Sustainability, x-Minute City and Isobenefit Models

In order to improve life quality, well-being, and social inclusion, the research is adopting urban planning tools to guide transformations along the principles of urban livability, defined as a behavior-related function of the interaction between environmental characteristics and personal characteristics (Ahmed et al., 2019). In this regard, the research is considering the Sustainable Development Goals presented by the United Nations, specifically Goal 11 "Sustainable cities and communities," which states that urban development will have to be more inclusive and sustainable, encompassing participatory, integrated, and sustainable settlement planning. In Italy, the targets set by the NRRP, represent tools to address urban regeneration issues in terms of innovation, sustainable mobility, cohesion, inclusion, and health.

The research, that aims at enhancing urban sustainability through the walkable city model, is evaluating best practices and experiences of it, and is implementing a literature review regarding theoretical aspects about nodes and networks evaluation. The walkable city model takes the long-standing idea of a city in which residents can do their main daily activities by walking. The concept is also present in D'Acci's Isobenefit Urbanism since 2013: "the Isobenefit Urbanism approach aims to create cities in which each dweller can do her/his usual main daily activities by walking or at maximum biking" (D'Acci 2013).

This theme is strongly linked with the individual and collective dimensions of urban society. In this framework, the research is moving toward crowdmapping methodologies.

3.2 Identification and Selection of Areas: The Crowdmapping Method

Crowdmapping can be defined as "the aggregation of crowd-generated inputs such as text messages and social media with geographic data to provide real-time interactive information about events, such as wars, humanitarian crises, crime, elections or natural disasters (the results are sometimes referred to as crisis maps)" (Quaintance, 2014). Thanks to residents' cooperation, these tools can drive the individuation of suitable locations for transformation based on their perception of their living environment in terms of needs, expectations, and vacancies. The crowdmapping method, being public and participatory, and connected to large possibilities of subjects through web 2.0 technologies (the set of all online applications that allow a high level of site-user interactions such as social media, forums, etc.) has lifted the spatial and temporal constraints associated with data collection in public participation processes (Diop et al., 2022).

What has been understood so far in the course of this initial investigation is that it might be useful to set up a platform where anyone can upload photographs, coordinates, characteristics, frequency of use, and state of conservation on locations that he deems to be susceptible – and in need of – the introduction of new use. The structure of the platform is based on a fixed number of typologies of places (under definition) and characterizers so that users will be guided to provide the information needed for the taxonomic classification.

The crowdmapping platform will be operational throughout the whole duration of the research and should be diffused and advertised both through institutional communication and through non-institutional communication, using social media and organizing meetings with residents, especially in the researchers' territories. The goal is to reach as many users as possible; for this purpose, digital crowdmapping should also be integrated with traditional forms (surveys, interviews) when possible, to include those with no access or familiarity with digital technologies, such as the elder population. The obtained data will be filtered and processed to achieve the classification of the places according to the defined characteristics, in terms of typology, morphology, dimensional parameters, accessibility, and state of conservation.

The working hypothesis for crowdmapping is based on a double level of quali-quantitative data input: one has a technical nature, while the other has an informal or communitarian one. In addition to formal quali-quantitative data (such as ownership, surface area, volume, state of the art, urban forecasting, etc.) that can be implemented by a technical nature component, for each space, it is possible to detect, through the input of additional information elements from the community, other social, community-related, and possible-use values (e.g., stories, local information, community desires, possible informal or improper uses, perceived dangerousness, etc.). The concepts of democratization of information are overlapped in a bottom-up production of information by users and users of places, inclusion of weaker actors, transparency of information, and empowerment of citizens who are involved in processes of reflection on their relationship with the territory (Parker, 2006). In addition, users who participate in mapping can contribute by providing the location (even an approximate one) of their home and the possible route to reach the main services, including the route to the mapped space.

3.3 Defining the Set of Possible Transformations

Once the areas have been identified, the next step is the actions to perform on them, through the codification of the functions to implement and the required – and feasible – transformations to realize them. This is in the process of being structured as an articulation of the function classes from the "x minutes city" model to define sets of specific functions, calibrated according to the variable needs of different social fabrics; then, the compatibility of each function with the typologies of locations is assessed, and the parameters for the evaluation of the results of the transformations are established, modeled, and codified. Hence, the accomplishment of this phase consists of the following elements:

- a set of functions.
- A matrix of transformations, showing the compatibility between the typologies of locations and the single functions, hence indicating the possibilities of transformations;
- A vector with the parameters that characterize the results of the transformations.

This will be compounded by a review and identification of the existing plans, agreements, and contracts supporting the development and management of these transformations and their products, which can also involve a co-management between original private owners (in the case of abandoned and unused businesses, for example) and the Municipalities, to achieve a complete operational framework.

In addition to the reconfiguration of abandoned spaces, at this early stage of research are emerging recent legislative and regulatory innovations that are aimed at facilitating and structuring processes of co-design or co-management of services in properties or spaces to be taken care of.

One of the recent introductions is the regulation for the Shared Administration of Common Goods, adopted by more than 80 Italian municipalities (including Turin) and in the process of approval in another 80 municipalities (such as the case of the Municipality of Rome), which provides for "Goods and pacts of collaboration" as implementation tools. The Collaboration Pact is the act through which citizens and administrations agree on the intervention of care, regeneration, and management of a common good in a shared form. On such assets (areas or buildings, including privately owned ones) it is possible to make interventions of social innovation, collaborative services, regeneration, and shared management by establishing, through the pact, objectives, and duration of the agreement, modes of action and collective use of the asset, governance tools, and mutual responsibilities.

3.4 Optimization of Possible Choices

Finally, in relation to the methodology for the selection of the optimal locations and transformations, the research is directing its gaze toward the category of Optimal Computing Budget Allocation tools. The intent is to inspire the operational approach to the industrial field while dealing with a deeply social and human-scale theme. On the one hand, the goal of producing the most effective improvement with respect to the budget will be drawn from the business sector; on the other hand, the multi-faceted and multi-actor nature of the urban field in which the project operates will lead to a careful analysis and modeling of the parameters that make up the evaluation system.

This is resulting in largely drawing from the field of multicriteria analyses: these methods serve as integrations to the main structure, providing the possibility to interpret and elaborate economic, social, environmental, and human benefits, in addition to aspects related to sustainability and resilience, by giving the correct weights to the complex characteristics that involve them.

The method, once fully operational, will compute all the possible transformations of the available locations by assessing the virtual benefits deriving from each of them and hence comparing them to establish which one produces the optimal results, and finally providing its user – identified with local administrations – with an overview of possible recommended choices.

Moreover, the research is including the multi-criteria evaluation models for social and environmental aspects. The review of recent application suggests considering the concept of social multi-criteria evaluation as a framework for a tool to implement a multi/inter-disciplinary approach (Munda, 2003) and focus on the issue of the complexity of social environments. This is also allowing the investigation of ways to enhance social aspects through the construction of matrices that consider the impact of the actors involved with qualitatively measurable criteria and aspects in environmental and economic matters through quantitative criteria (Baratta et al., 2021).

4   Conclusion

The complex set of actions proposed in this initial research reconnaissance survey need two steps that will need to be implemented:

- the specific in-depth study of each proposed step for theoretical verification and implementation.

– a series of concrete applications on one or more existing urban fabrics, aimed at experimental verifications of the proposed procedure.

In relation to the latter point, the choice of sites is based on the recognition of the 9 Italian cities involved in the "Structure for the Ecological Transition of Mobility and Infrastructure" (STIME): toward the end of 2021, the European Commission chose 100 European cities to participate in the "Climate-neutral and smart cities" mission within Horizon Europe program, and among them are the Italian cities Bergamo, Bologna, Florence, Milan, Padova, Parma, Prato, Rome, and Turin. These cities are set as front runners for the achievement of climate neutrality by 2030, requiring actions in several fields, including the improvement of energy efficiency, reduction of pollution, and the implementation of mobility strategies: with reference to the latter, the STIME report specifically focuses on integrated urban and transport policies and mentions several European best practices related to "15-min cities" –walkable communities, "20 min neighborhoods", and "superblocks" – since enhancing walking-distance services contributes to decarbonization.

Among the 9 cities of the program, 3 were chosen in light of their shared nature of congested, overpopulated cities:

– Florence (Tuscany), suffers from a strong dualism between the outstandingly touristic city center, specifically the quartier inside the mostly destroyed Medieval walls, and the peripheral areas out of the walls. The services used to be located in the center but now they moved to the peripheral areas increasing the process of emptying the downtown from residents. Out of the walls, the residential areas are mostly neglected from a service perspective as the basic ones are not grouped and no new small-scale center emerged;
– Rome (Latium), which is a monocentric city that suffers from the continued failure to transition to polycentrism and a slow process of administrative decentralization to the municipalities; dispersed from an urban perspective (often referred to as an archipelago territory) and, except for the central and semi-central areas, has tracks lacking essential services, far from the 15-min model, where community relations revolve around large commercial hubs. Due to its extension and heterogeneous urban management, a single Municipality will be chosen as a site for the application of the method, also to achieve similarity with the other ones.
– Turin (Piedmont), which suffers from extremely high levels of air pollution and, despite having a relatively good street network and public transport system, has the problem of congestion and difficulty in getting to pedestrianized areas; showing, also, criticalities in providing high social and urban quality spaces in its peripheral areas.

The same sites will also provide the local reference of the litmus test for the verification of the comprehensiveness of the taxonomic classification. The administrations of the three cities involved have already signed endorsement letters for the project, showing their interest in its development.

Concerning the validation, a key element for the comparison of the results is represented by proximity indicators. In particular, the ones proposed by the International Transport Forum of the OECD (an intergovernmental organization) include: a) Absolute Accessibility: Number of destinations reachable within a fixed amount of time with a given mode, i.e. accessible destinations. b) Proximity: Total number of destinations within a certain distance, i.e. nearby destinations. c) Transport performance: Ratio of accessible destinations to nearby destinations. The indicators are then calculated for different destinations through a set of parameters. Another research work (Pucci et al., 2021) developed an Inclusive Accessibility by Proximity (IAPI) based on the concept of basic accessibility understood as a minimum threshold that allows each person to take part in different activities, ensuring quality public spaces to support active mobility and to rethink a route design. Basic accessibility returns the ability to enjoy the activities that are presumed to be necessary to prevent the social exclusion of families.

Then, feedback will be collected from both the researchers in the RUs, and the residents and stakeholders involved in the transformations individuated by the methodology: concerning the latter, suitable inclusive processes will be chosen, adopted, tested, and codified in this context.

References

Acampa, G., Contino, F., Grasso, M., Ticali, D.: Evaluation of infrastructure: application of TOD to Catania underground metro station. In: AIP Conference Proceedings, vol. 2186, No. 1, p. 160010. AIP Publishing LLC (2019)

Ahmed, N.O., El-Halafawy, A.M., Amin, A.M.: A critical review of urban liveability. Eur. J. Sustain. Dev. 8(1), 165 (2019)

Baratta, A.F.L., Finucci, F., Magarò, A.: Generative design process: multi-criteria evaluation and multidisciplinary approach. TECHNE-J. Technol. Architect. Environ., 304–314 (2021)

Borghetti, F., Longo, M., Mazzoncini, R., Somaschini, C., Cesarini, L., Contestabile, L.: Relationship between railway stations and the territory: case study in Lombardy – Italy for 15 min station. Int. J. Transp. Dev. Integr. 5(4), 367–378 (2021)

Bottero, M., Oppio, A., Bonardo, M., Quaglia, G.: Hybrid evaluation approaches for urban regeneration processes of landfills and industrial sites: the case of the Kwun Tong area in Hong Kong. Land Use Policy 82, 585–594 (2019)

D'Acci, L.: Simulating future societies in isobenefit cities: social isobenefit scenarios. Futures 53, 3–18 (2013)

D'Acci, L.: Urban DNA for cities evolutions. Computers and Society (2014). arXiv:1408.2874

D'Acci, L.: A new type of cities for liveable futures. Isobenefit urbanism morphogenesis. J. Environ. Manage. 246, 128–140 (2019)

Diop, E.B., Chenal, J., Tekouabou, S.C.K., Azmi, R.: Crowdsourcing public engagement for urban planning in the global south: methods, challenges and suggestions for future research. Sustainability 2022, 14 (2022)

Graells-Garrido, E., Serra-Burriel, F., Rowe, F., Cucchietti, F.M., Reyes, P.: A city of cities: measuring how 15 minutes urban accessibility shapes human mobility in Barcelona. PLoS ONE 16, 1–21 (2021)

Griffin, G.P., Jiao, J.: The geography and equity of crowdsourced public participation for active transportation planning. Transp. Res. Rec. 2673, 1–9 (2019)

Jacobs, J.: The Death and Life of Great American Cities. Random House, New York (1961)

Burger, M.J., van der Knaap, B., Wall, R.S.: Polycentricity and the multiplexity of urban networks. Eur. Plan. Stud. 22(4), 816–840 (2014)

Mehaffy, M.W., Porta, S., Romice, O.: The "neighborhood unit" on trial: a case study in the impacts of urban morphology. J. Urbanism: Int. Res. Placemaking Urban Sustain. 8(2), 199–217 (2015)

MIMS Ministero delle Infrastrutture e della Mobilità Sostenibili (2022). Decarbonising Transport. Scientific Evidence and policy proposal. https://www.mit.gov.it/comunicazione/news/decarb onising-transport-scientific-evidence-and-policy-proposals. Last access on March 2023

Munda, G.: Multiple criteria decision analysis and sustainable development. In: Multiple Criteria Decision Analysis: State of the Art Surveys. International Series in Operations Research & Management Science, vol. 78. Springer, New York, NY (2005)

Munda, G.: Social multi-criteria evaluation: methodological foundations and operational conse-quences. Eur. J. Oper. Res. **158**, 662–677 (2003)

Parker, N.: Constructing community through maps? Power and praxis in community mapping. Prof. Geogr. **58**, 470–484 (2006)

Perry, C.: The Neighbourhood Unit: From the Regional Survey of New York and Its Environs, vol. VII. Neighbourhood and Community Planning, London, Routledge (1929)

Pucci, P., Carboni, L., Lanza, G.: Accessibilità di prossimità per una città più equa: sperimentazione in un quartiere di Milano, pp. 40–52 (2021)

Quaintance, K.: Concepts to Know: Crowdmapping (2014). http://kimoquaintance.com/2011/09/04/concepts-to-know-crowdmapping/

Short Paper (CAM 2023)

Accelerating the Simulations of Cardiac Arrhythmia with a Second-Order Numerical Method and High-Performance Computing

Guilherme Martins Couto$^{(\boxtimes)}$ (ORCID), Noemi Zeraick Monteiro (ORCID),
Bernardo Martins Rocha (ORCID), and Rodrigo Weber dos Santos (ORCID)

Federal University of Juiz de Fora, Juiz de Fora, MG, Brazil
`couto.guilherme@engenharia.ufjf.br`,
`{nzmonteiro,bernardomartinsrocha}@ice.ufjf.br`, `rodrigo.weber@ufjf.edu.br`

Abstract. Cardiac arrhythmia is a complex and potentially fatal condition affecting millions worldwide. Computational simulations are an essential tool for understanding the mechanisms of arrhythmia and developing new treatments. However, simulating arrhythmia with high accuracy can be computationally demanding. This paper presents a second-order numerical method for simulating arrhythmia that is parallelized using OpenMP. We demonstrate the effectiveness of our method by simulating arrhythmia in a two-dimensional cardiac tissue domain. Our results show that our method is more efficient than classical methods, with significant reductions in execution times and numerical errors. Additionally, we investigate the vulnerable window, a critical period during which the heart is most susceptible to arrhythmia, and show how the new method improves the computation of this metric. In summary, our novel second-order numerical method, parallelized using OpenMP, has demonstrated significant improvements in the efficiency of simulating cardiac arrhythmia. By providing faster and more accurate simulations, this work has the potential to accelerate research and aid in the development of new treatments for this complex condition.

Keywords: Second-order method · Spiral waves · Vulnerability window · Parallel computing

1 Introduction

Recent advances in computational biology have led to the development of computational models that aid in understanding complex phenomena of cardiac electrophysiology, such as the formation of reentry waves associated with cardiac arrhythmias. These reentry waves require triggers, such as premature ventricular extrasystoles on specific timings. The time window where an extrasystole induces cardiac arrhythmias is called vulnerability window [1].

O. Gervasi et al. (Eds.): ICCSA 2023 Workshops, LNCS 14112, pp. 103–113, 2023.
https://doi.org/10.1007/978-3-031-37129-5_9

Modeling cardiac tissue is challenging as the transmembrane potential signal requires interconnected intracellular and extracellular regions to allow for continuous exchange of currents. To simplify the complex microstructure, homogenization techniques are often used to produce smoothed equations that describe the dynamics of the transmembrane potentials. The monodomain model, a nonlinear system of partial differential equations (PDEs), is one of the most used homogenized models.

This paper presents a second-order numerical method based in [2], named Second-order Semi-Implicit Alternating Direction Implicit (SSI_{ADI}), for simulating cardiac arrhythmias with the monodomain model. We parallelized our novel method using OpenMP [3], resulting in significant improvements in the efficiency of cardiac simulations. In particular, our results demonstrate faster and more accurate simulations, when compared to the commonly used forward Euler (FE) method.

In Sect. 2, we present the monodomain equations. Section 3 describes the numerical methods, including the classic FE and the SSI_{ADI}. Section 4 presents the results of the vulnerability window and the performance of the methods, along with the speedups due to the parallel programming. We discuss the results and draw some conclusions.

2   Mathematical Model

We use the monodomain to model the cardiac tissue. Assuming that the intracellular and the extracellular conductivity tensors, σ_i and σ_e, are proportional, $\sigma_i = \alpha\sigma_e$, with α being a constant, the monodomain is given by:

$$\chi \left(C_m \frac{\partial V}{\partial t} + I_{ion} - I_s \right) = \nabla \cdot \sigma \nabla V, \tag{1}$$

where $\sigma = \frac{\sigma_i}{\sigma_i + \sigma_e}\sigma_e = \frac{\alpha}{1+\alpha}\sigma_e$, χ is the surface-to-volume ratio of cells (mm^{-1}), C_m is the specific membrane capacitance per unit area ($\mu\text{F mm}^{-2}$), V is the membrane voltage (mV), I_{ion} is the ionic current ($\mu\text{A mm}^{-2}$), σ is the conductivity tensor (mS mm^{-1}), and I_s is the stimulation density ($\mu\text{A mm}^{-2}$) [4].

FitzHugh-Nagumo (FHN) equations [5] are used to model the ionic current, I_{ion}. The FHN model is able to reproduce the dynamics of the action potential (AP) in a simplified form, using only two variables, one fast (v) and one slow (w). The fast variable has a cubic nullcline and is called the excitation variable, while the slow variable is called the recovery variable and has a monotonically increasing nullcline. The nullclines have a single point of intersection, which, without loss of generality, is considered at the origin.

Traditionally, the solution waveform of the FHN system shows a hyperpolarization of the potential in the refractory period. However, this feature is not characteristic of the cardiac AP and may adversely affect the model's recovery properties, particularly in reentrant activation patterns. Therefore, to adapt the model to the problem of cardiac AP, the hyperpolarization is suppressed with an adaptation presented before in [6] and [7], leading to the following equations:

$$\frac{\partial v}{\partial t} = Gv\left(1 - \frac{v}{v_{th}}\right)\left(1 - \frac{v}{v_p}\right) + \eta_1 vw, \tag{2}$$

$$\frac{\partial w}{\partial t} = \eta_2\left(\frac{v}{v_p} - \eta_3 w\right), \tag{3}$$

where G, η_1, η_2 and η_3 are positive coefficients, v_{th} is the threshold and v_p is the peak potential.

To model cardiac tissue electrophysiology, we couple the FHN Eq. (2) with the monodomain Eq. (1) and apply Neumann boundary conditions, obtaining

$$C_m\frac{\partial v}{\partial t} = \frac{1}{\chi}\nabla\cdot\sigma\nabla v - Gv\left(1 - \frac{v}{v_{th}}\right)\left(1 - \frac{v}{v_p}\right) - \eta_1 vw + I_s, \tag{4}$$

$$\frac{\partial w}{\partial t} = \eta_2\left(\frac{v}{v_p} - \eta_3 w\right), \qquad x \in \Gamma, \tag{5}$$

$$\partial_{\mathbf{n}} v(x,t) = 0, \qquad x \in \partial\Gamma, \tag{6}$$

where Γ is the domain, and $\mathbf{n}$ is the normal with respect to the boundary $\partial\Gamma$.

3 Numerical Methods

We use FE with operator splitting and SSI$_{ADI}$ methods, discussed below, to solve the system (4)–(6) for a 2D square tissue with $\Delta x = \Delta y$.

3.1 Forward Euler

In the Forward Euler method, also known as *explicit Euler*, the first-order derivative is approximated by progressive differences. Then, Eq. (5) is solved by

$$\frac{w_{i,j}^{n+1} - w_{i,j}^{n}}{\Delta t} = \eta_2\left(\frac{v_{i,j}^{n}}{v_p} - \eta_3 w_{i,j}^{n}\right). \tag{7}$$

Using $\delta_z^2 v_k = (v_{k-1} - 2v_k + v_{k+1})/\Delta z^2$ to represent a generic centered second-order derivative approximation, the Eq. (4) is solved in two steps. The first one deals with the reaction term:

$$\frac{v_{i,j}^{*} - v_{i,j}^{n}}{\Delta t} = \frac{1}{C_m}\left[-Gv_{i,j}^{n}\left(1 - \frac{v_{i,j}^{n}}{v_{th}}\right)\left(1 - \frac{v_{i,j}^{n}}{v_p}\right) - \eta_1 v_{i,j}^{n} w_{i,j}^{n} + I_s\right]. \tag{8}$$

The second step refers to the diffusion term:

$$\frac{v_{i,j}^{n+1} - v_{i,j}^{*}}{\Delta t} = \frac{\sigma}{\chi C_m}\left(\delta_x^2 v_{i,j}^{*} + \delta_y^2 v_{i,j}^{*}\right). \tag{9}$$

This scheme is conditionally stable, first-order accurate in time and second-order in space [8].

3.2   SSI-Alternating Direction Implicit

We applied the SSI$_{ADI}$ to Eq. (4), and, to (5), the Heun's method (modified forward Euler). Both are second-order accurate [8].

First, denoting by $\mathcal{R}$ the reaction term, a prediction v^* is calculated from Eq. (4) by explicit Euler scheme

$$v^* = v^n + \frac{\Delta t}{2\chi C_m}(\nabla \cdot \sigma \nabla v^n) + \frac{\Delta t}{2}\mathcal{R}(v^n, w^n). \tag{10}$$

Then, considering $\phi = \dfrac{\Delta t}{2}\dfrac{\sigma}{\chi C_m \Delta x^2}$, and

$$\mathcal{A}^1(v) = \left(v_{i-1,j}^{n+\frac{1}{2}} - 2v_{i,j}^{n+\frac{1}{2}} + v_{i+1,j}^{n+\frac{1}{2}}\right) + \left(v_{i,j-1}^n - 2v_{i,j}^n + v_{i,j+1}^n\right), \tag{11}$$

$$\mathcal{A}^2(v) = \left(v_{i,j-1}^{n+1} - 2v_{i,j}^{n+1} + v_{i,j+1}^{n+1}\right) + \left(v_{i-1,j}^{n+\frac{1}{2}} - 2v_{i,j}^{n+\frac{1}{2}} + v_{i+1,j}^{n+\frac{1}{2}}\right). \tag{12}$$

The resulting system of linear equations is solved with second-order ADI method [8]:

$$v_{i,j}^{n+\frac{1}{2}} - v_{i,j}^n = \phi\mathcal{A}^1(v) + \frac{\Delta t}{2}\mathcal{R}(v^*, w^*), \tag{13}$$

$$v_{i,j}^{n+1} - v_{i,j}^{n+\frac{1}{2}} = \phi\mathcal{A}^2(v) + \frac{\Delta t}{2}\mathcal{R}(v^*, w^*), \tag{14}$$

When rearranged, (13) and (14) can be expressed in the compact form:

$$-\phi v_{i-1,j}^{n+\frac{1}{2}} + (1+2\phi)v_{i,j}^{n+\frac{1}{2}} - \phi v_{i+1,j}^{n+\frac{1}{2}} = \mathbf{F}_i^n, \tag{15}$$

$$-\phi v_{i,j-1}^{n+1} + (1+2\phi)v_{i,j}^{n+1} - \phi v_{i,j+1}^{n+1} = \mathbf{F}_j^{n+\frac{1}{2}}, \tag{16}$$

where $\mathbf{F}_i^n$ and $\mathbf{F}_j^{n+\frac{1}{2}}$ are the following vectors:

$$\mathbf{F}_i^n = \phi v_{i,j-1}^n + (1-2\phi)v_{i,j}^n + \phi v_{i,j+1}^n + \frac{\Delta t}{2}\mathcal{R}(v^*, w^*), \tag{17}$$

$$\mathbf{F}_j^{n+\frac{1}{2}} = \phi v_{i-1,j}^{n+\frac{1}{2}} + (1-2\phi)v_{i,j}^{n+\frac{1}{2}} + \phi v_{i+1,j}^{n+\frac{1}{2}} + \frac{\Delta t}{2}\mathcal{R}(v^*, w^*). \tag{18}$$

Note that the matrices associated with each system of Eqs. (15) and (16) are tridiagonal. For example, the tridiagonal system of (15) has the following form:

$$\begin{bmatrix} 1+2\phi & -\phi & \cdots & \cdots & 0 \\ -\phi & 1+2\phi & -\phi & & \vdots \\ \vdots & \ddots & \ddots & \ddots & \vdots \\ \vdots & & -\phi & 1+2\phi & -\phi \\ 0 & \cdots & \cdots & -\phi & 1+2\phi \end{bmatrix} \begin{bmatrix} \mathbf{X}_1^{n+\frac{1}{2}} \\ \mathbf{X}_2^{n+\frac{1}{2}} \\ \vdots \\ \mathbf{X}_N^{n+\frac{1}{2}} \\ \mathbf{X}_{N+1}^{n+\frac{1}{2}} \end{bmatrix} = \begin{bmatrix} \mathbf{F}_1^n \\ \mathbf{F}_2^n \\ \vdots \\ \mathbf{F}_N^n \\ \mathbf{F}_{N+1}^n \end{bmatrix}, \tag{19}$$

where $\mathbf{X}_k$ for $k = 1, \ldots, N + 1$ is the system solution. The two tridiagonal linear systems are solved with Thomas algorithm [9].

Moreover, it is possible to prove, from [2], that SSI_{ADI} is an unconditionally stable method. However, in absence of diffusive terms, it degenerates into Heun's method, which is conditionally stable. This implies conditional stability in this work.

4 Numerical Experiments

The numerical experiments of this work were carried out considering an isotropic cardiac tissue of 2×2 cm. The spatial discretization is $\Delta x = \Delta y = 0.02$ cm and the total time of the simulation is $T = 400$ ms. The numerical methods were evaluated with different time steps. Each method was executed in two different phases. For the FE, the first part consists in calculating (7) and (8). Equation (9) is computed in the second part. On the other hand, for the SSI_{ADI}, initially the prediction (10) and the Heun's method are calculated. Secondly, for the diffusion, Eqs. (15) and (16) are solved.

Simulations were performed using the following set of parameters [6] (Table 1):

Table 1. Parameters

Parameter	Values
G	$1.5 \ \Omega^{-1}\mathrm{cm}^{-2}$
η_1	$4.4 \ \Omega^{-1}\mathrm{cm}^{-1}$
η_2	0.012
η_3	1
v_{th}	$13 \, \mathrm{mV}$
v_p	$100 \, \mathrm{mV}$
σ	$1.2 \cdot 10^{-3} \ \Omega^{-1} \, \mathrm{cm}^{-1}$
χ	$10^3 \ \mathrm{cm}^{-1}$
C_m	$10^{-3} \, \mathrm{mFcm}^{-2}$

Numerical errors and execution times for the calculation of both parts of the solution algorithms (the first part is the reaction term, while the second is the diffusion term) were analyzed. The parallel speedups were also measured. The code was implemented in C and parallelized with OpenMP. Simulations were performed in a computer equipped with a processor Intel® Core™ i5-12600.

4.1 Vulnerability to Reentry

In this study, we assessed how the time discretization and the choice of the method affect the vulnerability to reentry. To this end, we considered time steps varying from $\Delta t = 0.02$ to $\Delta t = 0.2$, and observed the velocity of the first stimulus S1. This relates to the vulnerability window in which the second stimulus S2 generates reentry. In these simulations, the S1 stimulus is applied at $t = 0$, during 1 ms, in the left edge $[0, 0.2] \times [0, 2]$. Then, the second stimulus S2 is applied during 3 ms in the quarter $[0, 1] \times [0, 1]$, at time t_{s2}. We vary the time t_{s2} with a discretization of 1 ms to calculate the vulnerable window, i.e., the times t_{s2} that lead to cardiac arrhythmia.

Table 2. Vulnerable window for reentry

Δt (ms)	S1 velocity (m/s)		Vulnerability window (ms)	
	FE	SSI_{ADI}	FE	SSI_{ADI}
0.02	0.599600	0.594845	[119, 130]	[119, 130]
0.04	0.601604	0.594452	[119, 130]	[119, 130]
0.06	0.603622	0.594059	[119, 130]	[119, 130]
0.08	0.606469	0.592105	[119, 130]	[119, 130]
0.10	–	0.592105	–	[119, 130]
0.20	–	0.580645	–	[120, 130]

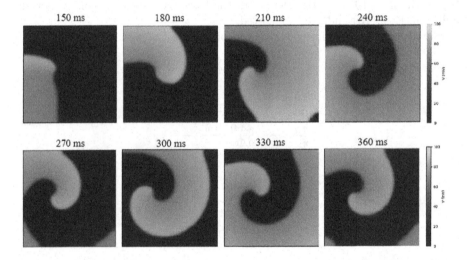

Fig. 1. Spiral snapshots - SSI_{ADI} method, with S2 applied at $t = 125$ ms

The results are presented in Table 2. We report instabilities with "–" in the tables. One can observe that the FE method presents an unstable behavior for large time discretizations, i.e., for $t > 0.08$.

It is possible to observe the reentry forming auto-sustained spiral waves, as indicated in the snapshots of the numerical solution shown in Fig. 1. However, there is also figure-of-eight formations in the right extreme of the windows, as showed in snapshots in Fig. 2.

4.2   Error, Execution Times and Parallel Performance

The S2 stimulus was applied at $t = 120$ ms for all tests in this Subsection. The error and the execution time of each method were analyzed for different Δt. Since

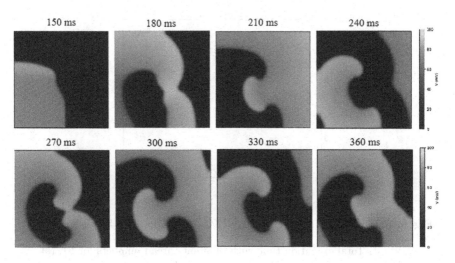

Fig. 2. Figure-of-eight snapshots - SSI$_{ADI}$, with S2 applied at $t = 130$ ms

there is no analytical solution for this problem, we consider the results obtained with FE using a small time step, of $\Delta t = 0.005$, as the reference solution. For the errors, we use the metric Relative Error in Percentage (REP):

$$REP = 100 \times \frac{\sqrt{\sum_{i=1}^{N_x} \sum_{j=1}^{N_y} \left(v_{i,j} - \hat{v}_{i,j}\right)^2}}{\sqrt{\sum_{i=1}^{N_x} \sum_{j=1}^{N_y} \hat{v}_{i,j}^2}}, \tag{20}$$

where $\hat{v}$ is the reference solution, and N_x, N_y are the number of spatial steps in each direction. The results are given by Table 3 and Fig. 3.

Table 3. Relative Error in Percentage (REP)

Δt (ms)	FE	SSI$_{ADI}$
0.02	1.6339	1.8227
0.04	3.9438	1.8008
0.06	6.0675	2.0656
0.08	8.7651	2.0854
0.10	–	1.9852
0.20	–	3.3317

It is important to observe that Table 3 and Fig. 3 do not concern the convergence study of methods. The goal is to see the relative error versus the time step, maintaining $\Delta x = \Delta y = 0.02$ fixed. We note that the error of SSI$_{ADI}$ with $\Delta t = 0.2$ is yet bellow the error of FE with $\Delta t = 0.04$.

For the parallel executions, the simulations were executed with 1, 2, 4 and 6 cores. The results for FE and SSI$_{ADI}$ are exhibited in Tables 4 and 5.

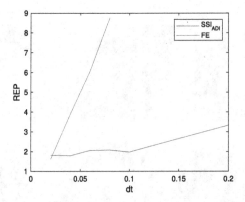

Fig. 3. Relative Error in Percentage (REP) versus time step for each method

Table 4. Total execution time with different thread numbers for FE (s)

Δt (ms)	1	2	4	6
0.02	2.500	1.338	0.826	0.639
0.04	1.293	0.713	0.480	0.391
0.06	0.874	0.495	0.362	0.307
0.08	0.676	0.396	0.307	0.292

Table 5. Total execution time with different thread numbers for SSI$_{ADI}$ (s)

Δt (ms)	1	2	4	6
0.02	8.768	4.550	2.534	1.924
0.04	4.409	2.298	1.332	1.026
0.06	2.968	1.560	0.926	0.734
0.08	2.237	1.177	0.733	0.583
0.10	1.806	0.964	0.612	0.494
0.20	0.931	0.518	0.373	0.317

For both methods, this total execution times come from two parts, or steps, as presented in Sect. 3. However, as the steps are different for the FE and the SSI$_{ADI}$ methods, each part has a different influence on the total execution time. Tables 6 and 7 show the proportion of each numerical step when executing the codes sequentially.

Next, we present speedup results for the particular case $\Delta t = 0.02$ ms in Tables 8a and 8b.

5   Discussion

For each time step and method, we analyse the vulnerable window for reentry. For this, we also study the S1 velocity in each case. Particularly, when $\Delta t = 0.2$

Table 6. Forward Euler proportion of time spent by each part (s)

	1st		2nd	
Δt (ms)	Time	% of total	Time	% of total
0.02	1.489	59.56	0.988	39.52
0.04	0.772	59.71	0.512	39.60
0.06	0.524	59.95	0.347	39.70
0.08	0.403	59.62	0.267	39.50

Table 7. SSI_{ADI} proportion of time spent by each part (s)

Δt (ms)	1st		2nd	
	Time	% of total	Time	% of total
0.02	3.640	41.51	5.126	58.46
0.04	1.833	41.57	2.575	58.40
0.06	1.233	41.54	1.735	58.46
0.08	0.927	41.44	1.309	58.52
0.10	0.749	41.47	1.057	58.53
0.20	0.387	41.57	0.544	58.43

Table 8. Speedups for each part with $\Delta t = 0.02$ ms

(a) FE method

Threads	1st	2nd	Total
2	1.886	1.875	1.868
4	3.030	3.174	3.027
6	4.113	3.959	3.912

(b) SSI_{ADI} method

Threads	1st	2nd	Total
2	1.948	1.914	1.927
4	3.556	3.406	3.460
6	4.806	4.421	4.557

ms, the SSI_{ADI} drives S1 stimulus at a velocity of 0.580645 m/s, which is still very close to the velocity observed with $\Delta t = 0.02$ ms, 0.594845 m/s. For $\Delta t = 0.2$, if S2 stimulus is applied at $t = 119$ ms, there is no spiral formation, but it is worth to note that SSI_{ADI} is able to compute almost the same window with larger Δt. It is also interesting to note, from Table 2, that the velocity of S1 is increasing with time step for FE, but decreasing with it for SSI_{ADI}.

In terms of performance, from Tables 3, 4 and 5, we note that, when comparing the two methods, the SSI_{ADI} was more efficient and accurate (see Table 3 and Fig. 3). To achieve an error smaller than 3.3317%, obtained by the fastest SSI_{ADI} solution ($\Delta t = 0.2$ ms), the FE takes 0.639 s, in the best case with 6 threads, while only 0.317 s are needed for the SSI_{ADI}. However, if the application demands an error lower than 5%, the FE performs slightly better and can delivery a result in 0.391 s, decreasing the distance to the SSI_{ADI}. Moreover, if the application has even greater flexibility, allowing an error of up to 10%, FE outperforms SSI_{ADI} and completes the simulation in just 0.292 s.

Tables 6 and 7 clearly show that FE execute all of its parts faster than SSI_{ADI}. These results are associated with the different approach each method adopts. While the first part of FE consists in calculating the ODE (7) and the reaction term (8), for the SSI_{ADI}, it involves the prediction (10), which has both diffusion and reaction, and the Heun's method. For the second part, the SSI_{ADI} also has more work to do, because it has to implicitly calculate the diffusion on one axis, as Eqs. (15) and (16), and to explicitly calculate the diffusion on the other, as shown in (17) and (18). The second part of FE only takes one diffusion computation, as shown in Eq. (9).

Also, it is possible to observe in Table 7 that the second part of the SSI_{ADI} took more time than the first one. This, however, occurs because the adapted FHN has only two variables. More realistic models, with multiple variables, take longer to compute the first part of the method as show [10].

In addition, the analysis of Tables 8a and 8b also allows observing that SSI_{ADI} has slightly more scalability with the increase in the number of threads. A speedup around 4.6 was obtained in a processor with only 6 cores. On the other hand, the maximum speed-up for FE was 3.9. These comes from the fact that both steps of SSI_{ADI} involve more calculations than those of the FE method.

6   Conclusions

In this study, we implemented the monodomain equation with an adapted version of the FitzHugh-Nagumo model to simulate cardiac cells. Two numerical methods, the Forward Euler and the SSI-Alternating Direction Implicit, were used and compared in both serial and parallel execution. We were able to reproduce reentry spiral auto-sustained and figure-of-eight formations in both methods, while also calculating the important metric of vulnerability window.

Our findings suggest that the SSI_{ADI} outperforms the FE method in terms of robustness and speed. Although the SSI_{ADI} is not commonly used for complex models, it is a powerful method for simpler ones in cardiac electrophysiology studies, due to its accuracy, stability, and speed compared to FE. Moreover, the parallel programming has the potential to enable fast simulations of heart dynamics and to support the development of new treatments and therapies for heart diseases, as demonstrated in [11].

Future research aims to test the SSI_{ADI} method with more complex cardiac cell models, such as the ten Tusscher-Noble-Noble-Panfilov model [12], which may provide more realistic results. Additionally, the results need to be extended to 3D simulations. In this regard, parallel programming with GPUs will be indispensable given the increasing complexity of models [10].

In summary, our newly developed second-order numerical method, parallelized with OpenMP, has demonstrated substantial improvements in the efficiency of simulating cardiac arrhythmia. By enabling faster and more accurate simulations, this work has the potential to accelerate research and facilitate the development of new treatments for this complex condition. Ultimately, our approach may aid in advancing our understanding of cardiac arrhythmia, leading to better clinical outcomes for patients.

Acknowledgements. This work has been supported by Universidade Federal de Juiz de Fora (UFJF), by a scholarship from Coordenação de Aperfeiçoamento de Pessoal de Nível Superior (CAPES) - Brazil - Finance Code 001. This research was funded by Conselho Nacional de Desenvolvimento Científico e Tecnológico (CNPq) e Empresa Brasileira de Serviços Hospitalares (Ebserh) grant numbers 423278/2021-5, 310722/2021-7, and 315267/2020-8; by Fundação de Amparo à Pesquisa do Estado de Minas Gerais (FAPEMIG) - Brazil.

References

1. Tran, D.X., Yang, M.J., Weiss, J.N., Garfinkel, A., Qu, Z.: Vulnerability to reentry in simulated two-dimensional cardiac tissue: effects of electrical restitution and stimulation sequence. Chaos Interdisc. J. Nonlinear Sci. **17**(4), 043115 (2007)
2. Pereira, R.R.: Métodos de diferenças finitas para problemas de difusão e reação não lineares. Ph.D. thesis, Laboratório Nacional de Computação Científica, Petrópolis (2018)
3. OpenMP Homepage. https://www.openmp.org/. Accessed 10 Apr 2023
4. Keener, J., James, S. (eds.): Mathematical Physiology II: Systems Physiology, 2nd edn. Springer, New York (2009). https://doi.org/10.1007/978-0-387-79388-7
5. FitzHugh, R.: Impulses and physiological states in theoretical models of nerve membrane. Biophys. J. **1**(6), 445–466 (1961)
6. Franzone, P.C., Pavarino, L.F.: A parallel solver for reaction-diffusion systems in computational electrocardiology. Math. Models Methods Appl. Sci. **14**(06), 883–911 (2004)
7. Rogers, J.M., McCulloch, A.D.: A collocation-Galerkin finite element model of cardiac action potential propagation. IEEE Trans. Biomed. Eng. **41**(8), 743–757 (1994)
8. Strikwerda, J.C.: Finite Difference Schemes and Partial Differential Equations. Society for Industrial and Applied Mathematics, Edition. SIAM (2004)
9. Sultanian, B.: Thomas algorithm for solving a tridiagonal system of linear algebraic equations. In: Gas Turbines: Internal Flow Systems Modeling. Cambridge Aerospace Series, pp. 337–339. Cambridge University Press, Cambridge (2018). https://doi.org/10.1017/9781316755686.012
10. Oliveira, R.S., Rocha, B.M., Burgarelli, D., Meira Jr, W., Constantinides, C., dos Santos, R.W.: Performance evaluation of GPU parallelization, space-time adaptive algorithms, and their combination for simulating cardiac electrophysiology. Int. J. Numer. Methods Biomed. Eng. **34**(2), e2913 (2018)
11. Kaboudian, A., Cherry, E.M., Fenton, F.H.: Real-time interactive simulations of large-scale systems on personal computers and cell phones: toward patient-specific heart modeling and other applications. Sci. Adv. **5**(3), eaav6019 (2019)
12. Ten Tusscher, K.H., Panfilov, A.V.: Alternans and spiral breakup in a human ventricular tissue model. Am. J. Physiol.-Heart Circulatory Physiol. **291**(3), H1088–H1100 (2006)

Short Papers (CAS 2023)

Survival Analysis of Organizational Network – An Exploratory Study

Paula Lopes[1] , Pedro Campos[1] , Luís Meira-Machado[2] ,
and Gustavo Soutinho[3(✉)]

[1] Faculty of Economics, University of Porto (FEP), 4200-464 Porto, Portugal
[2] Centre of Mathematics, University of Minho, 4704-553 Braga, Portugal
[3] Institute of Public Health (ISPUP), University of Porto, 4050-600 Porto, Portugal
gdsoutinho@gmail.com

Abstract. Organizations interact with their surroundings and with other organizations, and these interactions are critical for learning and evolution. To overcome the problems that they face during their existence, organizations must certainly adopt survival strategies, both individually and in groups. The aim of this study is to evaluate the effect of a set of prognostic factors (organizational, size, collaboration strategies, etc.) on the survival of organizational networks. Statistical methods for time-to-event data were used to analyze the data. We have used the Kaplan-Meier product-limit method to compute and plot estimates of survival, while hypothesis tests were used to compare survival times across several groups. In our study, we were confronted with one exploratory categorical variable, the strategy of the network, with a large number of levels. We have compared the corresponding survival curves through hypothesis tests, and we conducted a study that established three groups of strategies with the same risk or survival probability. Regression models were used to study the effect of continuous predictors and to test multiple predictors. Since violations of the proportional hazards were found for several predictors, accelerated failure time models were used to study the effect of explanatory variables on network survival.

Keywords: Accelerated Failure Time Model · Kaplan-Meier Estimator ·
Networks · Survival Analysis

1 Introduction

Organizations are adaptive at different levels of analysis: individually or as a group. In this work, we devote special attention to network formation and regard networks as new forms of organizations. To understand the interactions between firms and the different mechanisms of adaptation that include learning and evolution, we will use survival analysis, in particular to analyze the effects of a set of parameters (organizational density, size, and age) on the founding and mortality of organizations.

O. Gervasi et al. (Eds.): ICCSA 2023 Workshops, LNCS 14112, pp. 117–128, 2023.
https://doi.org/10.1007/978-3-031-37129-5_10

An inter-organizational network is a set of firms that interact through inter-organizational relations [1]. Johanson and Matsson [2] describe the network as a system of relationships based on a division of work in the network. The notion of an inter-organizational network is applied to a wide variety of relationships among organizations. The concept of inter-organizational networks can be applied to joint ventures, strategic alliances, industrial districts, consortia, social networks, and others. Hakansson [3, 4], Hakansson et al. [5], and others have studied the importance of relationships and learning in networks, making important contributions to the study of inter-organizational networks. Some authors study certain properties of the network structure that are interesting to analyse. One of them is the small-world effect, which was brought to the field of economics by many researchers such as Watts and Strogatz [6], Csermely [7], Latora and Marchoiri [8], etc. Watts and Strogatz [6] have shown that the connection form of some biological, technological, and social networks is neither completely regular nor completely random but somehow stays in between these two extreme cases. This type of network is named Small Worlds in analogy to the concept observed in social systems by Milgram [9]. Small-world networks are typically highly clustered, like regular matrices, but have a low path length, like random graphs. These properties are of great importance in economics. The work of Leskovec et al. [10] confirms what was said about the low path length of the small-world networks. In their work, graphs densify over time (i.e., the number of nodes increases), and at the same time the average distance between nodes decreases. The diameter of small-world networks decreases as well over time. We distinguish three main forms that characterize the most common processes of cooperation: linear, star, and multipolar networks. In a linear network (Fig. 1, top), each of the nodes of the network is connected to two other nodes. All the flow that is transmitted between nodes in the network travels from one node to the next node in a linear manner. In this case, activity A1 is managed by firm a1, activity A2 is managed by a2 and so on. No direction of the flows is identified in this graph, although the flow of resources can be unidirectional or bidirectional between nodes. Examples of this type of sequential network correspond to situations where firms collaborate with partners that are geographically close instead of searching for other networks that are already in action. The star network form (Fig. 1, left side) corresponds to the type of network form in which each of the nodes of the network is connected to a central node. Usually, firms rationalize resources and optimize activities when they form this configuration. The sharing of new technologies by a particular organization and the common benefit of resources are the main advantages of these topologies. Here the flows can also be bidirectional because the sharing of resources is not centralized but spread among the nodes of the network. Firms exchange, store, or get resources via the central activity A. In many situations, new firms are created to aggregate the activities of A: in this case, firm a5 contains activity A. One example of a network that follows this form is the grouping of suppliers. In this situation, firms are organized around a common client (usually a large client). This form of organizational network represents an interesting opportunity for the cooperating firms to organize their supplies more efficiently. In such a situation, the central activity is the goal of the network and constitutes the connection to the final client. The complementarities of the firms' competences are the key to the set of relationships that motivate this type of network, which is based on complementary vertical relationships. Among the several advantages that firms can take from these groups of suppliers, we can emphasize cost reduction, access to new markets, and risk reduction in the development of new products. The clustering of several organizations characterizes the multipolar network form (Fig. 1, right site). Typically, the relationships between organizations belonging to the same cluster are strong, but those between organizations that belong to different clusters are weak (although the relationships in this latter situation are stronger than those with any organization that is outside the network). This kind of network is typical of the automobile manufacturing sector, although it can also be found in other industries, as, for instance, in the textile and clothing industry.

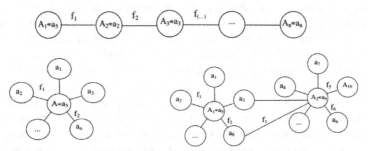

Fig. 1. Representation of the simplified forms of networks: linear network (top), star network (bottom, left side), and multipolar network (bottom, right side). Legend: ai denotes the individual agents or firms in the network; Ai denotes the cooperating activities (integrated into firms); and fi denotes the flow of resources (no direction of the flow is represented).

Firms typically join forces after adopting multiple cooperative strategies. According to Hitt et al. [11], a network cooperative strategy covers situations where several firms agree to form multiple partnerships to achieve shared objectives. Doing better than competitors (through strategic execution or innovation) and merging and acquiring other companies are the two primary means by which firms develop a cooperative strategy. Following Hitt et al. [11], cooperative strategies represent one of the major alternatives firms use to grow. Besides the network form (linear, star, or multipolar), the collaborative strategy adopted considers the following main variables of analysis: profit, stock of knowledge, marginal cost, and some other variable concerning network statistics (number of networks, nodes, etc.), at the firm or network level. These variables were collected for each strategy. The presence of the binary variable status (taking the value 1 if the network is alive at the end of follow-up and 0 otherwise) makes the use of survival analysis the appropriate statistical methodology for analyzing the survival time of the network (Age). Survival analysis will be used to study the distribution of lifetime as well as to compare the survival of two or more groups. Survival regression models will be used to study the relationship between life time distribution and explanatory (covariate) variables associated with each network. In order to be able to analyze the importance of these variables on the survival of the networks, data on inter-organizational networks is needed. It is possible to know how many firms are born and die every year according to the number of firms that exist in the same year. Therefore, it is possible to compute the organizational density and measure its impact on actual organizational birth and death (contemporaneous density). Nevertheless, it is very difficult to analyze the impact of the founding density (the density at the time of founding) for a particular firm. For that, we should have real time series from which we could capture information for every firm. That way we could follow firms during their lifetimes. Information should contain several time periods for the same firm and also cover many observations corresponding to different firms. The formation of networks also requires much information. Surveys can be implemented, in which we could collect data about the types of relationships and the reasons that force firms to link to networks. To analyze the evolution of the network, several time points would be needed, and therefore several interviews should be conducted. The shape of networks is also very dynamic, and reality would be difficult to measure by the mean of surveys. It is also important to introduce different scenarios concerning the economic situation to analyze its impact on the evolution of firms and networks. For the reasons presented above, we have chosen to use simulation. Simulation is a simplification of the world, and a well-recognized way of understanding it. It provides tools to substitute for human capabilities and the possibility of implementing different scenarios by constructing a virtual economic world. In this case, we use micro simulation, where world events are driven by agent (firm) interactions. Emergent behavior of aggregate variables is then captured, and the parameters can be reformulated in order to simulate different scenarios coming from different socio-economic perspectives. More information about the simulation methods used to model the interactions between organizational networks can be found in a related publication by one of the authors [12]. This source provides additional details of the rules that govern the network interactions and the assumptions made in the simulation process.

2   Survival Analysis of Organizational Network

This section analyzes how a set of explanatory variables influences the survival of organizational networks. Survival analysis is the appropriate tool to model the lifespan of organizational networks.

In this study, simulated data from a set of 500 companies is studied from birth until death or the end of the study. The response variable is the age at which the company 'died'. At the end of the study, 122 companies were still active (i.e., 'alive'), while 378 had 'died'. This means that we have 24.4% of right-censored observations in our data set. Besides the age or duration of life of the company, we have several explanatory variables that will be used to model the duration of life of the network. Tables 1 and 2 present a short statistical summary of these variables.

Table 1. Distribution of the categorical variables.

Categorical variables	N (%)	Censored (%)
Final status (status)		
0: alive	122 (24.4)	
1: dead	378 (75.6)	
Form of the network (form)		
1: when the shape is linear	352 (70.4)	92 (26.1)
2: when it is a single star	111 (22.2)	26 (23.4)
3: when it is a multipolar star	37 (7.4)	4 (10.8)
Collaboration Strategy (Strategy)		
A	56 (11.2)	18 (32.1)
B	94 (18.8)	18 (19.1)
C	51 (10.2)	22 (43.1)
D	58 (11.6)	8 (13.8)
E	56 (11.2)	12 (21.4)
F	82 (16.4)	20 (24.4)
G	49 (9.8)	10 (20.4)
H	54 (10.8)	14 (25.9)

Table 2. Mean and standard deviation for the scale variables.

Variables	Mean (SD)
Age (in years) (age)	4.914 (4.534)
Profit (in currency units) (profit)	9.421 (4.457)
Marginal Cost (in thousands euros) (mcost)	0.022 (0.023)
Number of existing networks at the time of its birth (netbirths)	1.604 (0.675)
Number of existing networks at the time of its death (netdeaths)	1.688 (0.709)
Number of existing nodes (firms) at the time of its birth (nodebirths)	6.708 (4.091)
Number of existing nodes (firms) at the time of its death (nodedeaths)	6.266 (3.891)
Stock of knowledge in Market X (stock1)	8253.5 (31144.9)
Stock of knowledge in Market Y1 (stock2)	17.163 (126.966)
Stock of knowledge in Market Y2 stock3	157.573 (1467.427)

3 Estimation of Survival

Empirical estimation of the survival function can be obtained using the Kaplan-Meier estimator [13], also known as the product-limit estimator. The Kaplan-Meier estimator is the most widely used method to estimate the survival function. It is a nonparametric estimator that computes the probability of observing the event of interest at a certain point in time, conditional on its survival up to that point. Figure 2a shows a graphical representation of the Kaplan-Meier estimator of survival for the lifetime of the organizational network. The corresponding curve shows the estimated survival probabilities against time. As shown in Fig. 2a, the survival function may not reach a value of 0 if the latest (largest) observations are censored. The Kaplan-Meier estimator can also be used to compute the median survival time, which is the time by which the probability of survival is 0.5. The median survival time can be appropriately estimated from the Kaplan-Meier curve as the x-axis (time) that crosses the horizontal line at 50% survival probability on the y-axis. According to this method, the network median survival is equal to 4.

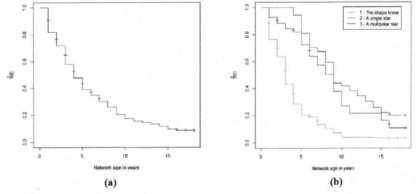

Fig. 2. (a) Kaplan-Meier estimator of survival; (b) Kaplan-Meier survival curves for each level of the covariable form.

Discrete covariates can be included in the Kaplan-Meier estimator by splitting the sample for each level of the covariate and applying the Kaplan-Meier method for each subsample. This is illustrated in Fig. 2b and Fig. 3a for variables form and Strategy, respectively. It is obvious from the analysis of Fig. 2b that those firms in a linear network (form = 1) have poorer survival than those classified in a single star network (form = 2) or a multipolar star network (form = 3). Table 3 reveals this issue too through the estimates of survival at 1, 3, 5, and 10 years since birth. Less differences can be appreciated when comparing the survival curves for form other than 1. In fact, it can be seen in Fig. 2b but also in Table 2 that the two curves cross. The median survival for firms in a linear star network is equal to 3, where those values increase to 9 for those in a single star network and multipolar star network.

Table 3. Kaplan-Meier survival estimates at 1, 3, 5, 10 and 15 years for each level of form and Strategy.

Categorical variables	1	3	5	10	15
Form					
1: The shape linear	0.764	0.434	0.204	0.039	0.031
2: A single star	0.928	0.846	0.724	0.420	0.220
3: A multipolar star	1.000	1.000	0.811	0.270	0.162
Strategy					
A	0.964	0.528	0.192	-	-
B	0.638	0.507	0.461	0.315	0.170
C	0.882	0.673	0.495	0.155	0.103
D	0.517	0.369	0.369	0.259	0.148
E	0.964	0.673	0.404	-	-
F	0.878	0.579	0.348	0.174	0.104
G	0.980	0.741	0.360	-	-
H	0.852	0.627	0.418	0.177	0.048

In Fig. 3a, we present the estimated probability of survival for each of the levels of the covariable strategy (Strategy) using the Kaplan-Meier estimator. In order to know if the survival of the organizational network can be influenced by the strategy, one can use a formal test to compare the survival distributions of the 8 samples. Under the assumption of proportional hazards, the log-rank test is optimal for testing the null hypothesis of equal survival distributions. However, as for covariable form, this assumption also seems to be violated for the covariable Strategy since several survival curves cross each other. Moreover, a test of the proportional-hazards assumption [14] indicated that the assumption is indeed violated in this case ($X^2 = 108.837$, $P = 1.6 \times e-20$). Under non-proportional hazards, log-rank is no longer the most powerful test [15]. The Peto & Peto [16] modification of the Gehan-Wilcoxon method [17, 18] can be a good choice in this case since it gives more weight to events at early time points. Results for the two methods (log-rank test and the Gehan-Wilcoxon test) are shown in Table 4 revealing that they can lead to different conclusions.

Table 4. Tests for comparison of survival curves.

Variable	Log-rank		Gehan-Wilcoxon	
	X^2 (df)	p-values	X^2 (df)	p-values
Form	110 (2)	$<2 \times e-16$	108 (2)	$<2 \times e-16$
Strategy	8.8 (7)	0.3	14 (7)	0.05

Table 5. P-values for the pairwise comparisons based on Peto & Peto test with corrections for multiple levels using the method proposed by Benjamini and Hochberg [19].

	A	B	C	D	E	F	G
B	0.619	-	-	-	-	-	-
C	0.196	0.308	-			-	-
D	0.061	0.308	0.061	-	-	-	-
E	0.066	0.619	0.780	0.061	-	-	-
F	0.619	0.619	0.619	0.061	0.619	-	-
G	0.061	0.619	0.780	0.061	0.986	0.619	-
H	0.585	0.619	0.649	0.078	0.780	0.780	0.789

Assuming the conclusion given by the Gehan-Wilcoxon test that at least one of these curves is different from the others, a naïve approach would be to perform pairwise comparisons. Results presented in Table 5 show the p-values from these comparisons with corrections for multiple levels using the one proposed by Benjamini and Hochberg [19]. The 8 groups lead to 28 pairwise comparisons with some p-values close to significance, in particular those involving groups 1 and 4, which correspond to the strategies A and D. When confronted with a considerable number of curves, one important question that tends to arise is if it is possible to group the curves in some manner. To this end, we have applied the methodology proposed by Villanueva, Sestelo and Meira-Machado [20], which allows us to ascertain whether these curves can be grouped or if all these curves are different from each other. Results from this methodology reveal the presence of three groups (i.e., strategies) with a similar survival pattern: Group 1 (A), Group 2 (B and D), and Group 3 (C, E, F, G, and H). The assignment of the curves to the three groups can be observed in Fig. 3b.

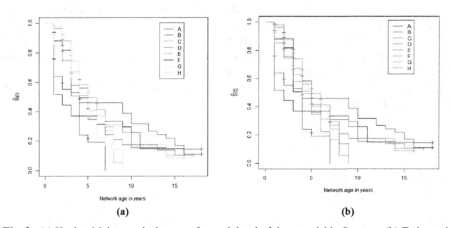

(a)   (b)

Fig. 3. (a) Kaplan-Meier survival curves for each level of the covariable *Strategy*; (b) Estimated survival curves for each of the levels of the variable "Strategy". A specific color is assigned for each curve according to the group to which it belongs (in this case, three groups).

4 The Accelerated Failure Time (AFT) Model

The Cox proportional hazards model [21] is the most commonly used method for investigating the effect of explanatory variables on survival. A key assumption of the Cox regression model is that the hazard curves for the groups of observations should be proportional and should not cross. There are several graphical methods for identifying this violation, but the simplest is an examination of the Kaplan-Meier curves, such as those depicted in Fig. 2b and Fig. 3a. A more formal test was introduced by Grambsch and Therneau [14]. When there is clear evidence of nonproportional hazards, one should look for an alternative approach. Since the Accelerated Failure Time (AFT) models [22, 23] do not exhibit proportional hazards, they can be considered as a good alternative to the Cox proportional hazards model. The AFT model describes a situation where the biological or mechanical life history of an event is accelerated (or decelerated). The hazard function of the AFT regression model can be written in the following form:

$$h(t|X) = h_0\Big(t\,exp(-\beta^T X)\Big)exp(-\beta^T X)$$

where X is a vector of explanatory variables, β is a vector of regression coefficients and $h_0(\cdot)$ is a baseline function of t, X and β. Under the AFT model, the effect of the explanatory variables on the survival time is direct, accelerating or decelerating the time to death or failure.

The survival distribution for the AFT is given by

$$S(t|X) = S_0\Big(t\,exp(-\beta^T X)\Big)$$

where $S_0(t)$ denotes the baseline survival function. The factor e^β is called the accelerated factor. This factor is the key measure of association obtained in the AFT model that can be used to evaluate the effect of predictor variables on survival time. Suppose we are considering a comparison of survival functions among two treatment groups. Then, the probability of surviving time point t in the treatment group is similar to the probability of surviving time point $te^{-\beta}$ in the control group.

The log-logistic and log-normal regression models are two of the most common examples of accelerated failure time models. The exponential and Weibull parametric regression models can be considered AFT models too. In our analysis, we considered several AFT models. Table 6 shows the models and the corresponding values for Akaike's Information Criterion (AIC), which led us to choose the AFT model with log-logistic distribution as the best model.

Table 7 shows the results for the univariable and multivariable log-logistic regression models. The interpretation of the parameter estimates shows us the impact of each prognostic factor on survival. A positive coefficient indicates higher survival times for the organizational network. For example, the coefficient for "form – single star" is 1.090, which indicates that the 'survival times' for organizational networks in this group are extended by a factor of 2.97 compared to those in the group "form – shape is linear". Similarly, it can be seen that the survival times are extended with an increase in the variables profit and stock1. On the other hand, a one-unit change in netbirths shortens survival time by a factor of 0.538.

Table 6. Akaike's Information Criterion values under different survival distributions for multivariable parametric survival regression models with covariates form, strategy, profit, netbirths, stock1 and stock2.

Parametric Survival Model	AIC
Exponential	2015.968
Weibull	1898.177
Log-normal	1847.173
Rayleigh	1928.973
Log-logistic	1842.017

Table 7. Univariable and multivariable Log-logistic survival regression models.

Covariable	Simple regression		Multiple regression	
	$\hat{\beta}$	P-value	$\hat{\beta}$	P-value
Intercept	-	-	1.310	$<2.0 \times e-16$
Form				
1 – shape is linear	-		-	-
2 – single star	1.090	$<2.0 \times e-16$	0.997	$<2.0 \times e-16$
3 – multipolar star	1.126	$<2.0 \times e-16$	1.170	$<2.0 \times e-16$
Strategy				
A	-	-	-	-
B	−0.009	0.963	−0.511	$1.7 \times e-04$
C	0.281	0.156	0.096	0.524
D	−0.459	0.019	−0.897	$6.7 \times e-10$
E	0.226	0.205	−0.190	0.166
F	0.110	0.515	−0.156	0.241
G	0.229	0.208	−0.310	0.026
H	0.164	0.382	−0.361	0.010
profit	0.050	$5.5 \times e-06$	0.031	$5.1 \times e-04$
mcost	−5.488	0.0039		
netbirths	−0.619	$< 2.0 \times e-16$	−0.211	$5.1 \times e-04$
netdeaths	−0.323	$1.5 \times e-06$		
nodebirths	−0.016	0.190		
nodedeaths	−0.034	0.008		
stock1	$2.88 \times e-05$	$1.8 \times e-06$	$1.4 \times e-05$	$7.2 \times e-04$
stock2	0.006	0.002	$1.61 \times e-03$	0.176
stock3	$4.3 \times e-04$	0.081		

5 Conclusions

A set of methods were used for analyzing the lifetime of organizational networks. The Kaplan-Meier method estimates the probability of surviving beyond a certain time point and uses a hypothesis test to compare survival curves between different groups. For categorical variables with a large number of levels, we have used newly developed methods by the author that can be used to establish groups of networks (levels of the variable) with the same risk or survival probability. Graphs for the estimated survival curves revealed that the survival curves for groups of observations crossed each other, revealing nonproportional hazards. More formal tests confirm this issue, revealing that the well-known and widely used Cox proportional hazards model is not recommended to study the effects of the exploratory variables through regression studies. Accelerated failure time models based on different distributions were compared, revealing that the log-logistic regression model was the one with the lower value for Akaike's Information Criterion.

Authorship and Contributions. Luís Meira-Machado and Paula Lopes were involved in the analysis of the survival data whereas Pedro Campos was mainly involved in the data preparation and brought different expertise to the project in the particular area of application. Gustavo acted as corresponding author and will take primary responsibility for presenting the work and communicating with the journal and the reviewers. He also participating in the last revision and rewriting of the paper.

References

1. Eiriz, V.: Dinâmica de relacionamento entre redes interorganizacionais. Inovação Organizacional **2**, 121–153 (2004)
2. Johanson, J., Matsson, L.-G.: Interorganizational relations in industrial systems: a network approach compared with transaction-costs approach. Int. Stud. Manage. Organ. **17**(1), 34–48 (1987)
3. Hakansson, H. (ed.): International Marketing and Purchasing of Industrial Goods – As Interaction Approach. Wiley, Chichester (1982)
4. Hakansson, H. (ed.): Industrial Technological Development: A Network Approach. Croom Helm, London (1987)
5. Hakansson, H., Havila, V., Pedersen, A.-C.: Learning in networks. Ind. Mark. Manage. **28**, 443–452 (1999)
6. Watts, D.J., Strogatz, S.H.: Collective dynamics of 'small-world' networks. Nature **393**(6684), 440–442 (1998)
7. Csermely, P.: Weak Links: Stabilizers of Complex Systems from Proteins to Social Networks. Springer, Germany (2006)
8. Latora, V., Marchoiri, M.: Economic small-world behavior in weighted networks. Eur. Physic. J. B **32**(2), 249–263 (2003)
9. Milgram, S.: The small-world problem. Psych. Today **1**, 62–67 (1967)
10. Leskovec, J., Kleinberd, J., Faloutsos, C.: Graphs over time: densification laws, shrinking diameters and possible explanations. In: Proceedings of the Conference on Knowledge Discovery in Data (KDD '05), pp. 77–187. Chicago Press (2005)
11. Hitt, M., Ireland, R.R., Hoskisson, R.E.: Strategic Management: Competitiveness and Globalization (concepts and cases), 6th edn. Mason, Thomson, South-Western (2005)

12. Campos, P., Brazdil, P., Mota, I.: Comparing strategies of collaborative networks for R&D: an agent-based study. Comput. Econ. **42**, 1–22 (2013). https://doi.org/10.1007/s10614-013-9376-9

13. Kaplan, E., Meier, P.: Nonparametric estimation from incomplete observations. J. Am. Stat. Assoc. **58**, 457–481 (1958)

14. Grambsch, P.M., Therneau, T.M.: Proportional hazards tests and diagnostics based on weighted residuals. Biometrika **81**(3), 515–526 (1994)

15. Li, H., Han, D., Hou, Y., Chen, H., Chen, Z.: Statistical inference methods for two crossing survival curves: a comparison of methods. PLoS ONE **10**, e0116774 (2015)

16. Peto, R., Peto, J.: Asymptotically efficient rank invariant test procedures. J. R. Stat. Soc. Ser. A Stat. Soc. **135**, 185–206 (1972)

17. Gehan, E.A.: A generalized Wilcoxon test for comparing arbitrarily singly censored samples. Biometrika **52**(1–2), 203–223 (1965)

18. Harrington, D.P., Fleming, T.R.: A class of rank test procedures for censored survival data. Biometrika **69**, 553–566 (1982)

19. Benjamini, Y., Hochberg, Y.: Controlling the false discovery rate: a practical and powerful approach to multiple testing. J. R. Stat. Soc. Series B Stat. Methodol. **57**(1), 289–300 (1995)

20. Villanueva, N.M., Sestelo, M., Meira-Machado, L.: A method for determining groups in multiple survival curves. Stat. Med. **38**(5), 866–877 (2019)

21. Cox, D.R.: Regression models and life-tables. J. Roy. Stat. Soc. B **34**, 187–220 (1972)

22. Bagdonavicius, V., Nikulin, M.: Accelerated life models: modeling and statistical analysis. Chapman & Hall/CRC (2019)

23. Hougaard, P.: Fundamentals of survival data. Biometrics **55**, 13–22 (1999)

The Kaplan-Meier Estimator: New Insights and Applications in Multi-state Survival Analysis

Luís Meira-Machado$^{(\boxtimes)}$ (iD)

Centre of Mathematics and Department of Mathematics, University of Minho,
Guimarães, Portugal
lmachado@math.uminho.pt
https://w3.math.uminho.pt/~lmachado/

Abstract. A topic that has received attention in statistical and medical literature is the estimation of survival for which the Kaplan-Meier product-limit estimator is the most commonly used estimator. This estimator is considered nonparametric because it does not rely on any assumptions about the probability distribution of the lifetime. The best known representation of the Kaplan-Meier estimator is based on a product of elementary probabilities whose underlying idea is the computation of conditional survival probabilities. The Kaplan-Meier estimator of survival can also be explained using the redistribution to the right algorithm, which removes the mass of a censored subject and redistributes this mass equally to all subjects who fail or are censored at later times. This paper presents additional alternative representations of this estimator, as well as applications and advantages of its use. One of these representations consists in defining the estimator as a sum of weights, which is a convenient form to estimate several quantities in the context of multi-state models. The estimator can also be represented as a weighted average of identically distributed terms, where the weights are obtained by using the inverse probability of censoring. The paper discusses how these formulations can be used to estimate several quantities in the context of multi-state models. Two real data examples are included for illustration of the methods.

Keywords: Censoring · Kaplan-Meier · Multi-state models · Survival Analysis

1 Introduction

Censored data analysis has several applications in longitudinal medical studies. In this type of data, it is frequent to have incomplete observations due to various factors such as loss of follow-up and dropout. The Kaplan-Meier product-limit estimator [1] has always been considered a standard method to obtain statistical summaries for such data. This method can handle right-censoring, which

Supported by Portuguese Foundation for Science and Technology, references UIDB/00013/2020, UIDP/00013/2020 and EXPL/MAT-STA/0956/2021.

is the most common type of censoring in survival analysis. It is implemented in almost all statistical software, including R, SPSS, and STATA. The survival package of the statistical software R is the most used package to implement the Kaplan-Meier method. To deal with other forms of censorship beyond right-censoring, other nonparametric estimators of survival, such as the Lynden-Bell and Turnbull estimators, have been developed. The Lynden-Bell [2] and Turnbull [3] estimators can be seen as generalizations of the Kaplan-Meier estimator, with the Lynden-Bell estimator designed to handle left-truncated and right-censored data, and the Turnbull estimator capable of handling interval-censored data in addition to right-censored data.

The Kaplan-Meier estimator can be generalized to inhomogeneous Markov processes with a finite number of states. This generalization was considered by Aalen [4] for the competitive risk model and independently by Aalen and Johansen [5] and Fleming [6] for the general case. Aalen and Johansen [5] introduced the so-called Aalen-Johansen estimator of the transition probabilities which can be seen as a matrix version of the Kaplan-Meier estimator. This relationship makes it possible to present a weighted version of the Aalen-Johansen estimator.

This article is organized as follows. In Sect. 2, the Kaplan-Meier estimator is introduced, and different representations of the estimator are presented. In Sect. 3, a modification of the Kaplan-Meier estimator is introduced that provides an estimator with less variability. In Sect. 4, it is shown how the different representations can be useful to estimate particular quantities in multi-state models. In Sect. 5, the methods are illustrated using two real data sets. The main conclusions of this research are deferred to Sect. 6.

2   The Kaplan-Meier Estimator of Survival

Let T_i be a random variable denoting the lifetime for $i = 1, \cdots, n$ individuals from a homogeneous population. Consider also that C_i is a random variable denoting the censoring time for the i-th individual. Due to this censoring variable, in practice, what is observed is $Y_i = \min(T_i, C_i)$ and $\Delta_i = I(T_i \leq C_i)$. The censoring is assumed to be independent in the sense that the additional knowledge of censorings before any time t does not alter the risk of failure at time t. This section aims to introduce the Kaplan-Meier estimators of survival $S(t) = P(T > t)$ using different formulations.

2.1   The Product-Limit Formulation

The best-known representation of the Kaplan-Meier estimator is based on a product of elementary probabilities of the occurrence of an event at a certain point in time, providing estimates that decrease according to the observations (failures or events) detected. This representation is discussed in most books on survival analysis. Consider lifetime data with the event of interest being a failure. Then, the expression of the Kaplan-Meier estimator involves calculating the number of individuals who fail at a given time, divided by the number of individuals at risk for failure at that same time. These successive probabilities are then multiplied by any earlier computed probabilities to get the final estimate.

Denote the J ordered failure times by $0 < t_1 < t_2 < \cdots < t_J$; and let d_j be the number of individuals who fail at time t_j, and r_j the number of individuals at risk just before that time. The idea behind the Kaplan-Meier estimator is to compute the conditional survival probabilities, $P(T \geq t_j | T \geq t_{j-1}) = 1 - d_j/r_j$. Then, the Kaplan-Meier survival estimator is the unconditional probability of survival, which is just the cumulative product of the conditional probabilities:

$$\widehat{S}^{KM}(t) = \prod_{j:t_j \leq t} \left(1 - \frac{d_j}{r_j}\right) \tag{1}$$

The expression for Eq. 1 can also be derived from maximum likelihood estimation of the hazard function [7,8].

The product-limit estimator is a nonparametric technique for estimating and plotting the survival probability as a function of time. The estimated survival plot is a step function that starts at the value 1 and has a series of decreasing horizontal steps that approach the shape of the population's true survival function. When there is no censoring, the Kaplan-Meier estimator is equivalent to the empirical estimator, for which every observation contributes equally to the size of the step. Confidence intervals are typically presented alongside the plot in order to demonstrate the level of uncertainty surrounding point estimates. One of the most common estimators that have been used to approximate its variance is Greenwood's formula. For more details on the calculation of the confidence intervals using the Greenwood method, please see Borgan [9].

2.2   The Weighted Version of the Kaplan-Meier Estimator

The Kaplan-Meier estimator can also be represented as a sum of weights, which is known as Kaplan-Meier weights. The weights correspond to the 'jump' of the estimator's distribution and are defined only for the event times. These weights can be obtained by the expression $W_j = \widehat{S}^{KM}(t_{j-1}) - \widehat{S}^{KM}(t_j)$, for $j = 2, \cdots, J$, with $W_1 = 1 - \widehat{S}^{KM}(t_1)$ and where $t_1 < \cdots < t_J$ are the ordered failure times. Then, the Kaplan-Meier estimator can be defined as follows:

$$\widehat{S}^{KM}(t) = 1 - \sum_{j=1}^{J} W_j I(t_j \leq t) \tag{2}$$

Next, an alternative notation is introduced that allows expressing how each failure time contributes to survival, even when there are tied failure times. For $i = 1, 2, \cdots, n$, let W_i be the Kaplan-Meier weight associated with Y_i when the marginal distribution of Y is estimated from pairs (Y_i, Δ_i)'s. That is,

$$W_i = \frac{\Delta_{[i]}}{n-i+1} \prod_{j=1}^{i-1} \left[1 - \frac{\Delta_{[j]}}{n-j+1}\right] \tag{3}$$

is the weight associated with $Y_{(i)}$, where $Y_{(1)} < \cdots < Y_{(n)}$ are the ordinal statistics obtained from Y_i's times and where $\Delta_{[i]}$ denotes the i-th concomitant. Ties between censored observations or between events are ordered arbitrarily. Ties between events and censoring times are treated so that the former (events) precede the latter (censoring).

For uncensored cases, the weight W_i is equal to $1/n$ for each i, while censored observations do not contribute to the weighting. The estimator of the Kaplan-Meier survival function can then be defined as follows:

$$\widehat{S}^{KM}(t) = 1 - \sum_{i=1}^{n} W_i I(Y_i \leq t) \tag{4}$$

As can easily be seen, the estimator is a step function with jump points located at the failure times. As will be shown below, the size of the weights (and the Kaplan-Meier 'jump') is a non-decreasing function. Later on, this form of representation of the Kaplan-Meier estimator will be used as a convenient way to introduce the idea of 'presmoothing'.

2.3 The Redistribution to the Right Algorithm

An alternative and equivalent representation of the product-limit formulation considers a redistribution to the right algorithm in which the weight of the censored observations is distributed over all observations to the right. The algorithm has the following four steps:

Step 1: Arrange the data in increasing order, with censored observations to the right of uncensored observations in the case of ties.

Step 2: Put equal mass $1/n$ at each of the n observations.

Step 3: Start from the smallest observation and move to the 'right'. Each time a censored observation is reached, redistribute its mass evenly to all observations to the right.

Step 4: Repeat Step 3 until all censored observations (except largest observations) have no mass.

The algorithm then attributes mass (weight, W_i) to each failure time ($\geq 1/n$) and null mass (weight) to censored observations. The estimator can then be defined as in Eq. 4.

2.4 Inverse Probability of Censoring Weighting

The Kaplan-Meier estimator can also be represented as a weighted average of identically distributed terms, where the weights are obtained by using inverse probability censoring weighting (IPCW). Satten and Datta [10] showed that this representation, by means of a weighted average, is convenient for the development of asymptotic theory and leads to an interesting variance decomposition of the Kaplan-Meier estimator. The resulting estimator is written as follows:

$$\widehat{S}^{IPCW}(t) = 1 - \frac{1}{n} \sum_{i=1}^{n} \frac{I(Y_i \leq t)\Delta_i}{\widehat{G}(Y_i^-)} \tag{5}$$

where $P(C > y) = G(y^-)$ and where $\widehat{G}$ denotes the Kaplan-Meier estimator of the censoring variable C that is computed using the pairs $(Y_i, 1 - \Delta_i)$'s; that is, $\widehat{G}$ is the estimator of the survival function for censored data using $\widehat{S}^{KM}(\cdot)$ but considering failure times as 'censored' observations and censored times as 'failures'. The equivalence of the IPCW estimator and the KM estimator is shown in [10]. The IPCW formulation has been used to deal with censoring in several contexts, such as to introduce nonparametric estimators of time-dependent ROC curves conditional on covariates [11], conditional transition probabilities [12] or the conditional cumulative incidence functions [13].

3   Presmoothed Kaplan-Meier Estimators

Presmoothing was used by [14] and by several authors later (see, for example [15] and references therein). The underlying idea is to replace each censoring indicator in the weighted version of the Kaplan-Meier estimator with a smooth fit of a regression model with a binary response. This replacement reduces the variability of the estimator, with a possible but low cost of bias.

Let $m(y) = P(\Delta = 1 \mid Y = y)$ be the conditional probability of observing the event given that $Y = y$ is observed. This function can be estimated parametrically (e.g., using a logistic regression model) or nonparametrically (using kernel or spline-type functions). The presmoothed estimator of the survival function is simply a modified version of the weighted version of the Kaplan-Meier estimator with smoothed weights that are obtained by replacing the censoring indicator variables. The term 'presmoothing' comes from the fact that smoothing is only used to obtain a modified version of the Kaplan-Meier estimator; the estimate itself is not smoothed. The new estimator is given by as follows:

$$\widehat{S}^{PKM}(t) = 1 - \sum_{i=1}^{n} W_i^{PKM} I(Y_i \leq t) \tag{6}$$

where

$$W_i^{PKM} = \frac{m_n(Y_{(i)})}{n - i + 1} \prod_{j=1}^{i-1} \left[1 - \frac{m_n(Y_{(j)})}{n - j + 1} \right] \tag{7}$$

and where $m_n(y)$ is an estimator of $m(y)$ based on the (Y_i, Δ_i)'s. This function can be estimated using a parametric estimator such as a logistic regression model or using the Nadaraya-Watson kernel type estimator [15]. Recent contributions suggest that the resulting estimator has less variability in the estimation, in particular in the right-hand tail, when compared to the original (nonparametric) estimator.

4   Application to Multi-state Models

In longitudinal medical studies, patients may observe multiple events in a given follow-up period. The analysis of these studies can be successfully performed by multi-state models [13,16,17]. A multi-state model is a stochastic process $(X(t), t \in T)$ with a finite state space, where $X(t)$ represents the state occupied by the process at time $t \geq 0$. One such model is the progressive illness-death model, shown in Fig. 1, which is fully characterized by three states and three transitions between them. The stochastic process of this model is characterized by its three potential transition times T_{hj}, from State h to State j. In this model, there are two competitive transitions leaving State 1, but only the transition with the lower time to occurrence is observed. Accordingly, denote by $\rho = I(T_{12} \leq T_{13})$ the indicator function of transition to State 2 in a given time and consider $U = \min(T_{12}, T_{13})$ the length of stay in State 1. Finally, denote by $T = U + \rho T_{23}$ the total time of the process. However, the vector (Z, Y, Δ_1, Δ) is observed in practice due to limitations in follow-up, follow-up losses, and other factors. Here, $Z = \min(U, C)$ denotes the length of stay in State 1, while $\Delta_1 = I(Z \leq C)$ is the corresponding indicator; $Y = \min(T, C)$ denotes the overall lifetime and $\Delta_1 = I(Z \leq C)$ the respective censoring indicator. Patients that are not in the absorbing state at the end of follow-up contribute with right censored observations. Here C denotes the potential censoring time that is assumed independent of the process, i.e. that C and (Z, Y) are independent.

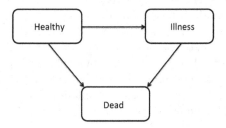

Fig. 1. The progressive illness-death model.

One of the main goals in clinical applications of multi-state models is the estimation of transition probabilities. These quantities have provided increasing interest as they allow for long-term predictions of the process. Several applications of the alternative representations of the Kaplan-Meier estimator are illustrated below to introduce estimators with lower variability for the transition probabilities.

4.1   The Aalen-Johansen Estimator

For two states h, j and $s < t$, introduce the so-called transition probabilities $p_{hj}(s, t) = P(X(t) = j \mid X(s) = h)$. Aalen and Johansen [5] introduced a nonparametric estimator of the transition probabilities for Markovian models. Their proposal can be thought of as the generalization of the Kaplan-Meier approach for the simple mortality model (model with two states and a single transition). Explicit formulae of the Aalen-Johansen estimator for the illness-death model are available [18].

Let $Z_{(i)}$ denote the ordinal statistics obtained from the Z_i's and let $\Delta_{1[i]}$ be the i-th concomitant. Similarly, introduce the $Y_{(i)}$ ordinal statistics obtained from the Y_i's and $\Delta_{[i]}$ be its i-th concomitant. According to this notation, the Aalen-Johansen estimator for the transition probability $p_{11}(s,t)$ is the Kaplan-Meier estimator defined as:

$$\widehat{p}_{11}^{AJ}(t) = \prod_{s < Z_{(i)} \leq t} \left(1 - \frac{\Delta_{1[i]}}{n M_{0n}(Y_{(i)})} \right) \tag{8}$$

and

$$\widehat{p}_{22}^{AJ}(t) = \prod_{s < Z_{[i]} \leq t, Z_{(i)} \leq Y_{(i)}} \left(1 - \frac{\Delta_{[i]}}{n M_{1n}(Y_{(i)})} \right) \tag{9}$$

where $M_{0n}(y) = \frac{1}{n} \sum_{i=1}^{n} I(Z_i \geq y)$ and $M_{1n}(y) = \frac{1}{n} \sum_{i=1}^{n} I(Z_i < y \leq Y_i)$. Finally, the transition probability $p_{12}(s,t)$ can be estimated by plug-in methods using the formulae in [18].

The introduction of this representation of the Aalen-Johansen estimator allows the use of presmoothing in the Aalen-Johansen estimator. As usual, the new estimators are obtained by replacing the censoring indicator variables with smooth functions that can be estimated parametrically or nonparametrically. Further details can be seen in [19]. These estimators are implemented in the statistical software R. The **mstate** package can be used to obtain estimates of the transition probabilities in any multi-state model while the **survidm** package [20] can only be used in the illness-death model.

4.2   Landmark Markov-Free Estimators

The Aalen-Johansen estimator is the usual estimator of the transition probabilities providing consistent estimates if the multi-state model is Markov. When the multi-state model is non-Markov, this is no longer the case. The Markov assumption states that future and past are independent given the present state. This means that the future evolution of the process is independent of the states already visited and the transition times between them. This simplifying assumption allows the construction of simple estimators but is violated in some applications [21]. This is a relevant observation, since the Aalen-Johansen estimator may be inconsistent if the process is non-Markovian [22]. This section briefly describes two alternative methods for estimating transition probabilities that do not rely on the Markov assumption. Both methods involve the concept of sub-sampling. The first estimator is due to de Uña-Álvarez and Meira-Machado [23] and uses a procedure based on (differences between) Kaplan-Meier estimators derived from a subset of the data consisting of all subjects observed to be in the given state at the given time. The second method, known as landmark Aalen-Johansen, is due to Putter and Spitoni [24] and is obtained by combining the Aalen-Johansen estimate of the state occupation probabilities derived from the same subset. Both approaches provide consistent estimators for the target that are free of the Markov condition.

In the illness-death model, the five transition probabilities can be expressed as depending on the joint distribution of (Z, Y). For example, $p_{11}(s,t) = P(U > t \mid U > s)$, $p_{12}(s,t) = P(U \leq t, Y > t \mid U > s)$ and $p_{22}(s,t) = P(U \leq t, Y > t \mid U \leq s, Y > s)$, whereas the two remaining transition probabilities $(p_{13}(s,t)$ and $p_{23}(s,t))$ can be obtained from those ones. To estimate $p_{1j}(s,t)$, $j = 1, 2, 3$, [23] consider the subsample of all subjects observed to be in State 1 at time s (i.e., those with a sojourn time in State 1 greater than s; $U > s$), whereas $p_{2j}(s,t)$, $j = 2, 3$, are estimated using the subsample of all subjects observed to be in State 2 at time s (i.e., those that have observed a transition to State 2 before time s and are still in that same state at time s; $U \leq s, Y > s$). Then, $\widehat{p}_{11}^{LM}(s,t) = \widehat{S}_U^{(s)}(t)$, $\widehat{p}_{12}^{LM}(s,t) = \widehat{S}_T^{(s)}(t) - \widehat{S}_U^{(s)}(t)$ and $\widehat{p}_{22}^{LM}(s,t) = \widehat{S}_T^{[s]}(t)$ where $\widehat{S}_U^{(s)}(t)$ is the Kaplan-Meier estimator of survival of the sojourn time in State 1 computed over the subsample of all subjects observed to be in State 1 at time s; $\widehat{S}_T^{(s)}(t)$ is the Kaplan-Meier estimator of survival of the total time computed over the same subsample, and $\widehat{S}_T^{[s]}(t)$ is the Kaplan-Meier estimator of survival of the total time computed over the subsample of all subjects observed to be in State 2 at time s.

The Landmark Aalen-Johansen approach introduced in [24] also uses a procedure that is based on the same subsamples of data. Assuming those subsamples, the transition probabilities are then estimated using the so-called Aalen-Johansen estimator, which in turn provides now consistent estimates since they can be seen as an occupation probability (consistency follows from [25]).

Both landmark approaches can use the presmoothing ideas described above to reduce the variability of the estimators. Presmoothing is highly recommended in landmark estimators since these methods lead to estimators that have greater variability due to their reliance on smaller datasets (subsampling).

5   Real Data Illustration

In this section, proposed methods are applied to two real data sets. The first comes from a bladder cancer study, whereas the second comes from a colon cancer study. Both data sets are available as part of the R **survival** package.

The present study aims to investigate multiple recurrence times in 85 patients with bladder tumors. To accomplish this, the estimated Kaplan-Meier survival curve (labeled as KM) and its presmoothed version (labeled as PKM) for the first and fourth recurrence times were obtained. Figure 2 shows the corresponding survival plots. As expected, the presmoothed method has less variability than the KM estimator, which has fewer jump points as t increases. The extra jump points of the presmoothed estimator (PKM) correspond to patients with censored values of the first recurrence (left hand plot) and fourth recurrence (right hand plot). Presmoothing was obtained using a logistic regression model.

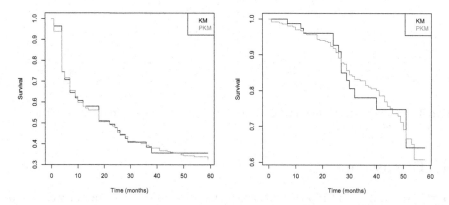

Fig. 2. Estimates of the survival for the first recurrence (left) and forth recurrence (right) using the original Kaplan-Meier (KM) estimator and the presmoothed Kaplan-Meier estimator. Bladder recurrence cancer data.

Data from a colon cancer clinical trial is also used, where patients were monitored from the date of cancer diagnosis until censoring or death from colon cancer. From the total of 929 patients, 468 developed a recurrence and among these 414 died. Thirty eight patients have died of causes unrelated to their disease and without evidence of recurrence. In addition to the two event times (recurrence and death) and corresponding censoring indicator functions, a vector of covariates are available.

The aim with this application is to illustrate the differences between the estimated transition probabilities from the Aalen-Johansen estimator (AJ), the Landmark estimator (LM), and the semiparametric estimators based on presmoothing (PAJ, PLM). Again, parametric presmoothing based on the logistic model is used. The left hand side of Fig. 3 depicts the estimates of $p_{12}(s = 1825; t)$ as functions of the time (for a fixed value of $s = 1825$, i.e., 5 years). Since the recurrence state (State 2) is transient, this curve is first increasing and then decreasing. The estimated curves reveal the lower variability of the presmoothed estimators. The PLM estimator seems to be the one that obtains more reliable curves. Similar conclusions can be obtained from the plots depicted on the right hand side of Fig. 3, in which the transition probability $p_{23}(s, t)$ is estimated through the four methods again for $s = 1825$.

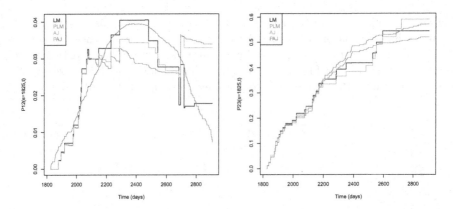

Fig. 3. Estimated transition probabilities for $p_{12}(s,t)$, (left), and for $p_{23}(s,t)$ for $s = 1825$. Colon cancer data.

6   Discussion

In this work, different representations of the Kaplan-Meier estimator were intro-duced. Based on one of these representations, new estimators were introduced for quantities of interest in the context of multi-state survival analysis. Specifically, estimators for the transition probabilities were introduced, although the same approach can be used to estimate other relevant quantities in medical applica-tions, such as the bivariate distribution function for censored gap times and the cumulative incidence function.

The proposed estimators can be extended to multi-state models beyond the progressive illness-death model. Specifically, it is possible to apply the new method based on the computation of Kaplan-Meier curves in subsamples to any progressive multi-state model.

References

1. Kaplan, E.L., Meier, P.: Nonparametric estimation from incomplete observations. J. Am. Stat. Assoc. **53**, 457–481 (1958)
2. Lynden-Bell, D.: A method of allowing for known observational selection in small samples applied to 3CR quasars. Monthly Notices Royal Astron. Soc. **2**, 95–118 (1971)
3. Turnbull, B.W.: Nonparametric estimation of a survivorship function with doubly censored data. J. Am. Stat. Assoc. **69**, 169–173 (1974)
4. Aalen, O.O.: Nonparametric estimation of partial transition probabilities in mul-tiple decrement models. Ann. Stat. **6**, 534–545 (1978)
5. Aalen, O.O., Johansen, S.: An empirical transition matrix for nonhomogeneous Markov chains based on censored observations. Scand. J. Stat. **5**, 141–150 (1978)
6. Fleming, T.R.: Nonparametric estimation for nonhomogeneous Markov processes in the problem of competing risks. Ann. Stat. **6**, 1057–1070 (1978)
7. Johansen, S.: The product limit estimator as maximum likelihood estimator. Scand. J. Stat. **5**(4), 195–199 (1978)

8. Feltz, C.J., Dykstra, R.L.: Maximum likelihood estimation of the survival functions of N stochastically ordered random variables. J. Am. Stat. Assoc. **80**(392), 1012–1019 (1985)

9. Borgan, Ø.: The Kaplan-Meier estimator. In: Armitage P, Colton T, eds. Encyclopedia of biostatistics, pp. 2154–2160. Wiley, Chichester (1998)

10. Satten, G.A., Datta, S.: The Kaplan-Meier estimator as an inverse-probability-of-censoring weighted average. Am. Stat. **55**(3), 207–210 (2001)

11. Rodríguez-Álvarez, M.J., Meira-Machado, L., Abu-Assi, E., Raposeiras-Roubín, S. (2016). Nonparametric estimation of time-dependent ROC curves conditional on a continuous covariate. Stat. Med. **35**(7), 1090–1102 (2016)

12. Meira-Machado, L., de Uña-Álvarez, J., Datta, S.: Nonparametric estimation of conditional transition probabilities in a non-Markov illness-death model. Comput. Stat. **30**, 377–397 (2015)

13. Meira-Machado, L., Sestelo, M.: Estimation in the progressive illness-death model: a nonexhaustive review. Biom. J. **61**(2), 245–263 (2019)

14. Dikta, G.: On semiparametric random censorship models. J. Stat. Plann. Inf. **66**, 253–279 (1998)

15. Cao, R., López, de Ullibarri, I., Janssen, P., Veraverbeke, N.J.: Presmoothed Kaplan-Meier and Nelson-Aalen estimators: Nonparamet. Stat **17**, 31–56 (2005)

16. Andersen, P.K., Borgan, O., Gill, R.D., Keiding, N.: Statistical Models Based on Counting Processes. Springer, New York (1993). https://doi.org/10.1007/978-1-4612-4348-9

17. Meira-Machado, L., de Uña-Álvarez, J., Cadarso-Suárez, C., Andersen, P.K.: Multistate models for the analysis of time to event data. Stat. Methods Med. Res. **18**, 195–222 (2009)

18. Borgan, Ø.: The Kaplan-Meier estimator. In: Armitage P, Colton T. (eds.) Encyclopedia of biostatistics, pp. 5–10. Wiley, Chichester (1998)

19. Moreira, A., de Uña-Álvarez, J., Meira-Machado, L.: Presmoothing the Aalen-Johansen estimator in the illness-death model. Electr. J. Stat. **7**, 1491–1516 (2013)

20. Soutinho, G., Sestelo, M., Meira-Machado, L.: survidm: an R package for inference and prediction in an illness-death model. R J. **13**(2), 70–89 (2021)

21. Soutinho, G., Meira-Machado, L.: Methods for checking the Markov condition in multi-state survival data. Comput. Stati. **37**(2), 751–780 (2022)

22. Meira-Machado, L., de Uña-Álvarez, J., Cadarso-Suárez, C.: Nonparametric estimation of transition probabilities in a non-Markov illness-death model. Lifetime Data Anal. **12**, 325–344 (2006)

23. de Uña-Álvarez, J., Meira-Machado, L.: Nonparametric estimation of transition probabilities in the non-Markov illness-death model: a comparative study. Biometrics **71**, 141–150 (2015)

24. Putter, H., Spitoni, C.: Non-parametric estimation of transition probabilities in non-Markov multi-state models: the landmark Aalen-Johansen estimator. Stat. Methods Med. Res. **27**(7), 2081–2092 (2018)

25. Datta, S., Satten, G.A.: Validity of the Aalen-Johansen estimators of stage occupation probabilities and Nelson-Aalen estimators of integrated transition hazards for non-Markov models. Statist. Probab. Lett. **55**, 403–411 (2001)

Improving Forecasting by Resampling STL Decomposition

Clara Cordeiro[1]([✉])[iD], M. Rosário Ramos[2][iD], and M. Manuela Neves[3,4][iD]

[1] Faculdade de Ciências e Tecnologia, Universidade do Algarve,
Faro, Portugal
ccordei@ualg.pt
[2] Universidade Aberta & CEG-UAb, Lisbon, Portugal
marosram@uab.pt
[3] Instituto Superior de Agronomia, Universidade de Lisboa, Lisbon, Portugal
manela@isa.ulisboa.pt
[4] CEAUL – Centro de Estatística e Aplicações, Faculdade de Ciências,
Universidade de Lisboa, Lisbon, Portugal

Abstract. The development of new forecasting algorithms has shown an increasing interest due to the emerging of new fields of application like machine learning and forecasting competitions. Although initially intended for independent random variables, *bootstrap* methods can be successfully applied to time series. The `Boot.EXPOS` procedure, which combines *bootstrap* and exponential smoothing methods, has shown promising results for forecasting. This work proposes a new approach to forecasting, which is briefly described as follows: using Seasonal-Trend decomposition by *Loess* (STL), the best STL fit is selected by testing all possible combinations of parameters. The best combination of smoothing parameters is chosen based on an accuracy measure. The time series is then decomposed into components according to the best STL fit. The `Boot.EXPOS` procedure is employed to forecast the seasonal component and the seasonally adjusted time series. These forecasts are aggregated to obtain a final forecast. The performance of this combined forecast is evaluated using real datasets and compared with other established forecasting methods.

Keywords: `Boot.EXPOS` · Forecast · Time series · Seasonal-Trend decomposition by *Loess*

1 Background and Motivation

A time series is a sequence of observations indexed by time, typically arranged at evenly spaced intervals and correlated. Time series studies have applications in almost all areas where Statistics is used, including economics, finance, the

Supported by national funds through FCT - Fundação para a Ciência e a Tecnologia under the project UIDB/00006/2020.

environment, and medical sciences. The most interesting and ambitious objective of time series analysis is forecasting future values based on past values.

Models are commonly fitted and used to predict future values of a time series. The most widely used forecasting methods are Exponential Smoothing Methods (EXPOS, named by [17]). These methods refer to a set of techniques that can be used to model and obtain forecasts. This versatile approach continually updates a forecast emphasising the most recent experience, that is, the recent observations receive more "weight" than the older ones. Its major attributes are its simplicity and robustness.

The *bootstrap* methodology has been widely applied in numerous research areas, including time series analysis, to produce estimates. This resampling technique is a popular methodology for independent data due to its simplicity and nice properties [18]. It is a computer-intensive method that provides solutions in situations where the traditional methods are unsuccessful or difficult to apply. However, classical Efron's *bootstrap* has been shown to be inefficient in the context of dependent data, such as in the case of time series, where the dependence structure must be preserved during the resampling scheme. Nonetheless, if the time series process is driven by independent and identically distributed (IID) innovations, another way of resampling may be employed. Efron's classical *bootstrap* can be easily extended to a dependent setup. This was the rationale behind the *sieve bootstrap* [1,2].

Boot.EXPOS is a procedure developed to obtain point forecasts and forecast intervals by combining the *sieve bootstrap* and EXPOS. Firstly, the Akaike Information Criterion (AIC) is employed to select the "best" exponential smoothing method. Secondly, the *sieve bootstrap* scheme is performed on the EXPOS residuals, and through a backward process, a sample path is obtained. Ultimately, a replica of the original time series is generated by using the fitted values of the best EXPOS and the sample path. Forecasts are obtained by employing the exponential smoothing parameters of the "best" EXPOS. The performance of Boot.EXPOS was compared with two widely used forecasting methodologies, EXPOS and ARIMA, as well as with the best forecasting methods used in M3[1] time series forecasting competitions [11,23]. Given reasonable assumptions such as stationarity, Boot.EXPOS has been demonstrated to be an effective tool for forecasting time series [11–14].

Inspired by [25], the suggestion is to decompose the time series into components using the Seasonal-Trend decomposition by *Loess* and forecasting each sub-series. The best STL fit is chosen based on an accuracy measure using the function stl.fit [10,15], which runs all possible parameters combinations, culminating in the selection of the optimal smoothing parameters linked to the best fit. The sub-series that will be forecast are the seasonal component and the seasonally adjusted time series (trend and irregular components), as in [20]. This research proposes the use of the Boot.EXPOS procedure for forecasting those sub-series and aggregating them into a single forecast. Furthermore, accuracy measures such as RMSE, MAE, and MAPE are employed to evaluate the

---

[1] More information in https://en.wikipedia.org/wiki/Makridakis_Competitions.

forecasting performance of the combined procedure. The initial findings are promising, indicating that the proposed forecasting combination has the potential to be a competitive approach.

This paper is structured as follows: Sect. 2 provides a description of the methodologies used. In Sect. 3, forecasting experiments are carried out on real time series of mean sea levels in the Pacific, and the results are presented based on out-of-sample point forecast evaluation. Finally, Sect. 4 concludes with closing remarks and additional comments.

2   Methodologies in Action

This study incorporates a combination of some procedures for time series decomposition and forecasting, described in the following subsections, aiming to obtain accurate forecasts.

2.1   Boot.EXPOS procedure

The Boot.EXPOS method involves selecting an appropriate EXPOS model based on the AIC criterion, followed by investigating the residuals for any remaining patterns. The error component is isolated and checked for stationarity. If it is not stationary, data transformation or differentiation is necessary. If stationarity is present, the residual sequence is filtered by an autoregressive model to estimate the autoregressive coefficients and obtain innovations. In the case of autoregressive (AR) models, the *bootstrap* can be applied by resampling the centred residuals and generating a dataset using the estimated AR coefficients and the resampled residuals. Since the AR residuals are IID, the classical *bootstrap* can be used. It is an easy procedure that has been considered a good alternative to conventional estimation and forecasting methods. The EXPOS fitted values and the reconstructed series are used to create a sample path of the simulated data. Forecasts are generated using the initial EXPOS model. This *bootstrap* process is repeated B times, and information is recorded in a matrix. An "optimal" point forecast is obtained by averaging each column of the matrix. More details can be found in [11–14].

2.2   Time Series Decomposition by *Loess*

Loess **Smoother.** Local regression methodology states that a regression function $g(x)$ with predictor x can be locally approximated by the value of a function in some specified parametric class. This is especially useful when a parametric function for the regression surface is not known. Such local approximations are obtained by fitting a regression surface to the data points within a chosen neighbourhood of the point x. There are several smoothing algorithms to proceed in fitting local polynomials. The focus here is on *Loess* (LOcally wEighted Scatterplot Smoothing) [4–9]. *Loess* is a computationally intensive smoothing algorithm that implements a nonparametric approach for estimating regression surfaces.

It is a very flexible procedure that does not need special assumptions about the parametric form of the regression surface and is a robust fitting method to the presence of outliers in the data. At a particular point x (or observation x_i in a data set), the loess fitting is obtained using weighted least squares to fit typically linear or quadratic polynomial functions of the predictors to a given number of points (or observations) in the neighbourhood of x. This number of points $n_\alpha = min(n, \lfloor \alpha n \rfloor)$, is determined by a smoothing parameter α and controls the smoothness of the estimated surface by local regression. Furthermore, α indicates the proportion of the data used for local regression and, therefore, should be a positive value between 0 and 1. The weighting scheme follows a smooth decreasing function assigning weights depending on their distance to x. In time series applications, the parameterization of loess smoothing span usually consider an integer $q = \lfloor \alpha n \rfloor$ for the number of closer neighbours (similar to the general case for $\alpha \leq 1$).

STL Decomposition and Forecast. A time series can be seen as the result of the combination of the following behaviours: T, a trend component, which represents an upward or downward movement over the time horizon; S, a seasonal component, which is a repetitive pattern over time; and I, an irregular component, remaining after the other components have been removed. One of the oldest commonly used methods is the time series decomposition method. The additive is one type of decomposition model and is described as

$$Y_t = T_t + S_t + I_t,$$

where $t = 1, \cdots N$, is the time period and N its length. The classical decomposition methods of time series allow to obtain estimates for the trend, the seasonality and the irregular components. However, these methodologies do not allow for a flexible specification of the seasonal component, and the trend component is generally represented by a deterministic time function, which is easily affected by outliers.

There are several methods that deal with this type of decomposition, but some time series recalls a more flexible approach, capable of identifying a seasonal component that changes over time, can deal with nonlinear trends and is robust in the presence of outliers. With these premises, the Seasonal-Trend decomposition of time series based on *Loess* [3] was chosen. The STL decomposition is already available within the ®R software through function stl [24].

To use STL, users typically need to pre-define the *Loess* smoothing parameters either based on their knowledge of the data or using default values. However, an algorithm proposed in [15] overcomes this limitation by automatically selecting the optimal smoothing parameters that minimise the error measure. The algorithm selects the best STL model with the smallest error measure achieved using a specific combination of s.window and t.window (see [15]). This approach is particularly useful for time series studies that require evaluation of inter-annual variability. The forecasting method proposed in [25] establishes the forecast as a linear combination of the individual forecasts for the trend, seasonal and error components obtained previously through STL decomposition. As described in [25], the decomposition procedure is supported by literature that points to improved forecasting performance of the models when distinct sub-series are used for their estimation. Assuming each sub-series follows its own structural model, the forecasting method is chosen according to accuracy measures. The final forecast is the aggregation of the extrapolations of each sub-series. In [25], four forecasting methods, namely ARIMA, Theta, Holt's Damped Trend, and Holt-Winters methods, were used as benchmarks to compare against the obtained results of the forecast approach proposed. Compared to standard statistical techniques, this approach performs relatively well in producing long-term forecasts for both the NN3 [16] and M1 [22] competition datasets. See [25] for more details.

2.3 Combining Procedures

The approach developed for the current study uses the STL decomposition [3]. As already explained, a remarkable characteristic of the STL decomposition is its robustness in the presence of outliers. Note that these observations are problematic since they influence parameter estimation (e.g., ARIMA models), which will mislead any statistical conclusion. Similar to all non-parametric regression methods, STL requires the subjective selection of smoothing parameters. The two main parameters are the seasonal (s.window) and trend (t.window) window widths. Therefore, to overcome this limitation, the stl.fit procedure [10,15] was used since it tries to obtain an "objective" choice of the STL smoothing parameters. Based on an accuracy measure, this algorithm selects the best STL model for each combination of s.window and t.window. This procedure has been developed to obtain "automatically" the seasonal and trend smoothing parameters by minimising an error measure.

After decomposing the time series using stl.fit, the Boot.EXPOS procedure is used to forecast the sub-series, and the "optimal" forecast will be obtained by summing the forecasts. The references [20,25] are the basis of this combined procedure, where the underlying idea was that better prediction accuracy could be achieved if the time series is split into smaller parts (or sub-series). In case of uncorrelated errors, the forecasting method is developed where each forecast combines the forecast obtained for the trend and seasonal component.

3 Mean Sea Level Case Study

Sea level trends, interannual and decadal variability, are types of patterns of sea level changes that have been studied due to their importance in forecasting mean sea-level rise for this century. This area of research is of great interest and has been the focus of numerous studies on time series of mean sea level.

This paper considers four monthly time series of the mean sea level from four locations in the Pacific Ocean[2] as seen in Fig. 1. Generally, a seasonal pattern and an upward trend are observed at different increase rates.

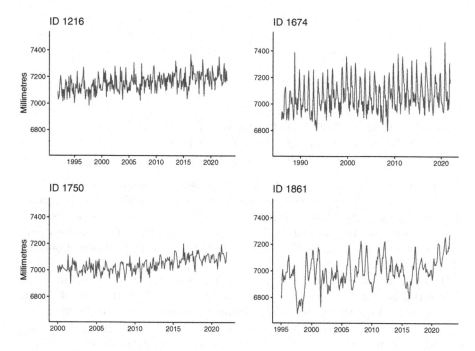

Fig. 1. The mean sea level time series from four locations in the Pacific Ocean.

The four time series are decomposed using `stl.fit` procedure, but it was necessary to check the existence of outliers according to [3]. Only the time series ID 1861 shows outliers, as seen in Fig. 2.

Furthermore, nine forecasting algorithms are used in this case study, and they are the following:

1. `auto.arima`: Fit best ARIMA model to univariate time series with AIC;
2. `ets`: Exponential smoothing state space model;
3. `bats`: Exponential smoothing state space model with Box-Cox transformation, ARMA errors, Trend and Seasonal components;
4. `baggedETS`: Bagging Exponential Smoothing Methods using STL Decomposition and Box-Cox Transformation;
5. `Boot.EXPOS`: Exponential smoothing state space model (`ets`), AR errors and classical *bootstrap* [11,12];
6. `stl + Boot.EXPOS`: `stl` followed by `Boot.EXPOS`;

---

[2] Permanent Service for Mean Sea Level (PSMSL), 2023, "Tide Gauge Data", Retrieved 7 April 2023 from http://www.psmsl.org/data/obtaining/.

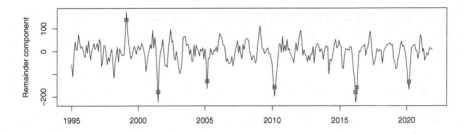

Fig. 2. ID 1861: outliers detection according to [3].

7. `stl.fit` + `Boot.EXPOS`: `stl.fit` followed by `Boot.EXPOS`;
8. `stlf` + `ARIMA`: `stlf` forecast followed by ARIMA;
9. `stlf` + `ets`: `stlf` forecast followed by `ets`.

The procedures 1, 2, 3, 4, 8 and 9 are available in package `forecast` [19,21] in Ⓡ software. In the previous procedures, the model selection was made using the AIC criterion, the *Mean Squared Error* (MSE) was the criterion adopted for the estimation of the parameters. Moreover, for algorithms 6 to 9, the robust approach was carried out for time series ID 1861 due to the presence of outliers, as seen in Fig. 2.

In order to evaluate and compare the performance of the algorithms, the time series is separated into two parts: the fitting set and the validation set, as seen in Table 1. All the procedures enumerated are applied to the fitting set $\{y_1, \cdots, y_{n-h}\}$ and forecasts are obtained. The validation set $\{y_{n-h+1}, \cdots, y_n\}$ is used to evaluate the forecasting capacity using some accuracy measures presented in Table 2. Let y_t denote the observation at time t and $\hat{y}_t$ the forecast of y_t, $t = 1, \cdots, n$. The forecast error is defined by $e_t = y_t - \hat{y}_t$. The forecasts are computed for a hold-out period $\hat{y}_n(1), \cdots, \hat{y}_n(h)$ and compared with the true values (the validation set) using the criteria in Table 2.

Table 1. The sea level time series.

ID	Station name	Fitting set	Validation set
1216	Spring Bay, Australia	January 1992–December 2021	Year 2022
1674	Quarry Bay, Hong Kong	January 1986–December 2020	Year 2021
1750	Napier, New Zealand	January 2000–December 2020	Year 2021
1861	Honiana-B, Solomon Islands	January 1995–December 2021	Year 2022

Table 2. Accuracy measures.

Acronyms	Definition	Formula
RMSE	Root Mean Squared Error	$\sqrt{(mean(e_t^2))}$
MAE	Mean Absolute Error	$mean(\lvert e_t \rvert)$
MAPE	Mean Absolute Percentage Error	$mean(100 \left\lvert \frac{e_t}{y_t} \right\rvert)$

Table 3. Results of the accuracy measures.

ID	Procedure	RMSE	MAE	MAPE
1216	auto.arima	53.62	48.56	0.67
	ets	**50.03**	**44.76**	**0.62**
	bats	55.79	49.73	0.69
	baggedETS	**49.08**	**43.66**	**0.61**
	Boot.EXPOS	**49.15**	**44.26**	**0.62**
	stl + Boot.EXPOS	50.81	45.18	0.63
	stlfit + Boot.EXPOS	66.16	56.44	0.79
	stlf + ARIMA	57.26	50.05	0.70
	stlf + ets	62.73	53.20	0.74
1674	auto.arima	76.29	65.90	0.93
	ets	102.48	83.02	1.18
	bats	78.76	63.23	0.90
	baggedETS	81.07	63.08	0.90
	Boot.EXPOS	**68.63**	**53.56**	**0.76**
	stl + Boot.EXPOS	**69.19**	**54.07**	**0.77**
	stlfit + Boot.EXPOS	**66.50**	**53.16**	**0.75**
	stlf + ARIMA	75.47	61.91	0.88
	stlf + ets	93.71	77.77	1.10
1750	auto.arima	39.31	32.81	0.46
	ets	46.48	38.84	0.54
	bats	40.01	33.66	0.47
	baggedETS	42.10	34.37	0.48
	Boot.EXPOS	48.02	40.37	0.57
	stl + Boot.EXPOS	**33.65**	**27.12**	**0.38**
	stlfit+Boot.EXPOS	**33.00**	**28.81**	**0.40**
	stlf + ARIMA	**30.30**	**24.43**	**0.34**
	stlf + ets	41.81	36.70	0.51
1861	auto.arima	127.18	118.01	1.64
	ets	68.49	61.60	0.86
	bats	126.59	117.22	1.63
	baggedETS	78.86	73.35	1.02
	Boot.EXPOS	**67.67**	**60.53**	**0.84**
	stl + Boot.EXPOS	**63.89**	**55.55**	**0.77**
	stlfit + Boot.EXPOS	**63.99**	**55.73**	**0.77**
	stlf + ARIMA	68.53	61.35	0.85
	stlf + ets	68.72	61.56	s 0.85

Note: The three best results are highlighted in **bold**.

Forecasts for twelve months (h=12) are obtained using the nine procedures, and their results are presented in Table 3. Based on these results, there is evidence that the forecasts achieved by the proposed combined procedures are in the top three best methods, except for the time series ID 1216. Concerning this time series, one possible solution for addressing this weak point could be to incorporate the option of implementing data transformation during pre-processing to stabilise the variance, such as the Box-Cox transformation.

4   Comments and Concluding Remarks

In this study, some procedures for time series decomposition and forecasting were combined in order to obtain accurate forecasts. The approach is a computational procedure for forecasting based on the combination of two procedures, stl.fit and Boot.EXPOS. The aim was to take advantage of flexible methods with fewer assumptions and provide properties for the estimators considered. This combination was applied to four real time series of mean sea levels with different lengths, seasonal patterns, trends and types of variability. The results were compared with other competing and established forecasting procedures, such as exponential smoothing and ARIMA models.

Furthermore, future work will involve the implementation of this procedure on various sets of time series and compare it with other forecasting procedures. This will constitute a major challenge to evaluate the effectiveness of the combined forecasting approach.

Acknowledgments. The authors thank the three referees for their constructive comments and valuable suggestions, which led to improvements to this work and will contribute to future work. The authors are partially financed by national funds through FCT – Fundação para a Ciência e a Tecnologia under the project UIDB/00006/2020.

References

1. Alonso, A.M., Peña, D., Romo, J.: Forecasting time series with sieve bootstrap. J. Stat. Plan. Infer. **100**(1), 1–11 (2002). https://doi.org/10.1016/s0378-3758(01)00092-1
2. Bühlmann, P.: Sieve bootstrap for time series. Bernoulli **3**(2), 123 (1997). https://doi.org/10.2307/3318584
3. Cleveland, R.B., Cleveland, W.S., McRae, J.E., Terpenning, I.: Stl: a seasonal-trend decomposition. J. Off. Stat **6**(1), 3–73 (1990)
4. Cleveland, W.S.: Robust locally weighted regression and smoothing scatterplots. J. Am. Stat. Assoc. **74**(368), 829–836 (1979). https://doi.org/10.1080/01621459.1979.10481038
5. Cleveland, W.S., Devlin, S.J.: Locally weighted regression: an approach to regression analysis by local fitting. J. Am. Stat. Assoc. **83**(403), 596–610 (1988). https://doi.org/10.1080/01621459.1988.10478639
6. Cleveland, W.S., Devlin, S.J., Grosse, E.: Regression by local fitting: methods, properties, and computational algorithms. J. Econometr. **37**(1), 87–114 (1988)
7. Cleveland, W.S., Grosse, E.: Computational methods for local regression. Stat. Comput. **1**, 47–62 (1991)
8. Cleveland, W.S., Grosse, E., Shyu, W.M.: Local regression models. In: Statistical Models in S, pp. 309–376. Routledge, Abingdon (2017). https://doi.org/10.1201/9780203738535-8

9. Cleveland, W.S., Loader, C.: Smoothing by local regression: principles and methods. In: Contributions to Statistics, pp. 10–49. Physica-Verlag HD (1996). https://doi.org/10.1007/978-3-642-48425-4_2
10. Cordeiro, C.: stl.fit(): Function developed in Cristina et al. (2016). https://github.com/ClaraCordeiro/stl.fit
11. Cordeiro, C., Neves, M.: Forecasting time series with boot.expos procedure. REVSTAT-Stat. J. **7**(2), 135–149 (2009)
12. Cordeiro, C., Neves, M.M.: Boot.EXPOS in NNGC competition. In: The 2010 International Joint Conference on Neural Networks (IJCNN). IEEE (2010). https://doi.org/10.1109/ijcnn.2010.5596361
13. Cordeiro, C., Neves, M.M.: Predicting and treating missing data with boot.expos. In: Advances in Regression, Survival Analysis, Extreme Values, Markov Processes and Other Statistical Applications, pp. 131–138. Springer, Heidelberg (2013). https://doi.org/10.1007/978-3-642-34904-1_13
14. Cordeiro, C., Neves, M.M.: Forecast intervals with Boot.EXPOS. In: Pacheco, A., Santos, R., do Rosário Oliveira, M., Paulino, C.D. (eds.) New Advances in Statistical Modeling and Applications. STAS, pp. 249–256. Springer, Cham (2014). https://doi.org/10.1007/978-3-319-05323-3_24
15. Cristina, S., Cordeiro, C., Lavender, S., Goela, P.C., Icely, J., Newton, A.: MERIS phytoplankton time series products from the SW Iberian peninsula (Sagres) using seasonal-trend decomposition based on loess. Remote Sens. **8**(6), 449 (2016). https://doi.org/10.3390/rs8060449
16. Crone, S.F., Hibon, M., Nikolopoulos, K.: Advances in forecasting with neural networks? empirical evidence from the NN3 competition on time series prediction. Int. J. Forecast. **27**(3), 635–660 (2011). https://doi.org/10.1016/j.ijforecast.2011.04.001
17. DeLurgio, S.A.: Forecasting Principles and Applications. McGraw-Hill/Irwin, New York (1998)
18. Efron, B.: Bootstrap methods: another look at the jackknife. Ann. Stat. **7**(1) (1979). https://doi.org/10.1214/aos/1176344552
19. Hyndman, R., et al.: forecast: Forecasting functions for time series and linear models (2023). https://pkg.robjhyndman.com/forecast/. R package version 8.21
20. Hyndman, R.J., Athanasopoulos, G.: Forecasting: Principles and Practice, 3rd edn. OTexts, Melbourne (2021). https://otexts.com/fpp3/. Accessed Mar 2023
21. Hyndman, R.J., Khandakar, Y.: Automatic time series forecasting: the forecast package for R. J. Stat. Softw. **26**(3), 1–22 (2008). https://doi.org/10.18637/jss.v027.i03
22. Makridakis, S., et al.: The accuracy of extrapolation (time series) methods: results of a forecasting competition. J. Forecast. **1**(2), 111–153 (1982). https://doi.org/10.1002/for.3980010202
23. Makridakis, S., Hibon, M.: The m3-competition: results, conclusions and implications. Int. J. Forecast. **16**(4), 451–476 (2000). https://doi.org/10.1016/s0169-2070(00)00057-1
24. R Core Team: R: A Language and Environment for Statistical Computing. R Foundation for Statistical Computing, Vienna, Austria (2023). https://www.R-project.org/
25. Theodosiou, M.: Forecasting monthly and quarterly time series using STL decomposition. Int. J. Forecast. **27**(4), 1178–1195 (2011). https://doi.org/10.1016/j.ijforecast.2010.11.002

Comparison of Feature Selection Methods in Regression Modeling: A Simulation Study

Vera Afreixo[(✉)] [iD], Jorge Cabral [iD], and Pedro Macedo [iD]

CIDMA – Center for Research and Development in Mathematics and Applications, Department of Mathematics, University of Aveiro, 3810-193 Aveiro, Portugal
{vera,jorgecabral,pmacedo}@ua.pt

Abstract. This simulation study explores the impact of different undesirable scenarios (e.g., collinearity, Simpson's paradox, variable interaction, Freedman's paradox) on feature selection and coefficients' estimation using traditional methodologies, such as automatic selection (e.g., stepwise using Akaike information criterion and Bayesian information criterion) and penalized regression (e.g., least absolute shrinkage and selection operator (LASSO), elastic net, relaxed LASSO, adaptive LASSO, minimax concave penalty and smoothly clipped absolute deviation penalty, penalized regression with second-generation p-values). Specifically, we compare wrapper and embedded methods regarding the feature selection, coefficients' estimation and models' performance. Our results show that the choice of the methodology can affect the number and the type of selected features, as well as accuracy and precision of coefficients' estimates. Furthermore, we find that the performance can also depend on the characteristics of the data.

Keywords: Simulation · Feature Selection · Coefficient Estimation

1 Introduction

Feature selection and coefficients' estimation are two fundamental topics in statistical modeling, particularly in regression analysis. Feature selection is the process of selecting a subset of the most important features (i.e., variables) that have a significant impact on the outcome variable, while ignoring irrelevant or redundant variables. The feature selection contributes to less complex models and to reduce the potential overfitting, in addition to promoting estimation stability. There are several feature selection methodologies that can be used, including: filter methods (e.g., association measures or test, information gain); wrapper methods (stepwise linear models); embedded methods (penalized regression models, extreme gradient boosting, random forest); genetic algorithms. There is no one-size-fits-all approach to feature selection. The choice of the method may depend on the type of data, the specific problem, and the outcome variable.

Automatic selection, as the name itself indicates, is a family of techniques that automatically select a subset of predictors to include in a regression model. These techniques aim to improve the adequacy of the regression model by selecting the most relevant predictors and removing irrelevant or redundant ones. In some way, they can be considered

O. Gervasi et al. (Eds.): ICCSA 2023 Workshops, LNCS 14112, pp. 150–159, 2023.
https://doi.org/10.1007/978-3-031-37129-5_13

traditional techniques, based on t tests and F tests, with some of their weaknesses being well-known, such as the computational burden and the possible incorrect identification of relevant predictors, usually known as the Freedman's paradox (Freedman 1983).

Penalized regression methods are a class of statistical techniques that are commonly used in regression analysis to address problems such as overfitting and collinearity (Belsley et al. 2004). These methods add a penalty term to the objective function being minimized, which promotes simpler models and more parsimonious solutions, where some coefficients are shrunk towards zero depending on the norm (or combination of norms) used. These methods have become increasingly popular in recent years, especially in high-dimensional data settings where the number of predictors is much larger than the number of observations. These methods can help to improve the predictive performance of models while also providing insight into the most important predictors (Hastie et al. 2009; Efron and Hastie 2016).

2 Methods

We consider a simulation study with different scenarios to demonstrate the performance of nine feature selection methods: stepwise selection of variables (Efroymson 1960; Hocking 1976) based on the Akaike information criterion (StepAIC) (Akaike 1974) and on the Bayesian information criterion (StepBIC) (Schwarz 1978), least absolute shrinkage and selection operator (LASSO) (Tibshirani 1996), adaptive LASSO (Zou 2006), relaxed LASSO (Hastie et al. 2017), elastic net (ENet) (Zou and Hastie 2005), smoothly clipped absolute deviation (SCAD) penalty (Fan and Li 2001), minimax concave penalty (MCP) (Zhang 2010), and second-generation p-values (ProSGPV) (Zuo et al. 2022).

We consider a number of simulation repetitions of $N = 50$ and different sample sizes of $n \in \{30, 100\}$. Continuous covariates (p) are drawn from a standard normal distribution considering $p \in \{5, 10, 15\}$, and random correlation matrices are generated based on the method proposed by Joe (2006), using values of $d \in \{0.1, 1, 100\}$ in order to generate different $n \times p$ matrices X. We firstly generate $Z = X\beta + \epsilon$, where ϵ is assumed to follow a normal distribution with a zero-mean and two different standard deviation (sd_ϵ), namely $sd_\epsilon \in \{1, 3\}$, and $\beta = (\beta_1, \beta_2, \ldots, \beta_p)$ is a vector of the true regression coefficients, where $(\beta_{p-4}, \beta_{p-3}, \ldots, \beta_p) \in \{(0, 0, 0, 0, 0), (1, -1, 1, -1, 1), (2, 2, 2, 2, 2), (2, 4, 6, 8, 10)\}$. Finally, when $p \in \{10, 15\}$, then $\beta_1 = \beta_2 = \ldots = \beta_{p-5} = 0$.

In scenarios where the Simpson's paradox (Simpson 1951) is present, Y is given by $Y = V_S + Z$, where V_S is defined by $V_S = \beta_{0S} + X_S \beta_{1S} + B_S \beta_{2S}$, X_S with a standard normal distribution, $N(0, 1)$, and B_S with a balanced Bernoulli distribution, $B(1, 0.5)$. V_S and X_S have a trend that disappear or reverses in the presence of B_S. We consider differences of means equal to 1 and 4 between the groups created by B_S in both V_S and X_S (Makowski et al. 2019).

In scenarios where the interaction between variables is present, each $Y_i \in Y$ is given by

$$Y_i = \begin{cases} 2 \times X_{Ii} + Z_i, \text{ if } B_{Ii} = 0 \\ -2 \times X_{Ii} + Z_i, \text{ if } B_{Ii} = 1 \end{cases},$$

with $i = 1, 2, \ldots, n$, $X_I \sim N(0, 1)$ and $B_I \sim B(1, 0.5)$. In the absence of either interaction or Simpson's paradox, then $Y = Z$.

The feature selection methods will be tested under different scenarios, namely: (1) in the absence of one of the variables (e.g., when $\left(\beta_{p-4}, \beta_{p-3}, \ldots, \beta_p\right) = (2, 4, 6, 8, 10)$ the methods will be evaluated in the presence of all the variables, in the absence of the variable with coefficient 2, and in the absence of the variable with coefficient 10); (2) the presence and absence of the variables implied in the Simpson's paradox; and (3) the variables interaction.

The 5-fold cross-validation root mean square error (CV-RMSE) will be determined for each scenario, method and repetition. Analyses will be performed in RStudio Version 2022.07.2+576 (Posit Team 2022) running R version 4.1.3 (R Core Team 2022). The R packages *glmnet* (Friedman et al. 2010), *MASS* (Venables and Ripley 2022), *ProSGPV* (Zuo et al. 2022a), *simstudy* (Goldfeld and Wujciak-Jens 2020), *clusterGeneration* (Qiu and Joe 2020) and *bayestestR* (Makowski et al. 2019) will be used. To organize the results, we develop a Shiny application that allows the visualization of the number of selected features and by each feature the percentage of selection, the coefficients' estimates, and the methods' performance through CV-RMSE (see the Appendix for two illustrations).

3   Results and Discussion

3.1   Only Noise Variables (Freedman's Paradox)

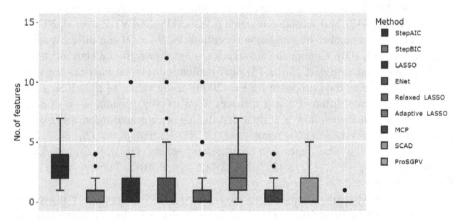

Fig. 1. Number of selected features by the methods under analysis in a complete noise scenario ($n = 100, p = 15, \beta = (0, \ldots, 0), sd_\epsilon = 1$) without relevant collinearity ($d = 100$).

In the scenario that only includes noise variables (i.e., only the variables with coefficients equal to zero), we observed that the more variables are included, the more variables tend to be selected. However, although several methods do not select any variable (in median), StepAIC, StepBIC and adaptive LASSO show a higher median number of selected features. ProSGPV is the method with the best overall performance and StepAIC the worst (see Fig. 1).

Adding collinearity to the models, the estimates obtained by the automatic selection methods are substantially different (and higher than) from the ones of the true regression coefficient vector (see Table 1).

Table 1. Descriptive analysis of the estimates (median [minimum, maximum]) by the methods under analysis in a complete noise scenario ($n = 100$, $p = 15$, $\beta = (0, \ldots, 0)$, $sd_\epsilon = 1$) with relevant collinearity ($d = 0.1$).

	StepAIC	StepBIC	LASSO	ENet	Relaxed LASSO	Adaptive LASSO	MCP	SCAD	ProSGPV
$\hat{\beta}_{15}$	0 [−6298.6, 7846.6]	0 [−4869.5, 2]	0 [−0.2, 0.1]	0 [−0.2, 0.1]	0 [−0.3, 0.2]	0 [−0.3, 0.2]	0 [−0.3, 0.1]	0 [−0.3, 0.1]	0 [−0.4, 0]
$\hat{\beta}_{14}$	0 [−7916.1, 5399.7]	0 [−7916.1, 0]	0 [−0.1, 0.1]	0 [−0.1, 0.1]	0 [−0.2, 0.1]	0 [−0.2, 0.1]	0 [−0.2, 0]	0 [−0.3, 0]	0 [0, 0]
$\hat{\beta}_{13}$	0 [−13135.5, 11891.2]	0 [−684.4, 90.1]	0 [0, 0.3]	0 [0, 0.3]	0 [0, 0.3]	0 [−0.1, 0.3]	0 [0, 0.4]	0 [0, 0.4]	0 [0, 0]
$\hat{\beta}_{12}$	0 [−10191.6, 1419.3]	0 [−1.3, 1419.3]	0 [−0.1, 0.1]	0 [−0.1, 0.1]	0 [−0.1, 0.2]	0 [−0.2, 0.3]	0 [0, 0.2]	0 [−0.1, 0.1]	0 [0, 0.3]
$\hat{\beta}_{11}$	0 [−28.1, 25866.4]	0 [−1.4, 442.9]	0 [−0.3, 0.1]	0 [−0.3, 0.1]	0 [−0.3, 0.1]	0 [−0.3, 0.3]	0 [−0.4, 0.1]	0 [−0.4, 0.1]	0 [0, 0.2]
$\hat{\beta}_{10}$	0 [−5472.4, 7120.8]	0 [−370.8, 2077.9]	0 [−0.1, 0.2]	0 [−0.1, 0.2]	0 [−0.2, 0.3]	0 [−0.2, 0.4]	0 [0, 0.4]	0 [−0.1, 0.4]	0 [0, 0]
$\hat{\beta}_{9}$	0 [−3322.1, 13299.5]	0 [0, 5229.2]	0 [−0.1, 0]	0 [−0.1, 0]	0 [−0.1, 0]	0 [−0.2, 0.1]	0 [0, 0]	0 [0, 0]	0 [0, 0]
$\hat{\beta}_{8}$	0 [−8837, 3451.3]	0 [−8837, 0.5]	0 [0, 0]	0 [0, 0]	0 [0, 0.1]	0 [−0.2, 0.2]	0 [0, 0]	0 [0, 0]	0 [0, 0]
$\hat{\beta}_{7}$	0 [−13420.5, 2469.5]	0 [−1.3, 1419.4]	0 [−0.1, 0]	0 [−0.1, 0.1]	0 [−0.2, 0]	0 [−0.2, 0.2]	0 [−0.3, 0]	0 [−0.3, 0]	0 [0, 0]
$\hat{\beta}_{6}$	0 [−23867.7, 5269.8]	0 [−4178, 0.3]	0 [−0.1, 0.1]	0 [−0.1, 0.1]	0 [−0.2, 0.1]	0 [−0.2, 0.2]	0 [−0.2, 0.1]	0 [−0.2, 0.1]	0 [0, 0]
$\hat{\beta}_{5}$	0 [−6322.6, 3659.5]	0 [−6322.6, 194.3]	0 [−0.1, 0.1]	0 [−0.1, 0.1]	0 [−0.1, 0.1]	0 [−0.2, 0.2]	0 [−0.1, 0.1]	0 [−0.1, 0.1]	0 [0, 0]

(*continued*)

Table 1. (*continued*)

	StepAIC	StepBIC	LASSO	ENet	Relaxed LASSO	Adaptive LASSO	MCP	SCAD	ProSGPV
$\hat{\beta}_4$	0 [−2120.3, 9488.3]	0 [−1.4, 9488.3]	0 [0, 0.1]	0 [0, 0.1]	0 [−0.1, 0.1]	0 [−0.1, 0.2]	0 [0, 0]	0 [0, 0]	0 [0, 0]
$\hat{\beta}_3$	0 [−21954.6, 3774.7]	0 [−186.8, 3774.7]	0 [−0.1, 0]	0 [−0.1, 0]	0 [−0.2, 0]	0 [−0.2, 0]	0 [−0.1, 0]	0 [−0.1, 0]	0 [0, 0]
$\hat{\beta}_2$	0 [−42352.6, 3398]	0 [−2193.7, 145.2]	0 [0, 0]	0 [0, 0.1]	0 [0, 0.2]	0 [−0.2, 0.3]	0 [0, 0]	0 [0, 0.1]	0 [0, 0]
$\hat{\beta}_1$	0 [−19749.4, 5098.8]	0 [−5985.8, 45.1]	0 [0, 0]	0 [0, 0]	0 [0, 0]	0 [−0.1, 0.2]	0 [0, 0]	0 [0, 0]	0 [0, 0]
$\hat{\beta}_0$	0 [−0.3, 0.2]	0 [−0.3, 0.2]	0 [−0.3, 0.2]	0 [−0.3, 0.2]	0 [−0.3, 0.2]	0 [−0.3, 0.2]	0 [−0.3, 0.2]	0 [−0.3, 0.2]	0 [−0.3, 0.2]

3.2 Five Explanatory Variables to Define the Outcome

When we have five explanatory variables (i.e., $(\beta_{p-4}, \beta_{p-3}, \ldots, \beta_p) \neq (0, 0, 0, 0, 0)$) to define the outcome (Y) without a relevant collinearity structure and without noise variables available (i.e., $p = 5$), we observed that, in general, the higher the magnitude of the coefficients, the easier the selection of variables and the better the estimation of coefficients, and the higher sd_ϵ the worse the performance of the methods under study (selection and estimation).

For the scenario with $(\beta_{p-4}, \beta_{p-3}, \ldots, \beta_p) = (1, -1, 1, -1, 1)$ with $sd_\epsilon = 3$, in general, the methods cannot select the five features (see Fig. 2). The ProSGPV presents in some cases the worst performance, selecting a smaller number of variables (less than five). For the scenario with the smallest standard deviation of the error ($sd_\epsilon = 1$), in general, all the methods present an adequate performance.

For the scenario with $(\beta_{p-4}, \beta_{p-3}, \ldots, \beta_p) = (2, 4, 6, 8, 10)$ and with $sd_\epsilon = 1$, all methods select the five explanatory variables in the different simulation scenarios. In this scenario we added noise variables (5 or 10) and we clearly observed that some methods select more than five variables (StepAIC, StepBIC, LASSO and ENet). It is observed that all methods present at least one scenario of exaggerated selection, although they are all consistent in the selection of variables of interest. Best results are obtained by adaptive LASSO, MCP, SCAD and ProSGPV (see Fig. 3).

When five explanatory variables (scenario with $(\beta_{p-4}, \beta_{p-3}, \ldots, \beta_p) = (2, 4, 6, 8, 10)$ and $sd_\epsilon = 1$) are generating the outcome with a relevant collinearity structure, without adding noise variables ($p = 5$), all methods tend to select fewer variables than expected (median = 4 for all methods except ENet).

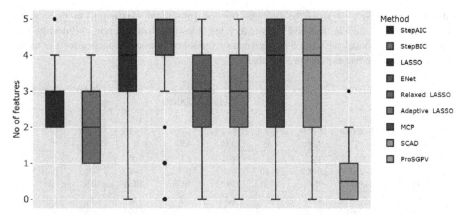

Fig. 2. Number of selected features by the methods under analysis for the scenario of five explanatory variables to define the outcome ($n = 30, p = 5, \beta = (1, \ -1, \ 1, \ -1, \ 1), sd_\epsilon = 3$) and without relevant collinearity ($d = 100$).

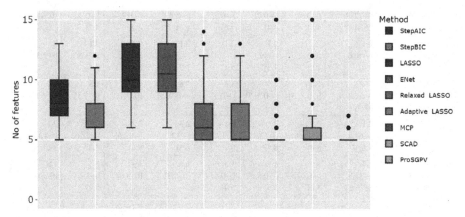

Fig. 3. Number of selected features by the methods under analysis for the scenario of five explanatory variables to define the outcome ($n = 30, p = 15, (\beta_{p-4}, \beta_{p-3}, \ldots, \beta_p) = (2, \ 4, \ 6, \ 8, \ 10)$, $sd_\epsilon = 1$) and without relevant collinearity ($d = 100$).

Again, it is observed that, in the presence of collinearity, the automatic selection methods can provide unstable estimates, with quite different values and with opposite signs when compared to the real coefficients (the range of values in the different simulations is very high). The methods' performance (measured through CV-RMSE) is better with ENet and worse with both automatic selection methods. Adding noise variables to the previous scenario, the best methods regarding feature selection are MCP, SCAD and ProSGPV. The well-known problems of the automatic selection methods are highlighted here, however the CV-RMSE of the different methods regarding the generation model are similar.

Table 2. Descriptive analysis of the estimates (median [minimum, maximum]) by the methods under study using models with five explanatory variables and with relevant collinearity. top) estimates for the model with the five explanatory variables; bottom) estimates for the model removing one of the five explanatory variables.

	StepAIC	StepBIC	LASSO	ENet	Relaxed LASSO	Adaptive LASSO	MCP	SCAD	ProSGPV
$\hat{\beta}_5$	1.7 [−35756.3, 986.6]	1.6 [−3004.8, 24.6]	1 [−1.9, 4.8]	1.4 [−1.9, 4.8]	1 [−2.7, 5.1]	1 [−1.8, 4.9]	1 [−1.9, 8]	1 [−1.9, 5.3]	0.9 [−2, 5.5]
	1.3 [−21.8, 24.6]	1.3 [−21.8, 24.6]	1.3 [−8.2, 10.7]	1.3 [−10, 10.7]	1.3 [−8.3, 10.8]	1.1 [−8.2, 10.7]	1.3 [−8.3, 10.9]	1.3 [−8.3, 10.9]	1.3 [−10.2, 10.9]
$\hat{\beta}_4$	1.3 [−23100.4, 34147.9]	1.3 [−2964.1, 74.2]	1.3 [0, 6.3]	1.7 [0, 4.8]	1.3 [−0.1, 6.3]	1.3 [0, 6.3]	1.7 [−0.9, 6.7]	1.8 [−0.9, 6.7]	1 [0, 6.3]
	3 [−5.7, 74.2]	3 [−5.7, 74.2]	2.9 [−5.6, 16.8]	2.9 [−5.6, 16.8]	2.9 [−5.6, 16.9]	2.4 [−5.6, 16.8]	2.8 [−5.7, 17]	2.9 [−5.7, 17]	3 [−6.7, 17.1]
$\hat{\beta}_3$	1.7 [−43167.1, 62593.6]	1.7 [−7222, 26.4]	1.5 [−0.3, 4.5]	1.8 [−0.7, 4.4]	1.5 [−0.7, 4.6]	1.6 [−0.4, 4.6]	1.7 [−0.2, 4.7]	1.7 [−0.4, 4.7]	1.5 [0, 4]
	2.6 [−40.6, 8.9]	2.1 [−40.6, 5.4]	2.1 [−2.3, 7.8]	2.1 [−19.8, 7.5]	2.1 [−2.4, 5.4]	2.1 [−2.3, 7.7]	2.1 [−3.6, 8.9]	2.1 [−3.6, 5.4]	2 [−3.3, 5.4]
$\hat{\beta}_2$	1 [−47710.6, 70377.6]	1 [−1139.4, 13.9]	1.6 [−0.3, 5]	1.9 [−0.3, 5]	1.6 [−0.3, 6.6]	1.8 [−0.9, 5]	1.9 [0, 7.1]	1.8 [0, 5.5]	1.7 [0, 5.3]
	2.1 [−61.4, 8.6]	2.1 [−61.4, 8.6]	2.1 [−12.4, 8.4]	2 [−12.4, 8.5]	2.1 [−12.5, 8.1]	2.3 [−12.4, 8.5]	2.3 [−12.6, 8.6]	2.3 [−12.6, 8.6]	2.1 [−12.7, 8.6]
$\hat{\beta}_1$	1.4 [−82648.3, 5876.5]	1.4 [−11.8, 5876.5]	1.6 [−0.6, 5.3]	1.7 [−0.8, 5.3]	1.3 [−0.6, 5.4]	1.6 [0, 5.3]	1.4 [0, 5.8]	1.3 [−1.2, 5.9]	1.3 [0, 6.6]
	−	−	−	−	−	−	−	−	−
$\hat{\beta}_0$	0.1 [−0.6, 0.5]	0 [−0.6, 0.5]	0 [−0.6, 0.5]	0 [−0.6, 0.5]	0 [−0.6, 0.5]	0 [−0.7, 0.5]	0 [−0.7, 0.5]	0 [−0.7, 0.5]	0 [−1.1, 0.7]
	0 [−0.6, 0.5]	0 [−0.6, 0.5]	0 [−0.6, 0.5]	0 [−0.6, 0.5]	0 [−0.6, 0.5]	0 [−0.6, 0.5]	0 [−0.6, 0.5]	0 [−0.6, 0.5]	0 [−1.1, 0.7]

When we remove an explanatory variable from a model with a strong collinearity structure, it is observed that the different methods provide more stable estimates. This elimination of a variable affects the coefficients' estimates of the StepAIC and StepBIC methods, both assuming much lower dispersion (see for example Table 2).

3.3 Two Variables to Define the Outcome

Simpson's Paradox
Considering two variables (one quantitative and the other dichotomous) incorporating the structure of Simpson's paradox and five noise variables without relevant collinearity structure to define the outcome, we observe that the LASSO and ENet methods, in general, select more variables than the other methods and more than expected (in line with what we had observed in previous scenarios when we have noise variables in the models). In the actual scenario, in general, all methods estimate well the coefficients of the two variables. However, when excluding the binary variable, all methods reveal the Simpson's phenomenon, noting that the estimate of the coefficient of the quantitative variable changes sign.

Variables Interaction
Considering that in the definition of the outcome we used two variables (one quantitative and the other dichotomous) that describe an interaction phenomenon and five noise variables without relevant collinearity structure, we noticed that the methods generally perform similarly by not selecting (in mean/median) neither of the two variables that define the interaction.

4 Discussion

In general, the performance of the methods depends on the characteristics/structure of the dataset. None of the methods under analysis can overcome the phenomenon of Simpson's paradox. In real data it would be important to quantify for each dataset the possibility of Simpson's paradox phenomenon occurrence and intensity due to missing variables, stablishing intensity measures and methods to evaluate the impact of the inclusion of unknown variables with potential moderator effects. Variables that define the outcome through interaction will not be selected by the usual methods under analysis. So, the traditional main effects regression models are not able to correctly identify the true explanatory variables.

The methods StepAIC, StepBIC, LASSO and ENet were the most sensitive to the presence of collinearity, revealing that in this context these methods do not have an adequate performance. In the presence of strong collinearity, the performance of the methods can benefit from the elimination of variables.

Funding. This research was partially funded by Portuguese funds through CIDMA, The Center for Research and Development in Mathematics and Applications of University of Aveiro, and the Portuguese Foundation for Science and Technology (FCT–Fundação para a Ciência e a Tecnologia), within projects UIDB/04106/2020 and UIDP/04106/2020.

Appendix

See Fig. A1 and Fig. A2 for two illustrations.

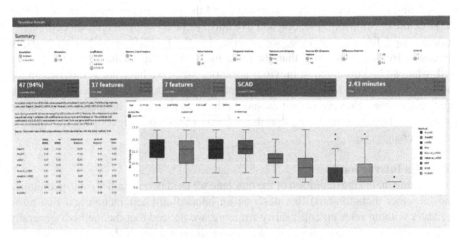

Fig. A1. Shiny app, view of the number of features.

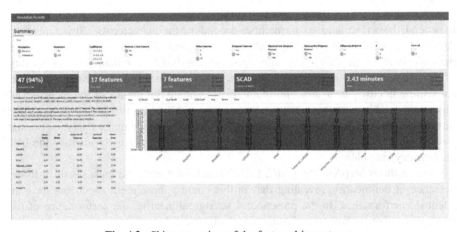

Fig. A2. Shiny app, view of the features' importance.

References

Freedman, D.A.: A note on screening regression equations. Am. Stat. **37**(2), 152–155 (1983)
Belsley, D.A., Kuh, E., Welsch, R.E.: Regression Diagnostics – Identifying Influential Data and Sources of Collinearity. Wiley, Hoboken, New Jersey (2004)

Hastie, T., Tibshirani, R., Friedman, J.: The Elements of Statistical Learning – Data Mining, Inference, and Prediction, 2nd edn. Springer, New York (2009)

Efron, B., Hastie, T.: Computer Age Statistical Inference. Cambridge University Press, Cambridge (2016)

Efroymson, M.A.: Multiple regression analysis. In: Ralston, A., Wilf, H.S. (eds.) Mathematical Methods for Digital Computers. Wiley, New York (1960)

Hocking, R.R.: The analysis and selection of variables in linear regression. Biometrics **32**(1), 1–49 (1976)

Akaike, H.: A new look at the statistical model identification. IEEE Trans. Autom. Control **19**(6), 716–723 (1974)

Schwarz, G.: Estimating the dimension of a model. Ann. Stat. **6**(2), 461–464 (1978)

Tibshirani, R.: Regression shrinkage and selection via the lasso. J. R. Stat. Soc. B **58**(1), 267–288 (1996)

Zou, H.: The adaptive lasso and its oracle properties. J. Am. Stat. Assoc. **101**(476), 1418–1429 (2006)

Hastie, T., Tibshirani, R., Tibshirani, R.J.: Extended comparisons of best subset selection, forward stepwise selection, and the lasso. arXiv:1707.08692 (2017)

Zou, H., Hastie, T.: Regularization and variable selection via the elastic net. J. R. Stat. Soc. B **67**(2), 301–320 (2005)

Fan, J., Li, R.: Variable selection via nonconcave penalized likelihood and its oracle properties. J. Am. Stat. Assoc. **96**(456), 1348–1360 (2001)

Zhang, C.H.: Nearly unbiased variable selection under minimax concave penalty. Ann. Stat. **38**(2), 894–942 (2010)

Zuo, Y., Stewart, T.G., Blume, J.D.: Variable selection with second-generation p-values. Am. Stat. **76**(2), 91–101 (2022)

Joe, H.: Generating random correlation matrices based on partial correlations. J. Multivar. Anal. **97**, 2177–2189 (2006)

Simpson, E.H.: The interpretation of interaction in contingency tables. J. R. Stat. Soc. B **13**, 238–241 (1951)

Posit Team. RStudio: Integrated Development Environment for R. Posit Software, PBC, Boston, MA (2022). http://www.posit.co/

R Core Team. R: A Language and Environment for Statistical Computing. R Foundation for Statistical Computing, Vienna, Austria (2022). https://www.R-project.org/

Friedman, J., Hastie, T., Tibshirani, R.: Regularization paths for generalized linear models via coordinate descent. J. Stat. Softw. **33**(1), 1–22 (2010)

Venables, W.N., Ripley, B.D.: Modern Applied Statistics with S, 4th edn. Springer, New York (2022)

Zuo, Y., Stewart, T.G., Blume, J.D.: ProSGPV: an R package for variable selection with second-generation p-values. F1000Research **11**, 58 (2022). https://doi.org/10.12688/f1000research.74401.1

Goldfeld, K., Wujciak-Jens, J.: simstudy: illuminating research methods through data generation. J. Open Source Softw. **5**(54), 2763 (2020)

Qiu, W., Joe, H.: clusterGeneration: random cluster generation (with specified degree of separation). R version 1.3.7 (2020). https://CRAN.R-project.org/package=clusterGeneration

Makowski, D., Ben-Shachar, M., Lüdecke, D.: bayestestR: describing effects and their uncertainty, existence and significance within the Bayesian framework. J. Open Source Softw. **4**(40), 1541 (2019)

Short Papers (CMSIM 2023)

A Numerical Scheme for Solving a Mathematical Model Derived from Larvae-Algae-Mussel Interactions

Ramoni Z. S. Azevedo[1] , Charles H. X. B. Barbosa[2] ,
Isaac P. Santos[1,3](✉) , José C. R. Silva[4] , Dayse H. Pastore[4] ,
Anna R. C. Costa[4] , Claudia M. Dias[2] , Raquel M. A. Figueira[5] ,
and Humberto F. M. Fortunato[5]

[1] Federal University of Espírito Santo, Vitória, Espírito Santo, Brazil
ramoni.sedano@aluno.ufes.br
[2] Federal Rural University of Rio de Janeiro, Seropédica, Rio de Janeiro, Brazil
mazza@ufrrj.br
[3] Federal University of Espírito Santo, São Mateus, Espírito Santo, Brazil
isaac.santos@ufes.br
[4] Federal Centers of Technical Education Celso Suckow da Fonseca, Rio de Janeiro,
Rio de Janeiro, Brazil
{jose.rubianes,dayse.pastore,anna.costa}@cefet-rj.br
[5] hubz, Rio de Janeiro, Rio de Janeiro, Brazil
{raquel.figueira,humberto.fortunato}@hubz.com.br

Abstract. In this work is proposed the use of a numerical strategy based on the operator splitting technique, for solving a mathematical model for the population of the golden mussel in its adult stage, larval stage and algae (its food source) in aquatic environments, presented in [1,19]. The model is composed of three unsteady and nonlinear advective-diffusive-reactive equations for species dynamics and the Navier-Stokes equations to simulate the water velocity field. We employ the operator splitting technique in order to effectively handle the reaction terms and the stiff processes associated with the model. The numerical methodology solves the transport problem in two stages: first, given the velocity field, we solve the advective-diffusive problem to obtain the densities of larvae, algae and mussels; then, we use this first step approximation as initial condition for solving the system of ordinary differential equations for the reactions terms. The new numerical formulation is then used in a 3D simulation of golden mussel proliferation in a section of the Pereira Barreto channel (Brazil), with a focus on population control actions. Preliminary results are discussed, as well as other considerations related to numerical strategy.

Keywords: Golden Mussel · Numerical Methods · Operator Splitting Technique

O. Gervasi et al. (Eds.): ICCSA 2023 Workshops, LNCS 14112, pp. 163–172, 2023.
https://doi.org/10.1007/978-3-031-37129-5_14

1 Introduction

The existence of the non-native species *Limnoperna fortunei*, also known as the golden mussel, in rivers and reservoirs can result in several impacts to the environment and economic activities [2]. In Brazil, this mollusk species is notably abundant within hydroelectric power plant reservoirs. Within these reservoirs, the mollusks possess the tendency to obstruct pipes, grilles, and heat exchangers, as these locations provide optimal conditions for their growth and reproductive activities due to the favorable temperature settings. To deal with this problem, a two-dimensional model capturing the interactions between larvae, algae, and mussels within aquatic environments was proposed in [19]. In this work we present the three-dimensional model to illustrate the population dynamics of mussels, considering the densities of adult mussels, mussel larvae, and algae in a stretch of the Pereira Barreto channel, located in Brazil, with a focus on population control actions. This channel was chosen as the study area because it artificially connects the reservoirs of two main hydroelectric plants in the Urubupungá Complex (Brazil) in order to maximize energy production, the Ilha Solteira HPP and the Três Irmãos HPP. Both plants have an advanced degree of golden mussel infestation, as does the channel itself. The extension of the model to the three-dimensional version is challenging since a new numerical treatment is necessary to avoid oscillations and deal with the computational complexity.

A numerical formulation for solving the mathematical model is presented. As the model is composed of three unsteady and nonlinear advective-diffusive-reactive equations for species densities coupled with the Navier-Stokes equations to simulate the velocity field of the water, we employ the operator splitting technique [20] in the finite element method context in order to effectively handle the reaction terms and the stiff processes associated with the model. The numerical methodology solves the transport problem in two stages: first, given the velocity field, we solve the advective-diffusive problem to obtain the densities of larvae, algae and mussels; then, we use this first step approximation as initial condition for solving the system of ordinary differential equations for the reactions terms. In the firs step, the nonlinear stabilized finite element method SUPG - Streamline Upwind Petrov-Galerkin [3] plus CAU - Consistent Approximate Upwind [6] and the BDF2 - two-step Backward Differentiation Formula of second order [8] are employed in the spatial and time discretizations. The nonlinear process is solved by a Picard fixed point iteration [4]. In the second step, the system of ODEs for reactions is approximated by the fourth-order Runge-Kutta scheme [4], as will be seen in the next section. Numerical simulations associated with a local validation of biological and environmental variables can be used to provide a more assertive and complete view of the hydrological and ecological dynamics of the studied environment. Thus, the results can serving as an additional tool for environmental agencies and operators to manage the golden mussel in Pereira Barreto channel.

This work is organized as follows. Section 2 is devoted to present the mathematical model. In Sect. 3, we present the numerical formulation. The results of the numerical simulations are shown in Sect. 4 and Sect. 5 concludes this paper.

2   Mathematical Model

The larvae-mussel-algae model consists of finding $L = L(\boldsymbol{x}, t)$, $M = M(\boldsymbol{x}, t)$ and $A = A(\boldsymbol{x}, t)$, the densities of larvae, mussels and algae, respectively, such that

$$\frac{\partial L}{\partial t} - D_L \Delta L + \boldsymbol{u} \cdot \boldsymbol{\nabla} L = R_L(L, M, A), \text{ in } \Omega \times [0, t_F], \tag{1}$$

$$\frac{\partial M}{\partial t} - D_M \Delta M = R_M(L, M, A), \text{ in } \Omega_M \times [0, t_F], \tag{2}$$

$$\frac{\partial A}{\partial t} - D_A \Delta A + \boldsymbol{u} \cdot \boldsymbol{\nabla} A = R_A(L, M, A), \text{ in } \Omega \times [0, t_F], \tag{3}$$

where $\Omega \subset \mathbb{R}^3$ is an open and bounded domain with a Lipschitz boundary Γ, $[0, t_F]$ is the temporal interval, with $t_F > 0$, $\Omega_M \subset \Omega$ is the spatial domain for the mussels, representing a layer close to the boundary walls (solid substrates and side walls), and

$$R_L(L, M, A) = r_1 M \left(1 - \frac{L}{K_L} \right) - (b_1 + \lambda_L) L, \tag{4}$$

$$R_M(L, M, A) = \lambda_M L \left(\frac{A^2}{c_1^2 + A^2} \right) \left(1 - \frac{M}{K_M} \right) - b_2 M, \tag{5}$$

$$R_A(L, M, A) = r_2 A \left(1 - \frac{A}{K_A} \right) - b_3 \left(\frac{A^2}{c_2^2 + A^2} \right) M \tag{6}$$

are the reactive terms.

The first component of the dynamics, described by Eqs. (1) and (4), pertains to the variation in larvae population. It accounts for the growth of larvae, which is related to the adult mussel population, conforming described in Cataldo & Boltovskoy [7]. The model further incorporates a logistic growth function, given as a function of the intrinsic growth rate of the larvae population, r_1, and the carrying capacity of the larvae population, K_L [10]. The rates of mortality and maturation of the larvae are denoted as b_1 and λ_M, respectively. In order to model the spatial propagation, the mathematical formulation incorporates diffusion and advection terms, with D_L representing the larval diffusion coefficient and $\boldsymbol{u}$ denoting the flow velocity field. The second equation in the model, Eq. (2) with R_M given by (5), characterizes the dynamics of the adult mussel population. In this case, the growth of mussels is influenced by both larval maturation and the availability of algae, with studies indicating seaweed algae as the primary food source for the golden mussel

[13]. The equation incorporates a logistic growth rate, where K_M represents the carrying capacity for mussels, c_1 denotes the half-saturation constant for adults, and b_2 signifies the mortality rate resulting from fish predation. The parameter D_M corresponds to the diffusion coefficient, a measure of mussel motility caused by their pedal locomotion mechanism and its concomitant byssal thread deployment [5,14,21]. Lastly, Eqs. (3) and (6) represent the dynamics of algae. This model assumes a growth rate, denoted as r_2, with logistic growth dynamics constrained by a carrying capacity, K_A, and a mortality rate due to predation by mussels, expressed as b_3. Additionally, the mathematical formulation incorporates diffusion and advection terms, where D_A signifies the diffusion coefficient governing algae dispersal. For a comprehensive understanding of this model, we refer the interested reader to Silva et al. (2022) [19].

Dirichlet boundary conditions for larvae and algae are imposed on the inflow of the channel, whereas homogeneous Neumann boundary condition are applied to the remaining portions of the boundary. The homogeneous Neumann boundary condition signify the absence of larvae and algae movement across the boundary. To simplify the computational implementation, we consider $M = 0$ in $\Omega \backslash \Omega_M$. The initial conditions are given by

$$L(\boldsymbol{x}, 0) = L_0(\boldsymbol{x}), \quad M(\boldsymbol{x}, 0) = M_0(\boldsymbol{x}), \quad A(\boldsymbol{x}, 0) = A_0(\boldsymbol{x}), \tag{7}$$

where L_0, M_0, A_0 are given non-negative functions representing the initial densities of larvae, mussels and algae, respectively. In the larvae and algae equations, Eqs. (1) and (3), the velocity field $\boldsymbol{u}$ is obtained from the unsteady incompressible Navier-Stokes equations [18].

3   Numerical Formulation

The model (1)–(3) is a unsteady and nonlinear system of advective-diffusive-reactive equations coupled through reactive terms. The free divergence velocity field, $\boldsymbol{u}$, which appears in the larvae and algae equations, is obtained from the unsteady incompressible Navier-Stokes equations. To solve the system of three transport equations, we use operator splitting technique, presented in [17,20]. This numerical scheme consists of solving the advection and diffusion terms separately from the reaction terms. This decomposition of operators is computationally efficient in solving advective-diffusive-reactive transport problems with complex reactive terms, especially in the common case when the timescale of reactive processes is much smaller than the timescale of advective/diffusive processes [17].

Thus, the approximate solution of (1)–(3), with suitable initial and boundary conditions, is obtained in two stages, which can be solved with different time steps. In the first stage the system of homogeneous advection-diffusion equations, given by (8)–(10), is solved by the finite element method in space, coupled with the nonlinear stabilized method, Consistent Approximate Upwind (CAU) [11], and by the two-step Backward Differentiation Formula (BDF2) in time. The resulting system of nonlinear equations is solved by a Picard fixed point iteration.

In the second stage the system of ODE's for the nonlinear reactions terms, Eqs. (11)–(13), is solved by the the fourth-order Runge-Kutta scheme. These stages are shown as follow.

Stage 01: solve the system of advective-diffusive equations:

$$\frac{\partial L}{\partial t} - D_L \Delta L + \boldsymbol{u} \cdot \boldsymbol{\nabla} L = 0, \tag{8}$$

$$\frac{\partial M}{\partial t} - D_M \Delta M = 0, \tag{9}$$

$$\frac{\partial A}{\partial t} - D_A \Delta A + \boldsymbol{u} \cdot \boldsymbol{\nabla} A = 0. \tag{10}$$

Stage 02: solve the ODE's system of reactive equations:

$$\frac{\partial L}{\partial t} = R_L(L, M, A), \tag{11}$$

$$\frac{\partial M}{\partial t} = R_M(L, M, A), \tag{12}$$

$$\frac{\partial A}{\partial t} = R_A(L, M, A). \tag{13}$$

The intermediate solution obtained in each time step, Δt, in the first stage, is used as initial condition for the reaction equations in the second stage, also calculated in Δt using a much more refined time step, $\Delta t_R = \Delta t / N_R$, where N_R is the number of small time steps for the Runge-Kutta scheme in each Δt. The numerical formulation for the Navier-Stokes model is based on the Characteristic Galerkin method [9].

4   Numerical Experiments

In this section we present the numerical experiments in order to evaluate the quality of the obtained solutions, comparing it to the densities observed in the field. Recent *in situ* measurements were carried out in December 2020 and August 2021, obtaining a mussel density of 3,936 gm^{-3} and 7,546 gm^{-3}, respectively.

We used the *FreeFEM++* software [12] to generate the mesh and to solve the transient incompressible Navier-Stokes equations to obtain the velocity field. A code in *MATLAB©* platform [15] was developed to solve the system of partial differential equations, given in Eqs. (1)–(3). The 3D domain Ω represents a stretch of the Pereira Barreto channel, corresponding to one third of its total length, that is 3,200 m long, close to the Três Irmãos HPP reservoir, located in the Tietê river basin, next to the municipalities of Pereira Barreto (SP) and Andradina (SP).

We considered a period of time of 9 months to evaluate the beginning of the golden mussel infestation. The following initial values were used for the populations: $L(\boldsymbol{x}, 0) = 0.0194115$ gl^{-1}, $M(\boldsymbol{x}, 0) = 1$ gm^{-3} and $A(\boldsymbol{x}, 0) = 0.001$ gl^{-1}. The parameters used in the simulations are described in Table 1.

Table 1. Parameters used in the numerical simulations.

Parameter	Value	Unit	Reference
D_A	1.2	m^2day^{-1}	[5]
D_M	0.0012	m^2day^{-1}	[16]
D_L	0.012	m^2day^{-1}	[14]
b_1	0.015	day^{-1}	inferred
b_2, b_3	0.02	day^{-1}	inferred
λ_M, λ_L	0.03	day^{-1}	inferred
r_1	0.07	day^{-1}	inferred
r_2	0.12	day^{-1}	inferred
K_L	20	gl^{-1}	inferred
K_M	1,732	gm^{-3}	inferred
K_A	0.01	gl^{-1}	inferred
c_1, c_2	0.001	gl^{-1}	inferred

The domain was discretized with 11,184 tetrahedral elements and 50,970 nodes, conforming mesh shown in Fig. 1.

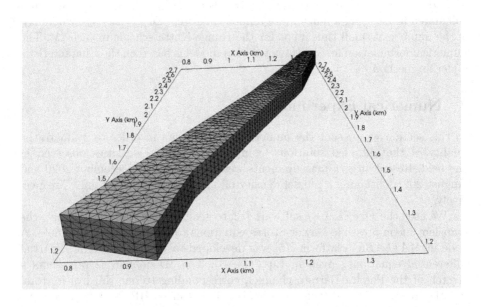

Fig. 1. Discretization of the spatial domain.

Figure 2 shows the velocity field. We use as initial condition for the Navier-Stokes equations, $u(x, 0) = 0$, in Ω. Also, a Dirichlet boundary condition on the channel inlet, for the velocity field, is given by $u = 0.13\,ms^{-1}$.

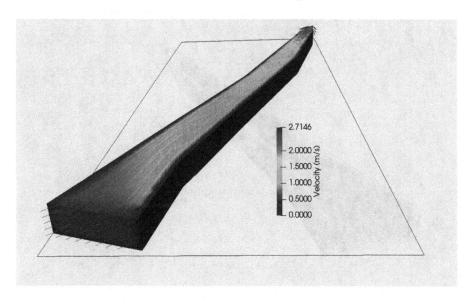

Fig. 2. Velocity field obtained from incompressible transient Navier-Stokes equations.

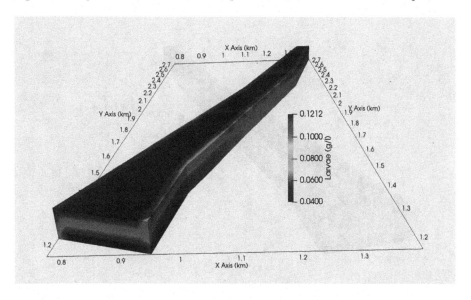

Fig. 3. Densities of Larvae after 9 months of infestation.

In the fist time step the time derivatives of the advective-diffusive equations are discretized by the Backward Euler (BDF1) method, since the BDF2 is a two-step scheme. Moreover, in each time step the algorithm performed $s_{max} = 20$ nonlinear iterations, using a Picard fixed point scheme.

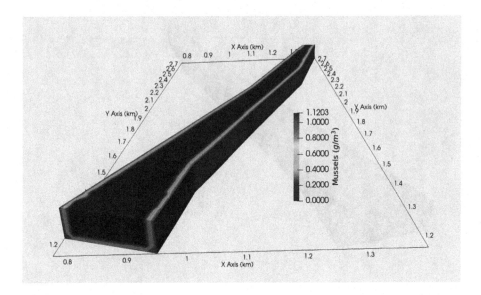

Fig. 4. Densities of Mussels after 9 months of infestation.

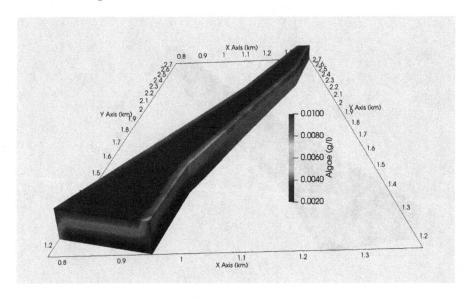

Fig. 5. Densities of Algae after 9 months of infestation.

The results for the densities of larvae, mussels and algae, in the period of 9 months, are shown in Figs. 3, 4 and 5, respectively. The larvae population at the inflow boundary is carried across the domain, due to the velocity field. In some regions far from the water flow and near the lateral boundary there is an increase in the larvae density. The mussel population, concentrated on the lateral boundary of the domain, grows as expected. The algae population is homogeneous throughout the domain with lower density near the lateral boundaries, where the mussels reside.

5 Conclusions

We have presented a numerical formulation employing the operator splitting technique to solve a complex system that arises from the interactions between larvae, algae, and mussels. This system contains both transient and nonlinear transport PDEs, making it a difficult problem to solve. To overcome this challenge, we adopted a two-stage approach where we first solved the advective-diffusive transport problems using the nonlinear stabilized finite element method, CAU, and the BDF2 scheme in time. Then, we used the fourth-order Runge-Kutta scheme to solve the system of ordinary differential equations for the reactions terms.

The work focused on studying the population dynamics of larvae, mussels, and algae over a short period of nine months. The preliminary results indicate that the model accurately represents the interaction between the populations during this initial period of infestation. The increase in mussel density supports the hypothesis that the Pereira Barreto channel serves as a nursery for the species. Additionally, the channel can serve as a passage for mussels to infest both the Tietê River, which feeds the Três Irmãos HPP reservoir, and the São José dos Dourados River, which feeds the Ilha Solteira HPP reservoir.

The operator splitting technique was very efficient in controlling the numerical oscillations generated by the complexity of the problem. In the future, we plan to run longer simulations using more refined meshes and a larger spatial domain to allow for more accurate comparisons between our numerical solutions and *in situ* data. Additionally, the numerical experiments suggest that the two-stage division scheme can significantly reduce computational time.

Acknowledgements. Research carried out within the scope of the project "Control of the Golden Mussel Infestation by Genetic Induction of Infertility" (PD-10381-0419/2019) with funding from CTG Brasil, SPIC Brasil and Tijoá Energia, within their ANEEL Research & Development Programs.

References

1. Azevedo, R.Z.S., et al.: Numerical solution of a 3d system of transient and nonlinear pdes arising from larvae-algae-mussels interactions. In: Lecture Notes in Computer Science, vol. 13377, pp. 684–697. Springer, Heidelberg (2022). https://doi.org/10.1007/978-3-031-10536-4_45
2. Boltovskoy, D., Correa, N., Cataldo, D., Sylvester, F.: Dispersion and ecological impact of the invasive freshwater bivalve limnoperna fortunei in the río de la plata watershed and beyond. Biol. Invas. 8, 947–963 (2006)

3. Brooks, A.N., Hughes, T.J.R.: Streamline upwind/petrov -galerkin formulations for convection dominated flows with particular emphasis on the incompressible navier-stokes equations. Comput. Methods Appl. Mech. Eng. **32**(1–3), 199–259 (1982)

4. Burden, R.L., Faires, J.D.: Numerical Analysis. Brooks/Cole, Cengage Learning (2011)

5. Cangelosi, R.A., Wollkind, D.J., Kealy-Dichone, B.J., Chaiya, I.: Nonlinear stability analyses of turing patterns for a mussel-algae model. J. Math. Biol. **70**(6), 1249–1294 (2015)

6. Carmo, E.G.D., Alvarez, G.B.: A new stabilized finite element formulation for scalar convection-diffusion problems: the streamline and approximate upwind/petrov-galerkin method. Comput. Methods Appl. Mech. Eng. **192**(31–32), 3379–3396 (2003)

7. Cataldo, D., Boltovskoy, D.: Yearly reproductive activity of limnoperna fortune(bivalvia) as inferred from the occurrence of its larvae in the plankton of the lower paraná river and the río de la plata estuary (argentina). Aquat. Ecol. **34**(3), 307–317 (2000)

8. Curtiss, C.F., Hirschfelder, J.O.: Integration of stiff equations. Proc. Natl. Acad. Sci. **38**(3), 235–243 (1952)

9. Donea, J., Huerta, A.: Finite Element Methods for Flow Problems. John Wiley & Sons, Ltd., Hoboken (2000)

10. Edelstein-Keshet, L.: Mathematical models in biology. Society for Industrial and Applied Mathematics (2005)

11. Galeão, A.C., do Carmo, E.G.D.: A consistent approximate upwind Petrov-Galerkin method for convection-dominated problems. Comput. Methods Appl. Mech. Eng. **68**, 83–95 (1988)

12. Hecht, F.: Freefem documentation. release 4.8 (2022). https://freefem.org/

13. Karatayev, A., Burlakova, L., Padilla, D.: The effects of dreissena polymorpha (pallas) invasion on aquatic communities in eastern Europe. J. Shellfish Res. **16**, 18–203 (1997)

14. van de Koppel A.D.M., Rietkerk, J., Herman, N.D.A.P.M.J.: Scale-dependent feedback and regular spatial patterns in young mussel beds. Am. Nat. 165(3), E66–E77 (2005)

15. MATLAB: Matlab manual switch (2022). https://www.mathworks.com/products/matlab.html

16. Montresor, L.C.: Implicações Ecotoxicológicas do controle químico de Limnoperna fortunei (Dunker 1857 (Bivalvia: Mytilidae). Ph.D. thesis, Universidade Federal de Minas Gerais (2014)

17. Odencrantz, J.E.: Modeling the biodegradation kinetics of dissolved organic contaminants in a heterogeneous two-dimensional aquifer. Ph.D. thesis, Graduate College of the University of Ilinois at Urbana-Champaign (1992)

18. Pritchard, R.R.F.A.P.J., McDonald, A.T.: Introdução à Mecânica dos Fluidos. Gen-LTC (2000)

19. Silva, J.C.R., et al.: Population growth of the golden mussel (l. fortunei) in hydro-electric power plants: a study via mathematical and computational modeling. Braz. J. Water Res. **27**, 1–15 (2022). https://doi.org/10.1590/2318-0331.272220210124

20. Wheeler, M.: Modeling of highly advective flow problems. In: Developments in Water Science, vol. 35, pp. 35–44. Elsevier (1988)

21. Zhou, D., Liu, M., Qi, K., Liu, Z.: Long-time behaviors of two stochastic mussel-algae models. Math. Biosci. Eng. **18**(6), 8392–8414 (2021)

The Role of the Essential Manifold in Data Mining – An Introductory Approach

Maria de Fátima Pina[1,2,3](✉) and Marina Alexandra Andrade[1,4]

[1] ISCTE - IUL, University Institute of Lisbon, Av. das Forças Armadas,
1649-026 Lisbon, Portugal
mfdpina@gmail.com, marina.andrade@iscte-iul.pt

[2] ISLA - Santarém, Superior Institute of Management and Administration of
Santarém, Rua Teixeira Guedes, 31, 2000-029 Santarém, Portugal

[3] ISR - UC, Institute of Systems and Robotics, Department of Electrical and
Computer Engineering, University of Coimbra, Rua Silvio Lima - Pólo II,
3030-290 Coimbra, Portugal
mfdpina@gmail.com

[4] ISTAR - IUL, Information Sciences and Technologies and Architecture Research
Center, University Institute of Lisbon, Av. das Forças Armadas,
1649-026 Lisbon, Portugal

Abstract. Interpolating data and the application of data mining techniques in nonlinear manifolds plays a significant role in different areas of knowledge, ranging from computer vision and robotics, to industrial and medical requests, and these growing number of applications have sparked the research interest of the scientific community to these topics. The Generalized Essential manifold, briefly, Essential manifold, consisting of the product of the Grassmann manifold of all k-dimensional subspaces of $\mathbb{R}^n$ and the Lie group of rotations in $\mathbb{R}^n$, for instance, plays an important role in the problem of recovering the structure and motion from a sequence of images, also known as stereo matching, which is a crucial problem in image processing and computer vision. A well-known recursive procedure to generate interpolating polynomial curves in Euclidean spaces is the classical De Casteljau algorithm, which is a simple and powerful tool widely used in the field of Computer Aided Geometric Design, particularly because it is essentially geometrically based. This algorithm has been generalized to geodesically complete Riemannian manifolds. Thus, having this in mind, in this work we present all the ingredients for a detailed implementation of the generalized De Casteljau algorithm to generate geometric cubic polynomials in the Essential manifold preparing the ground to solve different real interpolation problems in this manifold.

Keywords: Cubic polynomials · Essential manifold · De Casteljau algorithm · Geodesics · Data mining · Interpolating data

O. Gervasi et al. (Eds.): ICCSA 2023 Workshops, LNCS 14112, pp. 173–183, 2023.
https://doi.org/10.1007/978-3-031-37129-5_15

1   Introdution

Interpolation problems involving data on nonlinear manifolds is a topic that appears in a vast number of applications such that face recognition, biomedical image analysis, automobile safety, fingerprint recognition, and in many other problems where large sets of data allow the extraction of important information and identification of patterns.

For illustration, consider the problem of recovering structure and motion from a sequence of images, also known as stereo matching, which is a key problem in computer vision that continues to be one of the most active research areas with remarkable progress in imaging and computing. We refer, for instance, [3,10,15] and references therein for details concerning multiple applications.

The mentioned examples served as a motivation for our study and the main goal of this work is to present an approach for solving interpolation problems on the Generalized Essential manifold highlighting its contribution to data mining.

This manifold is the product of the Grassmann manifold $G_{k,n}$, consisting of all k-dimensional linear subspaces of the real n-dimensional Euclidean space, and the Lie group of rotations $SO(n)$. One particular case of that is the Normalized Essential manifold, corresponding to $k = 2$ and $n = 3$, which plays an important role in image processing. The classical problem of reconstructing a scene, or a video, from several images of the scene can be formulated as an interpolation problem on that manifold, since it encodes the epipolar constraint. Typically, it is given an ordered set of time-labeled essential matrices, $E_1, \ldots, E_j$, relating j different consecutive camera views (*snapshots*), and the aim is to calculate a continuum of additional virtual views by computing a smooth interpolating curve through the E_i's, $i = 1, \ldots, j$.

The De Casteljau algorithm has been used for a long time and on a widely variety of different areas. For a general introduction of the classical version of this algorithm and an overview of the historical evolution and existing works dealing with this concept we can mention, for instance, [6] and literature cited therein. Since most real life problems require the application of the De Casteljau algorithm in manifolds different from the Euclidean space $\mathbb{R}^m$, generalizations of this algorithm to other manifolds where performed, and there are known in the literature many references of works relating to the study of the algorithm, in other manifolds, and with different approaches. Just to name a few, see for instance, [1,4,11,12].

Although the existence in the literature of different methods for interpolating data in manifolds, the motivation to use, in this work, for the Essential manifold, the generalization of the classical De Casteljau algorithm for geodesically complete Riemannian manifolds, was based essentially in the fact that this algorithm is a powerful tool widely used and with a geometric and an algebraic feature that with recursive geodesic interpolation, allows to generate interpolating polynomial curves on manifolds.

In order not to be too exhaustive in this introductory section, more details concerned with this topic will appear in development sections.

2   Preliminaries and Notations

In this section, we provide preliminaries and introduce some notations that will be used throughout the paper. In this sense, we start to notice that the matrix groups are the most common examples of Lie groups which have greatest application in computer vision problems, robotics, engineering and control theory problems. These groups are all subgroups of the General Linear Group $GL_n(\mathbb{R})$, the group of all real $n \times n$ invertible matrices, whose Lie algebra is $\mathfrak{gl}(n)$, the set of all $n \times n$ matrices with real entries, equipped with the commutator of matrices $[A, B] = AB - BA$ as the Lie bracket. The adjoint operator in $\mathfrak{gl}(n)$ is defined by $\mathrm{ad}_A B := [A, B]$ and, in the sequel, we consider $\mathfrak{gl}(n)$ equipped with the Euclidean inner product

$$\langle X, Y \rangle = \mathrm{tr}(X^\top Y), \ X, Y \in \mathfrak{gl}(n). \tag{1}$$

Given $X \in \mathfrak{gl}(n)$, the *matrix exponential of* X, denoted by e^X, is the $n \times n$ real matrix given by the sum of the following convergent power series $\mathrm{e}^X = \sum_{k=0}^{+\infty} \frac{X^k}{k!}$, where X^0 is defined to be the identity matrix I.

The vector space of $\mathfrak{gl}(n)$ consisting of all symmetric matrices is denoted by $\mathfrak{s}(n)$, while $\mathfrak{so}(n)$ denotes the Lie subalgebra of $\mathfrak{gl}(n)$ consisting of all skew-symmetric matrices. It is well-known that $\mathfrak{gl}(n) = \mathfrak{s}(n) \oplus \mathfrak{so}(n)$, is a decomposition of the Lie algebra $\mathfrak{gl}(n)$, and that $[\mathfrak{so}(n), \mathfrak{so}(n)] \subset \mathfrak{so}(n)$, $[\mathfrak{so}(n), \mathfrak{s}(n)] \subset \mathfrak{s}(n)$ and $[\mathfrak{s}(n), \mathfrak{s}(n)] \subset \mathfrak{so}(n)$. Also, $\mathfrak{so}(n)$ and $\mathfrak{s}(n)$ are orthogonal with respect to the inner product (1). The rotation group $SO(n)$, having $\mathfrak{so}(n)$ as its Lie algebra, will also play a relevant role here.

It is important to mention that the logarithms of an invertible matrix B are the solutions of the matrix equation $\mathrm{e}^X = B$, and when B is real and doesn't have eigenvalues in the closed negative real line, i.e., when $\sigma(B) \cap \mathbb{R}_0^- = \varnothing$, where $\sigma(B)$ denotes the spectrum of B, there exists a unique real logarithm of B whose spectrum lies in the infinite horizontal strip $\{z \in \mathbb{C} : -\pi < Im(z) < \pi\}$ of the complex plane. In this work we will only consider this logarithm, usually called the *principal logarithm* of B and hereafter denoted by $\log B$. When B belongs to the rotation group $SO(n)$, then $\log B$ belongs to its Lie algebra $\mathfrak{so}(n)$. Further, when $\|B - I\| < 1$, $\log B$ is uniquely defined by the following convergent power series: $\log B = \sum_{k=1}^{+\infty} (-1)^{k+1} \frac{(B - I)^k}{k}$. This power series defines the principal logarithm for matrices which are close to the identity matrix. However, for $\alpha \in [-1, 1]$, $\log(B^\alpha) = \alpha \log B$, so that, making $\alpha = 1/2^k$, with $k \in \mathbb{Z}$, one has $\log\left(B^{\frac{1}{2^k}}\right) = \frac{1}{2^k} \log B$. Further, since $\lim_{k \to +\infty} \left(B^{\frac{1}{2^k}}\right) = I$, the previous expression allows to compute $\log B$ even for matrices B which are not close to the identity. This procedure is called *inverse scaling and squaring method* and can be found, e.g., in [7]. More properties of these matrices functions are available, for instance, in [7,8], but we emphasize here the identity

$e^A De^{-A} = e^{\mathrm{ad}_A} D = D + [A, D] + \dfrac{1}{2!}[A, [A, D]] + \cdots$, which plays an important role in this work.

3   The Geometry of the Essential Manifold

Let n be a positive integer and let k be a positive integer smaller than n. The Generalized Essential manifold $G_{k,n} \times \mathrm{SO}(n)$, briefly, Essential manifold, is the cartesian product of the real Grassmann manifold $G_{k,n}$, consisting of all k-dimensional (linear) subspaces of $\mathbb{R}^n$, and the rotation orthogonal group $\mathrm{SO}(n)$ of all orientation preserving rotational transformations in $\mathbb{R}^n$. Therefore, we have that

$$G_{k,n} \times \mathrm{SO}(n) = \{(S, R) : S \in G_{k,n},\ R \in \mathrm{SO}(n)\}. \tag{2}$$

This manifold is a smooth compact and connected manifold of real dimension $k(n - k) + n(n - 1)/2$ which can be seen as an embedded submanifold of $\mathfrak{s}(n) \times \mathbb{R}^{n \times n}$.

Each subspace of the Grassmann manifold $G_{k,n}$ can be associated to a unique operator of orthogonal projections onto itself, with respect to the Euclidean metric, and it is well-known that these operators (or, equivalently, its matrices, called projection matrices) are symmetric, idempotent, and have rank k. Therefore, in this work, similarly to [2,9], and [14] we use the following matrix representation of the Grassmann manifold

$$G_{k,n} := \left\{ S \in \mathfrak{s}(n) : S^2 = S \text{ and } \mathrm{rank}(S) = k \right\}, \tag{3}$$

which is also a smooth compact connected manifold of real dimension $k(n - k)$, and an isospectral manifold, where each element has the eigenvalues 1 and 0, with multiplicity k and $n - k$, respectively. Defining, for an arbitrary point $S \in G_{k,n}$, the sets of matrices

$$\mathfrak{gl}_S(n) := \{A \in \mathfrak{gl}(n) : A = SA + AS\}; \quad \mathfrak{so}_S(n) := \mathfrak{so}(n) \cap \mathfrak{gl}_S(n), \tag{4}$$

the tangent space at a point $P = (S, R) \in G_{k,n} \times \mathrm{SO}(n)$ can be defined by

$$\begin{aligned} T_P\left(G_{k,n} \times \mathrm{SO}(n)\right) &= \{([\Omega, S], RY) : \Omega \in \mathfrak{so}_S(n),\ Y \in \mathfrak{so}(n)\} \\ &= \left\{ \left(\mathrm{ad}_S^2(A), RY\right) : A \in \mathfrak{s}(n),\ Y \in \mathfrak{so}(n) \right\}. \end{aligned} \tag{5}$$

We consider the Essential manifold equipped with the Riemannian metric, induced by the Euclidean inner product on each tangent space, given by

$$\langle ([\Omega_1, S], RY_1), ([\Omega_2, S], RY_2) \rangle = \mathrm{tr}(\Omega_1^T \Omega_2) + \mathrm{tr}(Y_1^T Y_2). \tag{6}$$

Moreover, using the last description of the tangent space at $P \in G_{k,n} \times \mathrm{SO}(n)$, the normal space at P, with respect to the Riemannian metric (6), can be defined as follows

$$\left(T_P\left(G_{k,n} \times \mathrm{SO}(n)\right)\right)^{\perp} = \left\{ \left(A - \mathrm{ad}_S^2(A), RB\right) : A,\ B \in \mathfrak{s}(n) \right\}. \tag{7}$$

Bellow, we present a result for the Grassmann manifold $G_{k,n}$, that will be important to better understand further developments, and whose proof can be found in [13].

Lemma 1. *Let $S \in G_{k,n}$, $A, B \in \mathfrak{gl}_S(n)$ and $t \in \mathbb{R}$. Then,*

$$[A, S] = [B, S] \Leftrightarrow A = B; \tag{8}$$

$$e^{2tA}(I - 2S) = e^{\mathrm{ad}_{tA}}(I - 2S). \tag{9}$$

Now, we present some results about geodesics in the Essential manifold with respect to the Riemannian metric in (6).

3.1 Geodesics and Geodesic Distance

In this subsection, as mention, we present some results in order to compute explicitly, in $G_{k,n} \times \mathrm{SO}(n)$, the geodesic satisfying some initial conditions, the minimizing geodesic arc joining two points and the geodesic distance between two points of the Essential manifold.

Proposition 1. *The unique geodesic $t \mapsto \gamma(t)$ in $G_{k,n} \times \mathrm{SO}(n)$, satisfying the initial conditions $\gamma(0) = (S, R)$ and $\dot{\gamma}(0) = ([\Omega, S], RY)$, where $\Omega \in \mathfrak{so}_S(n)$ and $Y \in \mathfrak{so}(n)$, is given by*

$$\gamma(t) = (\gamma_1(t), \gamma_2(t)) = \left(e^{t\Omega} S e^{-t\Omega}, R e^{tY}\right) = \left(e^{t\,\mathrm{ad}_\Omega} S, R e^{tY}\right). \tag{10}$$

Proof. A detailed proof for the expression of γ_1 in $G_{k,n}$ can be found in [2], and since geodesics on $\mathrm{SO}(n)$ are translations of one parameter subgroups of $\mathrm{SO}(n)$ the proof of the expression γ_2 is immediate.

Remark 1. We note that any two points in the Essential manifold can be joined by a geodesic. This follows from the fact that $G_{k,n} \times \mathrm{SO}(n)$ is geodesically complete. However, to obtain an explicit formula for the geodesic that joins two points it is necessary to require some restrictions expressed in the following result.

Proposition 2. *Let $P = (S_1, R_1)$, $Q = (S_2, R_2) \in G_{k,n} \times \mathrm{SO}(n)$ be such that $\sigma\left((I - 2S_2)(I - 2S_1)\right) \cap \mathbb{R}^- = \varnothing$ and $\sigma(R_1^{-1}R_2) \cap \mathbb{R}^- = \varnothing$. Then, the minimizing geodesic arc in $G_{k,n} \times \mathrm{SO}(n)$, with respect to the Riemannian metric (6), that joins P (at $t = 0$) to Q (at $t = 1$), is parameterized explicitly by*

$$\gamma(t) = (\gamma_1(t), \gamma_2(t)) = \left(e^{t\,\mathrm{ad}_\Omega} S_1, R_1 e^{tY}\right), \tag{11}$$

or, equivalently, by

$$\gamma(t) = (\gamma_1(t), \gamma_2(t)) = \left(e^{t\,\mathrm{ad}_\Omega} S_1, e^{t\overline{Y}} R_1\right), \tag{12}$$

where

$$\begin{aligned} \Omega &:= \tfrac{1}{2}\log((I - 2S_2)(I - 2S_1)) \in \mathfrak{so}_{S_1}(n) \\ Y &:= \log(R_1^{-1}R_2), \quad \overline{Y} := \log(R_2 R_1^{-1}) \in \mathfrak{so}(n). \end{aligned} \tag{13}$$

Proof. The proof of the expression γ_2 is immediate. The proof of the expression γ_1, for the best of our knowledge, appeared for the first time in [2], and an easier alternative proof, taking in account Lemma 1, can be found in [13].

Remark 2. Notice that, since $\sigma(R_2 R_1^{-1}) = \sigma(R_1^{-1} R_2)$, we have that the condition $\sigma(R_1^{-1} R_2) \cap \mathbb{R}^- = \varnothing$, automatically, implies that $\sigma(R_2 R_1^{-1}) \cap \mathbb{R}^- = \varnothing$, and thus $\overline{Y}$ is well defined.

We end this section with the geodesic distance between two points P and Q in $G_{k,n} \times SO(n)$, witch is the length of the minimal geodesic curve connecting them. Therefore, considering the Riemannian metric (6), it is possible to reach the next result, whose proof is immediate.

Proposition 3. *Let $P = (S_1, R_1), Q = (S_2, R_2) \in G_{k,n} \times SO(n)$ be such that $\sigma((I - 2S_2)(I - 2S_1)) \cap \mathbb{R}^- = \varnothing$ and $\sigma(R_1^{-1} R_2) \cap \mathbb{R}^- = \varnothing$. Then, the geodesic distance between the points P and Q is given, explicitly, by*

$$
\begin{aligned}
d^2(P, Q) &= d_1^2(S_1, S_2) + d_2^2(R_1, R_2) \\
&= -\frac{1}{4}\mathrm{tr}\left(\log^2((I - 2S_2)(I - 2S_1))\right) - \mathrm{tr}\left(\log^2(R_1^{-1} R_2)\right)
\end{aligned}
\tag{14}
$$

or, equivalently, by

$$
d^2(P, Q) = -\frac{1}{4}\mathrm{tr}\left(\log^2((I - 2S_2)(I - 2S_1))\right) - \mathrm{tr}\left(\log^2(R_2 R_1^{-1})\right).
\tag{15}
$$

4   De Casteljau Algorithm in the Essential Manifold

We start this section by presenting a review of the generalized De Casteljau algorithm to generate cubic polynomials in geodesically complete Riemannian manifolds. Then, following the approach of [4] for connected and compact Lie groups and for spheres, and the work of [14] for the Grassmann manifold we present a detailed implementation of the De Casteljau algorithm for the generation of cubic polynomials in the Essential manifold.

4.1   Review of the Generalized de Casteljau Algorithm

Let M be a m-dimensional connected Riemannian manifold, which is also geodesically complete, so that any pair of points may be joined by a geodesic arc.

The classical version of the De Casteljau algorithm was developed at 1959 by Paul De Casteljau [5], and it is a recursive process to generate interpolating polynomial curves of arbitrary degree in the Euclidean space $\mathbb{R}^m$. These curves, generated by successive linear interpolation, are known in the literature as Bernstein-Bézier curves or, simply, Bézier curves (see, e.g., [6]).

The generalized De Casteljau algorithm is an extension of this classical version for an arbitrary manifold, and where the linear interpolation is replaced by geodesic interpolation, this being the reason why we need to assume that the manifold M is geodesically complete, at least in a sufficiently big neighbourhood of the given data points.

In what follows, we present a description of this general De Casteljau algorithm for generating geometric cubic polynomials on M. For the sake of simplicity, we parameterize the curves on the $[0, 1]$ interval, but notice that there's no loss of generality, since this interval can be replaced by any other interval $[a, b]$, $a < b$, just by choosing the reparametrization $(t \rightarrow s)$ defined by $t = (s - a)/(b - a)$.

Therefore, we have that given a set of four distinct points $\{x_0, x_1, x_2, x_3\}$ in M, a smooth curve $t \in [0, 1] \mapsto \beta_3(t) := \beta_3(t, x_0, x_1, x_2, x_3)$ in M, joining x_0 (at $t = 0$) and x_3 (at $t = 1$), can be constructed by three successive geodesic interpolation steps as follows.

Generalized de Casteljau Algorithm

Step 1. Construct three geodesic arcs $\beta_1(t, x_i, x_{i+1})$, $t \in [0, 1]$ joining, for $i = 0, 1, 2$, the points x_i (at $t = 0$) and x_{i+1} (at $t = 1$).

Step 2. Construct two families of geodesic arcs

$$\beta_2(t, x_0, x_1, x_2) = \beta_1(t, \beta_1(t, x_0, x_1), \beta_1(t, x_1, x_2)),$$
$$\beta_2(t, x_1, x_2, x_3) = \beta_1(t, \beta_1(t, x_1, x_2), \beta_1(t, x_2, x_3)),$$

joining, for $i = 0, 1$ and $t \in [0, 1]$, the point $\beta_1(t, x_i, x_{i+1})$ (at $t = 0$) with the point $\beta_1(t, x_{i+1}, x_{i+2})$ (at $t = 1$).

Step 3. Construct the family of geodesic arcs

$$\beta_3(t, x_0, x_1, x_2, x_3) = \beta_1(t, \beta_2(t, x_0, x_1, x_2), \beta_2(t, x_1, x_2, x_3)),$$

joining, for each $t \in [0, 1]$, the points $\beta_2(t, x_0, x_1, x_2)$ (at $t = 0$) and $\beta_2(t, x_1, x_2, x_3)$ (at $t = 1$).

The curve $t \in [0, 1] \mapsto \beta_3(t) := \beta_3(t, x_0, x_1, x_2, x_3)$ obtained in Step 3. of the previous Algorithm is called *geometric cubic polynomial* in M. It is important to observe that this curve joins the points x_0 (at $t = 0$) and x_3 (at $t = 1$), but does not pass through the other two points x_1 and x_2. We illustrate this situation in Fig. 1, for the particular situation when the manifold M is the Euclidean space $\mathbb{R}^m$.

These points are usually called by *control points*, since they influence the shape of the curve. This algorithm can also be used to generate $\mathcal{C}^2$-smooth *geometric cubic polynomial splines* by piecing together, in a smooth manner, several geometric cubic polynomials and which are interpolating curves of the data.

A few remarks should be made concerning the general applicability of this construction. In fact, although the geometry of a Riemannian manifold possesses enough structure to formulate the construction, the basic ingredients used, the geodesic arcs, are implicitly defined by a set of nonlinear differential equations. Therefore, this algorithm can be only practically implemented when we can reduce the calculation of these geodesic arcs to a manageable form.

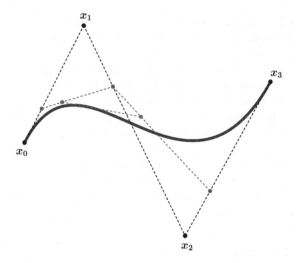

Fig. 1. Cubic polynomial defined by the De Casteljau algorithm in $\mathbb{R}^m$.

For this reason, in what follows we will present the implementation of the generalized De Casteljau algorithm, when the manifold M is the Essential manifold.

4.2   Implementation of the de Casteljau Algorithm in the Essential Manifold

Although the Essential manifold is geodesically complete, we have seen that an explicit formula for the geodesic that joins two points may be unknown in some particular situations. So, in this case the implementation of the De Casteljau algorithm is restricted to a convex open subset of the manifold where the expression to compute the geodesic arc joining two points is well-defined.

The generation of a geometric cubic polynomial in the Essential manifold $G_{k,n} \times SO(n)$, starts from four given points $x_0 = (S_0, R_0)$, $x_1 = (S_1, R_1)$, $x_2 = (S_2, R_2)$, $x_3 = (S_3, R_3)$ in $G_{k,n} \times SO(n)$.

Algorithm. Notice that, for $i = 0, 1, 2$ and $j = 1, 2, 3$, the superscripts in the operators Ω_i^j and V_i^j below are chosen according to the corresponding step.

Step 1. For $i = 0, 1, 2$, construct the geodesic arc joining the point x_i (at $t = 0$) with x_{i+1} (at $t = 1$), and given by

$$\beta_1(t, x_i, x_{i+1}) = (\beta_1(t, S_i, S_{i+1}), \beta_1(t, R_i, R_{i+1})) = \left(e^{t \, \mathrm{ad}_{\Omega_i^1}} S_i, \ R_i e^{t V_i^1} \right), \quad (16)$$

with

$$\begin{aligned}
\Omega_i^1 &:= \frac{1}{2} \log((I - 2S_{i+1})(I - 2S_i)) \in \mathfrak{so}_{S_i}(n) \\
V_i^1 &:= \log(R_i^{-1} R_{i+1}) \in \mathfrak{so}(n).
\end{aligned} \quad (17)$$

Step 2. Construct, for each $t \in [0, 1]$, two geodesic arcs. The first, joining the points $\beta_1(t, x_0, x_1)$ and $\beta_1(t, x_1, x_2)$, and defined by

$$\beta_2(t, x_0, x_1, x_2) = \left(e^{t \operatorname{ad} \Omega_0^2(t)} \beta_1(t, S_0, S_1), R_0 e^{t V_0^1} e^{t V_0^2(t)}\right), \qquad (18)$$

with

$$\begin{aligned}
\Omega_0^2(t) &:= \frac{1}{2} \log((I - 2\beta_1(t, S_1, S_2))(I - 2\beta_1(t, S_0, S_1))) \in \mathfrak{so}_{\beta_1(t,S_0,S_1)}(n) \\
V_0^2(t) &:= \log(e^{(1-t)V_0^1} e^{t V_1^1}) \in \mathfrak{so}(n).
\end{aligned} \qquad (19)$$

The second one, joining the points $\beta_1(t, x_1, x_2)$ and $\beta_1(t, x_2, x_3)$, and given by

$$\beta_2(t, x_1, x_2, x_3) = \left(e^{t \operatorname{ad} \Omega_1^2(t)} \beta_1(t, S_1, S_2), R_1 e^{t V_1^1} e^{t V_1^2(t)}\right), \qquad (20)$$

with

$$\begin{aligned}
\Omega_1^2(t) &:= \frac{1}{2} \log\left((I - 2\beta_1(t, S_2, S_3))(I - 2\beta_1(t, S_1, S_2))\right) \in \mathfrak{so}_{\beta_1(t,S_1,S_2)}(n) \\
V_1^2(t) &:= \log(e^{(1-t)V_1^1} e^{t V_2^1}) \in \mathfrak{so}(n).
\end{aligned} \qquad (21)$$

Step 3. Construct, for each $t \in [0, 1]$, the geodesic arc connecting the point $\beta_2(t, x_0, x_1, x_2)$ with the point $\beta_2(t, x_1, x_2, x_3)$, and defined by

$$\beta_3(t, x_0, x_1, x_2, x_3) = \left(e^{t \operatorname{ad} \Omega_0^3(t)} \beta_2(t, S_0, S_1, S_2), R_0 e^{t V_0^1} e^{t V_0^2(t)} e^{t V_0^3(t)}\right), \qquad (22)$$

with

$$\begin{aligned}
\Omega_0^3(t) &:= \frac{1}{2} \log((I - 2\beta_2(t, S_1, S_2, S_3))(I - 2\beta_2(t, S_0, S_1, S_2))) \in \mathfrak{so}_{\beta_2(t,S_0,S_1,S_2)}(n) \\
V_0^3(t) &:= \log(e^{(1-t)V_0^2(t)} e^{t V_1^2(t)}) \in \mathfrak{so}(n).
\end{aligned}$$
$$(23)$$

As a result, and taking into consideration (16), (18), (20) and (22), we obtain the geometric cubic polynomial in the Essential manifold.

Definition 1. *The curve* $t \in [0, 1] \mapsto \beta_3(t) := \beta_3(t, x_0, x_1, x_2, x_3)$ *defined by*

$$\beta_3(t) = \left(e^{t \operatorname{ad} \Omega_0^3(t)} e^{t \operatorname{ad} \Omega_0^2(t)} e^{t \operatorname{ad} \Omega_0^1} S_0, R_0 e^{t V_0^1} e^{t V_0^2(t)} e^{t V_0^3(t)}\right), \qquad (24)$$

with Ω_0^1, Ω_0^2, Ω_0^3, V_0^1, V_0^2 *and* V_0^3 *given by (17), (19) and (23), is called a* geometric cubic polynomial *in the Essential manifold* $G_{k,n} \times SO(n)$, *associated to the points* x_i, $i = 0, 1, 2, 3$.

Remark 3. Notice that, as expected, the curve just defined joins the points x_0 (at $t = 0$) and x_3 (at $t = 1$). It is obvious that $\beta_3(0) = x_0$. To see that $\beta_3(1) = x_3$, we start to observe that, from the definition of Ω_i^j and V_i^j, $i = 0, 1, 2$, $j = 1, 2, 3$, it can be easily derived the following boundary conditions:

- $\Omega_0^2(0) = \Omega_0^3(0) = \Omega_0^1$, $\Omega_1^2(0) = \Omega_1^1$, $\Omega_1^2(1) = \Omega_0^3(1) = \Omega_2^1$, and $\Omega_0^2(1) = \Omega_1^1$;
- $V_0^2(0) = V_0^3(0) = V_0^1$, $V_1^2(0) = V_1^1$, $V_1^2(1) = V_0^3(1) = V_2^1$, and $V_0^2(1) = V_1^1$.

Thus, considering these boundary conditions together with the definition of the geodesic arcs (16), we obtain that $\beta_3(1) = x_3$.

5   Conclusion and Future Work

We have presented all the details to implement the De Casteljau algorithm in the Essential manifold. As regarded, the implementation of the algorithm in this manifold requires that one knows how to compute matrix exponentials of skewsymmetric matrices and logarithms of orthogonal matrices.

For practical applications in data mining, one still has to rely on computing stable matrix exponentials and logarithms of structured matrices, since there are no explicit formulas to compute those matrix functions. However, when $k = 2$ and $n = 3$, we have explicit formulas to compute those matrices functions.

Efficient numerical methods to compute matrix functions have been developed along the years (see, for instance, [7]), and this is one of our future work.

Acknowledgements. The authors acknowledge Fundação para a Ciência e a Tecnologia (FCT) and COMPETE 2020 program for financial support to projects UIDB/00048/2020 and UIDB/04466/2020.

References

1. Altafini, C.: The De Casteljau algorithm on SE(3). In: Lecture Notes in Control and Information Sciences. Springer, London (2007). https://doi.org/10.1007/BFb0110205
2. Batzies, E., Hüper, K., Machado, L., Silva Leite, F.: Geometric mean and geodesic regression on grassmannians. Linear Algebra Appl. **466**, 83–101 (2015)
3. Bressan, B.: From Physics to Daily Life: Applications in Informatics, Energy, and Environment. Wiley-Blackwell, Hoboken (2014)
4. Crouch, P., Kun, G., Leite, F.S.: The De Casteljau algorithm on Lie groups and spheres. J. Dyn. Control Syst. **5**(3), 397–429 (1999)
5. de Casteljau, P.: Outillages Méthodes Calcul. Technical Report, André Citroën Automobiles SA (1959)
6. Farin, G.: Curves and Surfaces for Computer-Aided Geometric Design - A Practical Guide, 5th edn. Academic Press, New York (2002)
7. Higham, N.: Functions of Matrices: Theory and Computation. SIAM (2008)
8. Horn, R.A., Johnson, C.R.: Topics in Matrix Analysis. Cambridge University Press, New York (1991)
9. Hüper, K., Leite, F.S.: On the geometry of rolling and interpolation curves on S^n, SO(n), and Grassmann manifolds. J. Dyn. Control Syst. **4**, 467–502 (2007)
10. Ma, Y., Soatto, S., Kosecká, J., Sastry, S.: An Invitation to 3D Vision: From Images to Geometric Models. Springer, New York (2004). https://doi.org/10.1007/978-0-387-21779-6
11. Nava-Yazdani, E., Polthier, K.: De Casteljau's algorithm on manifolds. Comput. Aided Geom. Des. **30**(7), 722–732 (2013)

12. Park, F., Ravani, B.: Bézier curves on Riemannian manifolds and Lie groups with kinematics applications. ASME J. Mech. Des. **117**, 36–40 (1995)
13. Pina, F., Silva Leite, F.: Cubic splines in the Grassmann manifold generated by the De Casteljau algorithm. In: Preprint Series - Department of Mathematics - University of Coimbra, Portugal, no. 20–07 (2020)
14. Pina, F., Silva Leite, F.: Cubic splines in the Grassmann manifold. In: Gonçalves, J.A., Braz-César, M., Coelho, J.P. (eds.) CONTROLO 2020. LNEE, vol. 695, pp. 243–252. Springer, Cham (2021). https://doi.org/10.1007/978-3-030-58653-9_23
15. Szeliski, R.: Computer Vision: Algorithms and Applications. Texts in Computer Science, Springer, London (2011). https://doi.org/10.1007/978-1-84882-935-0

Short Paper (DTS 2023)

Experimental Comparison of Clustering Approaches for Personalized Federated Learning

Seohee Choi, Minjung Park, and Sangmi Chai[✉]

Ewha Womans University, Seoul, Republic of Korea
seohee.choi@ewhain.net, smchai@ewha.ac.kr

Abstract. Federated learning allows clients to collaboratively train a global model while preserving data privacy. However, personalized the global model is necessary for each device to prevent performance degradation caused by the heterogeneity of each client's local data. In this paper, we discuss previously studied client clustering techniques for personalized federated learning. We also evaluate the performance of personalized models generated by various federated learning and client clustering algorithms. Our research aims to bridge the research gap by evaluating the effectiveness of personalized models when applied to users.

Keywords: Clustering · Federated Learning · Personalized Federated Learning

1 Introduction

Federated learning is a method for training a unified global model in a distributed system without transferring data belonging to each client. It saves the computing resources of edge devices to train local models without requiring direct access to client-owned data, enabling model training while preserving data privacy. It has become increasingly important with the introduction of data privacy laws such as General Data Protection Regulation (GDPR).

In federated learning, heterogeneous local data distributions compared to the distributional level of the global model can lead to poor prediction performance. In a typical federated learning approach, local models trained on edge devices with highly distributed and diverse data sets are averaged to fit a global model. However, optimizing only the accuracy of the global model can lead to a degradation in personalization capabilities [1], resulting in significant performance degradation on end-user devices. It means that prediction accuracy may suffer if there is insufficient data available for the outcome being predicted during the global model training. This problem is similar to the sampling bias that occurs during the training of machine learning models. When training a model, if the number of samples between classes of data becomes too large, the recall for classes with fewer samples will be smaller, causing the model to overfit to certain classes. However, solving the sampling bias problem in a federated learning process is challenging as the class of data is not easy to determine. This is due to the fact that training participants cannot be identified and the client's data is difficult to access. To overcome this challenge, previous research in federated learning has suggested various techniques such as using metadata, applying noise to data, or applying contrastive learning for sampling the data without direct access to it. Due to the existence of heterogeneous learning environments and federated learning settings tailored to the purpose of various models, there is a need for research that can be personalized for different federated learning models.

Personalization is a relevant approach to address non-IID challenges and statistical heterogeneity present in each client. However, many studies only evaluate the accuracy of global models. In this paper, we aim to mitigate this research gap from the perspective of client clustering techniques, which is an intermediate approach between a single global model and local models [2] in federated learning personalization. Clustering is a similarity-based approach that considers group-level client relationships to model client relationships [3]. It provides a trade-off between generalization and distribution mismatch caused by heterogeneity in the data distribution across clients. This technique is simple to interpret and implement, especially when the number of clients is very large, and it can help improve non-IID handling.

2 Related Works

2.1 Federated Learning

The Federated averaging (FedAvg) algorithm is one of the most well-known federated learning algorithms [4]. FedAvg aggregates local model weights which are sent from clients to generate a global model. However, when the datasets produced by different clients are non-IID, the FedAvg algorithm achieve accuracy and system performance degradation [5]. Specifically, the non-IID setting can cause the global model to become biased towards the data of certain clients, resulting in poor generalization to other clients. As a result, various extensions to the FedAvg algorithm has been proposed to address the non-IID problem. For instance, Li et al. [6] demonstrated that strong convexity in client functions can improve the convergence rate in FedAvg. The authors argued that the divergence issue of averaging could be mitigated by not involving all clients in each round. Instead, clients could be selected with a certain probability or with a probability proportional to the size of their local dataset. Furthermore, in Federated Optimization in Heterogeneous Networks (FedProx) [7], to address the issue of local models deviating significantly from the global optima in federated learning, FedProx introduced a regularization term into the local objective function of the FedAvg algorithm. This term adjusts for the impact of local updates. This led to better convergence on heterogeneous data by restricting the impact of local updates on the global model. However, FedProx assigns the same weight to all devices in the aggregation step, similar to FedAvg, and does not account for device heterogeneity [8]. MOON [9] aimed to tackle the problem of weight deviation in non-IID data environments, which results in a widening of the representation gap between local and global models, by performing contrastive learning at the model level. By comparing the representations of different models, MOON accelerates convergence and maximizes the agreement between the local model learned by the client and the representation learned by the global model. SCAFFOLD [5] proposed a framework that utilizes additional control variables to facilitate the communication between the central server and participating clients, as well as estimate the update direction for both the global and local models. FedProx, MOON, and SCAFFOLD all aim to reduce the variance by introducing a function that compensates for local updates.

2.2 Personalized Federated Learning

The degree to which data is distributed differs for every client that possesses it, and the same is true for the devices of end-users who will be using the federated model. To mitigate the performance degradation caused by device heterogeneity, statistical heterogeneity, and data heterogeneity, which are inevitable during the federated learning process, personalization is necessary at the device, model, and data levels. Traditional machine learning approaches that can contribute to personalization by addressing data imbalances are not easily applicable to a federated learning mechanism that does not have direct access to local data owned by the client [10]. Therefore, additional processing is required to incorporate these techniques into the personalization process of federated learning.

Previous research [1] has suggested that for personalization in federated learning to be useful, three goals must be achieved simultaneously: (1) an improved personalization model for the majority of customers, (2) a robust initial model for customers with limited or no data for personalization, and (3) a fast convergence rate that allows high quality to be reached with fewer training rounds. Also, In [3], metrics were proposed to evaluate personalized federated learning. They consider three dimensions: (1) model performance; (2) system performance; and (3) trustworthy AI.

Google Research [2] has proposed three approaches to personalization: (1) user clustering – which involves grouping users into clusters and training a separate model for each group; (2) data interpolation – where some local data is combined with global data and used to train a model with the interpolated data combination; and (3) model interpolation – which first trains a global model and then trains a local model separately, combining each model afterwards. [2] states that personalized models serve as an intermediate step between purely local and global models. In [3], personalization techniques for federated learning are classified into two categories: Global Model Personalization and Learning Personalized Models. Previous research has attempted to personalize the global model, which closely replicates the training procedure of general federated learning for a single model. Since the generalization performance of the global model directly impacts the personalized model's performance, they optimized the global model to enhance subsequent personalization performance [3]. This involves additional training on each client's local dataset before utilizing the trained global model in the inference phase [10]. Representative algorithms included in this approach are Meta-learning. Meta-learning is a personalization technique for federated learning, which uses a small number of examples to train a model and then fine-tunes it for new tasks, allowing it to learn quickly. One meta-learning method, Model-Agnostic Meta-Learning (MAML) [11], has been used in personalization research. MAML has similarities between the personalization goals of MAML and federated learning (FL), and FedAvg can also be interpreted as a meta-learning algorithm [1]. And the latter approach, referred to as Learning Personalized Models, focuses on training models that are personalized to each individual client, instead of optimizing the global model for personalization. This trains a personalized model around the solution for each user's prediction, instead of training a single global model for personalization. Included in this approach are Multi-task learning and Client-clustering. Multi-task learning [12] is a learning paradigm used in various fields of machine learning, where multiple tasks are jointly learned to avoid the data sparsity problem when each task has less labeled data, and this knowledge can also be utilized by other tasks. From this research, we discuss clustering techniques that classify clients based on their similarities or preferences to improve accuracy by training personalized models.

2.3 Client Clustering Techniques

Clustering techniques refer to clustering and sampling that have been previously proposed in the machine learning. However, applying these algorithms to federated learning requires a lot of considerations due to the heterogeneity of the federated training environment. Client clustering in federated learning is a technique that assumes a common dataset among participating clients and their locally trained models. Client clustering techniques group different local data and the local models trained on them, i.e., clients, according to some characteristic or tendency. A group of users is a subset of the entire client group, and they are trained on the same task within the group. The idea is to learn the features of the data more efficiently by grouping similar users together, and increase the accuracy of global models trained on non-IID data.

While federated learning generally has the advantage that the identity of each participant is not disclosed and their data is protected, it also assumes significant challenges to personalization using clustering: (1) the identity of participating clients is unknown and they must be clustered without access to their data; (2) the classification criteria of clients and the subset to which they belong are disclosed, which can pose a security threat. In addition, if learning is required through additional communication, communication overhead can be a problem, and optimization of the learning process should be considered.

2.4 Federated Learning Personalization Based on Client Clustering

Client clustering techniques have been proposed as a solution to address the challenge of data heterogeneity in the personalization phase. This method enables efficient personalization by organizing de-identified data into a clustered structure.

In [13], the Iterative Federated Clustering Algorithm (IFCA) was proposed, which employs alternating minimization to estimate the identity of a cluster and minimize the loss function via gradient descent. The algorithm broadcasts the server model parameters to k clients and collect the model parameters after local learning. The central server performs gradient descent updates to the model parameters of clients with the same cluster identity estimate. This process is repeated several times to progressively cluster. In [14], a Stochastic Expectation Maximization (SEM) technique was proposed, which adds a step of dynamically updating W_i to Expectation-Maximization (EM) algorithm to design a multi-center federated loss. In this method, each client finds the global model closest to its learned value and proceeds with clustering. In order to use these methods, it is necessary to determine the appropriate number of clusters. In [15], a clustering structure was inferred based on the cosine similarity between clients' gradient updates, and clients were recursively separated in a top-down manner based on this clustering. This recursion stops when all clients are not far from a fixed value of the federated learning solution. Many of the previously proposed client clustering algorithms suffer from the drawback that clustering takes place over multiple rounds of communication, which can result in high communication costs. Therefore, in [16], the authors simplified the clustering process into a single step and trained a global model during a single round of communication. Clusters were generated based on the difference between the parameters of the global model and those of the local models.

3 Experiments

3.1 Experimental Setup

Datasets. We evaluate client clustering algorithms and compare their results using the MNIST [17] dataset and Federated Extended MNIST (FEMNIST), a publicly available federated benchmark dataset introduced in LEAF [18]. The MNIST dataset is a collection of handwritten digit vision images, and it is widely used to evaluate various federated learning environments. FEMNIST is suitable for testing more challenging and realistic environments, as it contains 26 handwritten 10-digit numbers, upper-and lower-case letters, and the image set is partitioned by writer. To construct datasets for clients, we select the same number of writers as the number of clients in both datasets. To implement the pathological non-IID setting in the MNIST dataset, we sort the data by label and partition the dataset so that a client has data for only two labels.

FL and PFL Algorithms. We use a pre-trained global model trained over 2000 iterations for each partitioned dataset. The global model is trained with FedAvg algorithm. A total of 100 clients participated in the training and the learning rate was 0.008. The final test accuracy was 0.82, and the final test loss was 0.63. We compare the performance of the IFCA [13], SEM [14], and CFL [15] algorithms by adjusting the percentage of clients participating in each training round, the number of clusters, and the number of communication rounds for clustering. We report the average test set accuracy for all clients, from immediately after the global model is created until the clustering task is complete, and the percentage of clients that reach the test set accuracy target at the end of the targeted communication rounds.

3.2 Experiments

We first used the IFCA algorithm to train a PFL model with client clustering. We experimented with fixing the number of clusters to k = 3. Also, existing research shows that the accuracy is not significantly different when k < 3. The experiment was run in the following environment: Batch size = 10, Participation clients in every round = 15, Learning rates = 0.03, Epoch = 1, Initial training rounds for client clustering = 30 (Figs. 1, 2 and 3).

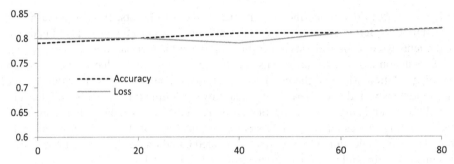

Fig. 1. Accuracy of the IFCA PFL model. FEMNIST datasets. Clients = 15.

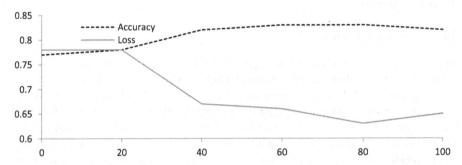

Fig. 2. Accuracy of the IFCA PFL model. FEMNIST datasets. Clients = 50

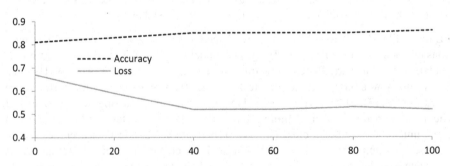

Fig. 3. Accuracy of the IFCA PFL model. FEMNIST datasets. Clients = 100

4 Conclusion

To measure the performance of the personalized federated models trained by client clustering methods, we personalized the global models generated by federated learning algorithms used in previous studies. In this personalization process, we adopted multiple client clustering methods and compared the outcomes in various experimental environments. Based on our evaluations of different client clustering techniques using MNIST and FEMNIST datasets, we present a comprehensive comparison of the performance and scalability of IFCA, SEM, and CFL algorithms in the context of personalization in federated learning. We believe that this study can help researchers and practitioners to select appropriate client clustering methods for their federated learning personalization tasks, with leading to improve its performance.

References

1. Jiang, Y., Konečný, J., Rush, K., Kannan, S.: Improving Federated Learning Personalization via Model Agnostic Meta Learning (2019). arXiv:1909.12488
2. Mansour, Y., Mohri, M., Ro, J., Theertha Suresh, A.: Three Approaches for Personalization with Applications to Federated Learning (2020). arXiv:2002.10619
3. Tan, A.Z., Yu, H., Cui, L., Yang, Q.: Towards personalized federated learning. IEEE Trans. Neural Netw. Learn. Syst. 1–17 (2022)
4. McMahan, B., Moore, E., Ramage, D., Hampson, S., Arcas, B.A.: Communication-efficient learning of deep networks from decentralized data. In: Artificial Intelligence and Statistics, pp. 1273–1282. PMLR (2017)
5. Karimireddy, S.P., Kale, S., Mohri, M., Reddi, S., Stich, S., Suresh, A.T.: Scaffold: stochastic controlled averaging for federated learning. In: International Conference on Machine Learning, pp. 5132–5143. PMLR (2020)
6. Li, X., Huang, K., Yang, W., Wang, S., Zhang, Z.: On the convergence of FedAvg on non-IID data (2019). arXiv preprint arXiv:1907.02189
7. Li, T., Sahu, A.K., Zaheer, M., Sanjabi, M., Talwalkar, A., Smith, V.: Federated optimization in heterogeneous networks. Proc. Mach. Learn. Syst. 2, 429–450 (2020)
8. Wahab, O.A., Mourad, A., Otrok, H., Taleb, T.: Federated machine learning: survey, multi-level classification, desirable criteria and future directions in communication and networking systems. IEEE Commun. Surveys Tutor. 23, 1342–1397 (2021)
9. Li, Q., He, B., Song, D.: Model-contrastive federated learning. In: Proceedings of the IEEE/CVF Conference on Computer Vision and Pattern Recognition, pp. 10713–10722 (2021)
10. Kairouz, P., et al.: Advances and open problems in federated learning. Found. Trends® Mach. Learn. 14, 1–210 (2021)
11. Finn, C., Abbeel, P., Levine, S.: Model-agnostic meta-learning for fast adaptation of deep networks. In: International Conference on Machine Learning, pp. 1126–1135. PMLR (2017)
12. Zhang, Y., Yang, Q.: A survey on multi-task learning. IEEE Trans. Knowl. Data Eng. 34, 5586–5609 (2022)
13. Ghosh, A., Chung, J., Yin, D., Ramchandran, K.: An efficient framework for clustered federated learning. Adv. Neural. Inf. Process. Syst. 33, 19586–19597 (2020)
14. Long, G., Xie, M., Shen, T., Zhou, T., Wang, X., Jiang, J.: Multi-center federated learning: clients clustering for better personalization. World Wide Web 26, 481–500 (2023)
15. Sattler, F., Müller, K.R., Samek, W.: Clustered federated learning: model-agnostic distributed multitask optimization under privacy constraints. IEEE Trans. Neural Netw. Learn. Syst. 32, 3710–3722 (2021)
16. Briggs, C., Fan, Z., Andras, P.: Federated learning with hierarchical clustering of local updates to improve training on non-IID data. In: 2020 International Joint Conference on Neural Networks (IJCNN), pp. 1–9. IEEE (2020)
17. Lecun, Y., Bottou, L., Bengio, Y., Haffner, P.: Gradient-based learning applied to document recognition. Proc. IEEE 86, 2278–2324 (1998)
18. Caldas, S., et al.: Leaf: a benchmark for federated settings (2018). arXiv preprint arXiv:1812. 01097

Short Paper (GeoForAgr 2023)

An Unpiloted Aerial System (UAV) Light Detection and Ranging (LiDAR) Based Approach to Detect Canopy Forest Structure Parameters in Old-Growth Beech Forests: Preliminary Results

Salvatore Praticò[1]([⊠]) [iD], Francesco Solano[2] [iD], Gianluca Piovesan[3] [iD], and Giuseppe Modica[4] [iD]

[1] Dipartimento di Agraria, Università degli studi 'Mediterranea' di Reggio Calabria, Reggio Calabria, Italy
salvatore.pratico@unirc.it

[2] Department of Agriculture and Forest Sciences (DAFNE), University of Tuscia, Viterbo, Italy

[3] Department of Ecological and Biological Science (DEB), University of Tuscia, Viterbo, Italy

[4] Dipartimento di Scienze Veterinarie, Università degli studi di Messina, Messina, Italy

Abstract. Due to the increasingly rapid trend of biodiversity loss triggered by global changes and considering the critical role played by forests in conserving biodiversity, it is of great interest the study the structural attributes of natural forest stands. Understanding forest structure parameters, such as canopy height vertical variation, is crucial in acquiring information about natural forest dynamics. Recently, unpiloted aerial systems (UAV) have been used for mapping forest structure parameters. Among these, light detection and ranging (LiDAR) sensors are gaining attention. The main aim of this study is to test the feasibility of using UAV-based LiDAR surveys in detecting and mapping forest structure heterogeneity of primary old-growth beech forests. UAV survey has been conducted by means of the Zenmuse L1, equipped on board of the multirotor DJI Matrice 300 RTK in two small plots of the old-growth beech forest of Val Cervara, within the Abruzzo, Lazio, and Molise National Park in Italy. The acquired data have been processed to obtain the canopy height model (CHM). CHMs maps showed marked differences in canopy height spatial pattern between the two sample plots. Plot 1 showed a one-layered canopy density curve and a higher number of trees, while Plot 2 was characterized by a bimodal canopy layer with a lower number of trees. The proposed approach, even if still a first attempt, could be proposed as tool for mapping and monitoring old-growth beech forests.

Keywords: Remote Sensing (RS) · *Fagus sylvatica* L. · Canopy Height Model (CHM)

© The Author(s), under exclusive license to Springer Nature Switzerland AG 2023
O. Gervasi et al. (Eds.): ICCSA 2023 Workshops, LNCS 14112, pp. 197–205, 2023.
https://doi.org/10.1007/978-3-031-37129-5_17

1 Introduction

Due to the increasingly rapid trend of biodiversity loss triggered by global changes [1, 2] and considering the critical role played by forests in conserving biodiversity and ecosystem services [3], it has now become of great interest the study the structural attributes of natural forest stands, in order to better describe their dynamics from a management and conservation perspective [4]. Understanding these dynamics means figuring out how a forest performs without anthropogenic disturbances. In old-growth stands, stand structure is related to the long-term ecological dynamics that govern the trees' death, regeneration and growth [5]. Small-scale natural disturbances often drive these dynamics causing the opening of single tree-fall gaps that influences the forest structure [6, 7] generating a complex canopy structure linked to high biodiversity [8]. Thus, understanding different forest structure parameters, such as the distribution and the shape of gaps [9], the canopy cover [10], and the canopy height vertical variation [11] is a crucial step to acquiring information about natural forest dynamics.

As the most widespread forest type in Europe [12], the primeval European beech forests are the object of several monitoring activities aimed at studying their dynamics after disturbance events [13–16]. Acquiring data about canopy structure parameters with terrestrial field survey campaigns is time-consuming [17]. In the last decades, remote sensing (RS) techniques, especially those related to the use of very high-resolution (VHR) data, have been shown to be able to achieve good results with high accuracy levels [18–22]. Recently, the use of unpiloted aerial system (UAV)-based surveying results have been used for mapping forest structure parameters [23, 24]. Among these, the use of light detection and ranging (LiDAR) sensors is gaining attention among researchers and practitioners [25–30].

The main aim of this study is to test the feasibility of using the UAV-based LiDAR surveys novel approach in detecting forest structure heterogeneity of old-growth beech forests in relation to past severe disturbances (e.g. avalanches), to support and enhance forest ecology and monitoring research. The proposed method was tested in two plot areas (1.39 ha) of the old-growth beech (*Fagus sylvatica* L.) forest of Val Cervara, within the Abruzzo, Lazio, and Molise National Park in Italy.

2 Materials and Methods

2.1 Study Area

The study area (Fig. 1) is the old-growth forest of Val Cervara. It is located inside the Abruzzo, Lazio, and Molise National Park and falls in the Abruzzo Region at an altitude between 1530 and 1900 m a.s.l. The forest is dominated by European beech (*Fagus sylvatica* L.) and is characterized by a mosaic of primary old-growth structural patches in different phases of development from seedlings to senescent and dead trees, with ancient individual trees of up to more than 600 years of age [31]. It is distributed over 24 ha, with an uneven age structure on soils developed on calcareous bedrock. In 2017, the forest was included in the UNESCO World Natural Heritage (UNESCO WH) of serial sites "Ancient and Primeval beech forests of the Carpathians and other regions of Europe" (https://whc.unesco.org/en/list/1133/ – last access 2023/04/21) for its exceptional ecological value. One of the plots was disturbed by an avalanche while the other show a typical complex structure linked to fine-scale disturbance.

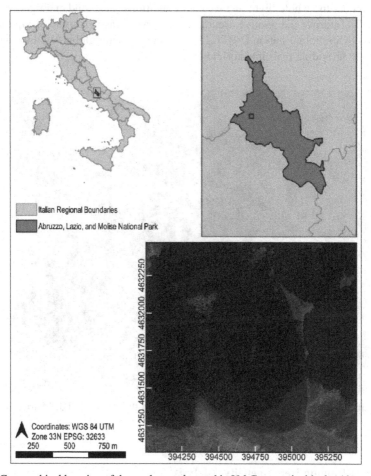

Fig. 1. Geographical location of the study area located in Val Cervara, inside the Abruzzo, Lazio and Molise National Park, in Abruzzo Region.

2.2 UAV Survey and Data Processing

The UAV survey has been conducted by means of the Zenmuse L1, equipped on board of the multirotor DJI Matrice 300 RTK on a 3-axis stabilized gimbal (Fig. 2). The Zenmuse L1 is a multisensory system, composed of three different sensors. The first one consists of a LiDAR sensor supporting 1 to 3 returns. The second one is an RGB camera used to collect photos obtaining true color 3D point-clouds. The last one is a high-accuracy inertial measurements unit (IMU), able to constantly check the flight parameters of the UAV during the flight.

The flight was conducted in a semi-automatic way. Taking-off and landing operations have been performed manually by the remote pilot, while the surveying flight was automated following a predetermined path. The height was set at 100 m a.g.l. and throughout the whole flight, the weather conditions (i.e., wind and light) remained constant. To improve the relative accuracy, the survey was performed using the high-precision GNSS mobile station D-RTK2 supporting all major global satellite navigation systems and providing real-time corrections.

Fig. 2. LiDAR sensor Zenmuse L1 equipped on board of the multirotor DJI Matrice 300 RTK.

2.3 Forest Canopy Heterogeneity Analysis

The main processing steps concerned the individual tree detection (ITD) and crown delineation within the two plots, to provide useful information regarding the vertical structure and the main properties of the forest canopy. The LiDAR derived CHM (0.5 m resolution) was first smoothed with a 3 × 3 pixels smoothing window size (SWS) for delating spurious potential local maxima, and a tree height threshold was set to 2.0 m for ITD. Tree tops were detected using local maximum (LM) algorithm by a 5 × 5 pixels fixed window size (FWS). Tree crown delineation was then performed following Silva et al. [32] using the Voronoi tessellation-based algorithm. For each plot we obtained the CHMs canopy profile, and the height frequency distributions and single tree crown area statistics were then derived. For comparing stand structure heterogeneity, we made use of variability and asymmetry measurements of tree heights [33] by computing Lorenz curves from the cubic power of tree heights, which has been observed to relate to Lorenz curves obtained from tree diameters [34]. Analysis was conducted using the treetop package [35] implemented in the R statistical software [36].

3   Results and Discussions

Results from a quick assessment of CHMs maps showed marked differences in canopy height spatial pattern between the two sample plots, highlighting a more complex structure for plot 2 (Fig. 3).

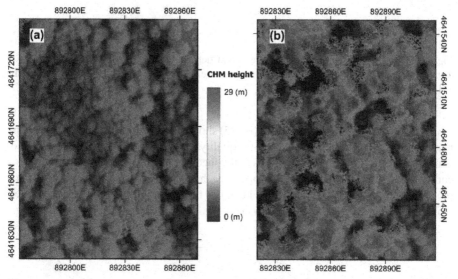

Fig. 3. LiDAR-derived Canopy height model (CHM) for plot 1 (a) and plot 2 (b) of the old-growth beech forest of Val Cervara (EPSG 32633 coordinate system).

Canopy metrics related to the plot confirm such differences. The maximum tree height was found in plot 2 (29 m) while in plot 1 reached 22 m (Fig. 4). Plot 1 showed a one-layered canopy density curve and a higher number of trees (456 canopy trees/ha) showing that this part of the forest was in the past disturbed by severe disturbance such as avalanches generating a unimodal and less-developed stands. Plot 2 was characterized by a bimodal canopy layer with a lower number of trees (244 canopy trees/ha), with the majority reaching the top of the canopy (Fig. 4). This more uneven-aged structure is the result of fine-scale disturbance driven single tree death where canopy gap pattern shapes tree recruitments. The greater space available for the trees reflects in the greater dimensions of the tree crowns of this plot. This complex vertical profile was also reported in other studies [5, 20] and seems to characterize the structure of old-growth beech forests where long-term growth dynamics are driven by fine-scale disturbances.

In our study, we chose to evaluate canopy heterogeneity in the canopy height, because tree height above the ground was the variable directly measured by the LiDAR.

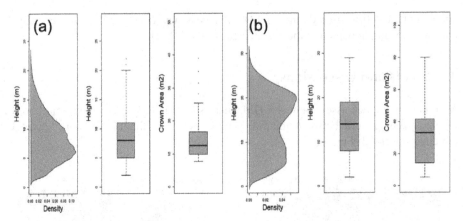

Fig. 4. Canopy height density profile, tree height density distribution and crown area density distribution from LiDAR-derived Canopy height model (CHM) for plot 1 (a) and plot 2 (b) of the old-growth forest of Val Cervara.

The Lorenz curve for the two plots (Fig. 5) showed an unequal distribution of canopy height as it lies above the line of absolute equality, suggesting different degree of homogeneity in their structure. The upper part of the shaded area shows the position of a Lorenz curve representing the maximum entropy over the Lorenz plot. It can be observed that plot 1 showed a lower variability in tree height by the low amplitude of its Lorenz curves, close to the diagonal (absolute equality) (Fig. 5).

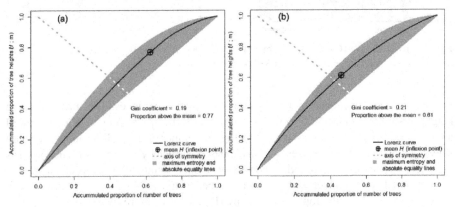

Fig. 5. Lorenz curve plot of LiDAR-derived tree heights for plot 1 (a) and plot 2 (b) of the old-growth forest of Val Cervara.

The Gini coefficient (GC) calculated as the ratio between the area enclosed by the equality line and the Lorenz curve, and the total area under the line of equality, obtained from both of stands was 0.19 and 0.21 respectively. Coefficient values confirms the Lorenz curve results [37]. The higher the coefficient, the more unequal the distribution is, suggesting that severe forest disturbance decreases GC, whereas fine-scale distur-bances and seed regeneration increases GC [38], and therefore gap dynamics could be characterized by shifts between hypothetical GC thresholds.

More apparent differences between the two beech forest plot can be observed when considering the measures of asymmetry. As suggested by Damgaard and Weiner [39], we evaluate the asymmetry of the Lorenz curve by comparing the position of its inflexion point against the axis of symmetry, specifically the location of the point at which the Lorenz curve has the same slope of the line of equality. Results reveals that plot 2 has a much more heterogeneous structure as the skewness of the Lorenz curve indicates understory development which is reflected by its uneven-sized tree height.

4 Conclusions

In this paper, which shows the preliminary results of still ongoing research, we used a UAV LiDAR-based CHM approach to detect forest structure heterogeneity in primary old-growth beech forests, to support studies in forest ecology and enhance monitoring research in this global change era. The differences shown by the two plots with different disturbance histories highlighted that the two different situations are easily detectable by the surveyed structure parameters. Further analyses and surveys are needed to refine the proposed method, also considering other indices. However, the analyses already presented in this study support the UAV approach as a tool for mapping and monitoring old-growth beech forests.

References

1. Erb, K.-H., et al.: Unexpectedly large impact of forest management and grazing on global vegetation biomass. Nature **553**(7686), 73–76 (2018). http://www.nature.com/articles/nature25138
2. García-Vega, D., Newbold, T.: Assessing the effects of land use on biodiversity in the world's drylands and Mediterranean environments. Biodivers. Conserv. **29**(2), 393–408 (2019). https://doi.org/10.1007/s10531-019-01888-4
3. De Frenne, P., et al.: Forest microclimates and climate change: Importance, drivers and future research agenda. Global Change Biol. **27**(11), 2279–2297 (2021). https://doi.org/10.1111/gcb.15569
4. Feldmann, E., Drößler, L., Hauck, M., Kucbel, S., Pichler, V., Leuschner, C.: Canopy gap dynamics and tree understory release in a virgin beech forest, Slovakian Carpathians. Forest Ecol. Manage. **415–416**, 38–46 (2018). https://doi.org/10.1016/j.foreco.2018.02.022
5. Solano, F., Modica, G., Praticò, S., Box, O.F., Piovesan, G.: Unveiling the complex canopy spatial structure of a Mediterranean old-growth beech (Fagus sylvatica L.) forest from UAV observations. Ecol. Indic. **138**, 108807 (2022). https://linkinghub.elsevier.com/retrieve/pii/S1470160X22002783
6. Brokaw, N.V.L.: The definition of treefall gap and its effect on measures of forest dynamics. Biotropica **14**(2), 158 (1982). https://www.jstor.org/stable/2387750?origin=crossref
7. Solano, F., Praticò, S., Piovesan, G., Modica, G.: Unmanned aerial vehicle (UAV) derived canopy gaps in the old-growth beech forest of Mount Pollinello (Italy): preliminary results. In: Gervasi, O., et al. (eds.) Computational Science and Its Applications – ICCSA 2021. LNCS, vol. 12955, pp. 126–138. Springer, Cham (2021). https://doi.org/10.1007/978-3-030-87007-2_10

8. Oettel, J., Lapin, K.: Linking forest management and biodiversity indicators to strengthen sustainable forest management in Europe. Ecol. Indic. **122**, 107275 (2021). https://linkinghub.elsevier.com/retrieve/pii/S1470160X20312152

9. Zellweger, F., Braunisch, V., Baltensweiler, A., Bollmann, K.: Remotely sensed forest structural complexity predicts multi species occurrence at the landscape scale. Forest Ecol. Manage. **307**, 303–312 (2013). https://linkinghub.elsevier.com/retrieve/pii/S0378112713004659

10. Smith, G.F., et al.: Identifying practical indicators of biodiversity for stand-level management of plantation forests. Biodivers. Conserv. **17**(5), 991–1015 (2008). https://doi.org/10.1007/s10531-007-9274-3

11. Müller, J., Brandl, R.: Assessing biodiversity by remote sensing in mountainous terrain: the potential of LiDAR to predict forest beetle assemblages. J. Appl. Ecol. **46**(4), 897–905 (2009). https://doi.org/10.1111/j.1365-2664.2009.01677.x

12. Packham, J.R., Thomas, P.A., Atkinson, M.D., Degen, T.: Biological flora of the British Isles: Fagus sylvatica. J. Ecol. **100**(6), 1557–1608 (2012). https://doi.org/10.1111/j.1365-2745.2012.02017.x

13. Di Filippo, A., Biondi, F., Piovesan, G., Ziaco, E.: Tree ring-based metrics for assessing old-growth forest naturalness. J. Appl. Ecol. **54**(3), 737–749 (2017). https://doi.org/10.1111/1365-2664.12793

14. Kenderes, K., Mihok, B., Standovar, T.: Thirty years of gap dynamics in a central European beech forest reserve. Forestry **81**(1), 111–123 (2008). https://doi.org/10.1093/forestry/cpn001

15. Petritan, A.M., Nuske, R.S., Petritan, I.C., Tudose, N.C.: Gap disturbance patterns in an old-growth sessile oak (Quercus petraea L.) – European beech (Fagus sylvatica L.) forest remnant in the Carpathian Mountains, Romania. Forest Ecol. Manage. **308**, 67–75 (2013). https://linkinghub.elsevier.com/retrieve/pii/S037811271300501X

16. Rehush, N., Waser, L.T.: Assessing the structure of primeval and managed beech forests in the Ukrainian Carpathians using remote sensing. Can. J. Forest Res. **47**(1), 63–72 (2017). https://doi.org/10.1139/cjfr-2016-0253

17. Milz, S., et al.: The HAInich: a multidisciplinary vision data-set for a better understanding of the forest ecosystem. Sci. Data **10**(1), 168 (2023). https://www.nature.com/articles/s41597-023-02010-8

18. White, J.C., Tompalski, P., Coops, N.C., Wulder, M.A.: Comparison of airborne laser scanning and digital stereo imagery for characterizing forest canopy gaps in coastal temperate rainforests. Remote Sens. Environ. 208, 1–14 (2018). https://linkinghub.elsevier.com/retrieve/pii/S0034425718300087

19. Aicardi, I., Dabove, P., Lingua, A., Piras, M.: Integration between TLS and UAV photogrammetry techniques for forestry applications. iForest Biogeosci. Forestry. e1–e7 (2016). http://www.sisef.it/iforest/?doi=ifor1780-009

20. Hobi, M.L., Ginzler, C., Commarmot, B., Bugmann, H.: Gap pattern of the largest primeval beech forest of Europe revealed by remote sensing. Ecosphere **6**(5), art76 (2015). https://doi.org/10.1890/ES14-00390.1

21. Messina, G., Lumia, G., Praticò, S., Di Fazio, S., Modica, G.: Preliminary results in the use of worldView-3 for the detection of Cork Oak (Quercus Suber L.): a case in Calabria (Italy), pp. 2153–2162 (2022). Springer International Publishing. https://doi.org/10.1007/978-3-031-06825-6_207

22. Vizzari, M.: PlanetScope, Sentinel-2, and Sentinel-1 data integration for object-based land cover classification in google earth engine. Remote Sens. **14**(11), 2628 (2022). https://www.mdpi.com/2072-4292/14/11/2628

23. Getzin, S., Nuske, R., Wiegand, K.: Using unmanned aerial vehicles (UAV) to quantify spatial gap patterns in forests. Remote Sens. **6**(8), 6988–7004 (2014). http://www.mdpi.com/2072-4292/6/8/6988

24. Sun, H., Yan, H., Hassanalian, M., Zhang, J., Abdelkefi, A.: UAV platforms for data acquisition and intervention practices in forestry: towards more intelligent applications. Aerospace **10**(3), 317 (2023). https://www.mdpi.com/2226-4310/10/3/317
25. Bartholomeus, H., et al.: Evaluating data inter-operability of multiple UAV–LiDAR systems for measuring the 3D structure of Savanna woodland. Remote Sens. **14**(23), 5992 (2022). https://www.mdpi.com/2072-4292/14/23/5992
26. Jin, C., Oh, C., Shin, S., Wilfred Njungwi, N., Choi, C.: A comparative study to evaluate accuracy on canopy height and density using UAV, ALS, and fieldwork. Forests. **11**(2), 241 (2020). https://www.mdpi.com/1999-4907/11/2/241
27. Cao, L., Liu, H., Fu, X., Zhang, Z., Shen, X., Ruan, H.: Comparison of UAV LiDAR and digital aerial photogrammetry point clouds for estimating forest structural attributes in subtropical planted forests. Forests **10**(2), 145 (2019). http://www.mdpi.com/1999-4907/10/2/145
28. Wallace, L., Lucieer, A., Watson, C., Turner, D.: Development of a UAV-LiDAR system with application to forest inventory. Remote Sens. **4**(6), 1519–1543 (2012)
29. Wallace, L., Lucieer, A., Malenovský, Z., Turner, D., Vopěnka, P.: Assessment of forest structure using two UAV techniques: a comparison of airborne laser scanning and structure from motion (SfM) point clouds. Forests **7**(3), 62 (2016). http://www.mdpi.com/1999-4907/7/3/62
30. Hu, T., et al.: Development and performance evaluation of a very low-cost UAV-LiDAR system for forestry applications. Remote Sens. **13**(1), 77 (2020). https://www.mdpi.com/2072-4292/13/1/77
31. Piovesan, G., Biondi, F., Di Filippo, A., Alessandrini, A., Maugeri, M.: Drought-driven growth reduction in old beech (Fagus sylvatica L.) forests of the central Apennines, Italy. Global Change Biol. **14**(6), 1265–1281 (2008). https://doi.org/10.1111/j.1365-2486.2008.01570.x
32. Silva, C.A., et al.: Imputation of individual longleaf pine (Pinus palustris Mill.) tree attributes from field and LiDAR data. Can. J. Remote Sens. **42**(5), 554–573 (2016). https://doi.org/10.1080/07038992.2016.1196582
33. Valbuena, R., Maltamo, M., Mehtätalo, L., Packalen, P.: Key structural features of Boreal forests may be detected directly using L-moments from airborne LiDAR data. Remote Sens. Environ. **194**, 437–446 (2017). https://linkinghub.elsevier.com/retrieve/pii/S0034425716303960
34. Hakamada, R.E., Stape, J.L., de Lemos, C.C.Z., Almeida, A.E.A., Silva, L.F.: UNIFORMIDADE ENTRE ÁRVORES DURANTE UMA ROTAÇÃO E SUA RELAÇÃO COM A PRODUTIVIDADE EM Eucalyptus CLONAIS. CERNE **21**(3), 465–472 (2015). http://www.scielo.br/scielo.php?script=sci_arttext&pid=S0104-77602015000300465&lng=pt&tlng=pt
35. Silva, C.A., et al.: treetop: a shiny-based application and R package for extracting forest information from LiDAR data for ecologists and conservationists. Methods Ecol. Evol. **13**(6), 1164–1176 (2022). https://doi.org/10.1111/2041-210X.13830
36. R Core Team. R: A Language and Environment for Statistical Computing. R Foundation for Statistical Computing, Vienna, Austria (2021). https://www.r-project.org/
37. Weiner, J.: Asymmetric competition in plant populations. Trends Ecol. Evol. **5**(11), 360–364 (1990). https://linkinghub.elsevier.com/retrieve/pii/016953479090095U
38. Valbuena, R., Packalen, P., Mehtätalo, L., García-Abril, A., Maltamo, M.: Characterizing forest structural types and shelterwood dynamics from Lorenz-based indicators predicted by airborne laser scanning. Can. J. Forest Res. **43**(11), 1063–1074 (2013).https://doi.org/10.1139/cjfr-2013-0147
39. Damgaard, C., Weiner, J.: Describing inequality in plant size or fecundity. Ecology **81**(4), 1139 (2000). http://www.jstor.org/stable/177185?origin=crossref

Short Papers (Geog-An-Mod 2023)

Current Spatial Aspects of Demographic Differentiation and Urbanization Process in Poland (Pilot Study)

Veranika Kaleyeva$^{(\boxtimes)}$ 🆔 and Piotr A. Werner 🆔

Faculty of Geography and Regional Studies, University of Warsaw, Krak. Przedm. 30, 00-927 Warsaw, Poland
v.kaleyeva@gmail.com

Abstract. The paper aims to analyze the balance between selected spatial demographic factors, i.e., elements of local demographic structure of population and intensity of urbanization process in Poland. Urbanization is currently perceived as an ambiguous process: people move to the metropolises (cities), but in turn, there is an observed decrease in fertility rates in urban areas. The hypothesis that rapidly urbanizing areas attract a cohort of young households at a fertile age is being investigated. It was assumed that there are specific regions that deviate from the general trend of an aging urban population. This would be reflected in the age distribution and higher fertility rate, especially in the settlement of selected growing urban, peri-urban, and rural areas of some cities. The sources of the data were the statistics of Poland (Polish CSO) at a certain given level of spatial (administrative) units (NUTS). As far as expected results are concerned, in the context of population characteristics and differentiation according to specific locations and geographical areas of Poland, our pilot study may have policy implications, such as the need for city planners to consider spatial variables in order to achieve the desired trade-off between meeting social needs and developing urban ecosystems in a sustainable manner. The starting point of the research methodology is a spatial matrix of correlations between selected demographic and urban process' characteristics.

Keywords: Urbanization · Demographic Differentiation · Poland

1 Introduction

In 2022, the global human population achieved a milestone of 8 billion [1]. Since 1975, the world has been adding another billion people every 12 years and is projected to surpass 9 billion around 2037 and 10 billion around 2058 (Fig. 1). Over the last decades, a persistent rise in population worldwide has significantly altered the landscape of urban fabric. Between 1975 and 2014, humanity has taken up more land for settlements than in all previous centuries [2].

Today, at least 56% of the population lives in cities, and urbanization is proceeding steadily worldwide. By 2050, approximately 7 out of 10 people will live in cities [4], with the urban population predicted to more than double from its current level [5].

© The Author(s), under exclusive license to Springer Nature Switzerland AG 2023
O. Gervasi et al. (Eds.): ICCSA 2023 Workshops, LNCS 14112, pp. 209–219, 2023.
https://doi.org/10.1007/978-3-031-37129-5_18

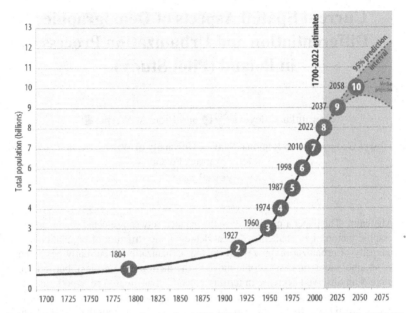

Fig. 1. Global population: estimates for 1700–2022 and projections for 2022–2100 [3].

In 2020, there were 1934 metropolises with more than 300,000 inhabitants, accounting for nearly 60% of the world's urban population, and it is expected that almost 1 more billion people will become metropolitan inhabitants in the next fifteen years [6].

In general, more economically developed regions have higher rates of urbanization than less developed regions [5, 7]. Total fertility rates have been lower than replacement rates in most economically developed regions for decades, though rates in less-developed economies remain higher [8]. The total population of the least developed countries is growing at a rate that is 2.5 times faster than the growth rate of the total population of the rest of the world [9]. In this context, population sizes in more economically developed, highly urbanized regions have recently declined, while those in the least-developed, least-urbanized regions have increased during the same period, reflecting fertility differences.

Cities expanded in size by 1.5% per year between 2000 and 2015. The land uptake by cities was higher in low-income countries (2.6%) than in middle-income countries (1.9% in lower middle and 1.5% in upper middle) or high-income countries (1%) [10]. Due to that expansion, many cities have grown beyond the boundaries of their central municipality. Simultaneously with global urban growth, there is an intensive urban sprawl process that forms low-density, often dispersed developments around the cities. Urban sprawl increased by 95% in 24 years worldwide, almost 4% annually, with built-up areas expanding by almost 28 km^2 per day. Europe has been the most sprawled and also the most rapidly sprawling continent, by 51% since 1990 [11].

In 2021, the population of Poland was declining. The population decline was for the first time during decades in both urban and rural areas; in previous years, the number of urban residents continued to decline, while the number of people living in rural areas increased (Fig. 2).

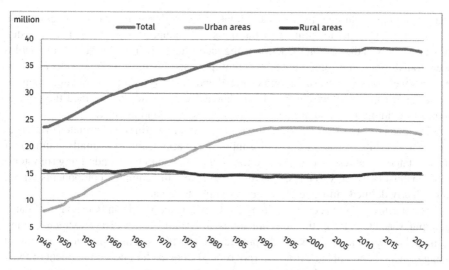

Fig. 2. Urban and rural population in Poland (1946–2021). Source: [12].

At the same time, in 2021, Poland's construction industry attained peak efficiency following impressive growth during the last decade [13]. In fact, 2020 was the first year that residential construction in Poland reached levels that were last seen during the communist era, with a high demand for additional housing as the post-war (WWII) baby-boomer generation entered the labour market. Earlier study portrays that the current construction boom is related to progressive suburbanization around Poland's mayor cities rather than inner urban growth of the central areas of metropolises [14].

The main aim of this paper was to reveal current latent factors specific to observed demographic and urbanization processes in Poland as well utilize some new portions of data collected within the completed in 2021 Polish National Population and Housing Census.

Accordingly, this study addresses the following questions: How demographic profile of inhabitants (families) interrelates to urban characteristics of settlement they reside? What are the differences in the combination of degree of urbanization and demographic structure of the population between spatial units? Are there any particular housing preferences associated with various cohorts of the population?

The main hypothesis is as follows: Rapidly urbanizing areas attract a cohort of young families at a fertile age.

The focus is on the year 2021 because this is the year of the most recent dataset available from the Central Statistics Office (annual editions) and the year of the last census, which is conducted in Poland once per decade.

2 Data and Methods

2.1 Methods

The applied procedure aimed to collect relative vast volume of data (variables) within the set of NUTS 4 administrative spatial units (380 counties in Poland). The next step of study involved dimension reduction using factor analysis (FA). Initial input variables were transformed into compound factors (components). Results of FA i.e. selected components were, in turn described, reinterpreted and visualized on cartographical maps to reveal their spatial differentiation, as the latent factors which determined the general trends of demographic and urbanization processes in Poland in 2021.

The objective of data reduction is to remove redundant (highly correlated) variables from the data file, replacing the entire input data variables with a smaller number of uncorrelated variables. Structure detection is used to examine the underlying (or latent) relationships between variables. The aim is to reveal the complex components with a very clearly defined influence of the observed phenomena.

The starting steps of FA were estimation of Covariance Matrix and Correlation Matrix of input variables. Then, the communalities of loading factors were extracted using principal component analysis (PCA) procedure. The PCA method produced a solution using principal component extraction (not rotated). For each of new component of PCA initial eigenvalues, individual percentage and cumulative percentage of variance were estimated. The components with eigenvalues were saved. The extraction communalities are estimates of the variance in each variable accounted for by the components. The high values of communalities indicate that the extracted components represent the variables well. These results was the starting point to FA aimed to reveal new insight into rotated components (Rotation Method: Varimax with Kaiser Normalization) and cut off the components with the diminished variance based on extraction rotation sums of squared loadings. The next steps of FA concerned only the chosen subset of initial components of PCA with a satisfactory level of representation and variance of the initial variables. Elimination of components was based on scree plot.

All procedures were completed using IBM SPSS software (ver.28).

2.2 Input Variables

The list of selected input variables involves characteristics concerning demographic, urbanization as well infrastructure data which (in opinion of authors) let reveal some specific spatial trends and heterogeneity of observed phenomena (Table 1). The acquired variables concern the data within the set of 380 spatial administrative units at NUTS 4 level (counties).

Table 1. Input statistical variables (by counties 2021).

Input Variable name	Description (per county in 2021)
RE2021Tot	Dwellings completed (per 10 000 inhabitants)
LQ2021	Location quotient of dwellings completed (relative measure; [15])
RoadsPow2021	Density of roads per 100 sq.km
Cars2021	Passenger cars (absolute number)
Stops2021	Active stops of public transport (absolute number)
RevPerPerson2021	Average gross monthly salaries
UEB2021	Share of urbanization %
PNPow2021	Natural increase
WSM0_17_2021	Migration balance index (0–17 years)
WSM0_64_2021	Migration balance index (17–64 years)
WSM64+2021	Migration balance index (over 64 years)
RodzinyTotal2021	Total number of households (families)
TotalRoDzieci	Total number of child families
RoDzieci0_2021	Total number of childless families
RoDzieci1_21	Total number of families with 1 child
RoDzieci2_21	Total number of families with 2 children
RoDzieci3_21	Total number of families with 3 children
RoDzieci4+21	Total number of families with 4 or greater children
TotalDzieci21	Total number of children
AvgDzieci	Average number of children per family
NieprodPer100Prod2021	Non-working age population per 100 people of working age
Wom15-34	Total number of women aged 15–34
Wom35-49	Total number of women aged 35–49

2.3 FA Results

There were four components extracted as compound measures of observed phenomena (Table 2). They explained 86.03% of total variance (from initial variables). The Varimax rotation method with Kaiser normalization was applied during FA.

Table 2. Total variance explained by selected FA components.

Component	Initial Eigenvalues Variance			Extraction Sums of Squared Loadings			Rotation Sums of Squared Loadings		
	Total	%	Cumulative %	Total	%	Cumulative %	Total	%	Cumulative %
1	11.88	51.67	51.67	11.88	51.67	51.67	10.81	47.00	47.00
2	4.31	18.74	70.41	4.31	18.74	70.41	3.95	17.16	64.16
3	2.55	11.07	81.48	2.55	11.07	81.48	2.87	12.46	76.62
4	1.04	4.54	86.03	1.04	4.54	86.03	2.16	9.40	86.03

Table 3. Rotated component matrix. Extraction Method: Principal Component Analysis. Rotation Method: Varimax with Kaiser Normalization. Rotation converged in 7 iterations (IBM SPSS software v.28).

Initial variables	Component				Initial variables description
	1	2	3	4	
RE2021Tot	0.25	0.83	0.29	0.14	Dwellings completed (per 10 000 inhabitants)
LQ2021	0.29	0.77	0.36	0.15	Location quotient of dwellings completed (relative measure; [15])
RoadsPow2021	0.26	-0.09	0.76	-0.04	Density of roads per 100 sq.km.
Cars2021	0.96	0.08	0.19	-0.02	Passenger cars (absolute number)
Stops2021	0.87	0.17	0.15	-0.01	Active stops of public transport (absolute number)
RevPerPerson2021	0.29	0.22	0.50	0.30	Average gross monthly salaries
UEB2021	0.11	-0.16	0.85	0.32	Share of urbanization %
PNPow2021	0.14	0.54	0.09	0.74	Natural increase
WSM0_17_2021	-0.03	0.80	0.44	0.05	Migration balance index (0-17 years)
WSM0_64_2021	0.25	0.92	-0.05	0.04	Migration balance index (17-64 years)
WSM64+2021	0.00	0.79	0.31	0.10	Migration balance index (over 64 years)
RodzinyTotal2021	0.97	0.11	0.21	0.00	Total number of households (families)
TotalRoDzieci	0.98	0.13	0.17	0.03	Total number of child families
RoDzieci0_2021	0.94	0.08	0.28	-0.06	Total number of childless families
RoDzieci1_21	0.96	0.09	0.22	-0.05	Total number of families with 1 child
RoDzieci2_21	0.97	0.18	0.13	0.07	Total number of families with 2 children
RoDzieci3_21	0.89	0.15	0.05	0.34	Total number of families with 3 children
RoDzieci4+21	0.70	0.05	0.19	0.52	Total number of families with 4 or greater children
TotalDzieci21	0.98	0.14	0.13	0.09	Total number of children
AvgDzieci	-0.12	-0.04	0.55	0.72	Average number of children per family
NieprodPer100Prod2021	-0.11	-0.16	0.23	0.68	Non-working age population per 100 people of working age
Wom15-34	0.96	0.09	0.21	0.05	Total number of women aged 15-34
Wom35-49	0.96	0.11	0.21	-0.01	Total number of women aged 35-49

The interpretation of FA components were based on comparison to initial variables using rotated component matrix, which is in fact the matrix of Pearson's correlation coefficients (Table 3).

1. **Mobile vital families.** The first factor was interpreted as the demographic component of mobile families (of childbearing age) with stable incomes in areas connected (communicated), with possible expansion of development.
2. **Migration families.** The second factor was interpreted as migration component of families with relatively stable incomes in areas of development expansion (including outside cities).
3. **Small rich families.** The third factor describes the demographic component of small, high-income families (including childless and multi-generational families) in cities and areas of urbanization and development expansion.

4. **Large immobile families**. The fourth factor describes the demographic component of immobile families with large numbers of children and low incomes outside cities.

2.4   Spatial Differentiation of FA Components

All values on maps represent adequate volume of variance of certain components.

Mobile Vital Families. This component is associated with stable-income families at fertile age inhabiting connected areas (reflected in high amounts of personal cars and bus stops) with possible expansion of urbanization. The area of representation of this component is heterogeneous (Fig. 3).

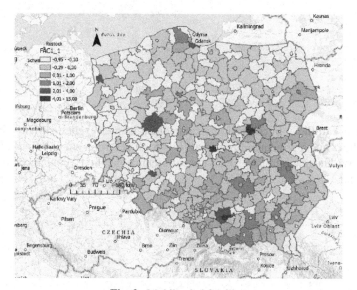

Fig. 3. Mobile vital families.

In some cases these are major Poland's cities, in others these are *"bagels"* surrounding the central municipality (mostly in a South East Poland).

Migration Families. This component is particularly interesting in the context of urban growth research because it's associated with the areas of intensive urbanization. This factor is defined by the high values of migration (positive balance), relatively high natural increase and stable income of inhabitants. The cartogram of the distribution of this component portrays overrepresentation of this cohort on the areas surrounding central cities of metropolitan areas (Fig. 4).

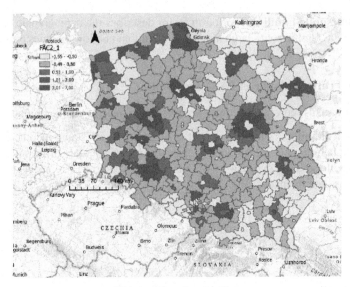

Fig. 4. Migration families

Small Rich Families. In contrast, this component is intensively distributed in central municipalities and highly urbanized areas (Fig. 5). It describes small (often childless or one kid) high-income families. This segment seems to be more pronounced in a North West Poland.

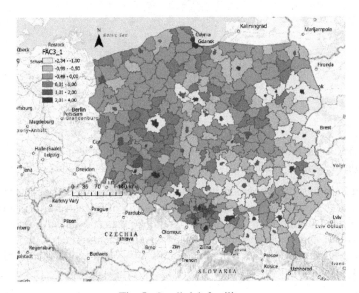

Fig. 5. Small rich families

Large Immobile Families. The fourth factor describes the cohort of large low income immobile families residing low urbanized areas. Geovisualizations of this factor provides unspecific picture (Fig. 6). This component seems to be widely distributed across country with, prevailing in outskirts of the cities.

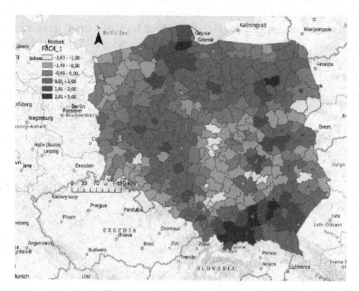

Fig. 6. Large immobile families

3 Discussion

Understanding population trends and anticipating demographic change are essential for national development planning and achieving continued progress towards the Sustainable Development Goals [3, 16–18] while drivers of human settlement distribution stays barely explored [19].

This pilot study identified compound factors specific to current sociodemographic and urbanization processes in Poland. Four extracted components (Mobile vital families (1), Migration families (2), Small rich families (3), Large immobile families (4) provided a range of latent determinants of the observed phenomena. The analysis suggests that the housing preferences of the settlers may be associated with their sociodemographic profile.

Thus, in all four cohorts the level of income of households plays a significant role. High income families are associated with residing highly urbanized areas. While stable income families are associated with the areas of intensive urbanization (the area of urban expansion) and wider unspecific areas. A further research is needed to assign the areas of overrepresentation of 'Mobile vital families' (1) component to better characterize the areas they inhabit.

In this study the low income families are associated with outskirt areas mainly. Another important characteristic of this cluster is immobility and high fertility rate. In contrast, high income families relate to having less (or no) kids.

The main hypothesis that the intensively urbanizing areas attract a cohort of young families at a fertile age was partially approved. The study reveal the interrelation of the areas of expansion and specific profile of settlers. They are 'Migration families' (2) characterized with stable income and relatively high level of natural increase on the area. On the other hand, no relevant age characteristic have been assigned to this group. The relation with the higher number of children haven't been confirmed either.

In the context of fertility research, mainly components three and four are on the focus of the interest. While 'Small reach families' (3) component resides cities and possess high incomes, the 'Large immobile families' (4) occupy lowly urbanized areas and tent to be poorly paid.

The fertility age was a significant parameter for components one and three, while there was no difference observed within the age category (defined for segment of 15–34 years and 35–49 years old).

Consideration of more variables describing infrastructure and urban/rural environment is recommended for future research.

4 Conclusions

The results of this study strengthen the evidence of interrelation between social profile of inhabitants and urban characteristics of settlement they reside. Complex causes likely underlie the detected spatial aspects of demographic differentiation and urbanization processes in Poland. There is a need to further examine the granularity of these disparities and the underlying causes for the observed discrepancies between different spatial units. Identifying housing needs and preferences associated with various cohorts of the population will remain a challenge for research and policymaking in the years to come.

5 Post Scriptum

The above study was prepared with consciousness that the observed phenomena dated for 2021 may change dramatically due to enormous flux of fugitives from Ukraine since February 2022. There were mainly women and children within estimated 1.6 million people. Some of them will settle in Poland, while others decide to transit or return to Ukraine. This change should be considered while multiplying this study for the following years data.

References

1. A World of 8 Billion. Future of the World. United Nations (2022)
2. Joint Research Centre (European Commission), Siragusa, A., Melchiorri, M., Pesaresi, M., Kemper, T.: Atlas of the Human Planet 2016: Mapping Human Presence on Earth With the Global Human Settlement Layer. Publications Office of the European Union, LU (2016)

3. World Population Prospects 2022: Summary of Results. United Nations, Department of Economic and Social Affairs, Population Division (2022)
4. World Bank: Urban Development. Overview. https://www.worldbank.org/en/topic/urbandevelopment/. Accessed 13 Apr 2023
5. World Urbanization Prospects: The 2018 Revision. United Nations, Department of Economic and Social Affairs, Population Division
6. Global State of Metropolis 2020. UN-Habitat (2020)
7. Muroishi, M., Yakita, A.: Urbanization and population contraction. Lett. Spat. Resour. Sci. 15, 543–553 (2022). https://doi.org/10.1007/s12076-022-00311-x
8. World Population Prospects, The 2019 Revision – Volume I: Comprehensive Tables. United Nations (2019). https://doi.org/10.18356/15994a82-en
9. World Urbanization Prospects 2018: Highlights. United Nations, Department of Economic and Social Affairs, Population Division
10. European Commission: Cities in the World: A New Perspective on Urbanisation. OECD (2020).https://doi.org/10.1787/d0efcbda-en
11. Behnisch, M., Krüger, T., Jaeger, J.A.G.: Rapid rise in urban sprawl: global hotspots and trends since 1990. PLOS Sustain. Transform. 1, e0000034 (2022). https://doi.org/10.1371/journal.pstr.0000034
12. Population. Size and structure and vital statistics in Poland by territorial division in 2021. As of 31 December. Statistics Poland (2022)
13. Statistics Poland. https://stat.gov.pl/en. Accessed 13 Apr 2023
14. Werner, P.A., Kaleyeva, V., Porczek, M.: Urban sprawl in Poland (2016–2021): drivers, wildcards, and spatial externalities. Remote Sens. 14, 2804 (2022). https://doi.org/10.3390/rs14122804
15. Kaleyeva, V., Werner, P.A., Porczek, M.: Driver factors, wildcards and spatial external effects of urban sprawl in Poland (2016–2022). In: Gervasi, O., Murgante, B., Misra, S., Ana, M.A., Rocha, C., Garau, C. (eds.) Computational Science and Its Applications – ICCSA 2022 Workshops: Malaga, Spain, July 4–7, 2022, Proceedings, Part I, pp. 325–337. Springer International Publishing, Cham (2022). https://doi.org/10.1007/978-3-031-10536-4_22
16. Chirisa, H., Campbell, M.: Spatial demography as the shaper of urban and regional planning under the impact of rapid urbanization: reconnoitering the future. In: The Palgrave Encyclopedia of Urban and Regional Futures, pp. 1–9. Springer International Publishing, Cham (2020). https://doi.org/10.1007/978-3-030-51812-7_96-1
17. Benti, S., Terefe, H., Callo-Concha, D.: Implications of overlooked drivers in Ethiopia's urbanization: curbing the curse of spontaneous urban development for future emerging towns. Heliyon. 8, e10997 (2022). https://doi.org/10.1016/j.heliyon.2022.e10997
18. World Cities Report 2022: Envisaging the Future of Cities. UN-Habitat (2022)
19. Hongtao, Y., Ting, M.: Changes in the geographical distributions of global human settlements. J. Resour. Ecol. 12, 829–839 (2021). https://doi.org/10.5814/j.issn.1674-764x.2021.06.011

Fire Severity and Vegetation Recovery Determination Using GEE and Sentinel-2: The Case of Peschici Fire

Valentina Santarsiero[1,4](✉) , Antonio Lanorte[2], Gabriele Nolè[2], Giuseppe Cillis[2], Francesco Vito Ronco[3], and Beniamino Murgante[4]

[1] CNR IGAG, Area della ricerca di Roma 1, strada provinciale 35d, 9, 00010 Montelibretti, RM, Italy
valentina.santarsiero@igag.cnr.it

[2] CNR IMAA, C.da Santa Loja, 85050 Potenza, Tito Scalo, Italy

[3] Apulia Region Civil Protection Department, Via delle Magnolie 6/8, 70026 Modugno, Bari, Italy

[4] School of Engineering, University of Basilicata, Viale dell'Ateneo Lucano 10, 85100 Potenza, Italy

Abstract. We propose an accurate and rapid methodology for the extraction of spatio-temporal fire features using Sentinel 2 products and the Google Earth Engine (GEE) platform. All Sentinel 2 images available in the GEE platform were clipped using the fire area mask and then the NBR, NDVI. dNBR and RdNBR indices were derived. The differential values of NBR, NDVI, dNBR and RdNBR were obtained by calculating the difference of the index values between two temporally adjacent images. The use of all available images in GEE restricted the time of occurrence of the images 5 days, excluding cloud-covered images and shortening the processing time of each satellite image. The results obtained showed that the proposed methodology allows for the rapid and accurate identification and classification of burnt areas, and also allows for the efficient and accurate extraction of the spatio-temporal characteristics of post-fire vegetation recovery. The results obtained can be used to implement targeted post-fire vegetation restoration practices.

Keywords: forest fire · remote sensing · GEE · GIS

1 Introduction

The factors that define the rate of vegetation regeneration after a fire are many and their complete identification is difficult. These factors are related to the characteristics of the fire environmental conditions and the characteristics of the plant species. Fire severity levels, topography (elevation, slope and orientation), post-fire climate and vegetation cover class are the most commonly used in estimates of regeneration [1]. Several studies have revealed that the influence of environmental factors on regeneration can vary between vegetation types [2].

O. Gervasi et al. (Eds.): ICCSA 2023 Workshops, LNCS 14112, pp. 220–231, 2023.
https://doi.org/10.1007/978-3-031-37129-5_19

Fire intensity represents the energy released during a fire. Topography, fuel type and condition, moisture content and chemical composition, and wind are the decisive factors in determining fire intensity. Therefore, fire intensity and fire duration take on opposite meanings in the presence of a given amount of fast-burning fuel. Consequently, high intensity fire with a low residence time may not be severe and may have low plant mortality. In contrast, low-intensity fires may damage the soil more than vegetation during combustion, e.g. burning litter or peat produce long-lasting heating resulting in increased severity. The vulnerability of vegetation to fire and post-fire responses are related to a set of characteristics that characterize each individual vegetation type. Remote sensing is often used in the monitoring of post-fire vegetation [1]. Indices derived from spectral bands have been widely used to estimate fire severity remotely [3, 4]. Fire causes changes in the spectral behavior of vegetation [5, 6]. Reflectance in the mid-infrared, which is sensitive to the water content of soil and vegetation, increases after fire, while in the near-infrared region the decline in reflectance occurs due to the fall in chlorophyll content of living vegetation.

Remote sensing is often used in the monitoring of post-fire vegetation [7, 8]. Indices derived from spectral bands have been widely used to estimate fire severity remotely. Fire causes changes in the spectral behavior of vegetation. Reflectance in the mid-infrared, which is sensitive to the water content of soil and vegetation, increases after fire, while in the near-infrared region the decline in reflectance occurs due to the fall in chlorophyll content of living vegetation.

Satellite earth observation is widely used to detect burnt areas [4, 9–12]. Satellite detection of burnt areas is commonly based on the detection of the effects of fire on the reflectance of vegetation. The increasing availability of medium spatial resolution sensors such as Landsat-OLI (30 m) or Sentinel-2 Multi Spectral Instrument (MSI) (10 m) can also overcome the limitations of lower resolution sensors in detecting smaller fires. In addition to improving fire detection and response times, there is also a need to improve the delineation, assessment and post-event monitoring of affected areas. Such post-event analysis can then be brought within the framework of strategies and policies for fire prevention, prediction, mitigation and response. The use of satellite imagery allows for accurate post-event delineation of fire extent and makes it possible to

- identify and estimate smaller areas affected by fires;
- avoid ground surveys in difficult areas to determine the location and extent of fires;
- use additional data in conjunction with satellite imagery to better assess, monitor and respond to fire-affected areas and communities;
- monitor environmental recovery, especially in relation to agricultural and forest areas.

To assess fire severity and vegetation regeneration using time series, several methodologies have been proposed, the most common being to monitor the state of vegetation from spectral indices. Among the most widely used indices are the Normalized Difference Vegetation Index (NDVI) [13–15]. Some studies have successfully applied NDVI, due to the relationship between the amount of vegetation consumed and fire intensity. In addition, specific indices have been developed that record the effects of fires with greater spectral contrast, such as the Normalized Burn Ratio (NBR). We propose an accurate and efficient framework for the extraction of spatio-temporal fire features using Sentinel 2 products and the Google Earth Engine (GEE) platform. All Sentinel 2 images available in the GEE platform were clipped using the fire area mask and then the NBR, NDVI and RdNBR indices were derived.

The Google Earth Engine (GEE) platform infrastructure allows for the production of complex geospatial products on various geographical and temporal scales, cloud-based processing and access to the platform, algorithms for classification and data processing [16–19].

There are still few works in the literature that have seen the application of GEE for monitoring fire severity and burnt areas [16, 20, 21].

Sentinel-2 is due to its innovative spectral properties, including red-edge bands suitable for characterizing chlorophyll content, which provide the means to create new indices for mapping fire severity [22, 23], is a useful source for monitoring burnt areas. Several previous studies have assessed forest fires using the normalized burn ratio (NBR). The NBR, in fact, exploits the near-infrared (NIR) and shortwave infrared (SWIR) regions of the electromagnetic spectrum [24] which makes it suitable for detecting fires in vegetation because changes in the NIR usually represent changes in photosynthetically active vegetation, which is reduced by fire, while changes in the SWIR reflect moisture content [25]. Indeed, fire causes a sharp contrast between NIR and SWIR recordings [26]. Furthermore, previous studies have used NBR variants, among which the differenced normalized burn ratio (dNBR) is commonly applied. The dNBR is a bi-temporal image differentiation performed on pre- and post-fire NBR images [5] to distinguish burn severity levels. The dNBR based on fire category has become a practical reference for obtaining information on burn severity [4, 27].

In this preliminary study, we present a rapid method for monitoring burnt forest areas and estimating post-fire vegetative recovery, using the NBR, dNBR, RdNBR and NDVI indices derived from Sentinel-2 within the GEE framework.

2   Material and Method

2.1   Study Area

The methodology was applied to the study of the fire of 24 July 2017, the area affected is approximately 3 km^2 and is located between the municipalities of Peschici and Vieste, in the province of Foggia. This area is a typical Mediterranean ecomosaic in which the driest periods are contextual with the hottest periods of the year [28, 29] Two pre-fire and immediate post-fire satellite images totally devoid of cloud cover were used to calculate the dNBR.

For an estimate of vegetation recovery following the fire, the NDVI was calculated for the entire available historical series (2016–2021). A map of the vegetation cover of the burnt areas was generated from the Nature Map (2013) in vector format (Fig. 1). The vegetation species affected by the fire mainly concern coniferous plantations, and to a lesser extent we find orchards, olive groves and agricultural areas. The topographic variables (altitude, slope and aspect) were generated from the DEM mosaic for the fire, resampled at a resolution of 20 m and projected in the WGS84 UTM 33N reference system. The average altitude is about 180 m above sea level, the area affected by the fire has fairly steep slopes, ranging from 0 to 15° in most of the area, accompanied by slopes with slightly milder slopes. The exposure of the slopes, takes into account the ability of the land to benefit from sunlight, in relation to its orientation with respect to the four cardinal points and the possible presence of mountains in the surroundings, or to suffer negative phenomena such as exposure to winds, which would be detrimental to cultivation. It is possible to divide the burnt area into two parts, one in which the vegetation is predominantly wooded and the prevailing exposure is from the east and south, while in the other part the prevailing exposure of the burnt area is from the east and north (Fig. 1).

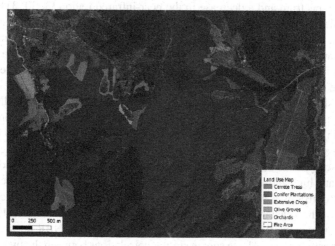

Fig. 1. Fire area and land use.

2.2 Methodology

The objective of the research is to implement an automatic procedure (tool) capable, starting from the processing of satellite images, of perimeter fires in a rapid and expeditious manner (i.e. as close as possible to the event) and to calculate severity indices that allow the mapping of first-order impacts (i.e. immediately after the event and second-order impacts (years after the event). The GEE software is the tool used for all data processing and spatial analyses. In particular, for the management of satellite images, which allows you to download satellite images and to pre- and post-process them. Images from the Sentinel-2 satellite were used to assess the severity of the fire.

The first analysis focused on estimating the fire severity of the entire burned area, through the calculation of the dNBR and RdNBR indices. The fire shows a very high severity (Fig. 2), with the presence of dNBR and RdNBR values higher than 1, in wooded areas. Subsequently, the severity was calculated in the years following the fire (from 2018 to 2021). During this pre-processing stage, proper masking of extremely dark pixels that do not represent burned-out areas plays a key role in reducing the generation of false positives, as well as reducing the computational effort.

After having identified and bounded the burned area and estimated the fire severity, we proceeded with the calculation of the NDVI index for the estimation of post-fire vegetative recovery.

3 Results and Discussions

3.1 Fire Severity Impact Assessment

As a consequence of a fire, vegetation shows a series of changes in the electromagnetic spectrum due to the effect of fire on chlorophyll. Fire destroys vegetation and, in many cases, leaves the ground bare, charring the roots of trees and also altering soil moisture.

This reduction in chlorophyll results in an increase in the visible region of the electromagnetic spectrum and a decrease in the near-infrared region [3, 30, 31]. There are many spectral indices used for the identification of burnt areas and the estimation of fire severity, among these the NBR (Normalized Burn Ratio) is one of the most widely used. This index combines near infrared and mid-infrared information and has been used extensively for the discrimination of burnt areas in the Mediterranean. The difference between the two pre/post-fire times allows us to estimate the dNBR, which in GEE has been reclassified from 0 to 1 based on the severity value (Fig. 2). The dNBR range values are fundamentally site-specific, no fixed thresholds are applied, but are classified according to the severity of the event by applying clustering algorithms to objectively assign fire severity classes to dNBRs based on an iterative breakdown of the data [32].

In this study, six classes of dNBR and RdNBR were selected: unburned; very low, low, moderate, high and very high.[33]. The dNBR shows the absolute value of change, while the RdNBR is a relative index which allows a certain independence from the conditions of the vegetation before the fire. Some studies have found that RdNBR is more accurate than dNBR [24] while others have found that RdNBR does not improve fire severity estimation and have shown similar correlations between the two indices and fire data field [33].

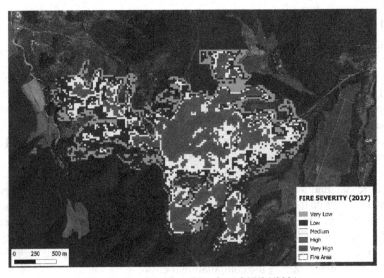

Fig. 2. Fire Severity of the fire of 07/24/2021.

Furthermore, several studies show that the RdNBR index is more sensitive to vegetation mortality and the dNBR to the severity of soil burn [34, 35]. The dNBR index, being linked to the variation of the NBR values calculated before and after the event, provides a measure of the effects of the fire and can therefore be used to characterize the degree of fire severity. The dNBR and RdNBR indices relating to the period of the event were first calculated and subsequently it was calculated over a period of 4 years (2017–2021). After the fire, we observe a mosaic of areas with different degrees of fire severity and this heterogeneity determines important implications in ecosystem recovery and land use possibilities (Fig. 2).

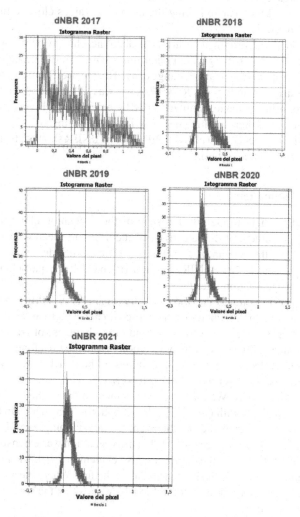

Fig. 3. Fire severity histograms for 2017 to 2021.

The fire shows a very high severity (Fig. 2), with dNBR and RdNBR values above 1 in the wooded areas. Subsequently, the severity was calculated in the years following the fire (from 2018 to 2021). Figure 3 shows the histograms with the fire severity values in the years following the event, what can be seen is that already starting from the year following the event, the severity values decrease significantly. In order to better photograph the evolution and impact of the fire in the affected area, the dNBR values calculated in the years following the event were compared with the dNBR value calculated immediately after the fire along 6 representative profiles. What emerges by analyzing the six profiles is a drastic decrease in the impact of the fire in the following years. The dNBR values significantly decrease going from severity values greater than 0.8 with peaks of 1.2 in 2017 to values of 0.4 the year following the event and values close to the non-burned threshold of 0.1 in 2021.

While the dNBR algorithm measures the absolute change between the pre- and post-fire images, the RdNBR algorithm determines burn severity based on the pre-fire reflectance and calculates the relative change caused by the fire. Similarly, to the processing listed previously for dNBR, the RdNBR value was calculated along the 6 profiles, also in this case, a fire behavior similar to dNBR emerges, with very high values, in some areas even higher than 1, which decrease in the following years.

The comparison of vegetation classes, RdNBR and dNBR showed, therefore, similar patterns of pixels classified as burnt.

3.2 Recovery Estimation

The spectral indices help to identify the state of the vegetation along the time series thanks to the improvement of the sensitivity of the different spectral bands. One of the most used indices is the Normalized Difference Vegetation Index, which is calculated by combining the near infrared (NIR) and red (R) bands, it is particularly useful for monitoring plant regeneration after fires.

Following the estimation of the impacts of the first order fire through the estimation of the fire severity and the perimeter of the burned area, a historical analysis of the vegetational state of the burned area was carried out through the use of NDVI. Specifically, an estimate was made of the state of the vegetation before the fire (June 2016–2017) and after the fire (June 2018–2021). Finally, the values of the dNBR pixels were compared with those of the historical series of NDVI, to verify how the vegetation responded to different degrees of severity. What can be seen in most of the studied area, even by carrying out a visual analysis with Google Earth orthophotos, is a change in the vegetation following the fire. Specifically, before the event the vegetation present belonged to the class of conifers, following the fire (year 2017) the vegetation was extensively damaged, in fact the effects of the fire on the shrubs are also evident in 2019, where the foliage of the plants remained standing still show the signs of the fire. Where the shrubs have been completely or almost totally destroyed, in the following years the vegetation present is mainly herbaceous (Fig. 4).

Comparing two images where the pre-fire vegetative cover is made up of coniferous forests, the fire has not completely destroyed this part of the forest, in fact the burned part of the forest, after a decrease in the NDVI index immediately following the event, shows a slow vegetative recovery of the same vegetation typology, as shown by the slight increase of NDVI in the following years (Fig. 5).

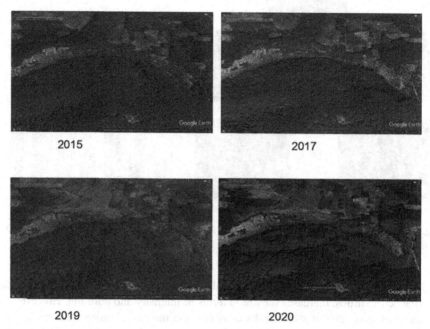

2015   2017

2019   2020

Fig. 4. Detail of the burnt area: pre-fire, during and post-fire images.

On the contrary, in an area of the forest completely destroyed by the fire, there was a drastic decrease in 2018 (following the fire) and a rapid rise in the index values which correspond to those of a meadow. In fact, in this part of the forest, following the fire, the trees were totally destroyed and/or removed following the fire, leaving space for the growth of bushes and meadows. This change of vegetation cover from woods to meadows is confirmed by the values of the historical series of NDVI which are higher following the fire than those pre-event in the same pixel. Comparing the areas in which the vegetation is composed of meadows and pastures, what emerges is a similar behavior of the NDVI both in non-burned areas and in areas affected by the fire with a severity greater than 1. This indicates the very of shrubs and meadows, so as not to highlight the presence of the fire starting as early as the following year. In areas covered by grass, the effects of fire are strongly influenced by the water content: if it decreases, dNBR and RdNBR increase because the fire resistance of the vegetation is lower. The dNBR values are also determined by the water content but in two opposite aspects: the residence time of the fire and the heat transferred to the ground. In fact, with the increase in water content, the duration of the fire increases while the amount of heat transferred to the ground decreases. The very high severity values in the meadows is probably due to the higher humidity of the same which, consequently, increases the duration of the fire.

It is interesting to note that the presence of shrubs mixed with grass compared to the presence of shrubs alone in a wooded area. This difference is fundamental in

Fig. 5. Fire area pixel detail, pre-, during and post-fire images with dNBR trend curve and NDVI historical series of the considered pixel.

understanding fire behavior, because due to the presence of tall grass the fuel load, added to the load of shrubs, increases the fire in terms of intensity and duration. However, the presence of grass mixed with shrubs increases the moisture content and reduces the likelihood of the fire reaching a high severity in this type of vegetation, contrary to what happens in the presence of dry shrubs. Remote sensing-based analysis of fire severity is an essential tool for assessing ecosystems in general at different spatial scales. Behavior varies within each vegetation class. In particular, the dNBR index in conifer plantations is more severe than in the other vegetation classes present in the area; in fact, the presence of shrubs (in this case conifers) causes the fire duration to increase.

4   Conclusions

The paper further demonstrates that the use of satellite data in activities related to the development, implementation and pre-operational management of systems for remote monitoring and mapping of forest and interface fires is very useful. In the scientific field, algorithms and forecasting models based on Earth observation technologies have been developed with the aim of obtaining, at different spatial and temporal resolution, information on parameters concerning the estimation of fire severity and vegetative recovery.

Therefore, the activities carried out in this paper were aimed at implementing a monitoring model with pre-operational purposes in order to carry out a correct perimeter of the effects of first and second order fire. For proper forest management, accurate identification and mapping of burnt areas is necessary, but field monitoring is complex and expensive, and not always accurate. With ready-to-use satellite data freely accessible in cloud-based Google Earth Engine (GEE), monitoring first- and second-order fire effects is much faster and cheaper. The results of this study demonstrate the great potential of Sentinel-2 satellite data and the use of GEE.

References

1. Pérez-Cabello, F., Montorio, R., Alves, D.B.: Remote sensing techniques to assess post-fire vegetation recovery. Curr. Opin. Environ. Sci. Heal. **21**, 100251 (2021). https://doi.org/10.1016/j.coesh.2021.100251
2. Ghermandi, B.L., Lanorte, A., Oddi, F., Lasaponara, R.: Assessing fire severity in semiarid **19** (2019)
3. Santarsiero, V., et al.: Assessment of post fire soil erosion with ESA sentinel-2 data and RUSLE method in Apulia region (Southern Italy). In: Gervasi, O., et al. (eds.) ICCSA 2020. LNCS, vol. 12252, pp. 590–603. Springer, Cham (2020). https://doi.org/10.1007/978-3-030-58811-3_43
4. Santarsiero, V., et al.: A remote sensing and geo-statistical approaches to mapping burn areas in Apulia region (Southern Italy). In: Gervasi, O., et al. (eds.) ICCSA 2021. LNCS, vol. 12954, pp. 670–681. Springer, Cham (2021). https://doi.org/10.1007/978-3-030-86979-3_47
5. Lanorte, A., Danese, M., Lasaponara, R., Murgante, B.: Multiscale mapping of burn area and severity using multisensor satellite data and spatial autocorrelation analysis. Int. J. Appl. Earth Obs. Geoinf. **20**, 42–51 (2012). https://doi.org/10.1016/j.jag.2011.09.005
6. Díaz-Delgado, R., Lloret, F., Pons, X.: Influence of fire severity on plant regeneration by means of remote sensing imagery. Int. J. Remote Sens. **24**, 1751–1763 (2003)
7. Gouveia, C., DaCamara, C.C., Trigo, R.M.: Post-fire vegetation recovery in Portugal based on spot/vegetation data. Nat. Hazards Earth Syst. Sci. **10**, 673–684 (2010). https://doi.org/10.5194/nhess-10-673-2010
8. Rahman, S., Chang, H., Magill, C., Tomkins, K., Hehir, W.: Spatio-temporal assessment of fire severity and vegetation recovery utilising sentinel-2 imagery in New South Wales, Australia, pp. 9960–9963. Department of Environmental Sciences, Macquarie University, Australia (2019)
9. Coppoletta, M., Merriam, K.E., Collins, B.M.: Post-fire vegetation and fuel development influences fire severity patterns in reburns. Ecol. Appl. **26**, 686–699 (2015). https://doi.org/10.1890/15-0225.1
10. Zheng, Z., Zeng, Y., Li, S., Huang, W.: A new burn severity index based on land surface temperature and enhanced vegetation index. Int. J. Appl. Earth Obs. Geoinf. **45**, 84–94 (2016). https://doi.org/10.1016/j.jag.2015.11.002
11. Nolè, G., Lasaponara, R., Lanorte, A., Murgante, B.: Quantifying urban sprawl with spatial autocorrelation techniques using multi-temporal satellite data. Int. J. Agric. Environ. Inf. Syst. **5**, 20–38 (2014). https://doi.org/10.4018/IJAEIS.2014040102
12. Scorza, F., Pilogallo, A., Saganeiti, L., Murgante, B.: Natura 2000 areas and sites of national interest (SNI): measuring (un)integration between naturalness preservation and environmental remediation policies. Sustainability **12**, 2928 (2020). https://doi.org/10.3390/su12072928
13. Ireland, G., Petropoulos, G.P.: Exploring the relationships between post-fire vegetation regeneration dynamics, topography and burn severity: a case study from the Montane Cordillera Ecozones of Western Canada. Appl. Geogr. **56**, 232–248 (2015)
14. Chen, X., et al.: Detecting post-fire burn severity and vegetation recovery using multitemporal remote sensing spectral indices and field-collected composite burn index data in a ponderosa pine forest. Int. J. Remote Sens. **32**, 7905–7927 (2011)
15. De Santis, A., Chuvieco, E.: GeoCBI: a modified version of the Composite Burn Index for the initial assessment of the short-term burn severity from remotely sensed data. Remote Sens. Environ. **113**, 554–562 (2009)

16. Xulu, S., Mbatha, N.: Burned Area Mapping over the Southern Cape Forestry Region, South Africa Using Sentinel Data within GEE Cloud Platform (2021)
17. Ye, J., Wang, N., Sun, M., Liu, Q., Ding, N., Li, M.: A New Method for the Rapid Determination of Fire Disturbance Events Using GEE and the VCT Algorithm—A Case Study in Southwestern and Northeastern China (2023)
18. Kumar, L., Mutanga, O.: Google Earth Engine applications since inception: usage, trends, and potential. Remote Sens. **10**, 1509 (2018)
19. Gorelick, N., Hancher, M., Dixon, M., Ilyushchenko, S., Thau, D., Moore, R.: Google Earth Engine: planetary-scale geospatial analysis for everyone. Remote Sens. Environ. **202**, 18–27 (2017)
20. Konkathi, P., Shetty, A.: Inter comparison of post-fire burn severity indices of Landsat-8 and Sentinel-2 imagery using Google Earth Engine. Earth Sci. Inf. **14**(2), 645–653 (2021). https://doi.org/10.1007/s12145-020-00566-2
21. Bar, S., Parida, B.R., Pandey, A.C.: Landsat-8 and Sentinel-2 based forest fire burn area mapping using machine learning algorithms on GEE cloud platform over Uttarakhand, Western Himalaya. Remote Sens. Appl. Soc. Environ. **18**, 100324 (2020). https://doi.org/10.1016/j.rsase.2020.100324
22. Puletti, N., Chianucci, F., Castaldi, C.: Use of Sentinel-2 for forest classification in Mediterranean environments. Ann. Silvic. Res. **42**, 32–38 (2018)
23. Filipponi, F.: Exploitation of sentinel-2 time series to map burned areas at the national level: a case study on the 2017 Italy wildfires. Remote Sens. **11**, 622 (2019)
24. Miller, J.D., et al.: Calibration and validation of the relative differenced Normalized Burn Ratio (RdNBR) to three measures of fire severity in the Sierra Nevada and Klamath Mountains, California, USA. Remote Sens. Environ. **113**, 645–656 (2009)
25. Key, C., Glacier Field Station Center: Evaluate sensitivities of burn-severity mapping algorithms for different ecosystems and fire histories in the United States. Final Report to the Joint Fire Science Program (2006)
26. Keeley, J.E.: Fire intensity, fire severity and burn severity: a brief review and suggested usage. Int. J. Wildl. Fire **18**, 116–126 (2009)
27. Nolè, G., et al.: Model of post fire erosion assessment using RUSLE method, GIS tools and ESA Sentinel data. In: Gervasi, O., et al. (eds.) ICCSA 2020. LNCS, vol. 12253, pp. 505–516. Springer, Cham (2020). https://doi.org/10.1007/978-3-030-58814-4_36
28. Lanfredi, M., Coluzzi, R., Imbrenda, V., Macchiato, M., Simoniello, T.: Analyzing space–time coherence in precipitation seasonality across different European climates. Remote Sens. **12**, 171 (2020)
29. Lanfredi, M., Coppola, R., D'Emilio, M., Imbrenda, V., Macchiato, M., Simoniello, T.: A geostatistics-assisted approach to the deterministic approximation of climate data. Environ. Model. Softw. **66**, 69–77 (2015). https://doi.org/10.1016/j.envsoft.2014.12.009
30. Nolè, G., et al.: Model of post fire erosion assessment using RUSLE method, GIS tools and ESA Sentinel DATA. In: Gervasi, O., et al. (eds.) ICCSA 2020. LNTCS, vol. 12253, pp. 505–516. Springer, Cham (2020). https://doi.org/10.1007/978-3-030-58814-4_36
31. Lanorte, A., Danese, M., Lasaponara, R., Murgante, B.: Multiscale mapping of burn area and severity using multisensor satellite data and spatial autocorrelation analysis. Int. J. Appl. Earth Obs. Geoinf. **20**, 42–51 (2013)
32. Shakesby, R.A.: Post-wildfire soil erosion in the Mediterranean: review and future research directions. Earth-Sci. Rev. **105**, 71–100 (2011). https://doi.org/10.1016/j.earscirev.2011.01.001
33. Soverel, N.O., Perrakis, D.D.B., Coops, N.C.: Estimating burn severity from Landsat dNBR and RdNBR indices across Western Canada. Remote Sens. Environ. **114**, 1896–1909 (2010). https://doi.org/10.1016/j.rse.2010.03.013

34. Roy, D.P., Boschetti, L., Trigg, S.N.: Remote sensing of fire severity: assessing the performance of the normalized burn ratio. IEEE Geosci. Remote Sens. Lett. **3**, 112–116 (2006). https://doi.org/10.1109/LGRS.2005.858485

35. Zhu, G., Blumberg, D.G.: Classification using ASTER data and SVM algorithms: the case study of Beer Sheva, Israel. Remote Sens. Environ. **80**, 233–240 (2002). https://doi.org/10.1016/S0034-4257(01)00305-4

Short Papers (MEETA 2023)

A Collaborative Spatial Decision Support System for Assessing Transformative Potential of Minimum Ecological Units (MEUs) in a Circular Regeneration Perspective

Stefano Cuntò[✉], Eugenio Muccio, Sabrina Sacco, and Piero Zizzania

Department of Architecture, University of Naples Federico II, via Toledo 402, Naples, Italy
{stefano.cunto,eugenio.muccio,sabrina.sacco,
piero.zizzania}@unina.it

Abstract. The need to respond to the challenges of our time requires a circular reinterpretation of the cultural and ecosystem heritage of our cities. In order to foster new ways of sustainable urban regeneration, it is essential to identify public green areas in which to promote cultural-based spatial regeneration processes consistent with the Circular Economy model. Different visions of urban landscape reform give an interpretation of these issues based on the model of the '15-Minute City' services and proximity logics contribute to the construction of enabling contexts, i.e. contexts in which the human beings are enabled to be active subjects, capable of pursuing their own well-being, that of their community and of their ecosystem. In particular, the ecosystem assets of cities can be read as a multitude of local proximity ecosystems or 'Minimum Ecological Units' (MEUs). Collaborative analysis of the use of MEUs can be the basis of Spatial Decision Support Systems (SDSS) which, through standardised techniques for accessing, understanding and interpreting data, facilitate stakeholders in decision-making processes. Starting from the results obtained by the multidisciplinary Collective "Needle Agopuntura Urbana", in the collaborative process of urban regeneration developed within the Needle Scampia (Naples) Living Lab, the contribution proposes the integration of Multi Criteria Decision Analysis (MCDA) tools with Participatory GIS (P-GIS) collaborative spatial survey practices. The proposed methodology aims to define a SDSS able to provide decision-makers and communities with a tool capable of considering qualitative factors with respect to the transformative potential of MEUs as well as providing the possibility of balancing these factors with quantitative dimensions.

Keywords: Spatial Decision Support System (SDSS) · Circular regeneration · Participatory GIS (P-GIS) · Multi-Criteria Decision Analysis (MCDA) · Minimum Ecological Unit (MEU)

O. Gervasi et al. (Eds.): ICCSA 2023 Workshops, LNCS 14112, pp. 235–252, 2023.
https://doi.org/10.1007/978-3-031-37129-5_20

1 Introduction

The need to guarantee timely responses to the many challenges that the present day calls us to face, gives rise to the need to reinterpret the cultural and ecosystemic heritage of our cities in a circular way [1]. This was evident during the COVID-19 pandemic, when urban green space was identified as the ideal place to deal with stress and anxiety [2], allowing for greater physical and social activity and helping to strengthen community relations [3, 4].

Identifying public green spaces in major Mediterranean cities in which to promote cultural-led spatial regeneration processes, consistent with the Circular Economy (CE) model, is crucial to foster new forms of sustainable urban regeneration. In this context, considering the idea of the "Third Landscape" [5] and the "cultural waste" [6–9], as a resource, can help to develop autopoietic systems [10] and to promote new processes of sustainable development based on the principles of common good and mutuality, as well as on the system of interpersonal and identity relations typical of Mediterranean cities [11].

Recently, various visions of urban landscape reform based on the valorisation of proximity relations [12] as a central element in the transition of cities towards sustainability have been widely echoed. The "Agenda for a green and just recovery" of the member cities of the C40 network "Cities Climate Leadership Group", interprets these issues with the definition of the "15-Minute City" strategy. The concepts underlying this approach stem from the "Neighbourhood Unit" model [13] complemented by proxemics studies [14] applied to the reading of urban spaces and research on the human scale of public space use [15].

As in the recent experiences of some cities in the C40 network [16], the interpretation of proximity services is increasingly linked to the concept of the common good [17, 18], focusing mainly on the relationships established between the good and the network of actors and users who inhabit the space. This network can be defined as a design community [19], i.e. communities that come together around a catalysing theme of ideas and collaborative projects [20]. According to this point of view, proximity services should be considered as enabling context factors through which human beings pursue their well-being and that of their community in a space in which they can share needs and foster the construction of shared projects and visions [21].

From a morphological point of view, the urban landscape can be interpreted as a complex expression of urbanisation processes of nature [22], which have led to a strong segmentation of the ecosystem heritage. From the perspective of proximity logics, the complex urban ecosystem can be read as a multitude of local neighbourhood ecosystems that can be identified as "Minimum Ecological Units" (MEUs) [21, 23] whose metabolism is as efficient as their ability to be self-sufficient [24], interconnected and supported by design communities. Reinterpreting the ecosystemic heritage of Mediterranean cities, from the perspective of proximity services, leads to prefigure planning and regeneration scenarios in which collaboration is at the basis of the public space use.

The most significant barriers to efficient planning and regeneration practices, which require new forms of governance, are related to the lack of involvement of citizens and local actors [25]. In this context, by monitoring, managing and evaluating the resources of the landscape in multidimensional contexts, the operational framework of Multicriteria

Decision Analysis (MCDA) has aided decision makers in efficiently making strategic decisions and defining concrete solutions [26]. The decision-making field has improved over the past three decades thanks to Spatial Decision Support Systems (SDSS) that combine MCDA and Geographic Information Systems (GIS) [27]. SDSS, by organising multidimensional knowledge layers, streamline the process of linking data to decisions through geographic mapping and GIS techniques [28, 29] and support choices through the MCDA. In this way, they enable decision-makers to perform sensitivity analysis, scenario analysis and optimisation to identify the most robust and efficient decision [30], facilitate stakeholder access to decision problems significantly outperforming previous decision support systems [27, 31, 32].

This contribution, identifies in the SDSS for planning [33–35], implemented in a GIS environment, a valid analysis tool that can support administrators and territorial communities in a transition process towards the enhancement of MEUs, i.e. towards the provision of proximity services based on the relations between urban public space and citizens. Such multidimensional and flexible tools are able to reconcile the experience and actual use of places and their potentials with the ambitions and needs of inhabitants, supporting multi-scalar choices related to spatial planning and urban design [36, 37].

In particular, the collaborative analysis related to MEUs, through the concept of Ecological Device (ED) [38], can underlie the construction of SDSS focused on the creation of new relationships and the strengthening of existing ones between human beings and ecosystems focusing on the mutual benefits that can be produced and experienced. The logic offered by EDs gives the opportunity to implement multi-scalar solutions for the transformation and management of the urban natural heritage in SDSSs, integrating collaborative processes of co-learning and co-design of urban public green spaces.

Starting from these considerations, the following research questions was identified: RQ1. Can the formal and informal use of the city's MEUs represent a criterion for assessing the capability of these areas to generate collaborative and enabling contexts for the formation of new design communities?; RQ2. Can these assessments support decision-making choices regarding new models of collaborative management and care of the city's green public spaces?

The article proceeds as follows: Sect. 2 describes the proposed methodology; Sect. 3 introduces the case study; Sect. 4 explains the data gathering and processing phases towards identification of criteria for SDSS; Sect. 5 presents the results and discussion; finally, Sect. 6 draw the conclusions, highlighting potentials and criticalities of the approach, and the research follow-ups.

2 Methodological Workflow

The goal is thus set: to identify, within a collaborative SDSS, sensitive areas for the activation of bottom-up circular regeneration strategies according to the areas' capability in delivering proximity services. The participatory process considers non-economic evaluations, which involve the collection of data related to the relevance or frequency of a given use or phenomenon, in the broader scope of social evaluations. Starting from the declared goal, a methodological workflow was developed (see Fig. 1).

The theoretical and operational background considers circular regeneration processes as a field on which to set up a collaborative SDSS to evaluate MEUs in their capability

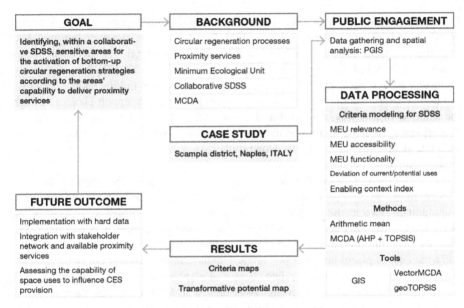

Fig. 1. The methodological workflow.

to deliver proximity services, by means of MCDA methods. The testing area consists of the case study of Scampia, a district of the municipality of Naples: a public engagement activity, involving a heterogeneous set of actors and citizens, constituted the data gathering phase, through the Participatory GIS (PGIS) tool. The data processing phase, on the other hand, was addressed to the modeling of criteria for SDSS, resulting in the following: MEU relevance; MEU accessibility; MEU functionality; Deviation of current and potential uses; Enabling context index. MEU values were thus obtained through arithmetic methods (the mean) and through multi-criteria evaluations, performed specifically through the AHP and TOPSIS methods with regard to the "enabling context" criterion. These methods were implemented in the GIS environment through the VectorMCDA package plugin.

In particular, the Analytic Hierarchy Process (AHP) method [39, 40] can be performed in involving local communities in the assessment, administering the matrix in community tables to define, by means of a pairwise comparison, a ranking of public green space uses according to their ability to define enabling contexts. The Technique for Order Preference by Similarity to Ideal Solution (TOPSIS) method [41], implemented in spatial contexts, makes it possible to graphically return an immediate representation of the values, resulting from the comparative evaluation of the criteria with respect to their concurrence in a specific area. This technique makes it possible to define two ideal alternatives, the first defined as the positive ideal point and the second as the negative worst point. The positive ideal point is that solution which maximises all criteria identified as gains and minimises all those identified as costs, the negative ideal point is defined according to the reverse logic. The two points are positioned at the extremes of a range of values from 0 to 1 in which all real alternatives are evaluated according to their distance from the two ideal points.

Lastly, two main results were obtained from such spatial data processing: the 5 criteria maps, and the transformative potential map, obtained through TOPSIS method.

3   The Case-Study

This contribution is based on a collaborative urban regeneration experience developed in Scampia, one of the suburbs of the city of Naples in southern Italy (see Fig. 2).

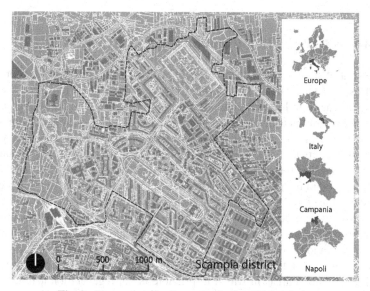

Fig. 2. The case study: Scampia district, Naples, Italy.

With an area of 4,23 sq. km and a resident population of more than 40.000 inhabitants, Scampia is the Naples municipality district with the highest amount of green areas. The Scampia district was born in a relatively recent period [42, 43], characterised, between the end of World War II and the 1970s, by unprecedented building growth interrupted abruptly by the 1980 earthquake that marked its definitive transition to "dormitory suburb" [44]. Between the 1980s and 1990s, the area was affected by multiple subsidised building projects and private cooperatives. The dislocation of the blocks of land, the cross-section and layout of the streets and the large number of buildings intended for infrastructures that was never completed, and above all the lack of maintenance of the public spaces and common areas, contributed to the degradation of the neighbourhood.

Between the 1990s and the early 2000s, the population of the Scampia neighbourhood recorded a high presence of criminal organisations, such as to give it the stigma of being "Europe's biggest drug-dealing square" [43]. The latest data collected by the "Parliamentary Commission of Inquiry into the conditions of security and the state of decay of cities and their suburbs" [45] show that the social and material vulnerability index is 121,1 (city mean 111,2), the index of non-completion of secondary schooling is 19,7 (city mean 10,7%), and the unemployment rate is 46,9% (city mean 27,8%). What emerges from the statistics, therefore, is the image of a neighbourhood in a constant state of emergency.

At the same time, a strong social cohesion has increasingly developed in the neighbourhood. More than twenty associations and third sector and private social actors coexist in the neighbourhood, promoting numerous informal experiences of civic and political activism. Since the early 2000s, the interest of participatory companies, universities, research centres, foundations, third sector associations, and participatory design groups has favoured the realisation of a number of highly innovative urban regeneration projects [46].

4   Towards Criteria Identification for SDSS

With the goal of setting up a database of MUEs and the types of formal, informal and potential uses of these areas, we provided appropriate research tools that were able to involve and activate local communities in both the survey and co-design phases of bottom-up regeneration actions and public space use and management activities.

The multidisciplinary Collective "Needle Agopuntura Urbana", together with the project partners, activated the "Needle Scampia"[1] Living Lab between 2019 and 2020, according to an action-research approach [47] focused on the community and territorial networks, framed in the perspective of "prosumers", and on MUEs, as resources to be reinserted into the productive and cultural cycle of the Scampia neighbourhood. The Living Lab activities were designed to start processes of 'taking charge' by the community (shopkeepers, territorial operators, administration, training bodies, etc.) of small areas of the neighbourhood concerned by urban transformation actions. The objectives underlying the approach adopted were: i. to implement a 'crowd-mapping' process to define potential green public areas in which to promote urban regeneration actions, according to the needs and capacities of the community; ii. to activate a 'design community', to coordinate participation in space management and use choices; iii. to guarantee 'in itinere' monitoring of activities.

The collaborative listening activity led to the identification by the community of 45 areas of perceived degradation, 14 areas of perceived maintenance and 3 inaccessible areas. For each of these areas, the perception of care was qualitatively assessed through the description of mapped structural elements. From the mapping exercise generated a fragmented perception of the neighbourhood by the participants themselves is revealed. This interpretation returns a spatially limited sociality, where the inhabitants mostly live in the areas surrounding the blocks of flats for short daily activities, and almost all work or leisure activities are carried out outside the neighbourhood, especially by the youngest.

---

[1] Initiative promoted by the Directorate General for Contemporary Creativity - DGCC and MIBACT, in the context of the 'Creative living Lab II edition' award. The "Needle Agopuntura Urbana" collective's members are: Abbate L., Cuntò S., Napoletano F., Pacera L., Dinardo M., Pone A., Sodano S., Diana S.. The project local partners are: Aps Jolie Rouge, Asd Stella Rossa 2006, Aps Banda Baleno, Gruppo di Risveglio dal Sonno GRIDAS, Centro Hurtado, Liceo Elsa Morante Scampia. The scientific partners are: Department of Architecture and Department of Social Sciences of University of Naples Federico II.

During the mapping process, the stakeholders reported the current uses of the identified areas, describing their morphology and social uses in relation to the accessibility and functionality dimensions of the area. The identification of uses was conducted collaboratively from a small pre-set that was implemented during the survey phases according to the alerts assigned to the MUEs. Once the structural elements of the territory were identified and current uses analysed, potential uses or uses to be enhanced were identified. The formal and informal uses of public space deduced from the process are the following: dog walking area, children's playground area, bus waiting area, proximity markets area, natural recreation area, skateboard area, recreational and social area, relaxation area, outdoor sport area, event area, mixed use area.

Finally, the research focused on the frequency of reports, in order to identify the most relevant areas for the community to choose as possible intervention areas. To do this, the 6 areas with the highest frequency were selected, in whose proximity there were associations that could support the regeneration process in terms of their capacity to take charge.

4.1 Public Engagement

The collaborative survey methodology was structured through numerous focus groups [48], a qualitative technique used in action research, in which a group of people, representative of more or less defined categories, are invited to talk, discuss and compare their personal attitudes towards a specific topic. In the investigation of the formal, informal and potential use of the public green space in the neighbourhood, the focus groups centralised on observing how a community interaction takes place and how a community creates a dialogue on the topic of MEUs.

In order to collect information from the focus groups at the same time as they took place, a Collaborative Mapping (CM) was performed. CM facilitated the identification of the structural components of the territory and the viewpoint of the relative communities by integrating it with the knowledge of technicians with respect to numerous issues, overcoming communication gaps between actors [49]. To explore and assess the critical elements of an area, as in the case of a neighbourhood, the involvement of the local community is a key factor [50, 51]. Indeed, the spatial representation of opportunities and critical issues can guide towards a participatory planning project that implements more accurate regeneration strategies [52, 53].

The 2D mapping, created on scale maps on which people drew with markers, pens, stickers and drawing pins, was implemented with Web-GIS[2] mapping methods to provide users with a simple, intuitive and inclusive tool to visualise the survey results. The process was based on models of "participatory GIS" (P-GIS), tools consisting of multiple methods and integrated technologies to enable collaborative planning and support inclusive public participation [54–57]. This device is oriented to the empowerment of a community [58], through the application of demand-driven research integrated with geospatial representation tools. Also, social data and geographic maps support the participatory approach as a wide-ranging 'policy process' [59] with the combination of experts and socially diversified knowledge generated from the community [60, 61].

---

[2] Needle Scampia - Collaborative Neighbourhood Uses Map, Available at: https://www.google.com/maps/d/u/0/edit?hl=it&mid=1FNBmdfqSMOvelZwreC5WCyH46T82IGIg&ll=40.899 578002260625%2C14.247766710674558&z=15.

4.2 Geo-Data Processing: Criteria Modeling

In order to assess the transformative potential of the selected MEU, a multi-criteria evaluation has been performed. This decision-making process involves evaluating and comparing several options based on multiple criteria. Defining criteria is a crucial step in the multi-criteria evaluation process because it helps to establish a clear and objective framework for assessing different options.

The data gathered in the previous phase was processed according to 5 relevant criteria for the objective of the assessment. Table 1 shows the list of criteria, the input data collected within the PGIS phase, and the processing method for each criteria. It should be noted that all processed data were standardised by rescaling the values of the variables on a common scale (from 0 to 1), in order to facilitate the comparison of variables with different units of measure and to make the visualisation of the data distribution easier.

Table 1. The criteria set.

ID	Criteria	Data input	Processing method
1	MEU relevance	Reporting frequency of MEU	-
2	MEU accessibility	Frequency of accessibility related to current uses	Mean
3	MEU functionality	Frequency of functionality related to current uses	Mean
4	Deviation of current and potential uses	Frequency of current uses and potential uses	Mean difference
5	Enabling context index	Score for typologies of current uses	MCDA: AHP
		Frequency of current uses	MCDA: TOPSIS

Below is a detailed description of each criterion and the related processing method:

1. **MEU relevance:** measured through normalised values of the reporting frequency of areas, with the aim of identifying the most highly acknowledged MEUs by the participants. The qualities attributed to the areas by the respondents, in terms of perceived care and degradation, were not taken into account for the purposes of the criterion, which only measures their frequency: this benefits the possibility of considering areas potentially sensitive to transformation beyond their conservation status.
2. **MEU accessibility:** measured through the normalised mean of the qualitative judgements values expressed on the accessibility of areas with respect to the uses reported in each of them. The objective is to identify the most perceived accessible MEUs with respect to the specific uses.
3. **MEU functionality:** measured through the normalised mean of the values of the qualitative judgements expressed on the functionality of the areas with respect to the uses reported in each of them. The objective is to identify the MEUs most perceived as equipped with respect to the specific uses.

4. **Deviation of current and potential uses:** measured through the normalised means of the reporting frequency of current and potential uses in each area, then calculating the difference between the values. The objective is to identify the extent of the distance between the supply of current uses and the demand for potential uses.

5. **Enabling context index:** obtained from the evaluation with TOPSIS method of the normalised mean values of the reporting frequency of current uses, weighted through AHP method according to the capability of uses to enhance enabling contexts, for each area. The objective is to identify the MEUs in which the uses most likely to generate enabling contexts are concentrated.

More specifically, the definition of this last index originated from the scores assigned by the participants to each use, according to four specific predetermined criteria: a) time spent in the area, i.e. the ability of an activity to maximise the time people spend using the place; b) involvement in the use of the area, i.e. the ability of an activity to effectively engage users in the physical use of the place; c) specificity of interest in the use of the area, i.e. the ability of an activity to satisfy a specific and shared need of the community in the use of the place; d) social aggregation capacity of the use of the area, i.e. the ability of an activity to involve the greatest number of people in the use of the place.

By assessing the uses against the above-mentioned criteria using the AHP method, the relative importance of each criterion was obtained. These values provided the weights to be associated with the uses in the TOPSIS evaluation, which was performed with respect to mean values of the reporting frequency of current uses. The resulting values shown in Table 2, then normalised, made it possible to obtain the enabling context indices for each area.

Table 2. The TOPSIS matrix.

Uses	AHP weight	Preference	Ideal point	Worst point
Recreational and social area	0,16	gain	1	0
Event area	0,15	gain	1	0
Outdoor sport area	0,12	gain	1	0
Children's playground area	0,1	gain	1	0
Skateboard area	0,09	gain	1	0
Relax area	0,09	gain	1	0
Proximity markets area	0,08	gain	1	0
Mixed use area	0,07	gain	1	0
Natural recreation area	0,07	gain	1	0
Dog walking area	0,03	gain	1	0
Bus waiting area	0,03	gain	1	0

5   Results and Discussion

The spatial values of the areas for each criterion were visualised through GIS maps. The maps follow the choropleth logic, in which data values are mapped to a colour scale, with each colour representing a range of data value, identifying areas with high or low values of a particular variable.

The relevance map (see Fig. 3) shows which MEUs are most recognised and reported by the community by defining their degree of relevance (increasing values from 0 to 1) in relation to the perception of the participants.

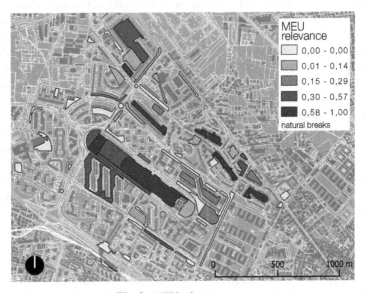

Fig. 3. MEU relevance map.

The results show the emergence of several clusters, the most consistent of which are: East Cluster, characterised by the presence of three MEUs that are part of economic and social housing complexes that are older than the rest of the neighbourhood, and are concentrated in an area where the architectural and urban characteristics guarantee greater conditions of proximity; North Cluster, which sees the presence of large green areas servicing large and dislocated residential complexes where, however, strong social values linked to the management practices of these areas are recognised; Central Cluster, made up of central territorial park MEUs, shows how the latter is perceived in a fragmented and non-homogeneous manner.

The accessibility map (see Fig. 4) shows which MEUs are most recognised as areas with good accessibility (increasing values from 0 to 1) with respect to the specific uses identified by the community.

The results confirm the definition of the first two clusters (East and North) deduced from the relevance map, and show how the Central Cluster's MEUs benefit from varying degrees of accessibility of use.

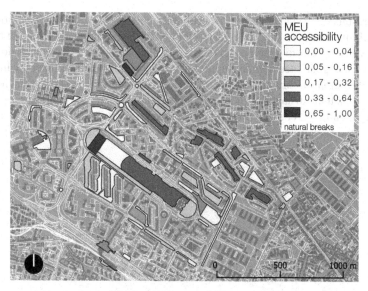

Fig. 4. MEU accessibility map.

The functionality map (see Fig. 5) shows which MEUs are most recognised as equipped areas (increasing values from 0 to 1) capable of supporting the specific uses reported by the community.

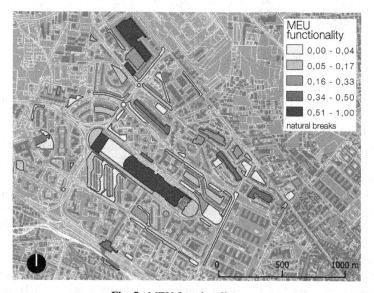

Fig. 5. MEU functionality map.

The results show that the degree of accessibility of MEUs is not always proportionate to their ability to support the uses that are identified. For example, the areas of the East cluster, which appear to guarantee good accessibility to the uses in the area, do not, on the other hand, guarantee optimal support for these uses in terms of functionality.

The deviation of current and potential uses map (see Fig. 6) shows which are the MEUs in which the distance of the supply of current uses over the demand for potential uses is concentrated, compared to the participants' reports, showing the community's interest in the need to increase the use of certain areas (decreasing values from 1 to 0).

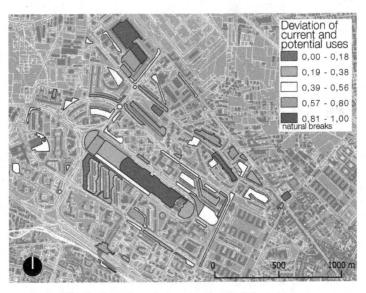

Fig. 6. Deviation of current and potential uses map.

The results identify 4 MEUs that are homogeneously distributed throughout the neighbourhood and are recognised as having great unexpressed potential. Here again, the East Cluster is found to be of interest.

The enabling context map (see Fig. 7) shows which MEUs have the highest concentration of uses that can promote the construction of enabling contexts (increasing values from 0 to 1).

The results confirm the presence of the three main clusters with a similar distribution of values in the areas. Each of them contains a focal area in which uses capable of creating enabling contexts are condensed. The surrounding areas result as satellites of the main MEUs characterised by gradually decreasing values.

Downstream of the values obtained for the 5 criteria, a TOPSIS assessment was performed to evaluate the areas according to their overall transformative potential. Equal weights were considered for all criteria, which were all meant as gain, with the exception of criterion 4 (Deviation of current and potential uses), which was meant as cost: this is due to the fact that during normalisation, the values that express the highest deviation between current and potential use are closer to 0.

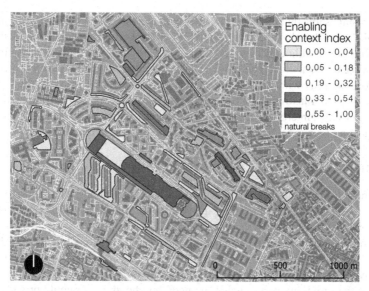

Fig. 7. Enabling context map.

The map of this potential (see Fig. 8), therefore, shows which MEUs are most likely to promote bottom-up urban regeneration processes aimed at activating design communities (values increasing from 0 to 1).

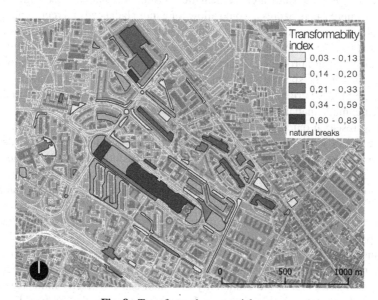

Fig. 8. Transformative potential map.

The results show that the areas most likely to activate such processes are condensed in the MEUs of the identified clusters. The Central Cluster contains two of the best-performing areas, although they are surrounded by MEUs with little transformative and networking capability. The North Cluster appears to have a defined core around which several areas with uneven values gravitate. The East Cluster has a number of MEUs with good transformation potential and a particular spatial distribution that itself suggests a possible interconnection between the areas, which are at medium-high values, foreshadowing scenarios of possible activation of design communities.

6   Conclusions

The proposed methodological process made it possible to build a collaborative SDSS enabling the identification of areas of transformation, thus setting up an MCDA-based and community-driven approach.

The main potentials are to be found in the involvement of communities and territorial networks, which makes it possible to collect the "insiders" points of view, since the data derived from the community are an expression of their needs and expectations with respect to the proximity services that the neighbourhood can or could provide. Moreover, the spatial dimension of the decision support system allows for clearer and more immediate communication between actors, according to the geographical visualisation of output values.

Some limitations of the methodology are related to the reliability of the collected information, which is tied to the quantity and type of actors involved, as well as their specific knowledge of the study area. A thematic division of the tables, also with respect to the power/interest they express, would allow for a more balanced and representative collection of judgements. Moreover, the survey process requires a time-consuming presence in the area, foreshadowing the need to set up permanent workshops and neighbourhood living labs to ensure proper continuity in the collection of judgements and monitoring of the areas. Finally, specific statistical tests to verify the correlation between the values obtained for the criteria should be carried out to refine the selection of criteria and improve the mathematical soundness of the process.

Future research outcomes concern the implementation of qualitative data inferred from the SDSS with quantitative information that could inform multilevel decision-making processes [62] aimed at different forms of transformation and management of MEUs according to climate change adaptation, such as projects to contrast urban heat island, flooding phenomena or foster solutions for disaster risk reduction. The integration of the performed assessment with the urban service and stakeholders network could enhance the construction of visions of transformation and co-management of urban public space through Geodesign practices on MEUs [63].

Ultimately, it is believed that this decision-making problem could also focus on the services that urban ecosystems provide and that directly affect human well-being, i.e. Ecosystem Services (ES), the availability of which can be directly influenced by the availability of neighbourhood services, and vice versa. In particular, Cultural Ecosystem Services (CES) are the only class of ES that do not represent purely ecological phenomena, but rather are the result of complex and dynamic relationships between ecosystems and humans, structured over long periods of time [64, 65]. From their assessment and implementation of the framework in SDSSs, it will be possible to structure urban landscape planning and management processes to identify place-based and bottom-up strategies [66].

References

1. Bosone, M., Nocca, F., Fusco Girard, L.: The circular city implementation: cultural heritage and digital technology. In: Rauterberg, M. (ed.) HCII 2021. LNCS, vol. 12794, pp. 40–62. Springer, Cham (2021). https://doi.org/10.1007/978-3-030-77411-0_4

2. Randrup, T.B., Buijs, A., Konijnendijk, C.C., Wild, T.: Moving beyond the nature-based solutions discourse: introducing nature-based thinking. Urban Ecosyst. **23**(4), 919–926 (2020). https://doi.org/10.1007/s11252-020-00964-w

3. Heymans, A., Breadsell, J., Morrison, G., Byrne, J., Eon, C.: Ecological urban planning and design: a systematic literature review. Sustainability **11**, 3723 (2019). https://doi.org/10.3390/su11133723

4. Shaw, A., Harford, D., Tolsma, K., Squires, E.: Climate Change, Equity, and COVID-19: Considerations in a Changing World. Integrated Climate Action for BC Communities Initiative (2020)

5. Clément, G.: Manifesto del Terzo paesaggio. Quodlibet (2016)

6. Hawkins, G., Muecke, S.: Culture and Waste: The Creation and Destruction of Value. Rowman & Littlefield (2003)

7. Ross, S., Angel, V.: Heritage and waste: introduction. J. Cult. Herit. Manag. Sustain. Dev. **10**, 1–5 (2019). https://doi.org/10.1108/jchmsd-02-2020-116

8. Huuhka, S., Vestergaard, I.: Building conservation and the circular economy: a theoretical consideration. J. Cult. Herit. Manag. Sustain. Dev. **10**, 29–40 (2019). https://doi.org/10.1108/jchmsd-06-2019-0081

9. Cerreta, M., Savino, V.: Circular enhancement of the cultural heritage: an adaptive reuse strategy for Ercolano Heritagescape. In: Gervasi, O., et al. (eds.) ICCSA 2020. LNCS, vol. 12251, pp. 1016–1033. Springer, Cham (2020). https://doi.org/10.1007/978-3-030-58808-3_72

10. Fusco Girard, L.: Toward a smart sustainable development of port cities/areas: the role of the "historic urban landscape" approach. Sustainability **5**, 4329–4348 (2013). https://doi.org/10.3390/su5104329

11. Argiolas, G.: Il valore dei valori. La governance nell'impresa socialmente orientata. Città Nuova (2014)

12. Alberti, F., Radicchi, A.: The Proximity City: a comparative analysis between Paris, Barcelona and Milan. TECHNE - J. Technol. Archit. Environ. **23**, 69–77 (2022). https://doi.org/10.36253/techne-12151

13. Perry, C.A.: Neighborhood and Community Planning: regional survey, volume VII comprising 3 monographs. The neighborhood unit. Regional plan of New York and its environs (1929)

14. Hall, E.T.: The Hidden Dimension. Anchor (1990)

15. Gehl, J.: Life Between Buildings: Using Public Space. Island Press (2011)

16. Àrea d'Ecologia Urbana: Pla clima 2018–2030. Ajuntament de Barcelona (2018)

17. Ostrom, E.: Governing the Commons. Cambridge University Press (2015)

18. Bauwens, M.: Peer-Produktion und Peer-Governance der digitalen Commons. In: Commons. Transcript Verlag, Bielefeld (2012)

19. Manzini, E.: Politiche del quotidiano. Progetti di vita che cambiano il mondo. Edizioni di Comunità (2018)

20. Latour, B.: We Have Never Been Modern. Harvard University Press (2012)

21. Manzini, E.: Abitare la prossimità: Idee per la città dei 15 minuti. EGEA spa (2021)
22. Heynen, N., Perkins, H.A., Roy, P.: The political ecology of uneven urban green space. Urban Aff. Rev. **42**, 3–25 (2006). https://doi.org/10.1177/1078087406290729
23. Charter for Ecosystemic Planning of Cities: Urban Ecology – urbanNext, https://urbannext.net/charter-for-ecosystemic-planning/. Accessed 14 Apr 2023
24. Rueda, S.: L'ecologia urbana i la planificación de la ciutat. Medi Ambient Tecnologia i Cultura. Repensar la ciutat **5**, 6–17 (1993)
25. Newig, J., Schulz, D., Jager, N.W.: Disentangling puzzles of spatial scales and participation in environmental governance—The case of governance re-scaling through the European water framework directive. Environ. Manag. **58**(6), 998–1014 (2016). https://doi.org/10.1007/s00 267-016-0753-8
26. Cerreta, M., Panaro, S., Poli, G.: A spatial decision support system for multifunctional landscape assessment: a transformative resilience perspective for vulnerable inland areas. Sustainability **13**, 2748 (2021). https://doi.org/10.3390/su13052748
27. Malczewski, J.: GIS-based multicriteria decision analysis: a survey of the literature. Int. J. Geogr. Inf. Sci. **20**, 703–726 (2006). https://doi.org/10.1080/13658810600661508
28. Malczewski, J., Rinner, C.: Multiattribute decision analysis methods. In: Malczewski, J., Rinner, C. (eds.) Multicriteria Decision Analysis in Geographic Information Science. AGIS, pp. 81–121. Springer, Heidelberg (2015). https://doi.org/10.1007/978-3-540-74757-4_4
29. Keenan, P.B., Jankowski, P.: Spatial decision support systems: three decades on. Decis. Supp. Syst. **116**, 64–76 (2019). https://doi.org/10.1016/j.dss.2018.10.010
30. Chen, Y., Yu, J., Khan, S.: Spatial sensitivity analysis of multi-criteria weights in GIS-based land suitability evaluation. Environ. Model. Softw. **25**, 1582–1591 (2010). https://doi.org/10.1016/j.envsoft.2010.06.001
31. Simon, H.A.: The New Science of Management Decision. Harper (1960)
32. Rodela, R., Bregt, A.K., Ligtenberg, A., Pérez-Soba, M., Verweij, P.: The social side of spatial decision support systems: investigating knowledge integration and learning. Environ. Sci. Policy **76**, 177–184 (2017). https://doi.org/10.1016/j.envsci.2017.06.015
33. Geertman, S., Stillwell, J.: Planning support systems: content, issues and trends. In: Geertman, S., Stillwell, J. (eds.) Planning Support Systems Best Practice and New Methods. GEJL, vol. 95, pp. 1–26. Springer, Dordrecht (2009). https://doi.org/10.1007/978-1-4020-8952-7_1
34. Emmanuel, R., Krüger, E.: Urban heat island and its impact on climate change resilience in a shrinking city: the case of Glasgow, UK. Build. Environ. **53**, 137–149 (2012). https://doi.org/10.1016/j.buildenv.2012.01.020
35. Gaffin, S.R., et al.: Bright is the new black—Multi-year performance of high-albedo roofs in an urban climate. Environ. Res. Lett. **7**, 014029 (2012). https://doi.org/10.1088/1748-9326/7/1/014029
36. Goodchild, M.F., Haining, R.P.: GIS and spatial data analysis: converging perspectives. In: Florax, R.J.G.M., Plane, D.A. (eds.) Fifty Years of Regional Science. ADVSPATIAL, pp. 363–385. Springer, Heidelberg (2004). https://doi.org/10.1007/978-3-662-07223-3_16
37. Cerreta, M., Poli, G.: Landscape services assessment: a hybrid multi-criteria spatial decision support system (MC-SDSS). Sustainability **9**, 1311 (2017). https://doi.org/10.3390/su9081311
38. Raciti, A., Saija, L.: From ecosystem services to ecological devices: the CoPED Summer School experience in the Simeto River Valley, Italy. J. Urban Manag. **7**, 161–171 (2018). https://doi.org/10.1016/j.jum.2018.04.005
39. Saaty, T.L.: The Analytic Hierarchy Process: Planning, Priority Setting, Resource Allocation (1990)
40. Saaty, T.L.: Decision Making for Leaders: The Analytic Hierarchy Process for Decisions in a Complex World. RWS Publications (1990)

41. Yoon, K.P., Hwang, C.-L.: Multiple Attribute Decision Making: An Introduction. SAGE Publications (1995)
42. Laino, G.: Le politiche per le periferie. In: Non è così facile. Politiche urbane a cavallo del secolo, pp. 67–104. FrancoAngeli (2007)
43. Amato, F.: Periferie plurali: Il caso di Scampia (Napoli) oltre gli stigmi. Geogr. Noteb. 4 (2021). https://doi.org/10.7358/gn-2021-002-ama1
44. Pugliese, E.: Oltre le vele: Rapporto su Scampia. Fridericiana Editrice Univ. (1999)
45. Camera dei Deputati: Commissione parlamentare di inchiesta sulle condizioni di sicurezza e sullo stato di degrado delle città e delle loro periferie, Relazione sull'attività svolta dalla Commissione. Stabilimenti Tipografici Carlo Colombo, Roma (2017)
46. Corbisiero, F., Napoletano, F.: Come rigenerare la città attraverso la tecnologia partecipata: il caso del PGIS applicato al quartiere Scampia di Napoli. Sociologia Urbana e Rurale (2023, forthcoming)
47. McCall, M.K., Peters-Guarin, G.: Participatory action research and disaster risk. In: Handbook of Hazards and Disaster Risk Reduction. Routledge (2012)
48. Morgan, D.L., Krueger, R.A.: The Focus Group Kit: Volumes 1-6. SAGE Publications (1997, incorporated).
49. Cerreta, M., Poli, G., Cuntò, S.: Un sistema spaziale collaborativo di supporto alla decisione per una pianificazione adattiva al cambiamento climatico: una sperimentazione per il quartiere Ponticelli. In: GIS day 2019. Il GIS per il governo e la gestione del territorio, p. 67. Aracne (2020)
50. Lees, L.: Gentrification and social mixing: towards an inclusive urban renaissance? Urban Stud. 45, 2449–2470 (2008). https://doi.org/10.1177/0042098008097099
51. Edwards, C.: Regeneration works? Disabled people and area-based urban renewal. Crit. Soc. Policy 29, 613–633 (2009). https://doi.org/10.1177/0261018309341902
52. Rambaldi, G., Kyem, P.A.K., McCall, M., Weiner, D.: Participatory spatial information management and communication in developing countries. Electron. J. Inf. Syst. Dev. Ctries. 25, 1–9 (2006). https://doi.org/10.1002/j.1681-4835.2006.tb00162.x
53. Norris, T.B.: Public participation GIS, participatory GIS, and participatory mapping. In: Geography. Oxford University Press (2017)
54. Cinderby, S.: Geographic information systems (GIS) for participation: the future of environmental GIS? Int. J. Environ. Pollut. 11, 304 (1999). https://doi.org/10.1504/ijep.1999.002263
55. Kingston, R.: Public participation in local policy decision-making: the role of web-based mapping. Cartogr. J. 44, 138–144 (2007). https://doi.org/10.1179/000870407x213459
56. Schuurman, N.: Critical GIScience in Canada in the new millennium. Can. Geogr./Le Géographe canadien. 53, 139–144 (2009). https://doi.org/10.1111/j.1541-0064.2009.00250.x
57. Attardi, R., Cerreta, M., Poli, G.: A collaborative multi-criteria spatial decision support system for multifunctional landscape evaluation. In: Gervasi, O., et al. (eds.) ICCSA 2015. LNCS, vol. 9157, pp. 782–797. Springer, Cham (2015). https://doi.org/10.1007/978-3-319-21470-2_57
58. Cinderby, S.: How to reach the 'hard-to-reach': the development of Participatory Geographic Information Systems (P-GIS) for inclusive urban design in UK cities. Area 42, 239–251 (2010). https://doi.org/10.1111/j.1475-4762.2009.00912.x
59. Orban-Ferauge, F.: Systèmes d'information géographique participatifs et aménagement du territoire: Expériences philippines citoyennes de désenclavement. Presses universitaires de Namur (2011)
60. Carley, M., Smith, H.: Urban Development and Civil Society: The Role of Communities in Sustainable Cities. Routledge (2013)

61. Arasteh, R., Ali Abbaspour, R., Salmanmahiny, A.: A modeling approach to path dependent and non-path dependent urban allocation in a rapidly growing region. Sustain. Cities Soc. **44**, 378–394 (2019). https://doi.org/10.1016/j.scs.2018.10.029

62. Fusco Girard, L., Cerreta, M., De Toro, P.: Towards a local comprehensive productive development strategy: a methodological proposal for the metropolitan city of Naples. Qual. Innov. Prosper. **21**, 223 (2017). https://doi.org/10.12776/qip.v21i1.779

63. Somma, M., Campagna, M., Canfield, T., Cerreta, M., Poli, G., Steinitz, C.: Collaborative and sustainable strategies through geodesign: the case study of Bacoli. In: Gervasi, O., Murgante, B., Misra, S., Rocha, A.M.A.C., Garau, C. (eds.) ICCSA 2022. LNCS, vol. 13379, pp. 210–224. Springer, Cham (2022). https://doi.org/10.1007/978-3-031-10545-6_15

64. Fagerholm, N., Käyhkö, N., Ndumbaro, F., Khamis, M.: Community stakeholders' knowledge in landscape assessments – mapping indicators for landscape services. Ecol. Ind. **18**, 421–433 (2012). https://doi.org/10.1016/j.ecolind.2011.12.004

65. Scholte, S.S.K., van Teeffelen, A.J.A., Verburg, P.H.: Integrating socio-cultural perspectives into ecosystem service valuation: a review of concepts and methods. Ecol. Econ. **114**, 67–78 (2015). https://doi.org/10.1016/j.ecolecon.2015.03.007

66. Opdam, P., et al.: Ecosystem services for connecting actors – lessons from a symposium. Change Adapt. Socio-Ecol. Syst. **2** (2015). https://doi.org/10.1515/cass-2015-0001

Measure Urban Regeneration: An Assessment Framework for European Cities

Stefania Regalbuto[✉] [iD]

Department of Management, University of Venice, San Giobbe, Cannaregio 873, 30121 Venice, Italy
stefania.regalbuto@unive.it

Abstract. Despite multiple definitions and understandings given both as part of the scientific and professional contexts, there is still no unequivocally recognized definition of urban regeneration. Under this expression are included a multiplicity of approaches ranging from recovery of abandoned areas and buildings to diversification of economic activities, redefinition of territorial development strategies, preservation or reuse of cultural heritage, recovery of public spaces and increase in the supply of services. Therefore, in this contribution, the indications provided by UN-Habitat revealing the complexity and multiplicity of the issues at stake, have been assumed. The paper aims to outline a tool to measure urban regeneration as part of a multidisciplinary and multi-level process able to include key qualitative and quantitative parameters specifically formulated for analyzing and monitoring European cities. The methodological framework has been developed in the context of the Horizon research project Bauhaus of the Seas Sailing (BoSS).

Keywords: urban regeneration · multidimensional evaluation · regenerative sustainability · indicators · port city

1 Introduction

An increasing focus on urban regeneration has been found over recent years. At the European level, echoing the political, economic, and social role recognized to design from the Bauhaus movement, which emerged in the 20th century, the New European Bauhaus (NEB) advocates the Green Deal implementation through regenerative approaches based on cultural values of aesthetics, sustainability, and inclusion [28]. Even public bodies of national relevance have expressed their views. Among them the National Order of Architects of Italy (CNAPPC), which has recently outlined some key principles as part of the "National Plan for Sustainable Urban Regeneration" [9] drawn in coordination with other relevant stakeholders, including the National Association of Italian Municipalities (ANCI), Region Authorities, National Association of Building Constructors (ANCE) and Italian Environmental League (Legambiente).

© The Author(s), under exclusive license to Springer Nature Switzerland AG 2023
O. Gervasi et al. (Eds.): ICCSA 2023 Workshops, LNCS 14112, pp. 253–266, 2023.
https://doi.org/10.1007/978-3-031-37129-5_21

In scientific literature, over the last decade, a steadily growing publication on urban regeneration topics should be noted and explored in the context of different fields of investigation. As inferable searching on Science Direct, from 2014 to 2024, 13,968 contributions on urban regeneration have been produced, only considering the fields of "Environmental Science" (10.923), "Social Sciences" (5.282) and "Business, Management and Accounting" (1.084), of which 798 in 2014 and 2.330 only in 2022.

Despite multiple definitions formulated, a uniform definition of urban regeneration is still lacking. Under this expression, both as part of the scientific and professional contexts, a multiplicity of approaches ranging from recovery of abandoned areas and buildings to diversification of economic activities, redefinition of territorial development strategies, preservation or reuse of cultural heritage, recovery of public spaces and increase in the supply of services have been included.

In this contribution, the indications provided by UN-Habitat [30], revealing the complexity and multiplicity of the issues at stake, have been assumed. Defined as a crucial tool for urban development until the 20th century, urban regeneration consists of the process through which it is intended to contrast economic, demographic, and social decline starting from interventions of recovery and reconversion of buildings and urban areas, which are currently widespread, especially in consolidated urban areas, such as those of Italian and European port cities.

The abovementioned definition is in continuity with the Regenerative Sustainability (RS) theoretical approach already systematized as part of the scientific literature as the most recent achievement gained in the context of the evolutionary process involving approaches for pursuing sustainability objectives [11, 17, 29].

Already Reed [23] pointed out the need for a new cultural approach to effectively pursue sustainability by focusing on the importance of adopting a multidimensional and place-based vision. Over time, the focus of sustainability paradigms has increasingly shifted away from minimizing the damage caused by excessive use of resources to defining development models inspired by the dynamics of ecological systems, to such an extent that some authors have begun to discuss the transition from Sustainable Development Goals (SDGs) to Regenerative Development Goals (RDGs) [1, 4, 13, 20].

Based on a holistic view of territorial contexts, regenerative sustainability has been made operational for over fifty years through the Regenerative Development (RD) approach leveraging on place-based development and design methodology, which has only recently been theorized [12, 15, 24].

Although the emerging field of Regenerative Development (RD) offers practical and theoretical guidelines in defining indicators and tools useful for the multidimensional assessment of sustainability, these last is still in its infancy [6, 16, 19]. Although focused on some relevant aspects such as biodiversity, energy, water, transport, climate, air quality, waste management, land use, poverty, and education, in fact, leaving out the ecological and socio-cultural components, the sustainability indicators are not yet able to fully grasp the complexity of the contexts of analysis [3]. Regarding RD evaluation tools, the achievements that have been found are useful on a hyperlocal, while a gap is highlighted against wider geographical levels.

Due to the complexities of coastal areas, stand out from the others some studies that have already investigated the regeneration of brownfield sites therein located, both from the point of view of theoretical models and in relation to the analysis of practices [2, 10, 18].

The contribution fits into the scientific-cultural debate on the definition of indicators and assessment tools for sustainability [3, 5, 7, 14, 22]. More specifically, recognizing some of the issues that emerged both from literature and from research contexts, the paper aims to outline a tool allowing for considering the hyperlocal context in relation to its broader territorial context and is useful for the analysis of practices and for the comparative study of territorial contexts distant from each other both culturally and geographically.

In this way, it is believed to support policymakers in identifying local strengths and opportunities and promote mutual exchange and learning between cities.

The tool proposed for the definition and evaluation of plans and programs assumed as dynamic processes, whose evolutionary logics are like those of living systems, in line with the perspective of Regenerative Development (RD), must be understood as a tool useful to carry on the analysis as a preparatory step for the implementation of Evolutionary Evaluation (EE) methods and techniques [27].

The analysis of the socio-economic, morphological, and environmental characteristics is considered essential and fundamental for the identification of specific criticalities and areas by intervening on which it is believed to be able to trigger regeneration processes which, over the short and medium-long term, should have positive impacts on a wider geographical context.

The framework has been developed as part of the Horizon research context Bauhaus of the Seas Sailing (BoSS) [36].

In summary, the first part of the paper (Sect. 2) describes the research context; the second one (Sect. 3) shows the methodological approach; in the third one (Sect. 4) the assessment framework is outlined; in the fourth part (Sect. 5) the early results obtained through the framework implementation are set out, and the last part (Sect. 6) concerns with discussion and conclusion.

2 Bauhaus of the Seas Sails Research Context

The contribution has been developed as part of the Horizon research project Bauhaus of the Seas Sails (BoSS) in the context of which, in line with the strategic objectives of the New European Bauhaus (NEB), is intended to leverage sustainability, social inclusion, and beauty to implement the Green Deal principles assumed as guidelines for Regenerative Development of coastal cities (Fig. 1).

In this perspective, port cities have been assumed as contexts of research and experimentation, with the aim to define and promote innovative and nature-based solutions as part of the design approach assimilating territories to complex and dynamic socio-technical-ecological contexts, in line with the theoretical approach provided by Regenerative Sustainability (RS) and the United Nations SDGs and EU strategic priorities.

In particular, in order to implement the objectives of the Horizon Europe mission, seven lighthouse demonstrators located in four different regions and aquatic ecosystems in Portugal (estuary), Italy (lagoon and gulf), Sweden/Germany (strait/northern sea/ river) and the Netherlands/Belgium (delta) have been selected as pilots to define and test innovative design solutions through which it is intended to provide tangible examples of mission-oriented approaches that are impactful, measurable, and targeted.

Furthermore, although concerning the local scale, the design solutions are conceived as an integral element of a wider context since the impacts that could be deployed up to the city and regional level have been considered.

Therefore, in the context of such a multi-level perspective, for each pilot, the project includes the proposal of an intervention on a local scale ("drop") generating impacts ("ripple effects") on the local context (demonstrator) at the city/region levels (demonstrating effects of scale) and at a broader level (demonstrating the replication). Hence the need for a framework to be understood as a decision support tool allowing both analysis and assessment of practices to allow their replicability.

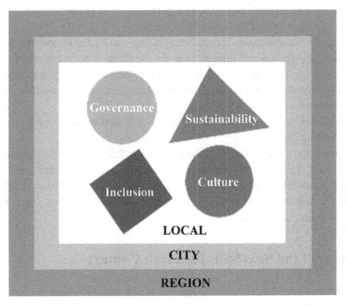

Fig. 1. The approach of BoSS research project

3 Methodological Approach

Assuming the measurement of urban regeneration as a crucial aspect both for the analysis of the territorial context preceding the definition of an urban regeneration plan (ex-ante), and for monitoring in the phase following its implementation (ex-post), the article focused on the definition of a framework of analysis for assessing a specific territorial context under the perspective of RD approach.

Therefore, in line with the Regenerative Development approach, the collection of quantitative-qualitative data has been carried on through the structuring of a place-based and multi-level assessment framework suitable both as a knowledge and management tool in exploring European contexts at the Regional and City level. In particular, the proposed framework has been structured, including the ecological, socio-cultural, and procedural components and the more purely technical ones.

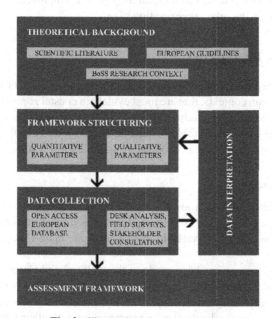

Fig. 2. The methodological approach

In this perspective, the methodological process (Fig. 2) that has led to the construction of the assessment framework is divided into four consecutive and consequential phases:

1. Theoretical background. This phase is focused on identifying the theoretical models based on which is intended to structure the assessment framework to measure urban regeneration. Hence, the investigation in the field of scientific literature and the exploration of the research project context has been carried out.
2. Framework structuring. It includes two distinct sections specifically formulated based on the type of data content. In the first section, the aspects considered significant to grasp ecological and socio-cultural components of the local context have been identified and described qualitatively. In the second section, recourse has been made to quantitative data, taken from specific European open-access databases. For each of the four thematic pillars proposed by the BoSS research project, in line with NEB recommendations, two key fields of investigation have been identified, each of them has been, in turn, considered in relation to both city and regional levels (Table 1).
3. Data collection. According to the framework structure, this phase is tackled in two distinct steps. For the collection of quantitative data, open access databases are consulted, while for the compilation of the information material expressed in qualitative

terms, a specific research phase. The latter could be based on information inferred from desk analysis, field surveys, interviews and/or consultation with stakeholders.

4. Data interpretation. This phase allows you to analyze the study context. Based on the findings, making some adjustments to the framework may be necessary. Data interpretation could also be carried out in relation to the specific features of different territorial contexts under a comparative perspective. Furthermore, the same analysis framework could be assumed as a monitoring tool, if employed before and after the implementation of the urban regeneration plan.

4 Assessment Framework

The selection of the parameters presented has been carried out based on the most frequent critical issues in urban contexts, that are most evident in coastal zones. However, considering the heterogeneity of the study contexts as well as the multiplicity of the issues at stake, the framework provided (Table 1) must be understood as a tool of general validity which has to be suitably modified according to specific local features.

4.1 Indicator Sources

To facilitate data retrieval, thus allowing immediate comparison among European cities and supporting the replicability of solutions, the proposed parameters have been selected and collected among the ones available from four of the main European databases set out below.

In particular, reference has been made to the Cultural and Creative Cities Monitor from Joint Research Center (JRC) - European Commission, whose composite indicators have been specifically designed to support policymakers and researchers in analyzing and monitoring their cities, also facilitating comparison with other urban centers on the role of culture and creativity in cities' social and economic well-being [32].

In analyzing and monitoring the environmental conditions, the European Environment Agency (EEA) database has been queried. Designed to support all stages of environmental policymaking, it includes indicators that report the trend (or state) of different phenomena analyzed in a given period in relation to the associated political objectives. Data collection refers to cities [33].

Some data have been inferred from the Eurostat database, the statistical office of the European Union, which publishes data referring to both cities and regions of the euro area, processed using data collected by national statistical authorities according to harmonized criteria and methodologies [34].

Other insights have been carried out by the Organization for Economic Cooperation and Development (OECD), with the aim of measuring regional welfare in policy assessment. In this perspective, each region has been measured against eleven themes (income, work, housing, health, access to services, environment, education, security, civic engagement and governance, community, and life satisfaction), each of which a quantitative score has been assigned [35].

While data inferred from JRC and EEA databases are related to the city level, OECD platform describes quantitatively the topics measuring regional well-being. Instead, Eurostat database includes both city and regional parameters.

Table 1. The assessment framework

Qualitative Parameters

Territorial features

Morphological features

Neglected and/or underutilized buildings and spaces

Local stakeholders

Main uses/cluster of uses

Government entities

Leading sectors and local know-how

Leading sectors of local economy

Relevant projects

Recent projects

Quantitative Parameters

Thematic Pillars	Key fields	Level	Parameters	Sources	Year
Sustainability	Human Impact	City	PM2.5 annual mean concentration	EEA	2021
		Regional	environment		
	Mobility	City	Local & International Connections	JRC	2019
		Regional	networks total railway lines, air transport of passengers, motorization rate, air quality (PM 2.5)	Eurostat, OECD	2017, 2022
Inclusion	Population	City	total population, foreigners as a proportion of population	Eurostat	2017
		Regional	total population, less than 15 years, 15–64, crude rate of net migration plus statistical	Eurostat	2017
	Employment	City	GDP per capita, employment rate, unemployment rate	Eurostat, JRC	2017, 2019

(continued)

Table 1. (*continued*)

		Regional	GDP (2020), employment rate, unemployment rate, economic activity rate, NEET	Eurostat	2020, 2021
Culture	Education and work	City	person (aged 25–64) with ISCED level 5, 6, 7 or 8 as the highest level of education, creative and knowledge-based jobs	Eurostat, JRC	2017, 2019
		Regional	tertiary educational attainment, adult participation in education and training	Eurostat	2019
	Human capital	City	human capital and education	JRC	2019
		Regional	human resources in science and technology	JRC	2019
Governance	Society	City	cultural participation and attractiveness	JRC	2019
		Regional	life satisfaction, access to services	OECD	2022
	Institution	City	quality of governance	JRC	2019
		Regional	civic engagement, community	OECD	2022

5 Venice Study Context

In order to test the assessment framework, a first implementation to analyse Venetian territorial context has been carried out. Venice is a seaside city, included within the administrative boundaries of Veneto Region, located in northern Italy.

Venice is a lagoon city, whose economy is mainly based on agriculture, fishing, handicrafts, industry and tourism. The analysis of the characteristics corresponding to the remaining qualitative parameters is more significant if conducted in relation to a circumscribed area and specific objectives.

From the analysis of the quantitative parameters collected (Table 2), on the other hand, although data referred to different geographical levels are not always directly comparable as they are taken from different databases elaborated in different moments in time, some issues emerge clearly.

Table 2. Venetian information framework

Quantitative Parameters

Thematic Pillars	Key fields	Level	Parameters	Data	Sources	Year
Sustainability	Human Impact	City	PM2.5 annual mean concentration	15–25 (poor air quality)	EEA	2021
		Regional	environment			
	Mobility	City	Local & International Connections	19.9	JRC	2019
		Regional	networks total railway lines, air transport of passengers, motorization rate, air quality (PM2.5)	68, 4293, 657, 19.0	Eurostat, OECD	2017, 2022
Inclusion	Population	City	total population, foreigners as a proportion of population	261.905 13.2	Eurostat	2017
		Regional	total population, less than 15 years, 15–64, crude rate of net migration plus statistical	4.879.133 633.774 1.135.667 3.2	Eurostat	2017
	Employment	City	GDP per capita, employment rate, unemployment rate	27.000–35.000, 70–75, 6.9	Eurostat, JRC	2017, 2019
		Regional	GDP (2020), employment rate, unemployment rate, economic activity rate, NEET	31.600, 70.8, 5.3, 69.4, 13.6	Eurostat	2020, 2021

(*continued*)

Table 2. (*continued*)

Culture	Education and work	City	person (aged 25–64) with ISCED level 5, 6, 7 or 8 as the highest level of education, creative and knowledge-based jobs	31.333, 30.5	Eurostat, JRC	2017, 2019
		Regional	tertiary educational attainment, adult participation in education and training	19.7, 10.6	Eurostat	2019
	Human capital	City	human capital and education	21.1	JRC	2019
		Regional	human resources in science and technology	35.4	JRC	2019
Governance	Society	City	cultural participation and attractiveness	61.9	JRC	2019
		Regional	life satisfaction, access to services	5.0, 5.8	OECD	2022
	Institution	City	quality of governance	39.4	JRC	2019
		Regional	civic engagement, community	7.9, 6.3	OECD	2022

Among the most relevant issues, the progressive depopulation that Venice port city is undergoing becomes evident. The resident population in Venice, in fact, is only a small part of that residing in the Veneto. Furthermore, the low incidence of the young population describes the phenomenon of demographic winter, which is accompanied by a consistent migratory trend that is also found at the city level. On the other hand, there is a discrete presence of foreigners.

However, there is good cultural liveliness in terms of civic participation and level of education. The degree of participation in "tertiary education" recorded at the regional level is in line with what was found at the city level in terms of "human capital and education". To the high rate of "cultural participation and attractiveness" found at the city level corresponds to comparable levels in terms of "civic engagement" and "community" at the regional level.

As for the labour market, Venice boasts a good score for "creative and knowledge-based jobs" and a good level of employment above 70%.

The environmental issue is quite critical. At the regional level, although there is a low "rate of motorization", the "air transport of passengers" is widely used, and there are low scores with respect to environmental quality. Both at the regional and city level, there are high levels of PM 2.5, one of the main air pollutants.

The main topics deriving from data interpretation are in line with the ones that emerged in the context of a cycle of focus groups wherein expert local stakeholders were asked to provide a critical synthesis of the local context under a multi-level and multidimensional perspective from a socio-economic viewpoint. The meetings have been organized as part of a collaboration between Ca' Foscari University of Venice and tertiary sector institutions, to investigate the main socio-economic issues concerning sustainability and competitiveness in northeast Italy [21, 26].

6 Discussion and Conclusion

Despite the growing interest in scientific and professional fields, a uniform definition of urban regeneration is still lacking. Assuming the indications recently provided by UN-Habitat [30], in line with the RS theoretical approach [11, 29], in this contribution, a place-based and multi-level framework as RD evaluation support tool [15, 16] has been outlined.

This approach is also consistent with the regulations in force on port planning, both in reference to the European regulation, which has already recognized Maritime Spatial Planning (MSP) [31] as a decision-making process, and to the Italian national one, wherein the careful analysis of the territorial context constitutes a crucial step prior to the definition of strategic planning documents, which are mainly focused on regeneration processes, as can be seen from the study of the approved documents.

The framework has to be understood as a first result in the attempt to define a tool to measure the regenerative development of European cities. It has been designed both as an analytic tool, to explore in depth a territorial context and as a monitoring tool, to evaluate urban transformation interventions and policies, configuring itself as a support tool in the context of RD evaluation.

Furthermore, since it has been developed as part of the BoSS research project, it has been also designed to compare different urban contexts. Therefore, considering the heterogeneity of the issues found at various levels, in the different territorial contexts, the framework is a specific and overarching tool, allowing for both in-depth analysis (wherein suitably tailored based on the specific objectives) and comparative analysis.

It should be noted that for the same key field of investigation, the parameters selected may vary according to the significance they assume in relation to the specific features of the study context, the availability of data and the scale of a given phenomenon. Despite the versatility of the tool, however, there are also limitations. The main drawbacks are related to the availability and comparability of data. In fact, the same data are not always available at both the city and region levels. (e.g. population is differently quantified at the city and regional level, whereas the classification of training varies from country to country). This could represent an obstacle in the exploration of a given phenomenon under a multi-level perspective.

Furthermore, as can also be seen from Table 1, it should be noted that not all the available data refer to the same year. This problem could be overcome by setting a time frame of 3–5 years, whose significance must be verified in relation to the specific historical moment. In this perspective, it is easy to understand that certain issues that emerge from the interpretation of the collected data could require an adjustment of the analysis framework or could highlight significant aspects to be considered in the subsequent phase of structuring the problem preparatory to the actual implementation of decision support methods and techniques in the context of RD evaluation.

Acknowledgments. The research presented in this paper has been developed within the EU-funded Horizon research project Bauhaus of the Seas Sailing (BoSS), Department of Management (DMAN), Ca' Foscari University of Venice.

References

1. Abson, D.J., et al.: Leverage points for sustainability transformation. Ambio **46**(1), 30–39 (2016). https://doi.org/10.1007/s13280-016-0800-y
2. Attardi, R., Bonifazi, A., Torre, C.M.: Evaluating sustainability and democracy in the development of industrial port cities: some Italian cases. Sustainability **4**(11), 3042–3065 (2012). https://doi.org/10.3390/su4113042
3. Bastianoni, S., Coscieme, L., Caro, D., Marchettini, N., Pulselli, F.M.: The needs of sustainability: the overarching contribution of systems approach. Ecol. Ind. **100**, 69–73 (2019). https://doi.org/10.1016/j.ecolind.2018.08.024
4. Benson, M.H., Craig, R.K.: The end of sustainability. Soc. Nat. Resour. **27**(7), 777–782 (2014). https://doi.org/10.1080/08941920.2014.901467
5. Cerreta, M., Poli, G., Regalbuto, S., Mazzarella, C.: A multi-dimensional decision-making process for regenerative landscapes: a new harbour for Naples (Italy). In: Misra, S., et al. (eds.) ICCSA 2019. LNCS, vol. 11622, pp. 156–170. Springer, Cham (2019). https://doi.org/10.1007/978-3-030-24305-0_13
6. Cerreta, M., Muccio, E., Poli, G., Regalbuto, S., Romano, F.: City-port circular model: towards a methodological framework for indicators selection. In: Gervasi, O., et al. (eds.) ICCSA 2020. LNCS, vol. 12251, pp. 855–868. Springer, Cham (2020). https://doi.org/10.1007/978-3-030-58808-3_61
7. Cerreta, M., Muccio, E., Poli, G., Regalbuto, S., Romano, F.: A multidimensional evaluation for regenerative strategies: towards a circular city-port model implementation. In: Bevilacqua, C., Calabrò, F., Della Spina, L. (eds.) NMP 2020. SIST, vol. 178, pp. 1067–1077. Springer, Cham (2021). https://doi.org/10.1007/978-3-030-48279-4_100
8. Cole, R.J.: Transitioning from green to regenerative design. Build. Res. Inf. **40**(1), 39–53 (2012). https://doi.org/10.1080/09613218.2011.610608
9. Consiglio Nazionale degli Architetti Pianificatori Paesaggisti Conservatori: Il Piano Nazionale per la Rigenerazione Urbana Sostenibile (2011). http://www.awn.it/attachments/article/731/CNAPPC_Piano_Nazionale_per_la_Rigenerazione_Urbana_Sostenibile.pdf. Accessed 29 Oct 2021
10. Craft, W., Ding, L., Prasad, D.: Understanding decision-making in regenerative precinct developments. J. Clean. Prod. **338**, 130672 (2022). https://doi.org/10.1016/j.jclepro.2022.130672
11. Du Plessis, C.: Towards a regenerative paradigm for the built environment. Build. Res. Inf. **40**(1), 7–22 (2012). https://doi.org/10.1080/09613218.2012.628548
12. Du Plessis, C., Brandon, P.: An ecological worldview as basis for a regenerative sustainability paradigm for the built environment. J. Clean. Prod. **109**, 53–61 (2015). https://doi.org/10.1016/j.jclepro.2014.09.098

13. Feleki, E., Vlachokostas, C., Moussiopoulos, N.: Characterisation of sustainability in urban areas: an analysis of assessment tools with emphasis on European cities. Sustain. Cities Soc. **43**, 563–577 (2018). https://doi.org/10.1016/j.scs.2018.08.025
14. Girard, L.F., Cerreta, M., De Toro, P.: Towards a local comprehensive productive development strategy: a methodological proposal for the metropolitan city of Naples. Qual. Innov. Prosper. **21**(1), 223–240 (2017)
15. Gibbons, L.V., Cloutier, S.A., Coseo, P.J., Barakat, A.: Regenerative development as an integrative paradigm and methodology for landscape sustainability. Sustainability **10**(6), 1910 (2018). https;//doi.org/10.3390/su10061910
16. Gibbons, L.V., Pearthree, G., Cloutier, S.A., Ehlenz, M.M.: The development, application, and refinement of a regenerative development evaluation tool and indicators. Ecol. Ind. **108**, 105698 (2020). https://doi.org/10.1016/j.ecolind.2019.105698
17. González-Márquez, I., Toledo, V.M.: Sustainability science: a paradigm in crisis? Sustainability **12**, 2802 (2020). https://doi.org/10.3390/su12072802
18. Hes, D., Stephan, A., Moosavi, S.: Evaluating the practice and outcomes of applying regenerative development to a large-scale project in Victoria, Australia. Sustainability **10**(2), 460 (2018). https://doi.org/10.3390/su10020460
19. Huang, L., Wu, J., Yan, L.: Defining and measuring urban sustainability: a review of indicators. Landsc. Ecol. **30**(7), 1175–1193 (2015). https://doi.org/10.1007/s10980-015-0208-2
20. Mang, P., Haggard, B.: Regenerative development and design: a framework for evolving sustainability (2016). (No Title)
21. Micelli, S.: The metropolitan area of Venice in the changing economy of the North East. In: European Cities and Global Competitiveness, pp. 130–150. Edward Elgar Publishing (2012)
22. Moosavi, S., Browne, G.R.: Advancing the adaptive, participatory and transdisciplinary decision-making framework: the case of a coastal brownfield transformation. Cities **111**, 103106 (2021). https://doi.org/10.1016/j.cities.2021.103106
23. Reed, B.: Shifting from 'sustainability' to regeneration. Build. Res. Inf. **35**(6), 674–680 (2007). https://doi.org/10.1080/09613210701475753
24. Robinson, J., Cole, R.J.: Theoretical underpinnings of regenerative sustainability. Build. Res. Inf. **43**(2), 133–143 (2015). https://doi.org/10.1080/09613218.2014.979082
25. Sacco, S., Cerreta, M.: A decision-making process for circular development of city-port ecosystem: the East Naples case study. In: Gervasi, O., Murgante, B., Misra, S., Rocha, A.M.A.C., Garau, C. (eds.) ICCSA 2022. LNCS, vol. 13378, pp. 572–584. Springer, Cham (2022). https://doi.org/10.1007/978-3-031-10562-3_40
26. Unicredit: Focus Group preparatori del Forum UniCredit Nord Est 2022 (2022)
27. Urban, J.B., Hargraves, M., Trochim, W.M.: Evolutionary evaluation: implications for evaluators, researchers, practitioners, funders, and the evidence-based program mandate. Eval. Program Plann. **45**, 127–139 (2014). https://doi.org/10.1016/j.evalprogplan.2014.03.011
28. von der Leyen, U.: A New European Bauhaus: Op-ed Article by Ursula von der Leyen, President of the European Commission (2020). Accessed 23 July 2022
29. Wahl, D.C.: Designing Regenerative Cultures. Triarchy Press (2016)
30. World Cities Report (2022)
31. European MSP Platform. Maritime Spatial Planning Country Information. EU MSP Platform, Venice, Italy (2018). https://www.msp-platform.eu. Accessed 10 May 2023
32. European Commission. Cultural and Creative City Monitor. https://composite-indicators.jrc.ec.europa.eu/cultural-creative-cities-monitor. Accessed 05 May 2023
33. European Union. European Environmental Agency. https://www.eea.europa.eu/ims. Accessed 05 May 2023
34. Organization for Economic Co-operation and Development. OECD Regional Wee-Being. https://www.oecdregionalwellbeing.org/. Accessed 05 May 2023

35. European Commission. Eurostat. https://ec.europa.eu/eurostat. Accessed 05 May 2023
36. European Commission. CORDIS EU research result. https://cordis.europa.eu/project/id/101 079995. Accessed 05 May 2023

Short Paper (MMIPU 2023)

Automatic Urine Sediment Detection and Classification Based on YoloV8

Sania Akhtar[1], Muhammad Hanif[1,2(✉)], and Hamidi Malih[1,2]

[1] Faculty of Computer Science and Engineering (FCSE), Ghulam Ishaq Khan Institute of Engineering Sciences and Technology, Topi, Swabi, Pakistan
`sania.akhtar@giki.edu.pk`
[2] Department of Electrical and Electronics, Kutahya Dumplupinar University, Kutahya, Turkey
`muhammad.hanif@giki.edu.pk, melih.saraoglu@dpu.edu.tr`

Abstract. The identification of urine sediment in human urine samples through microscopic images is a critical part of in vitro testing. Currently, automatic urine sediment analyzers are used by doctors to supplement manual examinations. However, the conventional technique of artificial feature extraction used by most analyzers can be labor-intensive and subjectively dependent on the professional's prior knowledge. To overcome these limitations, this work employs YoloV8, a recent version of the Yolo algorithm, to accurately detect and categorize urine particles. In addition, a data-centric strategy has been introduced to address difficulties with missing data, incorrect labeling, and class imbalance. This strategy aims to improve labeling reliability and remove noisy data points. Experimental findings on the dataset show that YOLOv8 has a greater detection accuracy than existing state-of-the-art techniques for detecting eleven different categories of urine sediments. The approach presented in this work outperforms other techniques, yielding a mean average precision (mAP) of 91%. Furthermore, the average detection time of the model is 0.6 microseconds.

Keywords: Urine Sediments · YoloV8 · object detection · Feature Extraction

1 Introduction

Urine sediment analysis is an essential medical diagnostic method used to detect various physical diseases. This low-cost method examines the active components present in urine. It involves qualitative detection of urine sediment cells and quantitative analysis of cell types, numbers, and shapes using microscopy. By studying the characteristics of urine sediment, doctors can determine whether the body is suffering from certain diseases [1,2]. For instance, even though urine with increased erythrocytes appears colorless to the naked eye, hematuria can be observed under a microscope [1]. Overall, urine sediment analysis plays a critical role in identifying potential health problems. When examining urine sediment,

O. Gervasi et al. (Eds.): ICCSA 2023 Workshops, LNCS 14112, pp. 269–279, 2023.
https://doi.org/10.1007/978-3-031-37129-5_22

elevated levels of leukocytes are often indicative of urinary system infections. If abnormal-shaped erythrocytes are observed under the microscope, the patient may have kidney disease. Additionally, the presence of epithelial cells in urine microscopy suggests that the patient's renal parenchyma has been damaged and requires treatment [1,2]. In short, the results of urine sediment analysis can provide valuable information to identify the underlying health issues affecting the urinary system and kidneys.

Urine microscopic images consist of various tiny and unevenly distributed particles, which makes it challenging to analyze. Therefore, the examination of urine sediment requires skilled laboratory physicians. However, this process is time-consuming and can be affected by the subjective will and working fatigue of the laboratory physicians due to the significant workload. Fortunately, with the advancement of digital image technology, automatic image recognition has become prevalent in the medical field. The conventional approach to image recognition, which involves "target segmentation + feature selection and extraction + classifier," has shown promising results in identifying and categorizing urine sediment images [1–3].

The field of computer vision has made significant progress with the emergence of convolutional neural networks through deep learning. This development has led to the creation of many outstanding object detection algorithms. Currently, object detection frameworks are typically divided into two categories: those based on regional recommendation and those based on dense sampling. In the former approach, the detector initially generates a rough regional proposal for the input image. Afterward, it more accurately classifies and locates the region of interest (ROI) produced [1,3]. Object detectors such as R-CNN [4], Fast R-CNN [5], Faster R-CNN [6], R-FCN [7], and FPN based on the two-stage detection framework have demonstrated exceptional performance. They operate in two stages, starting with the regional recommendation and then performing accurate detection. Due to this approach, they are commonly known as two-stage detectors [7]. In contrast, object detectors based on deep convolutional networks can use dense sampling [8] to directly detect objects by performing position regression and class prediction on all possible grid points on the detected feature layer. Examples of such one-stage detectors are SSD [9] and YOLO [8,10,11], which offer faster detection speed but comparatively lower accuracy. However, many outstanding algorithms and network structure enhancements have been introduced in recent years to improve the accuracy of one-stage detectors, achieving remarkable results.

2   Methodology

This paper describes the use of YOLOv8, an object detection and classification model, for identifying and categorizing different types of cells in urine sediment images. The dataset was labeled using Roboflow and included eleven classes of urine particles such as platelets, red blood cells (RBC), white blood cells (WBC), casts, crystals, epithelial cells (epith), transitional epithelial cells (epithn), erythrocytes (eryth), leukocytes (leuko), fungi (mycete), and background. Deep learning models were applied to the dataset to analyze the sample images and determine the number and types of cells present in the urine sediment.

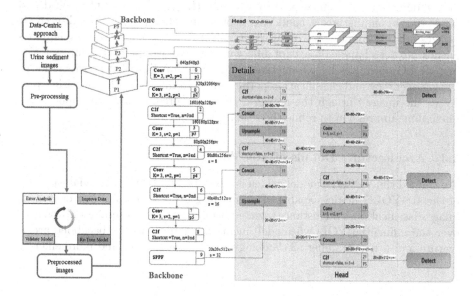

Fig. 1. Workflow of the proposed method.

2.1   Data-Centric Approach

Before training a deep learning model on any dataset, it is crucial to ensure that the data is of high quality and suitable for the intended purpose. In this context, the primary goal is to accurately identify and categorize different types of cells in urine sediment images. Therefore, the first step is to examine the data to detect any missing data, inaccurate labeling, or class imbalance issues.

Missing data refers to any data points that are not available or have not been recorded. Inaccurate labeling refers to any mislabeling of data points or incorrect assignment of class labels. Class imbalance issues occur when there is a significant disparity in the number of data points across different classes, which can lead to bias in the model's training. To address these issues, the data is carefully examined to identify any missing data points or incorrect labels. Any such data points are either removed or corrected to ensure that the dataset is of high quality and reliable. Additionally, the data is checked for any class imbalance issues, and appropriate measures are taken to balance the number of data points across different classes, such as oversampling or undersampling.

By ensuring the data is accurate, reliable, and balanced, the labeling reliability is boosted, and noisy data points are excluded. This process helps to ensure that the deep learning model trained on the dataset can accurately identify and categorize different types of cells in urine sediment images, leading to more accurate results and better insights.

2.2 Working of Yolo

YOLO (You Only Look Once) is an object detection algorithm that performs object detection in a single pass by dividing the input image into a grid and predicting bounding boxes, confidence scores, and class probabilities directly. It utilizes convolutional neural networks (CNNs) to extract features and employs anchor boxes to handle objects of different sizes and aspect ratios. During training, YOLO optimizes its parameters using a loss function that considers localization accuracy and classification performance. In inference, the algorithm processes the image through the network, generates predictions, and applies non-maximum suppression to refine the results.

2.3 Architectural Details of YoloV8

We trained the YOLOv8 model, which is developed by Ultralytics, a latest state-of-the-art YOLO model capable of performing tasks such as object detection, image classification, and instance segmentation. It includes several improvements over the influential YOLOv5 model, including changes in the backbone architecture and a new training methodology that enables faster and more efficient training.

2.3.1 Anchor Free Detection

Unlike models that rely on predefined anchor boxes to predict object location, YOLOv8 is an anchor-free model that directly predicts the center of an object. This approach eliminates the need for anchor boxes and simplifies the object detection process, leading to more accurate predictions. Earlier YOLO models had difficulties with anchor boxes as they might not represent the object box distribution in custom datasets, leading to inaccurate predictions. Anchor-free detection simplifies the object detection process by reducing the number of box predictions, resulting in faster Non-Maximum Suppression (NMS) during post-processing. NMS is a crucial step that filters out false positives and selects the most accurate detections after inference.

2.3.2 New Convolutions

The YOLOv8 model includes several architectural changes from earlier versions, such as replacing the first 6×6 convolution in the stem with a 3×3 convolution, using a new building block, and replacing C3 with C2f. The C2f module concatenates all the outputs from the Bottleneck, while in C3 only the output of

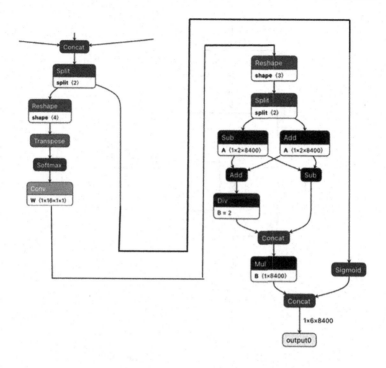

Fig. 2. The detection head for YOLOv8, visualized in netron.app.

the last Bottleneck was used. The module is composed of a Convolution layer, a Batch Normalization layer, and a SiLU activation layer, and the number of features is denoted as "f" while the expansion rate is denoted as "e". A diagram summarizing the module is provided in Fig. 2. The Bottleneck used in YOLOv8 is similar to that of YOLOv5, but with a change in the kernel size of the first convolution from 1×1 to 3×3. This change indicates a shift towards the ResNet block architecture, which was introduced in 2015. In the neck, feature concatenation is done without enforcing the same channel dimensions, which reduces the parameter count and the tensor size.

3   Experiments

3.1   Dataset

The accuracy of network recognition is greatly affected by the quality of datasets. In order to obtain a high-quality dataset for image recognition, several urine samples were collected using micro-photography equipment. From each sample, 650 high-definition images were captured, resulting in a total of 5632 images belonging to 10 different classes and 1 background, as shown in Fig. 4. The number of images per class is 284. The images were manually labeled using Robowflow and verified by the professional medical team and finally, 10 categories of urine

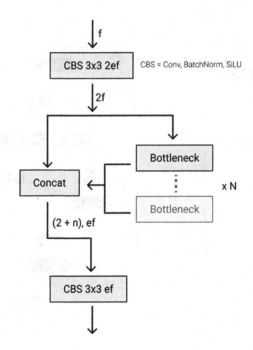

Fig. 3. The new YoloV8 c2f module.

sediment with medical significance were selected. These categories include RBC, WBC, casts, crystals, epithelial cells (epith), transitional epithelial cells (epithn), erythrocytes (eryth), leukocytes (leuko), and mycete.The dataset was divided into three sets - a training set, a validation set, and a test set - with random assignment of images. The training set consisted of 90% of the images, while the validation and testing set each contained 5% of the images.

3.2   Performance Metrics

The study assesses the performance of the model through the utilization of evaluation metrics such as precision, recall, F1 score, confidence interval, and micro-averaging.

Precision and recall are defined as.

$$Precision = \frac{TP}{TP + FP} \tag{1}$$

where TP is True Positives and FP is False Positives

$$Recall = \frac{TP}{TP + FN} \tag{2}$$

F 1 score is defined as.

$$F1 = \frac{2 * Precision * Recall}{Precision + Recall} = \frac{2 * TP}{2 * TP + FP + FN} \tag{3}$$

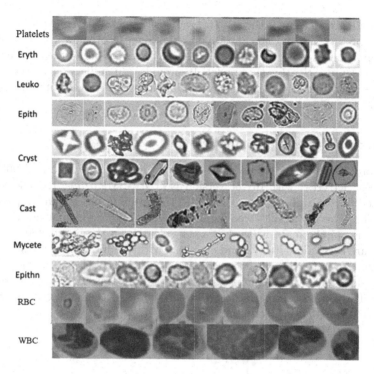

Platelets

Eryth

Leuko

Epith

Cryst

Cast

Mycete

Epithn

RBC

WBC

Fig. 4. The sample dataset for urine sediment is presented in the left column with their labels on the right

The F1 score is calculated by taking the harmonic mean of precision and recall. This is an appropriate choice because both precision and recall are rates. By taking the harmonic mean, the F1 score gives equal importance to both precision and recall in its calculation. Therefore, it can be said that the F1 score provides an average of precision and recall with equal weighting. Whereas evaluating multi-category recognition models, micro-averaging is a core indicator. It provides useful insights into the model's performance in multiple categories. To calculate the micro average for the given data, we sum up the number of true positive predictions for all the classes and divide it by the total number of actual positives, instead of predicted positives which are represented by the following equation.

$$PrecisionMicroAvg = \frac{TP1 + TP2 + ... + TPn}{TP1 + TP2 + ... + TPn + FP1 + FP2 + FP3 + ... + FPn} \quad (4)$$

The confidence measure is defined as

$$ConfidenceMeasure = \frac{TruePositive}{TruePositive + FalsePositive} \quad (5)$$

The confidence measure is the ratio of true positive predictions to the sum of true positive predictions and false positive predictions. In other words, it represents the proportion of correctly predicted positive instances out of the total instances predicted as positive by the model. It provides an indication of the model's accuracy in correctly identifying positive instances while taking into account the number of false positive predictions made.

3.3   Experiments and Analysis

The main network was trained and tested using an Intel Core i7-7700K CPU and Tesla T4 GPU with driver version NVIDIA-SMI 525.85.12. The learning rate used during training was 0.001, and the training process was repeated for 55 epochs. The test results were summarized in Fig. 7, which shows the confusion matrix of the main network.It's very clear from the figure that eryth and mycete are correctly detected and classified with the highest confidence of 97%. Whereas RBCs are the particles that are 81% correctly classified with the lowest confidence interval as compared to all other 10 particles. F1 score, precision, and recall are important performance metrics for detection and recognition tasks which are presented in Figs. 6 and 7.

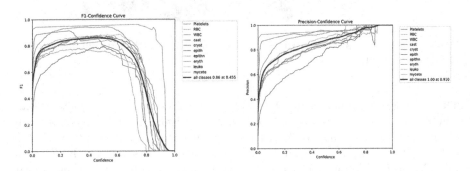

Fig. 5. F1 and Precision- confidence curve for all ten catagories.

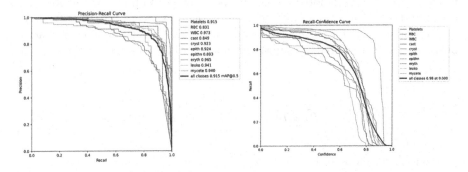

Fig. 6. Precision-Recall and Recall-confidence curve for all ten catagories.

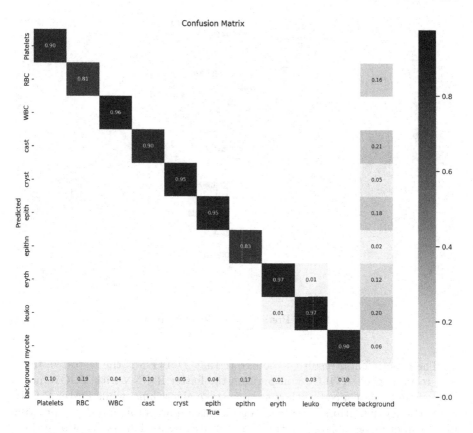

Fig. 7. Detection results on test set of ten catagories of urine sediment.

Table 1. Comparison of accuracy of detection methods from different research articles

N0	Methods	Dataset & categories	mAP	Infernece time
1	Our Method (Yolov8)	10 categories of RBC, WBC, cast, etc.	91%	0.6 ms per image
2 [12]	Faster RCNN+SSD	7 categories of RBC, WBC, Casts, etc.	84.1%	72 ms per image
3 [13]	CNN (DFPN)	7 categories of RBC, WBC, Crystals, etc.	86.9%	Not mentioned
4 [14]	DCNN	2 categories of RBC, WBC, Crystals, etc.	98.94%	2590 ms per image
5 [15]	Improved Yolov3	5 categories of RBC, WBC, Crystals, etc.	90.1%	0.047 s per fram

Figure 8 depicts the performance results obtained from testing a model on a dataset consisting of 10 distinct categories. The average mean precision accuracy achieved by the model was 91%, indicating that the model is capable of accurately classifying objects within the dataset. Furthermore, the inference time, which is the time it takes for the model to make a prediction on a single sample of data, was 0.6 ms, implying that the model is efficient and can make predictions quickly. Overall, the model appears to be reliable and efficient in performing its intended task of object classification.

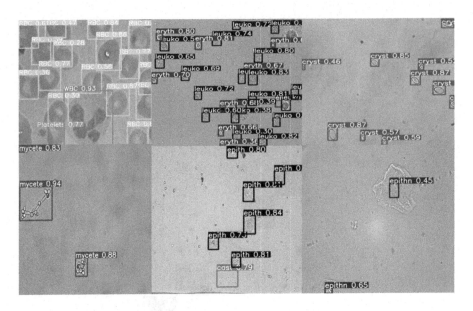

Fig. 8. Prediction results of YoloV8

The experimental results demonstrate that YOLOv8 is the fastest in terms of detection speed. YOLOv8 outperform the Faster R-CNN with VGG16 net in terms of detection speed as they are one-stage algorithms, while Faster R-CNN is a two-stage algorithm. Two-stage algorithms require a rough regional proposal for the input image, followed by more accurate classification and location estimation, which takes more time for detection. Although one-stage algorithms have faster detection speed, they are generally associated with lower accuracy. However, YOLOv8, despite being a one-stage algorithm, achieves high detection accuracy while maintaining fast speed. To further validate the effectiveness of the proposed method and other algorithms, we compare the detection of average class accuracy, which is presented in Table 1. Our method involves increasing the number of parameters and computations for determining the training samples. However, these modifications do not significantly impact the detection speed. Despite the requirement for fast detection, our model achieves a mean average precision (mAP) of 91%, which is superior to other algorithms. The detection time required for our model is 0.6 ms per image, which is slightly longer than improved YOLOv3's. Considering the real-time and accuracy requirements of automatic urinary sediment visible component detection, our model is a viable option.

4   Conclusion

This paper proposes a deep learning-based method for urine sediment image recognition, which is significant for the diagnosis of related diseases in urology and other departments. The traditional recognition methods have limitations, such as heavy workload and low accuracy. The proposed method uses a data-centric approach to enhance labeling reliability and overcome class imbalance and missing labeling data. The method employs YoloV8, a recent version of the Yolo algorithm, to accurately detect and categorize urine particles. The CNNs are trained on a dataset containing 5632 images, and the test set achieves an average mean precision of 91% with an average recognition time of 0.6 ms. Furthermore, the method has strong expandability and can introduce more categories for recognition in practical applications.

References

1. Goswami, D., Aggrawal, H., Agarwal. V.: Cell detection and classification from urine sediment microscopic images (2020)
2. Aglibot, K.P., Angeles, J.A., Gecana, J.F., Germano, A.B., Macalindong, J.A., Tolentino, R.E.: Urine crystal classification using convolutional neural networks. In: 2022 International Visualization, Informatics and Technology Conference (IVIT), pp. 245–250. IEEE (2022)
3. Ji, Q., Li, X., Zhiyu, Q., Dai, C.: Research on urine sediment images recognition based on deep learning. IEEE Access **7**, 166711–166720 (2019)
4. Uijlings, J.R.R., Van De Sande, K.E.A., Gevers, T., Smeulders, A.W.M.: Selective search for object recognition. Int. J. Comput. Vis. **104**, 154–171 (2013)
5. Girshick. R.: Fast R-CNN. In: Proceedings of the IEEE International Conference on Computer Vision, pp. 1440–1448 (2015)
6. Wang, Q., Bi, S., Sun, M., Wang, Y., Wang, D., Yang, S.: Deep learning approach to peripheral leukocyte recognition. PLoS ONE **14**(6), e0218808 (2019)
7. Redmon, I., Farhadi, A.: Yolov3: an incremental improvement. preprint. arXiv preprint arXiv:1804.02767, 4322 (2018)
8. Redmon, J., Divvala, S., Girshick, R., Farhadi, A.: You only look once: unified, real-time object detection. In: Proceedings of the IEEE Conference on Computer Vision and Pattern Recognition, pp. 779–788 (2016)
9. Redmon, J., Farhadi, A.: Yolo9000: better, faster, stronger. In: Proceedings of the IEEE Conference on Computer Vision and Pattern Recognition, pp. 7263–7271 (2017)
10. Li, Q., et al.: Inspection of visible components in urine based on deep learning. Med. Phys. **47**(7), 2937–2949 (2020)
11. Lin, T-y., Goyal, P., Girshick, R., He, K., Dollár, P.: Focal loss for dense object detection. In: Proceedings of the IEEE International Conference on Computer Vision, pp. 2980–2988 (2017)
12. Liang, Y., Kang, R., Lian, C., Mao, Y.: An end-to-end system for automatic urinary particle recognition with convolutional neural network. J. Med. Syst. **42**, 1–14 (2018)
13. Liang, Y., Tang, Z., Yan, M., Liu, J.: Object detection based on deep learning for urine sediment examination. Biocybernet. Biomed. Eng. **38**(3), 661–670 (2018)
14. Wang, Q., Sun, Q., Wang. Y.: A two-stage urine sediment detection method. In: 2020 International Conference on Image, Video Processing and Artificial Intelligence, vol. 11584, pp. 15–21. SPIE (2020)
15. Dong, S., Zhang, S., Jiao, L., Wang. Q.: Automatic urinary sediments visible component detection based on improved yolo algorithm. In: 2020 International Conference on Computer Vision, Image and Deep Learning (CVIDL), pp. 485–490. IEEE (2020)

Short Papers (MoveTo0 2023)

Ecosystem Services and Rural Innovation: The Liguria Region Case Study

Giampiero Lombardini[1] ⓘ, Angela Pilogallo[2](✉) ⓘ, and Giorgia Tucci[1] ⓘ

[1] dAD, University of Genoa, Stradone Sant'Agostino 37, 16123 Genova, Italy
{giampiero.lombardini,giorgia.tucci}@unige.it
[2] Department of Civil, Building-Architecture and Environmental Engineering, University of L'Aquila, Via G. Gronchi 18, 67100 L'Aquila, Italy
angela.pilogallo@univaq.it

Abstract. The exploitation of environmental resources and the growth of urbanization significantly altered natural ecosystems, turning over time into socio-ecological systems strongly influenced by urban regions. Spatial structures and ecosystems are required to address a mutually reinforcing symbiosis with environment and natural resources that can no longer be postponed, so as to combine the conservation needs with the reduction of socio-economic inequalities. The case study concerns the Liguria Region, characterized by a strong polarization between linear coastal conurbation and hinterland. This territorial structure is responsible for the mismatch between areas that provide most of Ecosystem Services (ES) and those with the highest population and urbanization density, which, on the other hand, are configured as major demand poles. This paper therefore aims to analyze the relationship between environmental values, in terms of ecosystem multifunctionality, and forms of rural innovation that contribute to support territorial competitiveness. The aim is to explore how a systemic approach can foster opportunities for integration between inner and coastal areas, qualifying the valley systems as new components of the anthropic-environmental structure of the region.

Keywords: Rural innovation · Ecosystem Services · ecosystem multifunctionality

1 Introduction

On our rapidly urbanizing planet, there is a need for planners to rethink human components and natural resources no longer as separate units but as part of a large socio-ecological system [1]. It represents a highly interconnected relationship between society and ecosystems [2] and is useful to jointly pursue natural resource conservation imperatives, economic development needs and the reduction of socio-economic inequalities, increasingly linked to differential access to ES [3]. The search for territorial structures suited to this new paradigm can no longer be postponed and must instead be seized as an opportunity to enhance those innovative characteristics of rural systems that stand as interface between anthropic and purely environmental systems [4].

O. Gervasi et al. (Eds.): ICCSA 2023 Workshops, LNCS 14112, pp. 283–290, 2023.
https://doi.org/10.1007/978-3-031-37129-5_23

This paper focuses on the case study of the Liguria Region (Italy), whose anthropic-settlement structure is essentially made up of the most important urban centers and the coastal conurbation, developing mainly along the east-west axis [5].

While showing a high potential in terms of natural capital and ecosystem multifunctionality [6, 7], this structure produces a significant spatial mismatch between the inner areas that provide most ES and the main demand poles represented by areas with the highest population and urbanization density.

According to a *bioregional* approach, based on the concept of urban bioregion that underpins balanced polycentric spatial patterns and supports self-reliant and fair local development [8], our research question is: can a systemic approach offer opportunities for integration between inner areas and coastal strips, qualifying the valley systems as new components of the regional anthropic-environmental structure?

The purpose of this paper is hence to investigate the relationship between ecosystem multifunctionality, defined as the capacity to simultaneously deliver several ES [9–11], and different forms of rural innovation that contribute to support territorial competitiveness and strengthen resilience [12, 13].

This work is organized as follows. Section 2 presents the overall methodology and describes methods used to assess the degree of rural innovation and the multifunctionality indicator. Section 3 illustrates the result of the comparison between spatial distributions of the two indicators and highlights correspondences interpreted in the light of territorial policies implemented and on-going settlement dynamics. Finally, the conclusions highlight a reciprocal multiplier effect between ES provision and the development of innovative contributions in rural systems.

2   Methodology

In order to analyze the relationship between innovation of rural systems and multifunctionality of ecosystems, two different spatially explicit indicators were calculated.

The first expresses the ability of ecosystems to provide multiple goods and services essential for human well-being. As part of this work, it was computed as the sum of 7 ES normalized with respect to time series.

The second measures rural systems' innovation degree and is representative of a set of characteristics of both socio-economic and political-technological dimensions.

With the aim of investigating the mutual relationship between these two indices, an autocorrelation analysis was performed to define innovation territorial cluster. They were then overlayed to ecosystem multifunctionality variation over the period 2000–2018.

The following paragraphs illustrate the methods used to calculate the two indices.

2.1   Ecosystem Multifunctionality

For the purpose of this study, we selected a set of 7 ES (Table 1) based on two criteria:

– relevance with respect to the study area;

– input dataset and layer availability to implement the calculation models, considering the 2000–2018 time series.

According to the Common International Classification (CICES v5.1) [14], they are included in two sections "Provision" and "Maintenance and regulation".

Table 1. Set of ES considered

Section	Class	Method/Model
Provision	Crop Production	InVEST
	Water yield	Budyko equation
Regulation and Maintenance	Regulation of chemical composition of atmosphere	InVEST
	Pollination	InVEST
	Maintaining nursery populations and habitats	InVEST
	Control of erosion rates	InVEST
	Regulation of the chemical condition of freshwaters	InVEST

The aforementioned ES were assessed and mapped for each available Corine Land Cover chrono sequences (2000–2006–2012–2018). The multifunctionality index used was calculated in the GIS environment by normalizing the current value compared to the historical series. This index was calculated with reference to 2000 and 2018. The difference between these two layers returns the spatial distribution of its variations over the period considered.

2.2 Rural Innovation

The second indicator was used to analyze sustainable territorial innovation processes and quantitatively measure the organizational characterizations of socio-economic structures.

For the purpose of computing this index, 7 indicators were selected, relating to aspects linked to the socio-economic dimension (multifunctional agriculture and agro-productive circuits; social and cultural actions; sustainable tourism) and 4 indicators describing political-technological aspects (governance policies; energy systems; digital networks).

By geolocating the presence of aforementioned innovation components over the regional territory, a regular hexagonal grid (size 500 m) was created in order to have a synthesis representation. Each grid cell shows the degree of innovation, i.e. the mean number of innovation components included within it.

3 Results and Discussion

This section illustrates the result of the cluster analysis carried out to define area where a more evident rural innovation is occurring. Then it shows the results from overlapping of rural systems innovation clusters with respect to the variation of ecosystem multifunctionality index.

To identify local clusters in the Innovation Degree (Fig. 1) we performed an autocorrelation analysis by the Univariate Local Moran's I index (LISA) [15] using the software GeoDa [16].

Results from this kind of geo-statistical analysis allow to identify *High-High* and *Low-Low* spatial clusters and, on the other hand, to classify *High-Low* and *Low-High* spatial outliers.

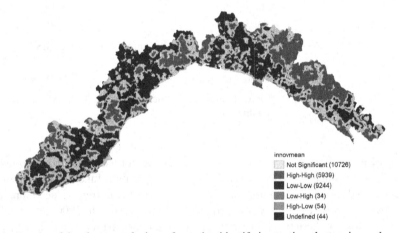

innovmean
Not Significant (10726)
High-High (5939)
Low-Low (9244)
Low-High (34)
High-Low (54)
Undefined (44)

Fig. 1. Results of the cluster analysis performed to identify innovation clusters in rural systems

These results confirm that different innovative actions create a field of mutual attraction, so they tend to have a tendency to have a certain degree of spatial concentration.

The representation of the clusters defined by the analysis is accompanied by the corresponding Significance Map (Fig. 2) that shows the locations with a significant local statistic ($p < 0.05$).

Results deriving from autocorrelation analysis were therefore used to extrapolate the areas of the regional territory that qualify as innovation clusters (*High-High* cluster) and to overlay them with the variation of the ecosystem multifunctionality index.

The highest values of multifunctionality are distributed in the inner part of the region near the mountainous areas characterized by predominantly forested and highly vegetated land covers, low anthropic pressure and geomorphological factors that have contributed to limiting the spread of urbanization processes.

On the other hand, the lowest values are found along the coastal strip in the most densely urbanised areas, where the highly fragmented settlement and production system, the massive adoption of intensive cultivation practices and the high density of road infrastructures contribute to low environmental performance.

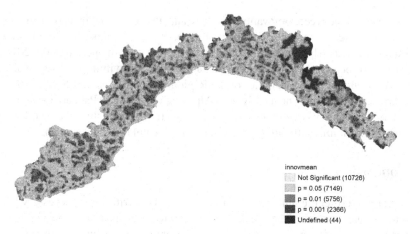

Fig. 2. Significance Map

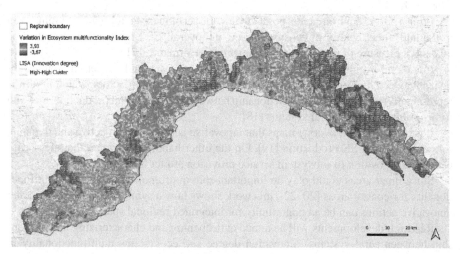

Fig. 3. Overlay between the rural systems innovation clusters and the spatial distribution of the variation of ecosystem multifunctionality index.

The overall picture shows a high variability of environmental performances as a function of urbanization intensity, with correspondences emerging between areas characterized by low to medium values and the main coastal conurbations.

The degree of innovation also takes on a rather fragmented distribution, assuming greater intensity where a multiplicity of innovative actions related to the tourism-accommodation, hiking and agro-production sectors are concentrated. A first level of innovation is also detected along the eastern coastal strip, linked to the initiation of regeneration projects and the presence of biodiversity in protected park areas.

The overlap between innovation clusters and the variation in ecosystem multi-functionality (Fig. 3) shows some correspondences: in fact, most innovation clusters correspond to areas where multifunctionality increased over the period 2000–2018.

It can also be seen that the major innovation hubs fall within the 4 regional Inner Areas. Also evident in the west part of the Region is the increase in ES where the Alta Valle Arroscia Inner Area and the Ligurian Alps Regional Natural Park are located. Thus, the synergy existing between innovation and protection actions through the creation of park areas that significantly affect regional environmental quality is evident.

4 Conclusions

To correctly interpret the innovation characteristics of a territory, it is necessary to consider their dynamic nature. These in fact are distributed over space and time in relation to a series of intrinsic factors such as contextual preconditions, resources, situational variables, capacity to accept risk and change, socio-cultural values and interests, absorption capacity [8, 17].

From a purely environmental point of view, the set of these factors can be summarized in the multifunctionality of ecosystems, i.e. the overall ES supply, which can thus be taken as a measure of territorial environmental performance [7].

It is therefore important to pursue a systemic approach and deepen the link established between the set of environmental values and innovation factors, which in turn is representative of the functional relationship between natural capital production sites and forms of innovation in rural systems [18].

It is clear from the overlay maps that innovative actions play an active and dynamic role in promoting ES production [19]. On the other hand, it is evident that areas with better predisposition to ecosystem service provision attract innovative actions.

Since inner areas could play an important role in promoting ecosystem multifunctionality for coastal areas [20–22], this work shows how a symbiosis of rural space and innovative actions can be an opportunity for integrated regional spatial development.

Research developments will be aimed at deepening and characterizing the relationship between rural systems' innovation degree and ecosystems multifunctionality in order to verify the opportunity to promote policies that enhance the conservation of natural resources as elements of competitive advantage for local development.

References

1. Alberti, M.: Cities that Think Like Planets: Complexity, Resilience, and Innovation in Hybrid Ecosystems. University of Washington Press (2018)
2. Francis, R., Bekera, B.: A metric and frameworks for resilience analysis of engineered and infrastructure systems. Reliab. Eng. Syst. Saf. **121**, 90–103 (2014). https://doi.org/10.1016/J. RESS.2013.07.004
3. Ronchi, S.: Ecosystem Services for Spatial Planning. Springer, Cham (2018). https://doi.org/ 10.1007/978-3-319-90185-5
4. Fanfani, D., Matarán Ruiz, A.: Bioregional Planning and Design. Volume II, Issues and Practices for a Bioregional Regeneration. Springer, Cham (2020). https://doi.org/10.1007/ 978-3-030-46083-9

5. Lai, S., Lombardini, G.: Regional drivers of land take: a comparative analysis in two Italian regions. Land Use Policy **56**, 262–273 (2016). https://doi.org/10.1016/J.LANDUSEPOL. 2016.05.003

6. Pilogallo, A., Scorza, F.: Ecosystem services multifunctionality: an analytical framework to support sustainable spatial planning in Italy. Sustainability **14**, 3346 (2022). https://doi.org/ 10.3390/SU14063346

7. Pilogallo, A., Scorza, F., Murgante, B.: An ecosystem services-based territorial ranking for Italian provinces. In: Gervasi, O., et al. (eds.) ICCSA 2021. LNCS, vol. 12955, pp. 692–702. Springer, Cham (2021). https://doi.org/10.1007/978-3-030-87007-2_49

8. Lombardini, G.: Bioregion as a knowledge and project tool for metropolitan territories. Genoa: the case of Polcevera Valley. Scienze del Territorio **10** (2022). https://doi.org/10.13128/SDT-13799

9. Selman, P.: Planning for landscape multifunctionality **5**, 45–52 (2017). https://doi.org/10. 1080/15487733.2009.11908035

10. Mastrangelo, M.E., Weyland, F., Villarino, S.H., Barral, M.P., Nahuelhual, L., Laterra, P.: Concepts and methods for landscape multifunctionality and a unifying framework based on ecosystem services. Landsc. Ecol. **29**, 345–358 (2014). https://doi.org/10.1007/S10980-013-9959-9/METRICS

11. Hansen, R., Pauleit, S.: From multifunctionality to multiple ecosystem services? A conceptual framework for multifunctionality in green infrastructure planning for Urban Areas. Ambio **43**, 516–529 (2014). https://doi.org/10.1007/S13280-014-0510-2/FIGURES/5

12. Sommariva, E., Canessa, N.V., Tucci, G.: Green actions for innovative cities. The new agri-food landscape. AGATHÓN|Int. J. Archit. Art Des. **11**, 150–161 (2022). https://doi.org/10. 19229/2464-9309/11132022

13. Gausa, M.N., Pericu, S., Canessa, N., Tucci, G.: Creative food cycles: a cultural approach to the food life-cycles in cities. Sustainability **12**, 6487 (2020). https://doi.org/10.3390/SU1216 6487

14. Haines-Young, R., Potschin, M.: Common International Classification of Ecosystem Services (CICES) V5.1 Guidance on the Application of the Revised Structure (2018)

15. Anselin, L.: Local indicators of spatial association—LISA. Geogr. Anal. **27**, 93–115 (1995). https://doi.org/10.1111/J.1538-4632.1995.TB00338.X

16. GeoDa on Github. https://geodacenter.github.io/. Accessed 21 Apr 2023

17. Panuccio, P.: Smart planning: from city to territorial system. Sustainability **11**, 7184 (2019). https://doi.org/10.3390/SU11247184

18. Montrasio, R., Mattiello, S., Zucaro, M., Genovese, D., Battaglini, L.: The perception of ecosystem services of mountain farming and of a local cheese: an analysis for the touristic valorization of an inner alpine area. Sustainability **12**, 8017 (2020). https://doi.org/10.3390/ SU12198017

19. Pilogallo, A., Scorza, F.: Mapping regulation ecosystem services specialization in Italy. J. Urban Plan. Dev. **148**, 04021072 (2022). https://doi.org/10.1061/(ASCE)UP.1943-5444.000 0801

20. Lombardini, G., Scorza, F.: Resilience and smartness of coastal regions. A tool for spatial evaluation. In: Gervasi, O., et al. (eds.) ICCSA 2016. LNCS, vol. 9788, pp. 530–541. Springer, Cham (2016). https://doi.org/10.1007/978-3-319-42111-7_42

21. de Castro-Pardo, M., Azevedo, J.C., Fernández, P.: Ecosystem services, sustainable rural development and protected areas. Land **10**, 1008 (2021). https://doi.org/10.3390/LAND10 101008

22. Lombardini, G., Pilogallo, A., Tucci, G.: The provision of ecosystem services along the Italian coastal areas: a correlation analysis between environmental quality and urbanization. In: Gervasi, O., Murgante, B., Misra, S., Rocha, A.M.A.C., Garau, C. (eds.) ICCSA 2022. LNCS, vol. 13380, pp. 298–314. Springer, Cham (2022). https://doi.org/10.1007/978-3-031-10542-5_21

Gender Dis-Equality and Urban Settlement Dispersion: Indices Comparison

Lucia Saganeiti[iD] and Lorena Fiorini[✉][iD]

Department of Civil, Building-Architecture and Environmental Engineering, University of L'Aquila, Via G. Gronchi, 18, 67100 L'Aquila, Italy
{lucia.saganeiti,lorena.fiorini}@univaq.it

Abstract. The challenge of "Gender equality" regards different sectors, such as empowerment and working conditions, cultural change, leadership, safety, economic security, health and wellbeing. For this reason, the gender mainstreaming is important for the coordination and integration of all other policies, including urban spatial planning.

Currently, it is fundamental to shift toward gender-sensitive territorial planning, which can be more focused on some specific areas of intervention such as: the localization of amenities, mobility and accessibility, and safety. In this context, the work presented aims to indagate the effect of urban dispersion on women's quality of life. Starting with a discussion related to the characteristics and limitations associated with the use of data from the "Sole 24 Ore" (a national Italian editorial journal), a new women's quality of life index (I_{QLw}) was developed. Subsequently, the I_{QLw} index, which includes demographic and economic factors, was compared with the urban dispersion index through a correlation analysis using LISA index (Local Indicator for Spatial Association).

Indeed, to be able to reach solutions and act toward the achievement of sustainability development goals and to influence changes in a positive way, it is crucial to know the phenomena and measure their dimensions through parameters and indicators useful for supporting transformational policies.

Keywords: Gender inequality · Urban sprinkling · Land planning · Indicator engineering

1 Introduction

"Gender equality", being a fundamental human right, is one of the 17 Sustainable Development Goals of the 2030 Agenda, and the achievement of gender equality is also one of the three cross-cutting priorities in terms of social inclusion in the National Recovery and Resilience Plan [1, 2].

From a study developed by the European Institute for Gender Equality (EIGE) in 2022 [3], it appears that the Gender Equality Index score for the EU is 68.6 points out of 100, with a 0.6-point increase since the 2021 index. In recent years this index has been increasing but this is occurring at a very slow rate in fact the current value is only 5.5 points higher than in 2010, with an average increase of only 1 point every 2 years.

O. Gervasi et al. (Eds.): ICCSA 2023 Workshops, LNCS 14112, pp. 291–300, 2023.
https://doi.org/10.1007/978-3-031-37129-5_24

Moreover, Gender equality levels change considerably among Member States, from 83.9 points in Sweden to 53.4 points in Greece. In particular, Italy ranks 14th in the EU in the gender equality index with a score of 65.0 points out of 100, so it is 3.6 points lower than the EU [4].

In this context, the promotion of gender equality is crucial and to be effective it must cover several areas, including the legislative one to regulate equal treatment, the strategic one through gender mainstreaming for better integration of all other policies, and the economic one by providing specific funding for the advancement of women [5]. It is all directly and undoubtedly related to Goal 5 Gender Equality but, when analysing the concept in relation to territorial transformations and urban policies, it links indirectly to Goal 11 Sustainable Cities and Communities of the 2030 Agenda.

The challenge of urban regeneration becomes as an objective to the achievement of which different sectoral public policies are required to be coordinated in a coherent and strategic framework of interventions, essential to deal with the consequences related to climate change, political instability, pandemic situation and so on and provide effective solutions. Indeed, all of these are challenges that need for cities to rethink their environmental, economic, social and cultural models [6, 7].

The sustainability of cities is achieved by orienting land use planning toward urban transformation models which must no longer be expansive but based on the regeneration of existing urban fabric, without the consumption of new soil, and in addition they must give attention to climate resilience, use of renewable energy, quality of urban liveability, gender and generational equality and social inclusion [8, 9].

To obtain this, it is also necessary to shift toward gender-sensitive territorial planning, which can be more focused on some specific areas of intervention such as: the localization of amenities, mobility and accessibility, and safety.

How can a dispersed urban context affect women's quality of life? This is the starting question from which the current research developed. In an urban context characterised by dispersed settlement, the location of public services will consequently be dispersed over the territory. This leads to excessive car use and longer travel times to reach workplaces, schools or other amenities [10, 11]. The result is an increase in costs that indirectly affect the quality of life [12, 13]. Moreover, in these contexts, women are disadvantaged by having fewer opportunities to enter into a structured and lasting work context, as the lack of care services such as nurseries or facilities for the aged forces women to stay at home to take care of these tasks. The Italian Institute of statistic in collaboration with Eurostat declares that in Italy there is a very high gap between men and women in the performance of household duties (60% gap) [14, 15].

Urban dispersion has made the management of time between work (and study), recreational activities and relationships among individuals even more complex. Scattered sites of interest over a wide, networked territory require multiple movements, and this necessity results in a constantly moving and consequently accelerated lifestyle, particularly for women [16]. For these reasons, it is essential to act by redefining cohesion and inclusion mechanisms centered on both social and occupational homogeneity and women's and neighborhood networks [17].

To be able to reach solutions and act toward the achievement of sustainability goals and to influence changes in a positive way, it is necessary to know the phenomena analysed and measure their dimensions through parameters and indicators useful for supporting transformational policies [18]. In this way it also would be possible to monitor their progress. One of the objectives of the work presented, in fact, was to analytically assess Italian women's quality of life so that it could then be compared with the urban dispersion index to highlight potential relationships, based on the first results obtained from previous research developed by the same authors [19].

The article will deal with the following aspects: critical analysis of the Italian women's quality of life indices proposed by the "Sole 24 Ore" (a national Italian editorial journal) in the last two years 2021 and 2022; description of the dataset used for the analysis; new women's quality of life index composed of six indicators and more related to economic aspects; description of the main results obtained; comparison of the new index calculated with that of the "Sole 24 Ore" and with the phenomenon of settlement dispersion; conclusions and future developments.

2 The Italian Woman's Quality of Life Indices, Criticisms and Comparison

As mentioned in the introduction, in the previous paper [19] the authors carried out an analysis from "Sole 24 Ore" data to investigate the influence of urban settlement dispersion on women's quality of life. Currently, an update of the "Sole 24 Ore" data (published to 2022) is available [20], so it would have been very interesting to make a comparison with the previous year, but it was not possible. The issue is that the two datasets, which were produced only one year apart, are not directly comparable with each other because the parameters used to calculate the total index are not always the same. As shown in Table 1, out of 12 indicators 4 have changed (accounting for one-third of the total) between 2021 and 2022.

Table 1. Differences between 2021 and 2022 of the "Sole 24 Ore" Women's quality of life indices.

	"Sole 24 Ore" 2021 Women's quality of life	"Sole 24 Ore" 2022 Women's quality of life
1	life expectancy at birth	life expectancy at birth
2	women's employment rate	women's employment rate
3	youth employment	youth employment
4	gender employment gap	gender employment gap
5	number of women-owned businesses	number of women-owned businesses
6	women administrators in businesses	women administrators in businesses
7	women administrators in municipalities	women administrators in municipalities
8	gender violence	gender violence
9	gender pay gap	number of paid working days
10	job non-participation rate	women graduate
11	performance in sports	women in sport
12	Olympic performance	Inadequate numeracy skills

Therefore, the two indices of women's quality of life cannot be compared in their total value but only by extracting those that have remained unmodified. This operation, however, is not easily done because the "Sole 24 Ore" makes available only the summary data download. In addition, among the indicators, which were changed in the year 2022, some are not very significant for the aim of evaluating women's quality of life, such as:

i) inadequate numeracy skills because it measures women's STEM skills but it based on tests taken in junior high school where women's age is not comparable to the other indicators;

ii) women in sports which is too generic with respect to the indicators used by the Council of Europe to assess the presence of women in sport. One among many is the indicator of "Women in decision-making positions of national sport federations" or "Proportion of women and men in decision-making positions in continental confederations of Olympic sports" [21]

iii) number of paid working days which is definitely less significant than the gender pay gap (measured in 2021) and which gives better information about the gender gap. In fact, the 2021 indicator was more comparable with the indicator used by the European commission: "gender pay gap".

The definition of indices, useful for comparing the phenomena investigated and assessing their variability in both time and space, characterizes many fields that use spatial analysis. However, the selection and the elaboration of indices must be precise and homogeneous so that the developed analyses are comparable [22].

On the other hand, the main problems are often related both to the different definitions, that cause confusion and difficulties in reporting the results obtained, and to the heterogeneity of the data by which the indicators are calculated (such as in the case of the "Sole 24 Ore" data).

3 Dataset

All data used for this analysis are open data freely downloadable from national reference sites. The data are aggregated by provincial territories, are all divided by gender and age classes and in some cases, approximations have been made to the data due to the different nomenclature and association of the Italian provinces. The data needed to compose the women's quality of life index were downloaded from different sources and for 4 years: 2018, 2019, 2020 and 2021. In particular: socio-demographic data on population, employment rates, life expectancy at birth are derived from the database of the Italian Statistical Institute (ISTAT [23]); data concerning the number of enterprises were downloaded from the open data explorer site of the chamber of commerce [24].

For the phase of comparing the quality of life of women with the spatial dynamics of urban transformation, the data of settlement dispersion on a provincial basis calculated with Moran's index was used; its methodology is reported in the report of the Institute for Environmental Protection and Research (ISPRA 2021) on the paper by Saganeiti et al. [25].

4 Index of Women's Quality of Life

The women's quality of life index (I_{QLw}) proposed in this research is a socio-economic one since it includes demographic and economic factors such as employment rates or the number of enterprises in the study area considered. The index is the composition of 6 indicators all normalized between 0 and 1 and it is expressed by the following formula:

$$I_{QLw} = LEx_w + EmplR_w + YEmplR_w + EntPC_w - \left(GAP_{empl} + GAP_{ent}\right) \qquad (1)$$

where:

LEx_w is the indicator of life expectancy at birth for women, measured at age 0. The higher the value of the indicator, the higher the age corresponding to life expectancy and consequently the better the quality of life.

$EmplR_w$ is the indicator of the employment rate of women for the age group considered to be 'active age', i.e. that in which one is able to work: 15 to 64 years. The higher the value of the indicator, the better the quality of life.

$YEmplR_w$ is the indicator of the youth employment rate for women for the 15–34 age group, which includes the social class of young people and young adults as defined by ISTAT. The higher the value of the indicator, the better the quality of life.

$EntPC_w$ this indicator expresses the number of women enterprises per capita i.e. per female residents of working age (15–64 years) in each province. Women's enterprises are defined as: cooperatives or partnerships with at least 60% female members and/or joint stock companies at least two-thirds of whose shares and members of the boards of directors are women. The higher the value of the indicator, the better the quality of life.

GAP_{empl} is the indicator of the employment gap between the employment rate of women and the employment rate of men. Like the other indicators, its (normalised) value range is between 0 and 1, but as the indicator increases, the quality of life decreases. In fact, a high value of the gap, e.g. 0.35, means that the value of the employment rate for women is 35 percentage points away from that of men. Inversely, a gap of 0 reflects gender equality.

GAP_{ent} is the indicator of the enterprise gap between the number of women's enterprises and the number of other enterprises generally composed of men. Since this is also a gap, like the previous one, it should be read the other way around, i.e. as the value of the indicator increases, the quality of life decreases, since the gap between the number of women's enterprises and the number of men's enterprises widens.

As mentioned, the women's quality of life index is composed of 6 normalized indicators (0–1) that can have both negative and positive values, and because of this, the I_{QLw} has a range of values between −2 and 4. Thus, when the index increases, the value of women's quality of life increases.

5 Women Quality of Life Results

In this work, I_{QLw} was calculated for the different Italian provincial territories and for 4 years: 2018, 2019 2020 and 2021. Between the two extreme dates, 2018 and 2021, the value of the variance of the index increases for the various provinces (+6%), thus not showing a homogeneous growth trend of the various indicators composing it. The maximum values diverge from the higher range of the index (+4) by an average of 1.4 points while the minimum values diverge by an average of 0.9 points. This shows how the index value for all provinces is shifted more towards its lower limit: −2, representing a lower quality of life for women. The graph in Fig. 1 shows the distribution of index values for the 4 years analysed (y-axis).

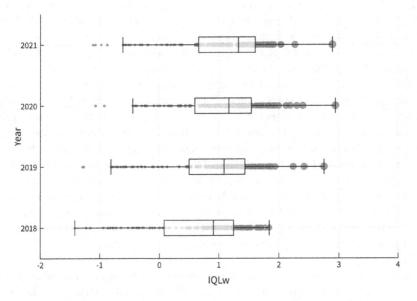

Fig. 1. Boxplot of the women's quality of life index for all provinces in different years.

The dots represent the provinces, the x-axis shows the index value, the rectangular boxes on each series are representative of the three quartiles. The positive aspect is that, albeit very slowly, the median value of the index is moving more and more towards the high values.

The maps in Fig. 2 show, in green shading, the values of the women's quality of life index by province. It is evident that the highest values are always concentrated in the provinces of central Italy. The lowest values of the index are instead distributed in the provinces of the south and in the region of Sicily with small variations over the 4 years. For the geographical repartition of the various provincial territories, see Fig. 3.

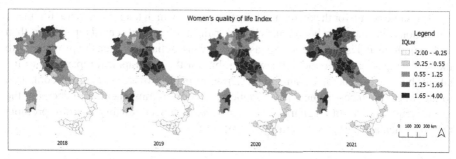

Fig. 2. Maps of woman's quality of life Index for years 2018, 2019, 2020 and 2021 for all provincial territory.

The boxplots in Fig. 3 represent the index of women's quality of life divided by the 5 geographical repartitions of the Italian territory: North-West, North-East, Centre, South and Islands (represented in the map in the center of Fig. 3). Each boxplot refers to an analysed year: 2018, 2019, 2020 and 2021. The provinces belonging to the northern and central repartitions have a much smaller variance (between 0.10 and 0.20) than those belonging to the southern and island repartitions (variance between 0.28 and 1.10).

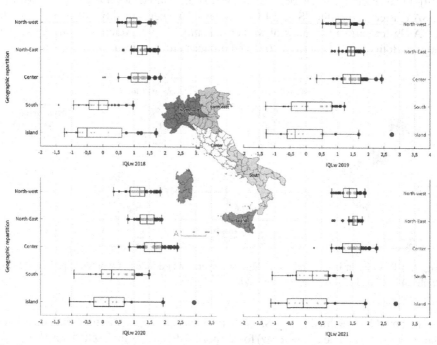

Fig. 3. Boxplot of the women's quality of life index for the geographic repartition in the four years. In the middle f picture there is a map of the geographic repartitions of Italy.

The same is true for the median value of the index, which tends to increase for all the repartitions over the years but remains higher in the northern and central repartitions than in the southern and island one. In the last three years Cagliari has been the province with the highest quality of life index for women, but for the geographical repartition of the islands but also in general it is an outlier. Certainly, in the province of Cagliari compared to the other provinces of the islands, policies have been implemented to decrease the gender gap. The city of Cagliari, in particular, has a gender equality board to promote the implementation of gender strategies [26].

6 Discussions and Future Developments

The above results show that the index of women's quality of life, with the exception of a few provinces, is higher in the provinces of northern and central Italy than in the provinces of the south and the islands. The southern provinces are also those characterised by often low-density and dispersed urban transformation associated in some cases with the urban sprinkling phenomenon [25, 27, 28].

The relationship between women's quality of life and urban dispersion was analysed with the LISA index (Local Indicator for Spatial Association), a spatial correlation index [29, 30]. This index was applied in previous research developed by the same authors [19]. In this case, the urban dispersion index at the national level is compared with the LISA cluster map of the "Sole 24 Ore" index of women's quality of life and with the LISA cluster map of the index of women's quality of life developed in this article (see Fig. 4). Both refer to data from 2021 and produce different results.

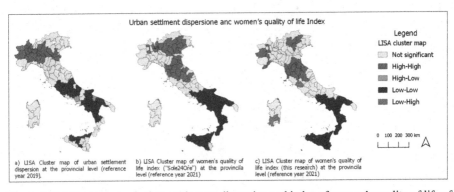

Fig. 4. LISA cluster map of urban settlement dispersion and index of women's quality of life of "Sole 24 Ore" and of this research (year 2021).

It should be specified that LISA statistical analysis applied to the urban dispersion index returns low values (Low-Low) for territories affected by high settlement dispersion and high values (High-High) for territories characterized by compact urbanization.

It is evident how in all three maps a clear distinction emerges between the provinces of northern and central Italy and those of the south. Two clearly separate clusters are formed where the blue colour corresponds to low values of both the index of women's quality of life and the urban dispersion index. Conversely, the red colour corresponds to high values of both the index of women's quality of life and the urban dispersion index.

The southern Italian provinces characterized by high settlement dispersion are also those where the quality of life index is lowest. The contrary is not true. It is not possible to affirm, even in general terms, that provinces with higher quality of life indices have a more compact urbanized form. This does not allow us to answer the research question of this article exhaustively, but it does allow us to open up some insights for further developments. The index introduced is powerful in monitoring the phenomenon on a territorial and temporal scale since it is composed of indicators that are regularly collected from institutional sources. It also makes it possible to identify the areas characterized by lower values of the quality of life in which to deepen the analyses in order to identify their relationship with the spatial distribution of the urbanized area. In fact, the analysis at the provincial level provides a first view of the phenomenon analyzed. Within the same province there are often different dynamics of territorial transformations from more compact forms to more dispersed forms and different urban policies.

Funding. This research is funded by the University Research Project for Basic and Initial Research 2022 (University of L'Aquila): "Gender dis-equality e dispersione insediativa" (Gender dis-equality and urban dispersion).

References

1. European Commission Eurostat: Sustainable development in the European Union: monitoring report on progress towards the SDGs in an EU context: 2022 edition. Publications Office of the European Union (2022)
2. Piano Nazionale di ripresa e resilienza #NextGenerationITALIA (2021)
3. EIGE: European Institute for Gender Equality|European Institute for Gender Equality. https://eige.europa.eu/. Accessed 23 Apr 2023
4. Cohen, G., Shinwell, M.: How far are OECD countries from achieving SDG targets for women and girls? Applying a gender lens to measuring distance to SDG targets. https://doi.org/10.1787/17a25070-en
5. European Commission: A Union of Equality: Gender Equality Strategy 2020–2025 EN. EUR-Lex. 4 (2020)
6. OECD: Building back better - A sustainable, resilient recovery after COVID-19. OECD Policy Responses to Coronavirus (COVID-19) 2–16 (2020)
7. Doytsher, Y., Kelly, P., Khouri, R., Mclaren, R., Mueller, H., Potsiou, C.: Rapid urbanization and mega cities: the need for spatial information management. In: FIG Congress 2010, p. 24 (2010)
8. The World Bank: Gender-Inclusive Urban Planning Design (2020)
9. Madlener, R., Sunak, Y.: Impacts of urbanization on urban structures and energy demand: what can we learn for urban energy planning and urbanization management? Sustain Cities Soc. 1, 45–53 (2011). https://doi.org/10.1016/J.SCS.2010.08.006
10. Olivieri, C., Fageda, X.: Urban mobility with a focus on gender: the case of a middle-income Latin American city. J. Transp. Geogr. 91, 102996 (2021). https://doi.org/10.1016/j.jtrangeo.2021.102996
11. Galiano, G., Forestieri, G., Moretti, L.: Urban sprawl and mobility. WIT Trans. Built Environ. 204, 245–255 (2021). https://doi.org/10.2495/UT210201

12. Manganelli, B., Murgante, B., Saganeiti, L.: The social cost of urban sprinkling. Sustainability. **12**, 2236 (2020). https://doi.org/10.3390/su12062236

13. Hough, J.A., et al.: The Costs of Sprawl (2004)

14. Un Ritratto Statistico: La vita delle donne e degli uomini in Europa Edizione (2020)

15. Wachter, I., Holz-Rau, C.: Gender differences in work-related high mobility differentiated by partnership and parenthood status. Transportation (AMST) 1–28 (2021). https://doi.org/10.1007/s11116-021-10226-z.

16. Hayati, A., Maryati, S., Pradono, P., Purboyo, H.: Sustainable transportation: the perspective of women community (a literature review). In: IOP Conference Series: Earth and Environmental Science (2020). https://doi.org/10.1088/1755-1315/592/1/012034

17. Borlini, B.: Il quartiere nella città contemporanea 13–29 (2010). https://doi.org/10.4000/QDS.717. http://journals.openedition.org/qds

18. Romano, B., Zullo, F., Saganeiti, L., Montaldi, C.: Evaluation of cut-off values in the control of land take in Italy towards the SDGs 2030. Land Use Policy **130**, 106669 (2023). https://doi.org/10.1016/J.LANDUSEPOL.2023.106669

19. Saganeiti, L., Fiorini, L.: Gender dis-equality and urban settlement dispersion: which relationship? In: Gervasi, O., Murgante, B., Hendrix, E.M.T., Taniar, D., Apduhan, B.O. (eds.) ICCSA 2022. LNCS, vol. 13376, pp. 278–284. Springer, Cham (2022). https://doi.org/10.1007/978-3-031-10450-3_23

20. Benessere delle donne: c'è Monza al vertice, al Sud più laureate - Il Sole 24 ORE. https://www.ilsole24ore.com/art/benessere-donne-c-e-monza-vertice-sud-piu-laureate-AEVHnTOC. Accessed 23 Apr 2023

21. Helfferich, B.: Balance in Sport (BIS). Mapping Existing Gender Indicators in Sports. Council of Europe 33 (2016)

22. Novelli, E., Occelli, S.: Profili descrittivi di distribuzioni spaziali: alcune misure di diversificazione (1999). http://journals.openedition.org/cybergeo. https://doi.org/10.4000/CYBERGEO.4930

23. Istat.it. https://www.istat.it/. Accessed 06 Apr 2023

24. Open Data Italia|Update: 09 marzo 2023|Camera di Commercio delle Marche|Dati Statistici sulle Imprese, Dataviz (Google Visualization API, JSON-stat, DCAT-AP, schema.org, RDF Data Cube). https://opendata.marche.camcom.it/. Accessed 15 Apr 2023

25. Saganeiti, L., Fiorini, L., Zullo, F., Murgante, B.: Consumo di suolo e dispersione insediativa in Italia. In: (a cura di) Munafò, M. (ed.) Consumo di suolo, dinamiche territoriali e servizi ecosistemici, pp. 261–265. SNPA/ISPRA (2021)

26. Gori, E., Romolini, A., Fissi, S.: Local authorities' policies for disseminating gender equality. Evidence from Italy. Transylv. Rev. Adm. Sci. **14**, 38–53 (2018). https://doi.org/10.24193/tras.53E.3

27. Romano, B., Fiorini, L., Zullo, F., Marucci, A.: Urban growth control DSS techniques for de-sprinkling process in Italy. Sustainability (Switzerland) **9**, 1852 (2017). https://doi.org/10.3390/su9101852

28. Romano, B., Zullo, F., Fiorini, L., Ciabò, S., Marucci, A.: Sprinkling: an approach to describe urbanization dynamics in Italy. Sustainability. **9**, 97 (2017). https://doi.org/10.3390/su9010097

29. Anselin, L.: Spatial Econometrics: Methods and Models, vol. 4. Springer, Dordrecht (1988). https://doi.org/10.1007/978-94-015-7799-1

30. Anselin, L.: Local indicators of spatial association—LISA. Geogr. Anal. **27**, 93–115 (1995). https://doi.org/10.1111/J.1538-4632.1995.TB00338.X

Short Paper (PCEI0T 2023)

Privacy and Ethical Considerations of Smart Environments: A Philosophical Approach on Smart Meters

Kamer Vishi[1,2]([⊠]) [iD]

[1] South-Eastern Norway Regional Health Authority, Sykehuspartner CERT,
Oslo, Norway
[2] Department of Informatics, University of Oslo, Oslo, Norway
kamer.vishi@sykehuspartner.no
https://sykehuspartner.no/

Abstract. This paper delves into the privacy and ethical concerns related to smart devices in IoT, particularly smart meters. It explores the regulatory framework governing data protection through the lens of GDPR. Our analysis identifies relevant GDPR articles and presents a case study that exposes the privacy risks associated with smart meters. Ethical considerations are explored using deontology and consequentialism, offering a thorough analysis of privacy and ethical issues for consumers, manufacturers, and policymakers. The paper emphasizes the complexity of these concerns and the need for a comprehensive assessment of potential benefits and harms to individuals and society. It also stresses the importance of ethical considerations and compliance with GDPR requirements when designing smart building systems to guarantee adequate privacy measures. Our concluding remarks advocate that manufacturers and suppliers prioritize consumer privacy and security over profit and consider stronger privacy protections, increased transparency, and alternative business models to address these concerns. The importance of IoT privacy concerns cannot be underestimated, given their impact on personal and organizational privacy.

Keywords: Privacy · GDPR · Security · Ethics · IoT · Smart
meters · Data protection · Data leakage · Malware

1 Introduction

The digital revolution has brought about transformative and irreversible changes to our society, with effects comparable to the upheavals of nineteenth-century industrialization or the invention of printing in the sixteenth century. One key driver of this revolution is the Internet of Things (IoT), which fosters the digitization of our lives by connecting everyday "things" (internet-enabled devices), making our environments or homes "smart" (intelligent). These everyday objects become informative, acting as physical access points to internet services. The internet expands invisibly into our familiar environment, integrating into our

O. Gervasi et al. (Eds.): ICCSA 2023 Workshops, LNCS 14112, pp. 303–313, 2023.
https://doi.org/10.1007/978-3-031-37129-5_25

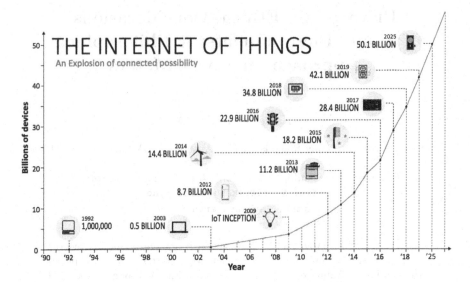

Fig. 1. The evolution timeline of the Internet of Things 1990–2025 (adapted from [19]).

homes and even "attaching" to our bodies through smart clothes, smartwatches, or fitness bracelets [18].

Different people may have varying interpretations of the IoT, but one undeniable aspect is the sheer number of connected devices and the vast amount of data generated.

Figure 1 illustrates the forecast provided by nternational Data Corporation (IDC) indicating that by 2025, there will be a total of 50.1 billion IoT devices, each capable of creating 79.4 zettabytes (ZB) of data individually. This explosion in connectivity and data production presents new ethical, legal, and social concerns [12,15].

As these devices connect to the internet, we confront various ethical and legal challenges, including security, privacy, transparency, data ownership, ethical and legal usage, data sharing, and the appropriateness of data collection. Smart meters, for instance, exemplify these concerns as the data they collect can potentially invade consumer privacy. Recent studies have highlighted that electricity consumption data may reveal private information such as household occupancy or economic status. In light of these concerns, it becomes increasingly crucial to examine the ethical implications of IoT technologies, particularly smart meters, and develop guidelines to address privacy issues and ensure responsible use [11].

2   Background

A smart environment can refer to a variety of locations, including but not limited to smart homes, businesses, and cities. The fundamental objective of smart environments is to increase the level of user comfort, access control, and building security, as well as to provide more effective administration of the facility.

According to Article 8 (Respect for your private and family life) of the European Court of Human Rights (ECHR), privacy is defined as follows:

"Everyone has the right to respect for his private and family life, his home and his correspondence." [2]

This right cannot be violated by a public authority, unless it is necessary to do so for legitimate reasons such as protecting national security, public safety, the country's economic well-being, preventing crime, promoting health or morals, or protecting the rights and freedoms of others.

The Global Privacy Network (GPEN) [9], in collaboration with 25 data protection authorities worldwide, conducted international research analyzing over 300 IoT devices, including smartwatches, fitness trackers, smart TVs, game consoles, and smart meters. Their research focused on examining how accurately companies inform their customers about privacy concerns. As these devices collect a significant amount of personal information, some of which is used to create targeted user profiles, companies must provide accurate information about privacy to their customers.

The study focused on how well companies communicated privacy matters to their customers. Furthermore, based on the research analysis, the following issues were identified:

- 59% of the IoT devices did not adequately explain how personal data is collected, processed, and used.
- 68% failed to provide information about how the collected information is stored.
- 72% did not provide information about data deletion.
- 38% did not provide contact information for customers to reach out if they have privacy concerns.

The study also raised concerns about medical devices that sent reports back to GPs via unencrypted email. As a result, data protection authorities considered action against any devices or services thought to have been breaking data protection laws.

According to the head of enforcement at the UK Information Commissioner's Office [9], the Internet of Things (IoT) technology could enhance various aspects of our lives, including our homes, health, and well-being. However, ensuring that privacy was not compromised in the process was essential. Companies that produced IoT devices needed transparency about protecting their customers' data. It was recommended that companies consider the privacy impact on individuals before bringing their products and services to market. Failure to do so could lead to consumer mistrust and reduced adoption rates.

This paper explores the "privacy paradox" [6] in the context of smart environments, with a specific focus on smart meters. Building on previous research, the paper examines the challenges posed by smart environments and investigates the factors that predict privacy attitude and behavior. The study includes an analysis of international research and industry practices to identify compliance with data protection laws and uphold individual privacy rights. By considering theoretical explanations for the privacy paradox, the paper provides a nuanced analysis of the privacy and ethical considerations of smart environments. The goal of the research is to ensure that privacy and security are prioritized in the development and use of IoT devices [6].

To address privacy concerns related to the Internet of Things (IoT), the European Commission has implemented a new data protection directive known as the *"EU General Data Protection Regulation (GDPR),"* [4] which was enforced on May 25th, 2018. Since IoT devices are all about data, privacy is a significant concern for IoT-related projects. The GDPR applies to the processing, storing, and using of personal data by "smart" devices used by EU consumers. Schouw [16], a leading IoT and Big Data expert, highlights the importance of complying with GDPR and the ePrivacy electronic communications regulation. According to Schouw, compliance with these regulations helps with governance and positively impacts buyers' perspectives. Providers that prioritize data privacy and take measures to comply with regulations can gain the trust of customers and improve their business.

Smart meters and the Internet of Things (IoT) raise important privacy and data protection concerns, which are addressed in the General Data Protection Regulation (GDPR) through several key articles. Specifically, the following GDPR articles are particularly relevant to smart meters and IoT [4]:

1. **Article 5** of the GDPR states that personal data must be processed to ensure appropriate security, including protection against unauthorized or unlawful processing, accidental loss, destruction, or damage. Any data collected by smart meters or IoT devices must be secured and protected appropriately.
2. **Article 25** of the GDPR requires data protection by design and default. This means that data protection measures must be built into smart meters and IoT devices from the outset and that default setting must ensure the highest level of privacy for the user.
3. **Article 30** of the GDPR requires organizations to record their processing activities. Companies that collect data from smart meters and IoT devices must keep records of the data they gather, how they process it, and how they protect it.
4. **Article 35** and **36** of the GDPR require organizations using smart meters and IoT devices to conduct data protection impact assessments (DPIAs) to assess and minimize potential privacy risks. DPIAs are necessary to identify risks and implement safeguards to protect individuals' rights and freedoms.

Generally, GDPR requires that personal data collected by smart meters and IoT devices must be processed in a secure and transparent manner, with appropriate safeguards in place to protect the privacy of individuals.

Apart from classic attack motives such as stealing sensitive data or damaging systems or people, a new trend has emerged in recent years: the blackmail of money. Cybercriminals are increasingly using Ransomware to prevent access to data or entire devices, only releasing it after receiving payment. This method has proven highly effective in generating funds, prompting cybercriminals to develop aggressive variants that bypass traditional security measures. Both private users and large companies have been victims of these attacks. Cybercriminals often use anonymization networks to hide their identities, making it difficult for law enforcement to tackle large-scale ransomware campaigns [5,17].

This type of threat is expected to continue to be a significant problem in the coming years, especially as the Internet of Things (IoT) becomes more prevalent. Even smart cars, watches, meters, household appliances, or entire homes can be taken hostage to extort a ransom. For instance, unauthorized access to a car's control systems or the front door can be prevented. Cybercriminals could turn off a refrigerator or alter the temperature control of a heating or air conditioning system, releasing it only after payment [10].

Furthermore, it is also worth mentioning that smart meters can support security policies against energy-related home attacks, as demonstrated by the BlackIoT botnet [20].

3 Case Study: Smart Meters

Figure 2 shows a smart meter, which is an intelligent electricity meter that can transmit energy consumption data in real-time to an energy supply company. With this data, the company can promptly respond to changes in energy consumption by adjusting their power plants and electricity storage accordingly. This enables energy providers to manage their energy supply more efficiently and effectively, ensuring a stable energy supply for their customers. Smart meters are an important component of the emerging smart grid infrastructure, which leverages advanced technology to optimize energy use, reduce costs, and minimize environmental impact.

Smart meters measure energy consumption and provide detailed information about an individual, family, or household, according to the Norwegian Data Protection Authority (Datatilsynet) [3]. Energy providers can access and retrieve data from smart meters even when we are at home or on vacation based on power consumption. Additionally, providers can monitor and control third-party devices such as smart TVs, thermometers, refrigerators, and doors. Researchers from Muenster University of Applied Sciences in Germany (Greveler et al. [7]) have demonstrated that smart meters can collect information about the TV channels and shows people watch. Network sniffing skills and tools were used to obtain this information. The data is sent unencrypted every two seconds from the smart meter to the provider server through the internet, potentially exposing user privacy.

Furthermore, according to Greveler et al. [7], companies can use the data collected by smart meters to create personalized ads for marketing or promotional purposes. By analyzing the data, they can determine if an individual is watching an illegal copy of a movie, for example. This highlights the potential

Fig. 2. An example of a smart electricity meter based on Open Smart Grid Protocol (OSGP), used in Norway and produced by Aidon. (Image courtesy of Aidon.com)

privacy implications of smart meters, as personal information can be shared with third-party companies without the user's consent.

Molina-Markham et al. [14] conducted a fascinating study on smart meters, demonstrating that off-the-shelf statistical methods can be used to extract complex user behavior and create user profiles from smart meter data, even without prior knowledge of household activities or training. Figure 3 illustrates power consumption segments for a day from one of the houses used in their experiment, showing variations and high-power consumption levels that indicate human activity, such as preparing food, taking a shower, or sleeping.

As discussed earlier, smart meters enable the monitoring of consumer behavior, which poses significant privacy concerns. These concerns are related to user behavior privacy, as described by Claude Castelluccia in *Chapter 2* of the book *European Data Protection: In Good Health?* [1]. Smart meters can intrude upon the privacy of consumers, and it is essential to address these concerns to ensure the protection of personal data.

4   A Philosophical Approach: Discussion and Critical Reflection

A philosophical approach to examining the privacy and ethical considerations of smart environments, particularly smart meters, provides a framework for understanding the underlying ethical principles and their application in practice. This approach helps to identify and evaluate the moral implications of different actions, and to determine what is morally right or wrong in a given situation. In this section, we discuss the ethical considerations of smart meters by analyzing them using different ethical theories or moral philosophies, including deontology

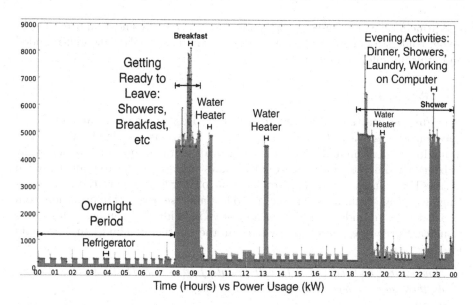

Fig. 3. An illustration of a power consumption trace at a second-level resolution that covers an entire day, including activity labels derived from a day's activity log (adapted from [14]).

and consequentialism. The aim is to provide a comprehensive analysis of the privacy and ethical issues associated with smart meters, and to critically reflect on the implications of these issues for consumers, manufacturers, and policymakers.

Before delving into the discussion and critical reflection sections, it is essential to have a brief understanding of the two ethical theories - deontology and consequentialism - that will be used to analyze the privacy concerns surrounding smart meters. Here is a brief summary of each:

- **Deontology:** This ethical theory, often associated with Immanuel Kant [13], focuses on the inherent moral value of actions rather than their outcomes. Deontological ethics argues that some actions are intrinsically right or wrong, regardless of their consequences. The central principle is the concept of duty, which implies that individuals should act according to moral rules or principles. In this framework, it is essential to adhere to these rules even if doing so might lead to less favorable outcomes.
- **Consequentialism:** This ethical theory focuses on the consequences or outcomes of actions to determine their moral value [8]. The most well-known form of consequentialism is utilitarianism, which posits that an action is morally right if it maximizes overall happiness or well-being for the most significant number of people. In this perspective, the ends justify the means, and an action is evaluated based on its potential to produce the best outcome.

Both deontological and consequentialist theories provide valuable insights for ethical decision-making. Deontology emphasizes the importance of moral duties and principles, while consequentialism focuses on the outcomes and overall well-being. Understanding both perspectives can help individuals make well-rounded and ethically informed decisions.

4.1 Discussion

Regarding ethical issues related to smart devices, an essential and universal question is: *what is right and wrong?* These questions are significant at both individual and community levels. They provide a framework for how we ought to behave in different contexts, from legal laws and regulations to informal social norms. For manufacturers and providers of IoT services, one of the most challenging ethical dilemmas is whether to collect and use personal information from smart devices to understand better and serve individual consumers. This raises significant privacy concerns, particularly in the Internet of Things, and prompts the question:

How ethical and legal is it to collect data from smart (IoT) devices, and do these devices pose a threat to data privacy?

In this paper, we discuss the ethical and legal considerations surrounding the collection of personal data by smart devices in the context of the Internet of Things (IoT). The question of whether it is ethical to collect data from smart devices is a complex one and can be analyzed through various moral philosophies such as deontology, consequentialism, virtue, and pragmatic ethics. For the sake of clarity and conciseness, we focus on consequentialism and deontology in this discussion.

We examine the relation between privacy and rights, harms, and interests to determine what morally important benefits data protection (privacy) can bring, and what morally important harms or violations of moral rights can result from a lack of data protection. We explore the potential benefits of data protection and the harms and violations that can result from breaches of privacy.

The most obvious harm that can occur from breaches of privacy is the unauthorized access, collection, use, and disclosure of personal information by smart devices such as sensors, smart meters, and smart TVs. This information may have personal, cultural, or social value that can be lost when the data is corrupted or misused. Moreover, any type of privacy breach is likely to cause some amount of psychological or emotional harm.

Furthermore, most of the information collected by smart devices is gathered without the consumer's knowledge or consent, which raises concerns about invasion of privacy. While some people view IoT devices as a revolutionary method of collecting data, others view it as a complete invasion of individual privacy.

To wrap up our discussion, in the context of smart meters and privacy, the two ethical theories, deontology and consequentialism, can offer different perspectives on data collection and usage:

From a deontological standpoint, collecting and using personal data from smart meters without user consent would be considered morally wrong, regardless of potential benefits. This is because privacy is a fundamental right that should not be violated. In this view, manufacturers and service providers have a duty to respect user privacy by obtaining consent and implementing robust data protection measures, even if it may impact their ability to optimize services or generate profits.

In a consequentialist analysis, the ethical nature of collecting and using personal data from smart meters depends on the overall consequences of such actions. If the data collection leads to improved energy efficiency, cost savings, environmental benefits, and better services for users, it might be considered morally right. However, if the negative consequences, such as privacy violations, unauthorized data sharing, and potential misuse of information, outweigh the benefits, then the data collection would be seen as morally wrong.

When evaluating smart meters and privacy concerns, it is essential to consider both deontological and consequentialist perspectives. By doing so, manufacturers, service providers, and policymakers can balance the need to respect user privacy with the potential benefits of data collection and usage in the context of smart environments. Implementing privacy-enhancing technologies, obtaining user consent, and ensuring transparency in data collection practices are some steps that can help address the ethical concerns raised by both theories.

4.2 Critical Reflection

In addition to analyzing the ethical considerations of collecting data from smart devices, it is important to consider the broader societal implications of such actions. One of the main concerns is the potential for increased surveillance and control by both private companies and government agencies. With the proliferation of smart devices, there is a risk that individuals may lose control over their personal data, and that this information could be used against them in a variety of ways. For example, data collected from smart devices could be used to create profiles of individuals that could be sold to third-party companies for advertising purposes, or even to insurance companies for risk assessment. This could lead to discriminatory practices that unfairly disadvantage certain groups of individuals.

Another concern is the potential for smart devices to be hacked or otherwise compromised, leading to a loss of privacy and security for individuals. As the Molina-Markham et al. [14] study showed, even seemingly innocuous data collected from smart meters can be used to infer sensitive information about individuals, such as when they are home or what they are doing. This information could be used to target individuals for criminal activity, or even to blackmail them. Additionally, smart devices could be used as a tool for cyber attacks, with hackers potentially able to take control of entire networks of devices and use them to launch large-scale attacks.

Given these concerns, it is important for individuals, companies, and policymakers to carefully consider the ethical and societal implications of smart devices and the data they collect. This may involve implementing stronger privacy protections, such as data minimization and encryption, as well as increased transparency around the types of data being collected and how it is being used. It may also involve exploring alternative business models that do not rely on the collection and monetization of personal data. Ultimately, any approach to smart devices and data collection must be grounded in a careful consideration of the ethical and societal implications, and a commitment to protecting the privacy and security of individuals.

5 Conclusion

In conclusion, the proliferation of smart environments and the Internet of Things (IoT) raises pressing concerns regarding individual privacy and data protection. Smart meters, in particular, can reveal intimate details about our daily lives, making this information valuable to various entities such as marketers, law enforcement, insurance companies, landlords, and employers.

Through a philosophical analysis of privacy and ethical considerations in smart environments, specifically focusing on smart meters, this paper has highlighted the importance of integrating both deontological and consequentialist perspectives in decision-making. Ethical considerations, in conjunction with the General Data Protection Regulation (GDPR), can guide manufacturers and service providers to ensure compliance with legal requirements and protect consumer privacy.

This paper emphasizes the critical role of consumer awareness and transparency in addressing privacy-related issues. Individuals have the right to know what information is being collected about them and how it is being used. The findings suggest that effective data protection and privacy preservation can be achieved through adherence to laws and regulations, as manufacturers and providers of smart devices often prioritize profit over consumer privacy concerns.

In light of these insights, it is imperative for consumers, manufacturers, and policymakers to adopt a comprehensive and ethical approach to smart environments, particularly smart meters, to mitigate privacy risks and ensure the responsible use of technology.

References

1. Castelluccia, C.: Behavioural Tracking on the Internet: A Technical Perspective, pp. 21–33. Springer, Dordrecht (2012). https://doi.org/10.1007/978-94-007-2903-2_2
2. Council of Europe: Guide on article 8 of the convention - right to respect for private and family life. In: European Convention on Human Rights, pp. 183–233. Bloomsbury Academic (2013). https://doi.org/10.5040/9781472561725.0014
3. Datatilsynet (Norwegian Data Protection Authority): Avanserte måle- og styringssystem (AMS) (June 2018), https://www.datatilsynet.no/personvern-paulike-omrader/overvaking-og-sporing/strommaling/. Accessed 12 Mar 2023
4. European Parliament and Council: Regulation (EU) 2016/679 of the European Parliament and of the Council of 27 April 2016 on the protection of natural persons with regard to the processing of personal data and on the free movement of such data, and repealing Directive 95/46/EC (General Data Protection Regulation) (Text with EEA relevance) (May 2016). http://data.europa.eu/eli/reg/2016/679/oj/eng

5. Fabrègue, B.F., Bogoni, A.: Privacy and security concerns in the smart city. Smart Cities **6**(1), 586–613 (2023)
6. Gerber, N., Gerber, P., Volkamer, M.: Explaining the privacy paradox: a systematic review of literature investigating privacy attitude and behavior. Comput. Secur. **77**, 226–261 (2018)
7. Greveler, U., Glösekötter, P., Justus, B., Loehr, D.: M0ultimedia content identification through smart meter power usage profiles. In: Proceedings of International Conference Information Knowledge Engineering (IKE) (January 2012)
8. Horta, O., O'Brien, G.D., Teran, D.: The definition of consequentialism: a survey. Utilitas **34**(4), 368–385 (2022). https://doi.org/10.1017/S0953820822000164
9. ICO: Privacy regulators study finds internet of things shortfalls (September 2016). https://www.aki.ee/en/news/privacy-regulators-study-finds-internet-things-shortfalls. Accessed 12 Mar 2023
10. Jakobi, T., Patil, S., Randall, D., Stevens, G., Wulf, V.: It is about what they could do with the data: a user perspective on privacy in smart metering. ACM Trans. Comput.-Hum. Interact. **26**(1), 1–44 (2019)
11. Kabulov, A., Saymanov, I., Yarashov, I., Muxammadiev, F.: Algorithmic method of security of the internet of things based on steganographic coding. In: 2021 IEEE International IOT, Electronics and Mechatronics Conference (IEMTRONICS), pp. 1–5. IEEE (2021)
12. Lucivero, F.: Big data, big waste? A reflection on the environmental sustainability of big data initiatives. Sci. Eng. Ethics. **26**(2), 1009–1030 (2020)
13. Misselbrook, D.: Duty, kant, and deontology. Br. J. Peneral Pract. R. Coll. Gen.l Practi. **63**, 211 (April 2013). https://doi.org/10.3399/bjgp13X665422
14. Molina-Markham, A., Shenoy, P., Fu, K., Cecchet, E., Irwin, D.: Private memoirs of a smart meter. In: Proceedings of the 2nd ACM Workshop on Embedded Sensing Systems for Energy-Efficiency in Building. ACM (July 2010). https://doi.org/10.1145/1878431.1878446
15. Reinsel, D.: How you contribute to today's growing datasphere and its enterprise impact (Mar 2023), https://blogs.idc.com/2019/11/04/how-you-contribute-to-todays-growing-datasphere-and-its-enterprise-impact/
16. Schouw, B.: GDPR and IoT: three things you need to know (July 2017). https://www.linkedin.com/pulse/gdpr-iot-three-things-you-need-know-bart-schouw. Accessed 12 Mar 2023
17. Singh, A.K., Kumar, J.: A secure and privacy-preserving data aggregation and classification model for smart grid. Multim. Tools Appl. **82**, 22997–23015 (2023)
18. Singh, R., et al.: Highway 4.0: Digitalization of highways for vulnerable road safety development with intelligent IoT sensors and machine learning. Saf. Sci. **143**, 105407 (2021)
19. SmartBear: Iot and it's impact on testing. https://smartbear.com/blog/internet-of-things-101/. Accessed 12 Mar 2023
20. Soltan, S., Mittal, P., Poor, H.V.: BlackIoT: IoT botnet of high wattage devices can disrupt the power grid. In: 27th USENIX Security Symposium (USENIX Security 18). pp. 15–32. USENIX Association, Baltimore, MD (August 2018). https://www.usenix.org/conference/usenixsecurity18/presentation/soltan

Short Paper (SCI 2023)

Classification of Malicious Websites Using Machine Learning Based on URL Characteristics

Muon Ha[1,2](✉) ⓘ, Yulia Shichkina[1] ⓘ, Nhan Nguyen[2], and Thanh-Son Phan[2]

[1] St. Petersburg State Electrotechnical University, St. Petersburg, Russia
muon.ha@mail.ru, strange.y@mail.ru
[2] Telecommunications University, Nha Trang, Vietnam
ptson@tcu.edu.vn

Abstract. This article focuses on evaluating the efficiency of machine learning classification algorithms in detecting malicious websites based on their URL addresses. A highly reliable dataset of URL addresses is used to train the machine learning classification model. The results show that the Random Forest algorithm achieves a high accuracy of 95.68% in detecting malicious websites and provides an effective solution to this problem. At the same time, software for detecting and warning of malicious website in two forms is also implemented: web applications and browser extensions.

Keywords: Malicious website detection · URL · machine learning · cybersecurity

1 Introduction

These days, malicious websites are tools that cybercrimes often use to attack end-users. The tricks they often use include:

- Phishing websites: created by criminals with the goal of obtaining confidential information of the users such as usernames, passwords, credit card numbers, one-time authentication codes, and related banking account information, etc.
- Defacement website – a kind of cyberattack that destroys a website and changes the display interface of the website. In other words, when a user visits the address of this website, the interface of another website will be displayed. Typically, the displayed content is a message that the hacker wants to convey.
- A website containing malicious code (malware) is a trick that uses the website as a tool for spreading and installing malicious code on the victim's computer in order to steal information or gain control of the victim's computer for malicious purposes.

O. Gervasi et al. (Eds.): ICCSA 2023 Workshops, LNCS 14112, pp. 317–327, 2023.
https://doi.org/10.1007/978-3-031-37129-5_26

According to statistics from the APWG [1] (Anti-Phishing Working Group), in the third quarter of 2022, there was a 47% increase in the number of detected phishing websites compared to the previous quarter.

Therefore, research on detecting and quickly preventing malicious websites has always been a particular interest to internet organizations and user communities. Nowadays, many researchers have also proposed numerous solutions to minimize cyberattacks via websites. However, cybercrimes always try to change their methods to evade detection. Thus, proposing an evolutionary solution is considered an effective method for detecting and blocking malicious websites (Fig. 1).

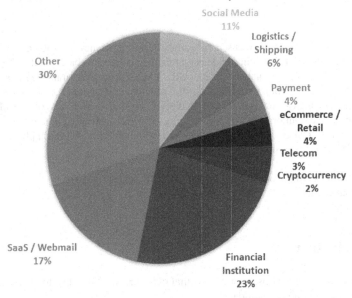

Fig. 1. The most targeted industries in the third quarter of 2022 [1]

The proposed approach is using machine learning methods to detect malicious websites based on URL characteristics. Different types of malicious websites, such as phishing, defacement, and web-spam, were taken into consideration in our work. To increase the accuracy of classification methods, we used a dataset updated from recent sources of URL data. In practice, we implemented a software tool for detecting and warning about malicious websites in the form of web applications and browser extensions.

The article is structured as follows. In the second section, a review of related works on the topic in the past few years is provided. In the third section, we developed a machine learning-based model for detecting malicious websites. In the fourth section, a description of the implemented software tool for detecting and warning about malicious websites is presented.

2 Related Works

Many studies have been conducted proposing different methods for detecting malicious URL addresses. One of them is maintaining a list of domain names or IP addresses of previously detected malicious websites [2–4]. This approach was used in [5], where the authors achieved 90% accuracy in classifying phishing websites after a three-week training using Google's phishing website blacklist. Or the Phishnet system presented in [6] uses a white list verification against a black list method. In this method, all URL addresses are checked against both the black and white lists respectively. Users are safe when the URL address is found in an official document; at the same time, users will be warned if the URL they visit is found in the black list. Another approach is presented as the use of shortened URL verification method, presented by the authors in [7–9], where if the attacker uses a URL shortening service, the user will receive a warning message about the risk of phishing attacks. DNS verification [10] of malicious URL addresses is also a widely used method.

Machine learning methods have been proven to quickly provide high accuracy in classifying objects based on available features. In studies [12–18], the use of machine learning methods in solving the problem of detecting malicious websites is presented. The rule-matching method, proposed in [19] for detecting malicious and safe URL addresses, uses 14 different features extracted from the URL address. The authors used the TF-IDF algorithm to search for high-frequency words in malicious URL addresses. Approximately 93.00% of malicious URL addresses were correctly identified by the Apriori algorithm in a dataset of 1400 URL addresses. In [20], the author presented the Phishing Alerting System (PHAS), capable of detecting and warning of all types of phishing emails, to help users make decisions. A dataset of email is used in this study and based on the extracted features, an accuracy of approximately 93.11% is proposed to be achieved using such machine learning methods as decision trees and random forests.

Although the above-mentioned works have achieved the main results, there are still some limitations, such as: firstly, the lack of flexibility in responding to new tricks of cybercriminals and the incomplete use of URL features for detecting malicious websites, and secondly, most of the existing works focus on detecting phishing websites and other types of malicious websites, such as defacement, web spam, are still limited. Thus, in this work, we propose the approach to the application of machine learning methods for the classification of multi-types of malicious websites based on their specific features.

3 Detection of Malicious Websites Using Machine Learning Methods

The malicious website detection model based on the proposed machine learning methods is divided into two stages, as shown in Fig. 2, as follows:

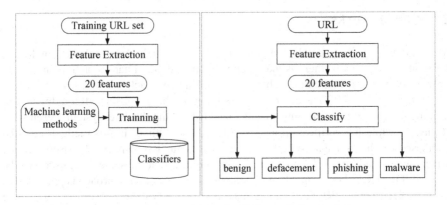

Fig. 2. Proposed model for classifying malicious websites

(a) Training stage: The training data file includes URLs of websites classified into 5 categories (labels): clean site, phishing, deception, spam web and malicious code website. The extracted URL features include 20 features. Using machine learning methods to train and provide classifiers.

(b) The detection stage: URLs are tracked and features are extracted using the trained classifier to identify malicious sites with URLs.

3.1 Feature Extraction URL

The basic structure of a URL consists of 3 main parts: protocol, host name, and path. Each URL has 24 features, but we only use 20 main features to judge whether a website is malicious or not. Some selected important features are shown in Table 1.

3.2 Machine Learning Classification Algorithms

Classification of objects based on feature extraction can use machine learning methods. There are several well-known machine learning methods such as:

- Decision Tree - A decision-making tool that uses a tree-like diagram or decision model and their possible outcomes, including the results of random events, resource expenditures, and benefits.
- Random Forest - A supervised learning algorithm that can solve both regression problems and classification tasks. Random forests generate decision trees on randomly selected data samples, predict for each tree and select the best decision by voting.
- K-Nearest Neighbors (K-NN) - one of the simplest supervised learning algorithms in machine learning. During training, this algorithm doesn't learn anything from the training data (which is also the reason why this algorithm is classified as lazy learning), all computations are done when it needs to predict the result of new data.

Table 1. Important features of URL

Features	Description
Having ip address	If the URL contains an IP address, it can be determined that the website is malicious. For example: http://192.70.12.33/phising.html
URL length	The average length of a URL address is 54 characters. If the URL address is longer than 54 characters, the website may contain malicious content
Shortening Service	The use of URL shortening service may be aimed at hiding the real address of the website and is also an indication that the website is not trustworthy
httpSecure	Cybercriminals can deceive users by attaching the "https" string to the URL address. For example: http://https-www-facebook.soft-hair.com/
Digit count	If a URL address contains too many characters and numbers, it is also a sign of a malicious website
Abnormal URL	This information can be extracted from the WHOIS database. For a legitimate website, the identifier is typically part of the URL address

- Adaptive Boost (AdaBoost) - a powerful learning algorithm that accelerates the creation of a strong classifier by selecting good features from a family of weak classifiers and linearly combining them using weights.

In this work, we will apply the aforementioned algorithms in succession for website classification and malicious site detection, thereby evaluating the performance of each algorithm to select the best algorithm for the implementation process of the malicious web site detection application for various popular web browsers.

3.3 Dataset

In this study, we have collected a sample of data from public and regularly updated data sources. Our sample dataset includes 213,345 URLs. They are divided into 5 groups and labeled as: Benign - 0; Defacement - 1; Phishing - 2; Malware - 3 and Spam - 4. The number of URLs in the dataset is distributed as shown in Fig. 3.

In this study, malicious URL addresses were collected from sources such as Open-Phish [22], Phishtank [23], Zone-H [24], and WEBSPAM-UK2007 [25]. For each data source, we collect the URL as a character string and its corresponding label, then merge them into a large dataset for training. The data preprocessing process includes feature extraction, removing duplicated URL addresses, and filtering out URL addresses that do not have the necessary features.

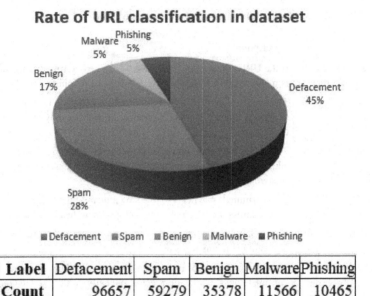

Label	Defacement	Spam	Benign	Malware	Phishing
Count	96657	59279	35378	11566	10465

Fig. 3. Count and ratio of groups of websites in the dataset

4   Results and Discussion

With the training data set, we used the most popular machine learning algorithms for 10-fold cross-validation to determine the model's performance. The performance metrics used to evaluate the models are Precision, Recall, accuracy, and F1-Score. Compared to some similar studies [12, 26], our model shows a significant effectiveness as demonstrated by the values mentioned above.

Based on the results in Fig. 4, with accuracy and F1-score values of 94.8388% and 95% respectively, the Random Forest method gives the best efficiency. Figure 5 shows its normalized confusion matrix, from which it can be seen that the model's recognition accuracy with data labels ranges from 4.3% to 56.37%. Meanwhile, the false recognition rate is relatively low, with the highest being 1.59%. This demonstrates the high diagnostic efficiency of the model. Therefore, we choose the Random Forest method in the implementation step of the application for detecting and warning against malicious websites based on URL characteristics.

The final step of the research involves implementing software to detect and prevent malicious website using the Random Forest method. To increase the program's efficiency, we combine the Random Forest method and the blacklist check method. The input URL address will first be checked in the database of malicious URL addresses, and then it will be verified using the machine learning model. Figure 6 shows the process of the malicious website detection and prevention program.

Our software has been implemented in two forms: a web application and a browser extension. The web application is built using programming languages JavaScript and Python, and its interface shows in Fig. 7.

MACHINE LEARNING MODELS SCORES COMPARISON

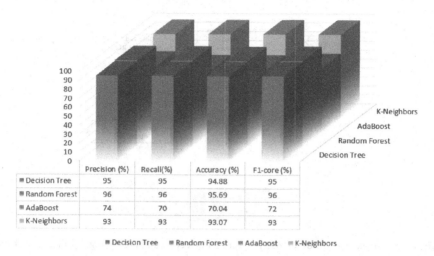

	Precision (%)	Recall(%)	Accuracy (%)	F1-core (%)
▪ Decision Tree	95	95	94.88	95
▪ Random Forest	96	96	95.69	96
▪ AdaBoost	74	70	70.04	72
▪ K-Neighbors	93	93	93.07	93

▪ Decision Tree ▪ Random Forest ▪ AdaBoost ▪ K-Neighbors

Fig. 4. Performance metrics for a malicious dataset URL with different classifiers

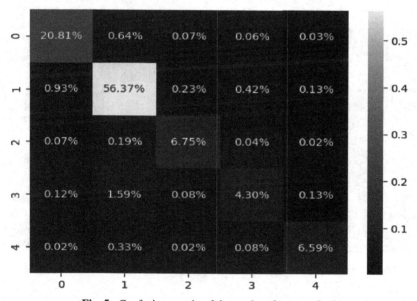

Fig. 5. Confusion matrix of the random forest method

The browser extension is a small part of the software used for configuring the web browser. The browser extension for detecting malicious websites is built using HTML, JavaScript, and CSS, while the Random Forest model was implemented using the Python programming language. Figures 8 shows the results of the browser extension check for a malicious website.

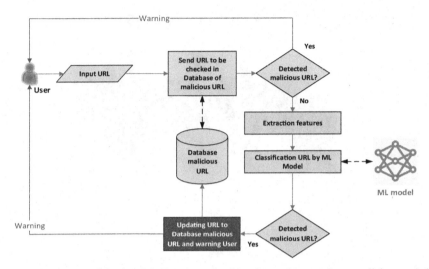

Fig. 6. The process of the developed program for detecting and preventing a malicious website

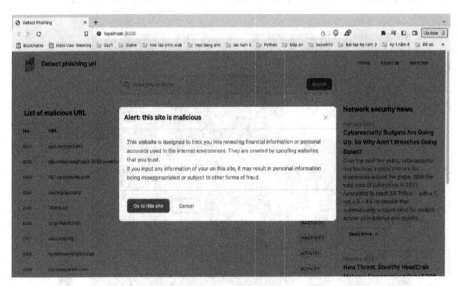

Fig. 7. Web application interface for detecting and warning a malicious website.

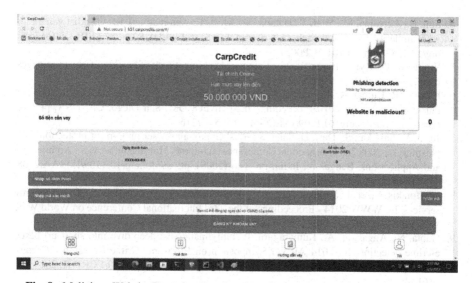

Fig. 8. Malicious Website Detection Results of Developed Browser Extension Application

5 Conclusion

Thus, this article presents an approach to using machine learning methods for classifying malicious websites based on URL characteristics. The results of the tests showed that the Random Forest method provides the best efficiency. This work also created software in the form of a web application and a browser extension for detecting and warning against malicious websites using random forest methods and blacklists. In the future, we will continue to explore different feature sets and use larger data sets to more accurately and efficiently detect malicious websites.

Acknowledgment. This work was supported by the Ministry of Science and Higher Education of the Russian Federation by the Agreement № 075-15-2022-291 on the provision of a grant in the form of subsidies from the federal budget for the implementation of state support for the establishment and development of the world-class scientific center «Pavlov center Integrative physiology for medicine, high-tech healthcare, and stress-resilience technologies».

References

1. Phishing activity trends reports. APWG. https://apwg.org/trendsreports/. Accessed 12 Feb 2023
2. Akiyama, M., Yagi, T., Hariu, T.: Improved blacklisting: Inspecting the structural neighborhood of malicious urls. IT Prof. **15**, 50–56 (2013). https://doi.org https://doi.org/10.1109/MITP.2012.118
3. Hong, J., Kim, T., Liu, J., Park, N., Kim, S.-W.: Phishing URL detection with lexical features and blacklisted domains. In: Jajodia, S., Cybenko, G., Subrahmanian, V.S., Swarup, V., Wang, C., Wellman, M. (eds.) Adaptive Autonomous Secure Cyber Systems, pp. 253–267. Springer, Cham (2020). https://doi.org/10.1007/978-3-030-33432-1_12

4. Sun, B., Akiyama, M., Yagi, T., Hatada, M., Mori, T.: Automating URL blacklist generation with similarity search approach. IEICE Tran. Inf. Syst. **E99**(D), 873–882 (2016). https://doi.org/10.1587/transinf.2015ICP0027

5. Whittaker, C., Ryner, B., Nazif, M.: Large-scale automatic classification of phishing pages. In: Network and Distributed System Security Symposium (2010)

6. Prakash, P., Kumar, K., Kompella, R., Gupta, M.: PhishNet: predictive blacklisting to detect phishing attacks. In: 2010 Proceedings IEEE INFOCOM, San Diego, CA, USA, pp. 1–5 (2010). https://doi.org/10.1109/INFOCOM.2010.5462216

7. Joshi, Y., Saklikar, S., Das., D, Saha, S.: PhishGuard: a browser plug-in for protection from phishing. In: 2008 2nd International Conference on Internet Multimedia Services Architecture and Applications, Bangalore, India, pp. 1–6 (2008). https://doi.org/10.1109/IMSAA.2008.4753929

8. Nikiforakis, N., et al.: Stranger danger: exploring the ecosystem of ad-based URL shortening services. In: WWW 2014 - Proceedings of the 23rd International Conference on World Wide Web, pp. 51–62 (2014). https://doi.org/10.1145/2566486.2567983

9. Gupta, N., Aggarwal, A., Kumaraguru, P.: bit.ly/malicious: deep dive into short url based e-crime detection. In: 2014 APWG Symposium on Electronic Crime Research (eCrime), Birmingham, AL, USA, 2014, pp. 14–24 (2014). https://doi.org/10.1109/ECRIME.2014.6963161

10. Singh, C., Meenu: Phishing website detection based on machine learning: a survey. In: 2020 6th International Conference on Advanced Computing and Communication Systems (ICACCS), Coimbatore, India, 2020, pp. 398–404 (2020). https://doi.org/10.1109/ICACCS48705.2020.9074400

11. Chou, N., Ledesma, R., Teraguchi, Y., Mitchell, J.: Client-side defense against web-based identity theft. In: Proceedings of the Network and Distributed System Security Symposium, San Diego, California, USA (2004)

12. Sharma, A., Thakral, A.: Malicious URL classification using machine learning algorithms and comparative analysis. In: Raju, K.S., Govardhan, A., Rani, B.P., Sridevi, R., Murty, M.R. (eds.) Proceedings of the Third International Conference on Computational Intelligence and Informatics. AISC, vol. 1090, pp. 791–799. Springer, Singapore (2020). https://doi.org/10.1007/978-981-15-1480-7_73

13. Wu, T., Xi, Y., Wang, M., Zhao, Z.: Classification of malicious urls by CNN model based on genetic algorithm. Appl. Sci. **12**(23), 12030 (2022). https://doi.org/10.3390/app122312030

14. Dutta, A.K.: Detecting phishing websites using machine learning technique. PLoS ONE **16**(10), e0258361 (2021). https://doi.org/10.1371/journal.pone.0258361

15. Monther, A., Rami, A.: MALURLS: a lightweight malicious website classification based on URL features. J. Emerg. Technol. Web Intell. **4**(2), 128–133 (2012). https://doi.org/10.4304/jetwi.4.2.128-133

16. Patgiri, R., Katari, H., Kumar, R., Sharma, D.: Empirical study on malicious URL detection using machine learning. In: Fahrnberger, G., Gopinathan, S., Parida, L. (eds.) ICDCIT 2019. LNCS, vol. 11319, pp. 380–388. Springer, Cham (2019). https://doi.org/10.1007/978-3-030-05366-6_31

17. Alsaedi, M., Ghaleb, F.A., Saeed, F., Ahmad, J., Alasli, M.: Cyber threat intelligence-based malicious URL detection model using ensemble learning. Sensors. **22**(9), 3373 (2022). https://doi.org/10.3390/s22093373

18. Alsmadi, M., Alsmadi, I., Wahsheh, H.A.M.: URL links malicious classification towards autonomous threat detection systems. In: Al-Emran, M., Al-Sharafi, M.A., Al-Kabi, M.N., Shaalan, K. (eds.) ICETIS 2021. LNNS, vol. 322, pp. 497–506. Springer, Cham (2022). https://doi.org/10.1007/978-3-030-85990-9_40

19. Jeeva, S.C., Rajsingh, E.B.: Intelligent phishing URL detection using association rule mining. HCIS **6**(1), 1–19 (2016). https://doi.org/10.1186/s13673-016-0064-3

20. Fon, K.H., Lashkari, A., Ghorbani, A.: A phishing email detection approach using machine learning techniques. Int. J. Comput. Inf. Eng. **44**, 2340 (2017)

21. Firake, S.M., Soni, P., Meshram, B.B.: Tool for prevention and detection of phishing e-mail attacks. In: Wyld, D.C., Wozniak, M., Chaki, N., Meghanathan, N., Nagamalai, D. (eds.) CNSA 2011. CCIS, vol. 196, pp. 78–88. Springer, Heidelberg (2011). https://doi.org/10.1007/978-3-642-22540-6_8

22. Phishing intelligence. OpenPhish. https://openphish.com/. Accessed 12 Feb 2023

23. Join the fight against phishing. PhishTank. https://phishtank.org/. Accessed 12 Feb 2023

24. Zone-H. Zone. http://www.zone-h.org/archive. Accessed 12 Feb 2023

25. Webspam-UK2007 (current dataset). In: WEBSPAM-UK2007. https://chato.cl/webspam/datasets/uk2007/. Accessed 12 Feb 2023

26. Das, A., Das, A., Datta, A., Si, S. and Barman, S.: Deep approaches on malicious URL classification, In: 2020 11th International Conference on Computing, Communication and Networking Technologies (ICCCNT), Kharagpur, India, 2020, pp. 1–6 (2020). https://doi.org/10.1109/ICCCNT49239.2020.9225338

Short Paper (SCOPUR 2023)

Non-knowledge and the Unexpected in Planning: An Experimentation Account

Maria Rosaria Stufano Melone[✉] and Domenico Camarda

DICATECh, Polytechnic University of Bari, Bari, Italy
mariarosaria.stufanomelone@poliba.it

Abstract. In previous research stages we have reflected on how uncertainty and the unknown are elements that one can't avoid dealing with during the territorial and environmental planning process. Our lives (in our individual and private choices) and our plans for a city or a territory have to cope with unexpected events, uncertainties, and often with unwanted consequences of our own decisions. We have explored literature and methods and took the first steps toward applied ontologies as a useful conceptual tool for managing non-knowledge aspects affecting decisions in planning. In the present step of our research, we describe an activity which was carried out with the students of the Regional planning program in Polytechnic University of Bari for two consecutive years.

Keywords: spatial planning · uncertainty · knowledge management · ontology

1 Introduction

The topic of uncertainty and the unknown and more specifically of non-knowledge has been widely recognized as inescapable when dealing with life in general, in particular when dealing with decisions that have to define and model strategies and choices for environment, territorial management or urban government. This is because such kind of decisions, strategies and plans has the propriety of being pointed to the future, trying to model one of the possibilities, and trying to give a direction to actions.

In the 1960's the model of all-knowledge and comprehensive rationality removed the heavy burden of the consciousness about the non-knowledge – so promoting, we could say, 'violent' actions in relation with environment and territories, their dynamics and their ecologies. That approach caused consequences of blind choices and therefore unexpected events (indeed more and more frequent). In the following decades consciousness arose about the side effect of actions of transformation.

When managing knowledge, the other coin side of non-knowledge emerges, made of uncertainty, ambiguities, deep unknowns that fatally affect the results of a strategic plan or, more in general, of the efficacy of environmental and planning choices.

This research was financially supported by the Italian National Operational Program for "Research and Innovation" 2014-2020; Area: Smart Secure and Inclusive Communities, Project: "Resilient City- Everyday Revolution" (ARS01_00592). Within a common research work, D. Camarda wrote Sect. 5 and M.R. Stufano Melone wrote all other sections.

O. Gervasi et al. (Eds.): ICCSA 2023 Workshops, LNCS 14112, pp. 331–340, 2023.
https://doi.org/10.1007/978-3-031-37129-5_27

A part of this aspect of the unknown (i.e., unexpected effects generated as consequences of actions) belongs to the set of the deeply unknown (as previously explored [1–3].

The topic of the unexpected events has been treated according to a different point of view in Gaurino and Borgo [4] where this kind of events are treated with a neutral gaze to better understand their intrinsic nature and not according a point of view that has as a-priori focus their riskiness or dangerousness (treated as properties). At the same time a different reading of unexpected is about black unicorns [5]. But still this topic can't be said as completely explored. First, this is due to an ontological (in philosophical terms) and intrinsic propriety of the deep unknown that surrounds our knowledge not only about the future [6]. Also, it depends on our wider present [6], where our individual gaze can't reach (even if arguably a distant present lays in a future present given by the distance needed to reach it). Still, there is the aspect of the the unknown that leads to unexpected events, manifesting themselves through clues and seeds that insurging dynamics form in reality and arise in the final event.

There are two global examples. One is climate change, whose clues devised by scientists and scientific literature tried to sensibilise public opinion. More recently, SARS-COVID-19 outbreak hit us 'unexpectedly' and now we could recognize that the problem was in 'the air' (maybe literally) because there were warnings and previous events that went in that direction. In fact, bird flu, ebola, mad cow disease, etc. had occurred, and also in this case there were comments on literature and warnings from science [7].

Therefore, as argued in previous work, the subject of non-knowledge and the unexpected is complex and multifaceted. With the hindsight, another event that could be expected if not avoided could be the outbreak of war in Ucrayne. Over the last year, this proved to be a shocking event that has affected our lives in general, and our environment too.

The paper is organized as follows. After this brief introduction, we try to sketch out possible paths towards a definition about non-knowledge in planning in Sect. 2. Then a synthetic description of the experimentation follows in Sect. 3. In Sect. 4 some reflexions are carried out about the experimentation responses obtained, followed by some final remarks in the conclusive section.

2   About Non-knowledge in Planning, Search for a Definition

The decisions we make both in our individual lives and in our design, planning, organization and planning activities are primarily based on cognitive materials of knowledge and intentions. It would be interesting to be able to define which genetic material builds intentions intended as objectives, expected and pursued results, both at the individual level and in the actions and decisions which set the management of the territory and the environment. This fascinating topic runs through the vast literature in various scientific disciplines, crossing philosophical, psychological, sociological reflections, as well as spatial planning and cognition reflections, passing through cognitive studies on artificial intelligence, data management and knowledge representation.

In fact, the point is crucial and often remains hidden, in a sort of background where it would be better to go and investigate, shedding light and clarity, in order to be able to act and organize, even before making decisions. It would be a decision-making system that eliminates blind spots as far as possible and that is aware of the inherent, and too often implicit, risk in the folds of non-knowledge.

The unawareness of non-knowledge can lead to decisions that have often turned out to be harmful, moving in the illusion [8] of a comprehensive rational decision-making cognitive environment. It can lead to drawing lines of action that are too often clear-cut, authoritative and lacking elements of monitoring-mitigation-flexibility, in addition to the (mis)intention to apply the least impact in entering the complex dynamic balance of urban and regional ecosystems.

We have previously addressed some aspects in the definition of a concept such as unawareness, which can be highly elusive due to its negative and unacknowledged nature [2]. On the other hand, by exploring the literature it has been possible to describe, if not define, different nuances of uncertainty and unknown that those who work in planning also for the city often face [1, 9], in addition to the methods and tools that have been developed to act in conditions of deep uncertainty [10–12].

To give an example referring to the city, clearly cities are complex and fundamentally uncertain objects, and urban planning has to constantly deal with 'wicked' problems [13] and since Simon's time there was a conscious sight about the highly distinctive problem of social choice under conditions of uncertainty [14, 15].

In particular, in this contribution we want to reflect on two other aspects when speaking of non-knowledge. One is the concept of belief, that is what is believed and is assumed to be true almost in a dogmatic or uncritical way. The other is the illusion of knowing, i.e. the conviction of not having to implement one's own load of knowledge regarding certain aspects or tasks.

In fact there is a literature exploring this topic. Human judgment under uncertainty has been shown as involving consistent departures from normative rationality. Often humans tend to over-estimate the probability of events with positive personal returns while under-estimating the probability of events with a negative return [16–18].

From the studies carried out for example by Evans [16] it seems that the decision-making aspects even in an environment of uncertainty (and therefore by extension, and even more so, of non-knowledge) are characterized by a sort of blind optimism, and that rather the depressed subjects are bearers of a sort of 'depressive realism'. Dealing with uncertainty is a common problem for agent systems. The ability to reason with uncertain information is an indispensable requirement for modeling intelligent behavior in a complex and dynamic environment [16]. The research was aimed at verifying how adaptive and resilient this trait of optimism was.

3   Starting an Experimentation

We thus began to think about war, an extreme anthropic event, as the possible future of any territory, even other than Ukraine, even close to Italian, in particular southern Italian, areas. Of course we could be differently interested by this kind of destroying event if occurring in our lives and on our territories. Our interest was about how people would react and organize, in a similar circumstance. This was an exercise that led people to imagine situations in which one has to deal with something laying in the layer of the unknown, as hypothesized p.es. in Stufano and Camarda [1].

We envolved students of the Regional planning program at the Polytechnic University of Bari, Italy, for two consecutive academic years in answering a questionnaire about reactions, scenarios and consequences of a possible war event nearby.

In the first year, the questions were formulated in three sections focusing on economy, society, and the environment. Each section was composed of four questions, dealing with economic consequences, which actors would be involved, and what actions would be expected by the decision-makers to cope with the consequences of the war event. In the second year, an additional section four was added, aiming at eliciting comments and suggestions regarding the organization of the questionnaire - for example a missing question, or further categories that could have been added.

In the first year, students were in a situation in which an actual war had unexpectedly started off in Europe, indeed. Their responding mood was of bewilderment and surprise and probably new anguish began to creep latently in their minds. In the second year the same event was still ongoing (it is still ongoing), and the scenario in front of the students was still different. The first reaction of dismay was followed by a sort of long-term concern, looking at the economic consequences of a situation of international tension and uncertainty.

Below is the introduction to the questionnaire, with the instructions (Table 1) and the questions asked, divided into sections (Table 2).

Table 1. Instructions for the questionnaire

Instructions
In recent months we have all been concerned about the war in Ukraine, in particular about the humanitarian catastrophe generated by a conflict on Europe's doorstep. Even the involvement of our Country, currently limited to infrastructural support, raises concerns in each of us.
In this dramatic situation, we ask you a reflexive contribution that can be useful both in terms of study and research.
This exercise consists of three sections of questions, to which you should answer according to your point of view, placing yourself in the situation described.
After filling in a brief personal data section, we ask a reflective stretch of your imagination. Imagine that the war could directly affect Italy and especially the area of your city in the next future (but let's hope not...).
Then answer the questions below, according to your point of view.

The present study reports our reflections and analysis about the first seven responses from the second-year exercitation and all the responses from the first year (just seven indeed, as few students were in the class of the first survey) to have a coherent sample. Even if it is a small sample, we think it is useful for a first step of reflection. In the following section, we discuss these first reflections and insights with an eye forward, to the possibility of developing ontology-based models.

Table 2. Questions asked in the questionnaire

Section 1
1.1. What economic damage could the war cause and in which places and sectors of the local organization in your city?
1.2. Which local agents would be involved?
1.3. What behaviors and/or activities would those local agents develop as a result of the damage caused?
1.4. What activities would they develop to promote local recovery/development?
Section 2
2.1. What social damage could it cause and in which places and sectors of the local organization in your city?
2.2 Which local agents would be involved?
2.3. What behaviors and/or activities would local agents develop as a result of damage caused?
2.4. What activities would be developed to promote local recovery/development?
Section 3
3.1. What environmental damage could it cause and in which places and sectors of the local organization in your city?
3.2 Which local agents would be involved?
3.3. What behaviors and/or activities would local agents develop as a result of the damage caused?
Section 4
Any final comments
Below you can express your free comments and suggestions regarding the organization of the questionnaire (for example which question you think is missing, or which other categories you would add.

4   What We Can Elicit from This Sample of Responses

As anticipated in the conclusion of the previous section, the sample available to us is not very large. For the first year we received eight responses of which seven are processable as the eighth seems to be a duplication. In the second year of experimentation we instead obtained 64 responses, all processable.

We would like to point out that this was our first attempt to build a structured experimentation related to this topic, i.e. non-knowledge, in relation to a possible unexpected event (in this case of an anthropic nature). In fact, nothing tells us whether this event could actually occur or not, especially if we go back to the status of knowledge before February 2022 - the event breakout. As a matter of facts, while some of us here were experimenting the pleasantness of a placid dawn, a couple of thousand kilometers away hell was just starting off.

The questions posed to the students were aimed at collecting an effect of absolute surprise (non-knowledge) with respect to an event that from one day to the next triggered an absolutely improbable event, something that until the day before was considered simply impossible.

The questions reported in the previous table (Table 2) invited to reflect on the repercussions relating to the environmental, social and economic spheres of a possible conflict that could affect the territory where the respondents live.

At the moment we are at the first considerations on how to analyze this material, in such a way that it tells about the non-knowledge and possible strategies for limiting this cognitive property (individual and collective). In these conditions, and considering a symmetry of the sample, it was decided in a first screening to explore in parallel the seven responses from the 2022 academic year and seven more responses from the 2023 academic year.

Primarily, two characteristics emerge that seem to differentiate the responses between the two datasets: (i) the first responses come from a homogeneous sample of inhabitants of the city of Taranto in the Apulia region (southern Italy), while the second ones are a non-homogeneous sample of responses, each generated by an inhabitant of a different city in the Apulia region; (ii) the first-year responses were given at a time when emotional surprise and bewilderment were very high and widespread in the public opinion, while the second-year responses come after the constant news experience of a year of conflict.

From these two premises, at least two considerations emerge: (i) for the first sample, the attention towards a focus on the city of Taranto and its present and atavistic problems [19, 20], not being eroded even in the perspective of a disruptive event induced by war; (ii) comparing the responses obtained just after the start of the war and after the first year of conflict, different lengths and articulation of the responses can be noted, thus suggesting a different emotional status between the first and second set - although in the last year the general geopolitical framework seems to be more complicated and less decipherable.

If we reflect on the issues relating to the concept of non-knowledge, indeed what we can deduce seems to relate just to what is not written down. First of all, a real immersion in a non-known scenario does note seem to show up. Yet having to actually face a war scenario, primary issues such as the risk of survival etc. seem to have been underrated if not discarded. Instead, the hypothetical future of the war disaster on one's own territory receives a scenario projection that is often a translation of the economic, social and environmental problems known to the writer's present time.

Another useful note for the comparative reading of the responses received is a greater habituation to news reports and some dynamics relating to a war context. Indeed, explicit emotional participation is apparently lacking, and once again the perception of an unknown and potentially unexpected local war scenario does not sound plausible in the responses, not even in the future - near or far.

Moreover, we can try to sketch out some reference categories relating to the concept of belief and the illusion of knowledge, previously anticipated. To try to outline the cognitive system of non-knowledge, albeit with the risk of a logical oxymoron, we can imagine it with the property of a shape placed in the negative, which has credences and bielefs as an internal boundary. These categories are a most fine grained gaze on concepts of uncertainty and unknown, or better, they are on a different layer, more abstract, pertaining to epistemological philosophical disciplines.

We can find prodromic significant reflections in this regard in Hume [21], analysing how the cultural context changes these beliefs. For the Maya, the possible non-rising of the sun the next day was a real risk, whereas in Hume's world the sun rising the next day was an established belief, even if perhaps not confirmed - but the opposite was considered as unlikely to occur.

The concept of credence emerged from the work on subjective probability put down by contemporary epistemologists, who highlight a close connection between credence and the more familiar notion of confidence (e.g., Elisabeth Jackson [22]). Here we could find non-knowledge in a form of belief relating to the fact that the respondents to the questionnaire place themselves in a position in which the event, even if they try to articulate hypotheses, would never take place. This seems to be understood in the broad 'sense' and in the tenor of the responses, and matches with an illusion of knowing that the event may never occur - in relation to the habit of life experiences up to now conducted by participants.

5   Conclusion

In dealing with the organization of the questionnaire, we must say that it is always difficult to build up a framework able to capture background emotional aspects, to bring out the psychological attitudes or the individual mental frames from which each response follows. Furthermore, the need to induce the participants to imagine themselves in a different situation (actually quite different) from current events, although necessary in this case, is not easily successful: it is not simple, it strongly depends on the different individual abilities and it is difficult to be operationally managed [23, 24].

In general, a life context with already high risks at present can influence responses often in an optimistic sense (the so-called normalization of deviance already mentioned), thus inducing inadvertently reckless actions (e.g. in business economics [25]). In the case of Taranto, an atavistic familiarity with risk seems to normalize the probable effects of future catastrophes within the same current problem areas, even though they may be exacerbated, thus making the unexpected dangerously implausible.

In general, the two experiments present aspects that are not entirely comparable, as they are diachronically interesting but contextually different situations - a specific area vs. more areas. This contextual 'bio' diversity can be interpreted as bearer of initial bias towards the interpretation of non-knowledge, of the unexpected and the imagination of future scenarios. Furthermore, the redundancy of chronicle and journalistic information of our times determines habituation towards the problematic aspects, thus diminishing their possible scope and range. Our experimentation has therefore, if possible, induced more reasons for reflection than manageable responses.

But we certainly do not expect straight and simplified decision support when speaking of an intrinsically complex conceptual context such as the regional and urban ecosystem. And after all, on closer consideration, all these aspects of reflection, positive or negative, in-depth or superficial, precious or modest, all cognitive behaviors conformist or eccentric, aware or approximate, rational or emotional, contribute thoroughly to constructing meanings and useful relationships to conceptually characterize an ontology of non-knowledge.

For this reason, ontological approaches and models applied to non-knowledge seem useful to feed decision support architecture construction paths, even in complex fields such as environmental futures in spatial planning. Attempts to use foundational ontologies as analyzers and relational descriptors of the present socio-environmental complexity are already reported in the recent literature, with non-definitive but encouraging results [26–28]. An example is reported in Fig. 1.

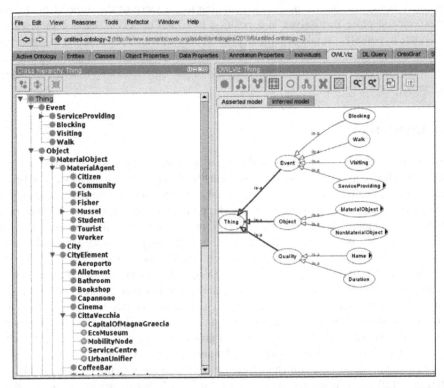

Fig. 1. Example of city classes, properties and features in ontological analysis [29, p. 434]

In the end, we acknowledge that the experiment itself is limited, as the survey had a restricted number of respondents on its first year which conditioned the use of a same sample size in the next year. As a matter of facts, from a scientific point of view, it can be just considered as a pilot experiment, in order to check the importance of carrying out new more robust experiments and reflections with a larger dataset in as a future step. Actually, the whole dataset available in the second year of experimentation includes a fairly numerous population, i.e. 64 respondents. This remarkable increase was due to the extension of the regional area of the experimentation, which will be kept also in the third experiment to be carried out, so possibly envisaging more statistically significant analyses next year. Indeed, that will be the appropriate context to develop also quantitative or quali-quantitative analysis, which in the present case is not properly carried out due to the objective limitations induced by the small sample.

By now, the intriguing results emerged from this small pilot study did encourage us to further develop the investigation and perhaps consolidate final results. From this perspective, the acknowledgement of this possibility is the most robust result of the pilot study.

Based on the results and theoretical and experimental reflections such as the above, the efforts of our research group will be oriented towards investigating the potential of these models also for the dimensions of the unexpected and non-knowledge, typically embedded in many areas of planning space. In the short term, activity will be instead oriented to increase the develop a closer and a more extensive analysis of the whole sample of experimentation, toward more robust and interpretable results.

References

1. Stufano Melone, M.R., Camarda, D.: Reflections about non-knowledge in planning processes. In: La Rosa, D., Privitera, R. (eds.) INPUT 2021. LNCE, vol. 146, pp. 205–212. Springer, Cham (2021). https://doi.org/10.1007/978-3-030-68824-0_22

2. Stufano Melone, M.R., Camarda, D.: About non-knowledge in knowledge management for planning: towards an applied ontological approach. TeMA J. Land Use Mobil. Environ. **15**, 79–87 (2022)

3. Stufano Melone, M.R., Rabino, G.: The creative side of the reflective planner. Updating the Schön's findings. TeMA J. Land Use Mobil. Environ., 2550 (2014)

4. Borgo, S., Guarino, N.: Ontological analysis and extreme events classification. In: De Lucia, C., Borri, D., Kubursi, A., Khakee, A. (eds.) Economics and Engineering of Unpredictable Events, pp. 266–277. Routledge, London (2015)

5. Taleb, N.N.: The Black Swan: The Impact of the Highly Improbable. Random House Publishing Group, New York (2007)

6. Gumbrecht, H.U.: Our Broad Present: Time and Contemporary Culture. Columbia University Press, New York (2014)

7. Quammen, D.: Spillover: Animal Infections and the Next Human Pandemic. WW Norton & Company, New York (2012)

8. Newell, A., Simon, H.A.: Human Problem Solving. Prentice-Hall, Englewood Cliffs (1972)

9. Schubert, D.: Cities and plans: the past defines the future. Plan. Perspect. **34**, 3–23 (2019)

10. Marchau, V.A.W.J., Walker, W.E., Bloemen, P.J.T.M., Popper, S.W. (eds.): Decision Making under Deep Uncertainty: From Theory to Practice. Springer, Cham (2019). https://doi.org/10.1007/978-3-030-05252-2

11. Buurman, J., Babovic, V.: Adaptation pathways and real options analysis: an approach to deep uncertainty in climate change adaptation policies. Policy Soc. **35**, 137–150 (2016)

12. Zimmermann, K.: Local climate policies in Germany. Challenges of governance and knowledge. Cogent Soc. Sci. **4**, 1482985 (2018)

13. Rittel, H.W.J., Webber, M.M.: Dilemmas in a general theory of planning. Policy Sci. **4**, 155–169 (1973)

14. Moroni, S., Chiffi, D.: Uncertainty and planning: cities, technologies and public decision-making. Perspect. Sci. **30**, 237–259 (2022)

15. Simon, H.A.: Reason in Human Affairs. Stanford University Press, New York (1983)

16. Evans, D., Heuvelink, A., Nettle, D.: The evolution of optimism: a multi-agent based model of adaptive bias in human judgement. In: AISB'03 Symposium on Scientific Methods for the Analysis of Agent-Environment Interaction, pp. 20–25. University of Wales, Aberystwyth (2003)
17. Miller, D.T., Ross, M.: Self-serving biases in the attribution of causality: fact or fiction? Psychol. Bull. **82**, 213 (1975)
18. Zuckerman, M.: Attribution of success and failure revisited, or: the motivational bias is alive and well in attribution theory. J. Pers. **47**, 245–287 (1979)
19. Camarda, D.: Building sustainable futures for post-industrial regeneration: the case of Taranto, Italy. Urban Res. Pract. **11**, 275–283 (2018)
20. Camarda, D., Rotondo, F., Selicato, F.: Strategies for dealing with urban shrinkage: issues and scenarios in Taranto. Eur. Plan. Stud. **23**, 126–146 (2014)
21. Hume, D.: A Treatise of Human Nature. John Noon, London (1739)
22. Jackson, E.G.: The relationship between belief and credence. Philos. Compass **15**, e12668 (2020)
23. Tasso, A.: Simulazione mentale: come e perché pensiamo situazioni alternative alla realtà. Giornale italiano di psicologia **31**, 753–792 (2004)
24. Fauconnier, G.: Mental spaces. Ten Lectures on Cognitive Construction of Meaning, pp. 1–23. Brill, Boston (2018)
25. Center for Chemical Process Safety of the American Institute of Chemical Engineers (CCPS): Recognizing and Responding to Normalization of Deviance. Wiley, New York (2018)
26. Silavi, T., Hakimpour, F., Claramunt, C., Nourian, F.: Design of a spatial database to analyze the forms and responsiveness of an urban environment using an ontological approach. Cities **52**, 8–19 (2016)
27. Jung, C.-T., Sun, C.-H., Yuan, M.: An ontology-enabled framework for a geospatial problem-solving environment. Comput. Environ. Urban Syst. **38**, 45–57 (2013)
28. Borgo, S., Borri, D., Camarda, D., Stufano Melone, M.R.: An ontological analysis of cities, smart cities and their components. In: Nagenborg, M., Stone, T., González Woge, M., Vermaas, P.E. (eds.) Technology and the City. Philosophy of Engineering and Technology, vol. 36, pp. 365–387. Springer, Cham (2021). https://doi.org/10.1007/978-3-030-52313-8_18
29. Camarda, D., Stufano Melone, M.R., Borgo, S., Borri, D.: Toward clarification of meanings via ontological analysis method in environmental planning processes and actions. In: Leone, A., Gargiulo, C. (eds.) Environmental and territorial modelling for planning and design, pp. 427–435. FedOAPress, Napoli (2018)

Short Paper (SSIC 2023)

Does Living on an Island Make You Happier?

Dimitris Ballas[1]([✉]) [iD] and Richard Rijnks[2] [iD]

[1] Department of Economic Geography, University of Groningen, Landleven 1,
9747 Groningen, AD, The Netherlands
d.ballas@rug.nl

[2] Department of Planning, University of Groningen, Landleven 1, 9747 Groningen, AD,
The Netherlands
r.h.rijnks@rug.nl

Abstract. This paper revisits the literature on the economics and spatial economics of happiness with a particular focus on geographical and environmental features pertaining to islands and related characteristics and concepts such as insularity. It includes preliminary statistical analysis of suitable secondary data in Europe including most of the variables that are thought to be associated with subjective well-being measures and examines whether and the extent to which insularity and living on an island may have a statistically significant impact on happiness when compared to mainland areas. To that end the paper makes a start in addressing aspects of a new research agenda for happiness and islands, which considers a number of attributes of islands that are typically seen as negative from an regional economic performance perspective (mostly relating to remoteness and poor accessibility to the mainland) but which might be considered as positive in terms of happiness and well-being.

Keywords: well-being · insularity · geographical handicaps · remoteness

1 Introduction

This paper revisits the literature on the economics and spatial economics of happiness with a particular focus on geographical and environmental features pertaining to islands and related characteristics and concepts such as insularity and 'islandness'. It has long been argued that islands are special cases for sustainable economic and social development. They are relatively isolated and 'on their own' compared to mainland areas, yet they are also more dependent and need to be well-connected to other areas more than mainland areas. The dominant economic development model, which is based on high population concentrations, specialization, large-scale production, and agglomeration economies does not directly apply to most islands, especially the smaller and medium-sized ones.

The paper presents preliminary statistical analysis of suitable secondary data in Europe including most of the variables that are thought to be associated with subjective well-being measures and examines whether and the extent to which insularity and living

O. Gervasi et al. (Eds.): ICCSA 2023 Workshops, LNCS 14112, pp. 343–350, 2023.
https://doi.org/10.1007/978-3-031-37129-5_28

on an island may have a statistically significant impact on happiness when compared to mainland areas. To that end the paper also considers a number of attributes of islands that are typically considered as 'negative' from an regional economic performance perspective (mostly relating to remoteness and poor accessibility to the mainland) but which might be considered as positive in terms of happiness and well-being (as is also evident by the popularity of many remote islands as tourist destinations).

The paper also considers and discusses the policy implications of the analysis, including issues pertaining to alternative sustainable futures (also drawing on the ongoing work as part of the new Erasmus Mundus International Master programme and consortium ISLANDS [1]).

2 Happiness, Space, Place, Islands and Insularity

There is a well-established 'happiness field' within the social sciences cutting across a range of themes including economics, sociology, psychology, demography, planning and more recently geography [2–5]. In this context there has been a significant body of studies aimed at analyzing the socio-economic and demographic determinants of subjective happiness and well-being with the use of self-reported measures of well-being measured in social surveys. Economists have been making significant contributions to this field with analysis mostly focusing on individual or household level determinants of well-being. According to recent reviews and summaries of relevant literature [6] with references to more extensive reviews [2, 7], a list of such determinants includes income and employment status, health status, education, social contacts and inter-personal relationships, trust, social capital and migration status.

There has also been an increasingly sustained effort by scholars working in economic geography and regional science to add a spatial dimension to the analysis of happiness by considering the role of space and place the upon subjective well-being of individuals [3, 4, 8]. It has been increasingly argued [3] that from a methodological perspective there is a need for a "comprehensive geographical approach to the analysis of subjective happiness and well-being in order to attempt to quantify the extent to which subjective happiness can be attributed to 'individual' (e.g. employment status, age-group), 'household' (e.g. household income, accommodation type and size), and/or wider 'contextual' circumstances and characteristics (e.g. climate, socio-economic environment) across the world, and to establish the relative importance of such characteristics in different countries and within regions and cities in a country". To that end, a regional science and economic geography approach in the analysis of happiness and its determinants can be adopted to address questions such as [3]:

- "Is the source of happiness or unhappiness purely personal, or do spatial/contextual factors matter? (and if they do, to what extent?)
- Are there happiness spatial spillover effects? Does the happiness level of an individual affect that of their neighbors?
- If social comparisons are important, what is the spatial scale at which people make their social comparisons?
- Do the levels of happiness among individuals reflect different characteristics of residents in different districts and regions and areas (compositional effects) or are there

environmental, geographical, or other factors (e.g. amenities, social capital and cohesion, socio-economic inequality) of places that cause their inhabitants to be happy or unhappy (contextual effects). In other words, should we talk of Happy People, Happy Households, or Happy Places?" [3].

The work presented in this paper is part of a wider project and research effort aimed at extending the above 'geography of happiness research agenda' by engaging with the literature on the field of island studies [9, 10]. In particular, our paper builds on the literature that explores the possible impact of the physical environment upon happiness and to that end, insularity and islandness is seen as physical geography feature. There is already significant research that considered the impact of location-specific factors upon happiness and associated factors, such as, for example, the work of Brereton et al. 2008 [11] who used GIS-based methods to explore the impact of location-specific factors (including distance from natural amenities) upon subjective life satisfaction and well-being in Ireland. Also of relevance is the work of Mitchell [12] who examined the relationship between green spaces and measures of health in Scotland and highlighted the importance of access to green spaces in relation to mental health and life satisfaction. There has also been extensive work exploring urban planning, the natural environment and public health measures in the US and urban/rural differentials [13–16].

The work presented in this paper builds on this literature by adding an islandness and insularity dimension to geographical as well as human geography features. In particular, we consider the importance of islandness defined in relation to the geography of islands, their physical, economic, societal and symbolic characteristics, including (but not limited to) issues of place and cultural identity, geographical specificities and geographical handicap and local and regional population dynamics of island regions. We also consider key qualities of islands including their remoteness, small size (compared to the mainland), vulnerability, isolation and inter-dependencies with the mainland and other islands. This paper makes a start to that direction by utilising data from the European Social Survey and local data (building on recent work by one of the authors of this paper [6] and focusing on Greece, an EU member state in which islands play a very prominent role in terms of the country's social and cultural identity, tradition and history. A country with 6,000 islands and islets (of which only 227 islands are inhabited) [17].

3   Data and Methods

As noted in the previous section, there is a rapidly growing number of research studies which involve the quantification and analysis of subjective happiness and well-being measures and their socio-economic and spatial determinants. These studies are typically based on self-reported measures of happiness and well-being included in social survey datasets. One of these datasets is the European Social Survey (ESS), which is an academically driven cross-national survey, conducted biennially across Europe since 2001 with the use of face-to-face interviews conducted with newly selected cross-sectional samples [17]. The survey includes a wide range of demographic and socio-economic data, including subjective happiness and life satisfaction but also social attitudes and human values. In this study we use the sub-dataset for Greece and also build on recent work by one of the authors of this paper [6] including a dummy variable for islands.

In particular, we used a subjective happiness measure as our dependent variable, which is measured on a 0–10 scale on the basis of the question: How happy are you? We z-transformed and centred it and assumed it is a happiness continuous dependent variable. In addition, we included relevant individual level demographic and socio-economic explanatory and control variables and in particular, age (age and age squared, centred to regional averages) and dummy variables in relation to gender, employment status, income category, trust in institutions and health status but also information on whether a respondent has been a victim of crime, as well as a dummy variable relating to subjective financial conditions (the extent to which respondents feel they are coping financially on their present income). We also added a dummy variable referring to whether the respondent is based on an island (taking the value of 1 if they are) or not (taking the value of zero).

4 Results

Table 1 presents the results of regression analysis of the data for Greece in the 2010 wave of the European Social Survey [18] with the added island dummy as discussed above. As can be seen the following variables have significant positive main effects on happiness (as defined in this study): individual income, subjective financial circumstances (those who feel living comfortably or coping on present income compared to those who do not), health status, cohabiting status (respondents living with husband, wife, partner report higher happiness scores than those who do not). On the other hand, being unemployed has a significant negative main effects These results are widely consistent with previous research on the correlates of happiness which were briefly reviewed and referred to in Sect. 2.

As can also be seen in the table presenting preliminary statistical analysis and with regards to the question posed in the title of this paper, the results suggest that the answer is positive: there is a statistically significant positive effect on subjective happiness of individuals living on a Greek island when compared to those living on the mainland. Nevertheless, it should be noted that there is a need to consider additional variable that may be associated with insularity (as discussed in Sect. 2). The results presented in this paper give just a flavor of the potential that there is and a proof of concept for a more comprehensive model and discussion. The following section discusses further some of the key issues that would need to be considered when building a more comprehensive model (Table 2).

Table 1. Does living on an island make you happier? Regression analysis results

Dependent variable: happy	Coef.	p-value
Age (centred)	−0,019	0,000
Age squared	0.001	0.000
Female (ref: Male)	0.171	0.032
Secondary education attainment (ref: primary)	0.061	0.549
Tertiary education attainment (ref: primary)	0.102	0.382
Income missing (ref: low income	0.063	0.518
Medium income (ref: low income)	0.366	0,001
High income (ref: low income)	0.705	0.000
Living comfortably or coping on present income (ref: finding it difficult or very difficult)	0.809	0.000
Cohabiting with husband/wife/partner (ref: not cohabiting)	0.639	0.000
Unemployed	−0.463	0.001
Health very good or good (reference: fair. Bad and very bad)	0.607	0.000
Living on an island	*0.467*	*0.000*
Constant	4.226	0.000

Table 2. Does living on an island make you happier? Regression model diagnostics

Number of observations	2,669
F (13, 2655)	33.03
Prob > F	0.0000
R-squared	0.1392
Adj R-squared	0.1350
Root MSE	2.0128

5 Discussion

This paper presents preliminary analysis of relevant secondary data that can be used to study the possible impacts on and/or links between insularity, islandness and subjective happiness and well-being. As also noted in the previous section, the preliminary results presented are just a starting point and give a flavor of the potential for further analysis. There is a need to acknowledge and take into account in the analysis that there are significant differences between islands and to that end we can consider relevant typologies and classifications. Of particular relevance here is previous work that classified the Greek islands to the following clusters/typologies [19]:

- Cluster 1: Small, remote from EU and agriculture dependent comprising the following islands: Agios Efstratios, Amorgos, Anafi, Antiparos, Folegandros, Irakleia, Kea, Kimolos, Kythera, Kythnos, Schinoussa, Serifos, Sifnos, Sikinos, Skyros
- Cluster 2: Small, remote from Athens and the EU and agriculture dependent, comprising the following islands: Agathonisi, Astipalaia, Inousses, Ios, Kalymnos, Karpathos, Kasos, Leipsoi, Nisyros, Patmos, Psara, Symi, Thirasia, Tilos
- Cluster 3: Accessible, successful and diversified, comprising: Andros, Chios, Donoussa, Kos, Leros, Lesvos, Milos, Mykonos, Naxos, Paros, Rhodes, Samos, Santorini, Syros,, Tinos
- Cluster 4: Ionian islands, large, dependent on agriculture and tourism – these are: Erikoussa, Ithaki, Kefalonia, Kerkyra, Lefkada, Othoni, Paxi, Zakynthos
- Cluster 5: Inshore, diversified, but mixed economic performance, comprising Aegina, Agistri, Alonissos, Evia, Hydra, Poros, Salamina, Skiathos, Skopelos, Spetses
- Cluster 6: Crete

Also of relevance (and with potential to include in our analysis) is the work of island scholars aimed at building indices of accessibility of islands (with a particular emphasis on transport modes and choices), focusing on Greece [20, 21]. The research presented in this paper may also have important policy implications, as it relates to regional and island-related policies. In particular, it is particularly relevant to debates pertaining to social and territorial cohesion as well as so called geographical handicaps and quality of life [22].

There is also potential to synthesize the happiness research agenda and key questions posed in Sect. 2 with key questions that are being addressed by scholars in the island studies field. In particular, as pointed out in a recent key textbook on island studies, such questions include (adopted from [10]):

- Are islands and islanders marginalised and vulnerable to global changes, or are they resilient and capable of responding quickly to external pressures?
- Are islands and island societies isolated and remote physically, cultural, and economically, or are they open and connected to the world around them?
- To what degree do islands share common features?
- Are islands and islanders diverse, heterogeneous and unique, or do they share standard characteristics that may allow us to think of them as part of one or more relatively homogenous, coherent, groups? [10].

6 Concluding Comments

This paper presented preliminary analysis and a research agenda regarding the possible impact of insularity and islandness upon subjective happiness and well-being. The preliminary results suggest that the response to the title posed in the title of this paper is positive. Nevertheless, as briefly outlined in Sect. 5, these preliminary findings are the basis for further work that will take into account more factors and methodological and conceptual issues, engaging with and building upon relevant work by scholars in working on the spatial economics of happiness as well as island studies. There is also significant potential for GIS, geoinformatics and related methodologies in the social sciences [23] to be applied extensively in order to consider a wide range of variables and factors associated with insularity (including remoteness and inder-dependencies of islands from/to other islands and the mainland as well as more sophisticated accessibility indicators).

References

1. Islands and Sustainability, Erasmus Mundus international programme and consortium, accessibility of islands: towards a new geography based on transportation modes and choices. Island Stud. J. **9**, 293–306
2. Nikolova, M., Graham, C.: The economics of happiness. In: Zimmermann, K.F. (eds.) Handbook of Labor, Human Resources and Population Economics. Springer, Cham (2020). https://doi.org/10.1007/978-3-319-57365-6_177-1
3. Ballas, D.: The economic geography of happiness. In: Zimmermann, K.F. (eds.) Handbook of Labor, Human Resources and Population Economics. Springer, Cham (2021). https://doi.org/10.1007/978-3-319-57365-6_188-1
4. Ballas, D.: What makes a 'happy city'? Cities **32**, s39–s50 (2013)
5. Layard, R.: Happiness: Lessons From a New Science. Penguin Books, Allen Lane (2005)
6. Ballas, D., Thanis, I.: Exploring the geography of subjective happiness in Europe during the years of the economic crisis: a multilevel modelling approach. Soc. Indic. Res. **164**, 105–137 (2022). https://doi.org/10.1007/s11205-021-02874-6
7. Clark, A.E.: Four decades of the economics of happiness: where next? Rev. Income Wealth Ser. **64**(2) (2018). https://doi.org/10.1111/roiw.12369
8. Rijnks, R.: Subjective well-being in a spatial context, PhD thesis, University of Groningen, Groningen, The Netherlands (2020)
9. Baldacchino, G.: The coming of age of island studies. J. Econ. Soc. Geogr. **95**, 272–283 (2004)
10. Randall, J.E.: An Introduction to Island Studies, Rowman (2021)
11. Brereton, F., Clinch, J.P., Ferreira. S.: Happiness, geography and the environment. Ecol. Econ. **65**, 386–396 (2008)
12. Mitchell, R.: Is physical activity in natural environments better for mental health than physical activity in other environments? Soc. Sci. Med. **91**, 130–134 (2013). https://doi.org/10.1016/j.socscimed.2012.04.012
13. Brereton, F., Bullock, C., Clinch, J.P., Scott, M.: Rural change and individual well-being: the case of Ireland and rural QoL. Eur. Urban Reg. Stud. **18**(2), 203–227 (2011)
14. Burger, M., Morrison, P., Henriks, M., Hoogerbrugge, M.: Urban-rural happiness differentials across the world. In: Helliwell, J.F., Layard, R., Sachs, J.D., De Neve, J. (eds.) World Happiness Report 2020. Sustainable Development Solutions Network, New York, Chapter 4 (2020). http://worldhappiness.report
15. Morrison, P.S.: Wellbeing and the region. In: Fischer, M., Nijkamp, P. (eds.) Handbook of Regional Science. Springer, Heidelberg (2020). https://doi.org/10.1007/978-3-642-36203-3_16-1
16. Berry, B.J.L., Okulicz-Kozaryn, A.: An Urban-Rural Happiness Gradient. Urban Geogr. **32**(6), 871–883 (2011)
17. Islands- visit Greece. https://www.visitgreece.gr/islands. Accessed 27 Mar 2023
18. European Social Survey. https://www.europeansurvey.org/. Accessed 27 Mar 2023

19. Armstrong, H., Ballas, D., Staines, A.: A comparative classification of labour market characteristics of British and Greek islands. Eur. Urban Reg. Stud. **21**, 222–248 (2014)

20. Spilanis, I., Kizos, T., Petsioti, P.: Accessibility of peripheral regions: evidence from Aegean Islands (Greece). Island Stud. J. **7**(2), 199–214 (2012)

21. Karampela, S., Kizos, T., Spillanis, I.: Accessibility of islands: towards a new geography based on transportation modes and choices. Island Stud. J. **9**, 293–306 (2014)

22. European Commission: Mountains, Islands and Sparsely Populated Areas (2020). https://ec.europa.eu/regional_policy/en/policy/themes/sparsely-populated-areas/

23. Ballas, D., Clarke, G.P., Franklin, R.S., Newing, A.: GIS and the Social Sciences: Theory and Applications, Routledge (2017). https://www.routledge.com/GIS-and-the-Social-Sciences-Theory-and-Applications/Ballas-Clarke-Franklin-Newing/p/book/9781138785120

Short Paper (Spatial_Energy_City 2023)

A Model to Detect Low Income Urban Areas to Plan Renewable Energy Communities Against Energy Poverty

Alessandra Marra[✉] [iD]

Department of Civil Engineering, University of Salerno, 84084 Fisciano, SA, Italy
almarra@unisa.it

Abstract. This work is included in a broader research project, aimed at promoting the development of Renewable Energy Communities (RECs) through urban planning in priority areas for intervention. According to a methodology already proposed by the author, priority areas, mapped on an infra-urban scale, are intended to be located where a minimization of the constraints and a maximization of the benefits deriving from the RECs establishment are expected, with particular reference to the reduction of energy poverty. The aim of this work is to detail the already proposed methodology, in order to better assess energy poverty. To this end, a model for the construction of a composite index of urban poverty is proposed, starting from basic indicators, selected following a review of the technical-scientific literature on urban poverty and deprivation or distress. The spatialisation of the obtained index makes it possible to obtain a more detailed map of energy poverty with respect to the previously proposed methodology. The model is applied to the case study of Pagani, in Campania Region (Italy), which is the study area investigated in the article that precedes this work, which allows to compare the results already obtained and appreciate the progress made by the model presented in this paper.

Keywords: Urban and Energy Poverty · Renewable Energy Communities · Urban Planning

1 Introduction

The goal of carbon neutrality, promoted by the European Green Deal by 2050, has been made legally binding by the recent European climate legislation, which introduces the ambitious goal of reducing net greenhouse gas emissions by at least 55% by 2030, compared to the levels of 1990 [1].

At the same time, in Europe the phenomenon of energy poverty is increasing significantly [2], to the point that the issue of the 'expensive bill' is constantly on the news. Due to the Russia-Ukraine war crisis, which has led to turbulence in energy markets, price volatility and global energy insecurity, the phenomenon of energy poverty no longer affects only low-income families, "but also those with lower-middle income and potentially others in some Member States as well" [3], threatening the achievement of the ambitious European decarbonisation targets.

O. Gervasi et al. (Eds.): ICCSA 2023 Workshops, LNCS 14112, pp. 353–363, 2023.
https://doi.org/10.1007/978-3-031-37129-5_29

Renewable Energy Communities (RECs) arouse growing interest for the fight against energy poverty and, in general, for the contribution of numerous environmental benefits, including: the energy efficiency of existing buildings; the promotion of the use of energy from renewable sources and the social acceptance of the latter; the reduction of climate-changing emissions [4–6].

According the European Directive "RED II", RECs are coalitions of citizens, small-medium enterprises and local authorities, including municipal administrations, which are able to produce, consume and exchange energy produced from renewable sources, with the main purpose of providing environmental, economic or social benefits to the community itself or to the local areas in which it operates [7]. The link with the local areas in which they are established makes the RECs a relevant tool for urban planning, in order to protect vulnerable people from the current price increase and ensure a just transition of cities towards climate neutrality.

This work is included in a broader research project, aimed at promoting the RECs development through urban planning. As part of the project, a methodology to identify priority areas in which to address this action was proposed, according to a place-based approach, as published in a previous study [8].

Priority areas, mapped on an infra-urban scale, are located where a minimization of the constraints and a maximization of the benefits deriving from the RECs establishment are expected. Constraints are defined as all factors for which an urban or rural area is not suitable for the installation of RES plants. Among the benefits provided by RECs, particular reference was made to reducing energy poverty, as this topic is little explored in the identification of RECs potential spatial configurations in the relevant literature.

In the absence of an agreement in the international scientific community on the methods and techniques for measuring energy poverty, it is evaluated with reference to two main proxy variables: the energy performance of residential buildings and the low income of residents. As no open data is available at the chosen spatial level, these variables are in turn estimated with specific methodologies. However, the second variable was evaluated expeditiously by associating public (ERP) and social (ERS) housing neighborhoods with low-income areas.

The aim and the novelty of this work compared to the previous work is to detail the already proposed methodology, with particular reference to the assessment of low income urban areas, since an increasing number of families are at risk of energy poverty, not only those residing in ERP and ERS neighborhoods. To this end, a model for the construction of a composite index of urban poverty is proposed. The index is constructed starting from basic indicators, selected following a review of the technical-scientific literature on the topic of poverty, deprivation or distress affecting urban areas.

The model is applied to the case study of Pagani, in Campania Region (Italy), in the context of studies and research conducted for the formation of the Municipal Urban Plan, by virtue of an institutional agreement between the Municipality and the Department of Civil Engineering (DiCiv) of the University of Salerno[1]. In addition, Pagani is the

---

[1] This study is developed within the research project "Agreement between DiCiv and municipality of Pagani for studies and research to support the formation of the Municipal Urban Plan". Prof. Roberto Gerundo is the project scientific responsible, while Alessandra Marra is principal investigator and technical coordinator of the research group.

study area investigated in the article that precedes this work, which makes it possible to compare the results already obtained and appreciate the progress made by the model presented here.

To this end, the following Sect. 2 describes the proposed methodology, applied to the case study described in Sect. 3. The results of this application are presented and discussed in Sect. 4, while Sect. 5 reports the main conclusions of the study and future developments of the research.

2 Materials and Methods

2.1 Selection of Basic Indicators

In the Italian geographical context, the territorial variation of per capita income is not known at the intra-city or neighborhood detail. In fact, the Ministry of Economy and Finance provides this data with reference to a lower spatial level, i.e. for each Italian municipality, with the exception of some large cities.

However, to overcome this problem, it is possible to consider other variables, measurable at the local level, considered to be expressive of a potential socio-economic hardship of resident families, according to the technical-scientific literature on urban poverty. These proxy variables have been traced in order to identify measures other than income, since incomes tend to fluctuate over time. Moreover, it is likely to run into problems of under-reporting, especially with reference to income derived from private entities [9]. The literature relating to the phenomenon of urban deprivation or distress also offers criteria and indicators useful for identifying urban areas or neighborhoods characterized by urban poverty [10–12].

The economic value of the house is notoriously considered a proxy variable for estimating the income of its inhabitants. In Italy, the real estate prices can be deduced by consulting the data from the Observatory of the Real Estate Market (OMI), thanks to which the Revenue Agency has mapped urban and rural areas of different market value for the whole Italian territory [13]. However, the level of spatial detail does not offer differentiation within urban fabric, i.e. on an infra-urban scale.

According to a technical report drawn up for the Italian metropolitan cities, there are three indicators that are best able to estimate the income vulnerability of families in Italy: low schooling rate, active employment rate, discouraged unemployment rate [14]. The same report also suggests further indicators, specifying that the choice must be made with reference to the urban system under study. For example, the ratio of rented houses to total dwellings is an appropriate indicator, as it is a typical feature of areas where urban poor are spatially concentrated.

The indicators proposed in the aforementioned report can be measured through simple algebraic operations starting from the census variables, the data of which are periodically released by the National Institute of Statistics for each census zone of the Italian territory, i.e. on an infra-urban scale, therefore they are considered suitable and selected in this study (Table 1). Overall, these indicators can be traced back to several domains or dimensions of urban poverty: Employment; Education and Culture; Demographic Structure; Building quality; Property deed.

Table 1. Selected indicators, with their definition and domain of reference.

Domain	Indicator	Definition
Employment	I_1 - Active unemployment rate	Ratio between the unemployed population looking for new employment and the population belonging to the total labor force
	I_2 - Unemployment rate discouraged	Ratio of people not in the labor force, i.e. those not classified as employed or seeking work, to the population in the total labor force
Education and Culture	I_3 – Low schooling rate	Ratio between the population with an educational qualification equal to or less than a lower secondary school diploma (middle school) on the total resident population aged 6 and over
Demographic Structure	I_4 - Old age index	Ratio of the population of 65 years of age and older and the population of age 0–14 years
	I_5 - Incidence of large families	Ratio between the number of families with 6 or more members and the total number of families
	I_6 – Vulnerable migration rate	Ratio of foreigners from low-income countries to total resident population
Building quality	I_7 – Building degradation index	Ratio between residential buildings in poor and mediocre state of conservation and total residential buildings
Property deed	I_8 – Rate for rental housing	Ratio of rented occupied dwellings to total occupied dwellings

2.2 Construction of the Urban Poverty Index

The construction of the composite index is carried out by first normalizing the m basic indicators (I_m, with $m = 1, \ldots, 8$) using the "Min-Max" method. Among the possible normalization techniques, this procedure makes it possible to relate the unique values of a single input indicator ($x_{m,i}$) to the maximum ($x_{m,i_{max}}$) and minimum ($x_{m,i_{min}}$) value that the indicator itself assumes in the territory under study, consisting of n census sections (with i $= 1, \ldots, n$). In the chosen set all the indicators have positive polarity, i.e. an increase in their value corresponds to an increase in criticality in the corresponding domain. Thus, the linear correlation formula that yields the respective normalized values ($y_{m,i}$) can be written as follows:

$$y_{m,i} = \begin{cases} 0 & x_{m,i} \leq x_{m,i_{min}} \\ \frac{x_{m,i}-x_{m,i_{min}}}{x_{m,i_{max}}-x_{m,i_{min}}} & x_{m,i_{min}} < x_{m,i} < x_{m,i_{max}} \\ 1 & x_{m,i} \geq x_{m,i_{max}} \end{cases}$$

The domain of each normalized indicator consists of the interval [0, 1], where 1 corresponds to the maximum degree of criticality, while 0 represents the minimum.

The composite index of urban poverty for each section (UPI_i) is obtained expeditiously through a weighted average of the normalized indicators, each of which is assigned a weight (w_m):

$$UPI_i = \frac{\sum_m w_m y_{m,i}}{\sum_m w_m}$$

If the indicators are not linearly correlated to each other, it is possible to adopt equal weights, so that the denominator of the previous formula will be equal to the total number of uncorrelated indicators. One of the suitable methods to investigate the possible existing linear correlation is to calculate the Pearson index. The correlation analysis must be carried out upstream of the normalisation, thus avoiding incurring any distorting effects caused by this operation. This type of analysis also makes it possible to reduce the number of basic indicators selected to that represented by the uncorrelated variables [15, 16].

In order to identify different levels of urban poverty, the classification is carried out on the basis of the Natural Break method, which is also suitable for any non-uniform data distributions [17]. Given the number of classes, for example equal to five (Very Low, Low, Medium, High, Very High), this method allows to maximize the variance between the classes and minimize the variance within each class.

3   Case of Study

The city of Pagani is part of a dense intermunicipal conurbation, called 'Agro-Nocerino-Sarnese', located in the Salerno Province of Campania Region (Italy). Pagani is characterized by a high population density, concentrated in an urban continuum that connects to the metropolitan area of Naples, to the east, and to the urban pole of Salerno, to the west. This vast settlement area is characterized by a high degree of urbanization, which has led to a serious fragmentation of the rural landscape (Fig. 1).

With Executive Decree n. 17 of 4 March 2020, Campania Region updated the summary index of housing deprivation in the regional territory. This index, elaborated on a municipal basis, aggregates the municipalities into four different ranges, corresponding to the following classes: High, Medium-High, Medium-Low and Low. The synthetic index was constructed starting from the following indicators: the ratio between occupied dwellings and total dwellings, variable that takes the name of 'Housing Intensity Index'; the reciprocal of the ratio between the inhabited municipal area and the resident municipal population, a variable called 'Index of pressure on the housing stock'. As a result, the Municipality of Pagani is one of those with high housing deprivation, ranking as the 44th one out of a total of 550 Campania Region municipalities. Within the urban fabric, there are various districts of Public Residential Building (Fig. 2), implemented under the current General Regulatory Plan (PRG). The new Municipal Urban Plan (PUC), which will update the PRG, is formally approved in the preliminary component for now (PUC Preliminary), while the definitive project is being finalized.

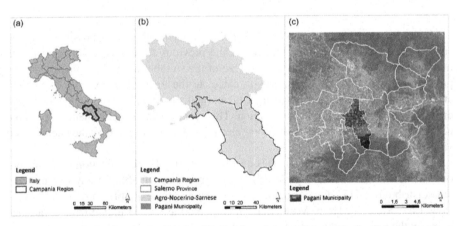

Fig. 1. Campania Region in the South of Italy (a) and the study area in the Salerno Province of Campania Region (b), with the Pagani municipal territory highlighted among all the Agro-Nocerino-Sarnese municipalities (c).

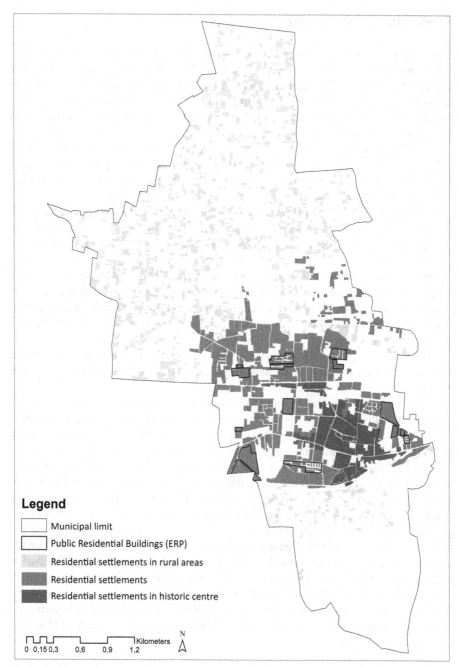

Legend

☐ Municipal limit

☐ Public Residential Buildings (ERP)

▨ Residential settlements in rural areas

▨ Residential settlements

▨ Residential settlements in historic centre

0   0,15 0,3   0,6   0,9   1,2   Kilometers   N

Fig. 2. Residential land use of Pagani Municipality. Author's elaboration on the Urban Land Use Map of PUC Preliminary.

4   Results and Discussion

The proposed methodology is applied to the case study, starting from the acquisition and preparation of the data needed to measure the basic indicators. As mentioned, data is available on a census basis for the entire national territory, but only those referring to each section belonging to Pagani Municipality were extrapolated. Since open data is not available at a more detailed spatial level, the census tract is identified as the minimum territorial unit for thematic mapping.

In a GIS environment, by building a *geodatabase*, in which the values of the input indicators are associated with the spatial polygons representing each section, it is possible to implement the formulations contained in the methodological proposal for the construction of the UPI index.

For the study area, all the proposed indicators merged into the composite index aggregation procedure, as Pearson's correlation analysis revealed little correlation between the selected variables. In fact, the values of Pearson's *r coefficient* are in the range 0.00008–0.134.

In this way, once the index values are known for each minimum spatial unit and by performing a classification with the Natural Breaks method in five intervals, the representative map of the territorial variation of socio-economic hardship in the territory in question is obtained. More precisely, the value of the composite index varies from a minimum of 0.075 to a maximum of 0.56.

This map is subsequently intersected with the urban land use map, with specific reference to the areas with a predominantly residential function, to which the input data refer (Fig. 3).

The final map shows that the composite index reaches its highest levels not only in areas traditionally considered low-income, i.e. public housing districts. Numerous other neighborhoods are affected by conditions of potential socio-economic hardship, both in the more central areas and in the rural areas of settlement sprawl.

The ERP districts, affected by a high and very-high index, are confirmed as urban areas representative of an income vulnerability of the residents, therefore their location is a valid criterion for the territorialisation of the phenomenon. However, the case in question demonstrates how they are not sufficient to capture the areas susceptible to potential socio-economic hardship in their entirety. A more detailed knowledge of the territorial distribution of this phenomenon is useful for more accurately mapping urban areas at risk of energy poverty. It follows a different and more precise spatial distribution of the priority areas for the promotion of RECs, compared with the priority areas map achieved in in the previous study that this work intends to integrate (Gerundo & Marra 2022). So, it is possible to use the simplified method when drawing up the preliminary plan, while the more detailed method is suitable for the definition of the final plan.

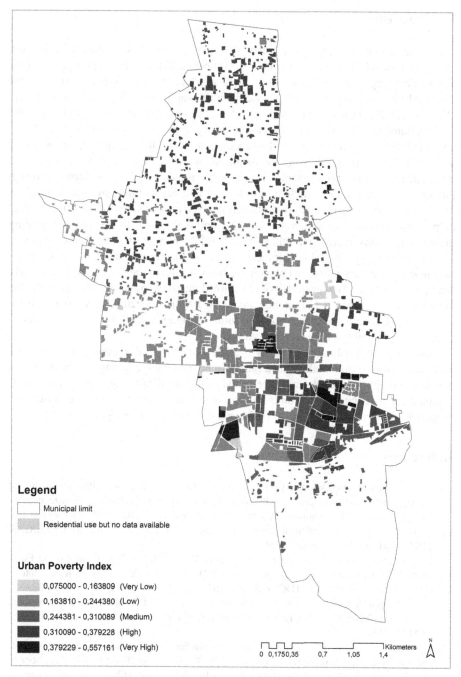

Fig. 3. Urban Poverty Map for the study area.

5 Conclusion

In an international context where urban and energy poverty is on the rise, this work proposes a model for the construction of a composite index of urban poverty, with the aim of detecting low and medium-low income urban areas. The spatialisation of the proposed index allows to obtain a more detailed map of energy poverty with respect to the previously proposed methodology, along the same research project in which the work is framed [8]. In fact, in the previous model energy consumption is evaluated with an articulated methodology, while low-income areas are located quickly in public or social housing districts. Although the results show that the latter is a good criterion to use, especially in the preliminary drafting of the municipal plan, the methodological proposal presented in this article allows to take into account the multiple dimensions of urban poverty in the computation of energy poverty. Consequently, the priority areas map for the promotion of Renewable Energy Communities can also be updated, guiding planning decisions in greater depth, which is useful when drafting the definitive plan.

The developed methodology for the aggregation of the basic indicators is easily practicable in the ordinary municipal planning activity, which in Italy is already particularly long and articulated. However, it should be noted that it is possible to further refine the methods for combining the input indicators [18, 19], in order to build a more accurate map. This advance represents a possible future development of the work, in order to improve the reliability of the results obtained.

Since the input data are ordinarily available in municipal planning processes, the proposed method is potentially transferable to other geographical contexts. Furthermore, the methodology is scalable to lower levels of spatial detail, aggregating the results obtained for higher territorial units. In this direction, the methodology exposed can support RECs promotion actions to be framed in territorial planning.

References

1. EU, European Commission: Regulation 2021/1119 of the European Parliament and of the Council of 30 June 2021 establishing the framework for achieving climate neutrality and amending Regulations (EC) No 401/2009 and (EU) 2018/1999 («European Climate Law») (2021). https://eur-lex.europa.eu/legal-content/EN/TXT/PDF/?uri=CELEX:320 21R1119&from=IT. Accessed 31 Mar 2023
2. EU, European Commission: State of the Energy Union 2021 – Contributing to the European Green Deal and the Union's recovery (2021). https://eur-lex.europa.eu/legal-content/EN/TXT/?uri=CELEX:52021DC0950&qid=1635753095014. Accessed 31 Mar 2023
3. EU, European Commission: State of the Energy Union 2022 (2022). https://eur-lex.europa.eu/legal-content/EN/TXT/?uri=CELEX%3A52022DC0547&qid=1666595113558. Accessed 31 Mar 2023
4. Brummer, V.: Community energy – benefits and barriers: a comparative literature review of community energy in the UK, Germany and the USA, the benefits it provides for society and the barriers it faces. Renew. Sustain. Energy Rev. **94**, 187–196 (2018). https://doi.org/10.1016/j.rser.2018.06.013
5. McCabe, A., Pojani, D., Broese van Groenou, A.: Social housing and renewable energy: community energy in a supporting role. Energy Res. Soc. Sci. **38**, 110–113 (2018). https://doi.org/10.1016/j.erss.2018.02.005

6. Koltunov, M., Bisello, A.: Multiple impacts of energy communities: conceptualization taxonomy and assessment examples. In: Bevilacqua, C., Calabrò, F., Della Spina, L. (eds.) NMP 2020. SIST, vol. 178, pp. 1081–1096. Springer, Cham (2021). https://doi.org/10.1007/978-3-030-48279-4_101

7. EU, European Commission: Directive (EU) 2018/2001 of the European Parliament and of the Council of 11 December 2018 on the promotion of the use of energy from renewable sources (2018). https://eur-lex.europa.eu/legal-content/EN/TXT/?uri=CELEX%3A02018L2001-20181221. Accessed 31 Mar 2023

8. Gerundo, R., Marra, A.: A decision support methodology to foster renewable energy communities in the municipal urban plan. Sustainability **14**(23), 16268 (2022). https://doi.org/10.3390/su142316268

9. Baker, J., Schuler, N.: Analyzing urban poverty. A summary of methods and approaches, Policy Research Paper No. 3399, World Bank, Washington, DC, USA (2004)

10. Conway, M., Konvitz, J.: Meeting the challenge of distressed urban areas. Urban Stud. **37**, 749–774 (2000). https://doi.org/10.1080/00420980050004008

11. Cordoba Hernández, R., Gonzáles García, I., Guerrero Periñan, G.: Urban poverty partnership: report about urban deprivation/poverty observatories in the European Union. Monograph (Otros), ETS Arquitectura (UPM), European Commission, Brussels, BE (2018)

12. Marra, A.: Peripheralization risk in urban and metropolitan areas. A methodological proposal for the analysis and mitigation. Ph.D. thesis in risk and sustainability in civil, architectural and environmental engineering systems, University of Salerno (2020)

13. Italian Revenue Agency: Database of real estate prices (2022). https://www1.agenziaentrate.gov.it/servizi/geopoi_omi/index.php. Accessed 31 Mar 2023

14. NUVAP, Evaluation and Analysis Unit for Programming, Department for Cohesion Policies of Italian Prime Minister Office. Poverty Maps. Territorial analysis of socio-economic disadvantage in urban areas. An exercise for the 14 Italian metropolitan cities. Technical reports (2017). https://www.forumdisuguaglianzediversita.org/wp-content/uploads/2018/05/Report_Poverty-MAPS_2017-07-20_CASAVOLA-et-AL.pdf. Accessed 31 Mar 2023

15. Manly, B.: Multivariate Statistical Methods. Chapman & Hall, UK (1994)

16. OECD: Organization for Economic Cooperation and Development. In: Handbook on Constructing Composite Indicators. Methodology and User Guide, OECD Publications, Paris, FR (2008)

17. Jenks, G.F.: The data model concept in statistical mapping. In: Frenzel, K. (eds.) International Yearbook of Cartography, no. 7, George Philip, London, UK (1967)

18. Gerundo, R., Marra, A., De Salvatore, V.: Construction of a composite vulnerability index to map peripheralization risk in urban and metropolitan areas. Sustainability **12**(11), 4641 (2020). https://doi.org/10.3390/su12114641

19. Grimaldi, M., Sebillo, M., Vitiello, G., Pellecchia, V.: Planning and managing the integrated water system: a spatial decision support system to analyze the infrastructure performances. Sustainability **12**(16), 6432 (2020). https://doi.org/10.3390/su12166432

Short Paper (VRA 2023)

Experience of Using PBL and Gamification as an Active Methodology in Time of Pandemic in Ecuador

Gomez José Manuel[✉] [iD]

Indoamerica University, Ambato EC180103, Ecuador
josegomez@uti.edu.ec

Abstract. During the COVID 19 pandemic, the use of innovative and attractive strategies within educational environments has been demonstrated, where teaching is focused on the student, in the development of skills. These strategies conceive learning as a constructive and motivating process. To do this, a topic that generates great interest in the current educational scenario was analyzed: the active methodologies applied within the current situation experienced by the pandemic; which is eminent because through its use it is possible to continue with the teaching/learning process between teacher and student in difficult times such as those currently experienced by society in general. The objective is to know the experiences of teachers in the application of PBL and Gamification as strategies of active methodologies in the teaching process. The methodology is qualitative approach. The sample consisted of 15 teachers from the Sierra del Ecuador educational system. The survey technique was applied. In conclusion, it has been confirmed that the application of active methodologies encourages students to learn, in a practical way, useful and concrete knowledge that they will usually find in their daily context and curiosity about learning is rewarded.

Keywords: Gamification · PBL · teaching

1 Introduction

The COVID-19 pandemic has caused great challenges for the education system around the world, and Ecuador has not been the exception. School closures and social distancing restrictions have forced educators to quickly adapt to distance learning, using alternative methods to ensure continuity of learning. In this context, the use of the Problem Based Learning (PBL) methodology and gamification has emerged as a promising strategy to maintain student engagement and motivation during remote education.

Problem-Based Learning (PBL) is a methodology that involves students in solving real and significant problems, fostering collaboration and critical thinking. On the other hand, gamification implies the incorporation of game elements and mechanics in the educational process to increase the motivation and commitment of students. These two methodologies can be combined to create an engaging and interactive learning environment, even in times of pandemic.

O. Gervasi et al. (Eds.): ICCSA 2023 Workshops, LNCS 14112, pp. 367–373, 2023.
https://doi.org/10.1007/978-3-031-37129-5_30

In Ecuador, the adoption of PBL and gamification during the pandemic has had mixed results. Some educators have been able to successfully implement these methodologies in remote learning, while others have faced significant challenges. The availability of appropriate technological platforms and tools has been a crucial factor for the success of these methodologies. Educators who have had access to digital resources and online platforms have been able to design interactive and gamified learning experiences, which has helped keep students engaged.

However, the implementation of PBL and gamification has also presented challenges. The adaptation of educational content to the PBL format and the identification of authentic and relevant problems has required an additional effort on the part of educators. In addition, the proper design of gamified activities and assessments has been essential to prevent gamification from becoming a distraction or excessive focus on playful aspects instead of substantive learning.

The use of digital tools as means for the development of active methodologies in the teaching-learning process allows to diversify and innovate teaching processes. In this way, by taking advantage of technology from a structured and dynamic approach, indicators such as interest and motivation of the learner, active participation of all students in planned activities, autonomy when developing tasks and self-regulation of learning can be significantly improved.

In addition to this, there are numerous technological tools that can be used to mediate the cognitive processes of students, since new generations considered as digital natives have lived closely related to the new information and communication technologies and therefore, they show a higher level of interest and motivation to work with these tools. Consequently, by incorporating technological tools in the educational process from a didactic approach, it seeks to attend to two fundamental elements in the XXI century education, the strengthening of education and the development of new digital skills in students.

From this perspective, active methodologies have the potential to engage the student participatively, by encouraging their curiosity allowing adequate spaces for their own reflection and activity within the learning experience; that is, placing him as a key and active actor in the teaching and learning process and not only as a recipient of the knowledge and content that the teacher exposes. According to Mendes (2019) the fundamental purpose of this kind of methodologies lies in promoting the autonomous learning of the student, that is, the ability to learn to learn, to be aware of their own cognitive processes to regulate their learning inside and outside the classroom.

It is necessary to point out that, although the autonomy of the student is promoted, does not mean that the teaching role has less importance, but on the contrary, acquires a deeper function that consists of promoting the appropriate experiences and guiding the student so that he assumes his own learning with responsibility. In this way, Robledo et al. (2015), considers that learning becomes more efficient and meaningful by relying on competences that interrelate conceptual knowledge with procedural knowledge, that is, they not only stay in theory, but focus on the practical application of knowledge, which favors the development of propitious skills and competencies to school and work performance.

Active methodologies include Problem-Based Learning (PBL), Flipped Classroom, and Gamification. Problem-Based Learning refers to a methodology that is focused on the development of content and concepts through a problem of the particular context of the student and his interest in general, in which, through certain guidelines, the student is actively involved in the construction of his knowledge. On the other hand, the gamification methodology focuses on taking advantage of the principles of the game for the development of skills and abilities in the student. It should be noted, that these two methodologies were selected, since they are in accordance with the study problem of this research work.

In the Ecuadorian territory is promoted, from the legal bodies, the development of a quality educational process and centered on the human being, where active methodologies are applied. The development from a perspective of integrality that is intended to be generated in Basic Education, constitutes an essential step for the development of the capacities, abilities and skills that the person needs to face the challenges of today's world.

The problem has been shown that through the research work developed in the master's degree in education of the Indoamerican Technological University of Ecuador, where the participants have made use of innovative digital tools that allowed improving learning. That is why, it is necessary to know the different innovative activities with active methodologies based on PBL and Gamification in basic education, beating out the traditional methods that are beginning to dislike the empowerment of knowledge.

In this analysis, we will further explore the experience of using PBL and gamification as an active methodology in times of pandemic in Ecuador. We will examine the challenges and opportunities that have arisen in the implementation of these methodologies, as well as the observed results in terms of student motivation and engagement. The importance of technological tools and the appropriate adaptation of educational content in this context will also be analyzed.

2   Method

It was based on an investigation of a qualitative nature, due to the collection of information through the interview of the Sierra system of the Ecuadorian educational system. Qualitative research has made it possible to relate all the problematic aspects of active methodologies on PBL and Gamification.

The population of this research was 15 teachers attending the master's degree in education at the Technological University, who made innovative proposals that resulted in the application of active methodologies.

3   Results

The population of this research was 15 teachers attending the master's degree in education at the Technological University, who made innovative proposals that resulted in the application of active methodologies (Table 1).

Table 1. Table with the teachers interviewed with the description of the proposal

Teachers	Area	Level	Type	Description
Wilma Yolanda, Moreno Moreno	Mathematics	10th Year of General Education	PBL	Propose the generating question: Whatsocial, educational, environmental problems exist in your community? With the answers of the students, make brainstorm ideas to propose various problems of the context Activities Make four working groups where each of the issues raised are distributed Explain to students about statistics, variables, research instruments, the collection process, tabulation, and measures of central tendency Development Each group performs the operationalization of the variables of the selected problem. They prepare the data collection instrument and apply it through Google Forms They carry out the data tabulation and the frequency distribution table. Calculate the measures of central tendency, the arithmetic mean, the mode and the median • Conclusion In the conclusion students expose their group interpretation related to recollected data
Santiago Chávez, Zully Sánchez, Jeymy Villagómez	Mathematics	First Year EGB: 5-year-olds	Gamification	Learning experience: ¡¡Jambato SapitoSapón!! (The name of the application that was attached to it) Gamification of scope of RLM in Preparatory First Year EGB: 5-year-olds children – Numbers from 1 to 10 – Count to 10 – Ascending and descending series Steps to the learning process: 1. Observe and identify numbers 2. Associate the quantity with the numeral 3. Identify the numeral and represent itgraphically 4. Sort numbers ascending and descending Gamification Link interactivity https://es.educaplay.com/recursos-educat ivos/12567808-sapito_sapon.html

(*continued*)

Table 1. (*continued*)

Teachers	Area	Level	Type	Description
Marlene de Jesus, Sailema Amancha	Mathematics	4th Grade of Basic General Education	Gamification	Give the respective explanations of how the didactic game works to the students – Apply the didactic game with fourth grade boys and girls – Enter the Kahoot! platform (teacher and students) – Start the game – The teacher explains the operations to be solved and the answer options to choose from – Students solve the operations and answer the correct answer immediately within 20 s to give way to the next addition or subtraction game Challenge 1: https://create.kahoot.it/share/jugando-con-las-sumas-y-restas/248 82540-d253-4356-b786-20d8ac26f296 Challenge 2: https://create.kahoot.it/share/jugando-con-las-sumas-y-restas/248 82540-d253-4356-b786-20d8ac26f296 Challenge 3: https://create.kahoot.it/share/jugando-con-las-sumas-y-restas/248 82540-d253-4356-b786-20d8ac26f296
Teran Cortez, Darwin Patricio	Social Sciences	9th Year of General Education	Gamification	This gamification seeks to understand the nature of democracy, based on the study of its characteristics, duties and citizen rights, the structure of the Ecuadorian State and the role of the Constitution to stimulate the exercise of critical, responsible and committed citizenship. https://quizizz.com/admin/quiz/5f8f24c90487ba001c99afcc
Mauricio Altamirano, Geomaira Guachamín, Reyna Mendoza, Lara Sayra, Franco Calderón	Mathematics	2nd year of basic education	Gamification	1. Understanding of the concept of basic operations: Activities that allow know the concept of addition, subtraction, multiplication and division 2. Introduction of basic operations: Activities focused on discovering the four basic operations and how to use them 3. Practice of basic operations: Activities to practice the use of the four basic operations productively or systematically 4. Consolidation of basic operations: Activities aimed at using the basic operations in various situations. https://view.genial.ly/62c05f7a59ebc800169280a7/interactive-content-videojuego-matematicas

4 Conclusion

It concludes with the different proposals presented for different activities with active methodologies based on digital tools to improve learning in the Education of the Ecuadorian system, through which contributes to motivation, active participation and the construction of significant learning in the student.

The conclusions of this research show the need to propose various attractive strategies for students and, thus, they can obtain significant learning in the classroom.

The adoption of the Problem Based Learning (PBL) methodology and gamification in the context of the pandemic in Ecuador has proven to be a promising strategy to maintain student engagement and motivation during remote education. Although there have been challenges in its implementation, especially in terms of access to technological platforms and resources, those educators who have managed to overcome these obstacles have seen positive results.

The use of PBL has allowed students to become actively involved in authentic and relevant problem solving, fostering critical thinking and collaboration. On the other hand, gamification has provided a playful and motivating experience that has maintained the interest of students. Both methodologies have proven to be effective in promoting more meaningful and applicable learning in real situations.

To guarantee the success of these methodologies, it is essential to have adequate technological tools and careful planning in the adaptation of educational content. Educators must ensure that they provide digital resources and online platforms that facilitate interaction and collaborative learning. Furthermore, it is essential to balance gamification effectively, preventing it from becoming a distraction and making sure that the main focus remains on substantive learning.

In summary, the use of PBL and gamification as active methodologies during the pandemic in Ecuador has provided opportunities to maintain student engagement and motivation in a remote educational environment. Although challenges have arisen, those educators who have managed to adapt and overcome them have experienced positive results in terms of engagement, skill development, and application of knowledge. These methodologies offer a promising approach for the future of education, even beyond the pandemic, as they foster more meaningful and problem-oriented learning.

In general, the experience of using PBL and gamification as an active methodology in times of pandemic in Ecuador has been positive. These methodologies have demonstrated their ability to sustain student interest, foster problem-solving skills, and promote more meaningful learning. However, it is important to recognize that its successful implementation requires a careful approach and proper planning, taking into account the needs and circumstances of the students. Ultimately, the combination of PBL and gamification offers a promising approach for the future of education in Ecuador and around the world.

References

1. Mendes, I.A.: Active methodologies as investigative practices in the mathematics teaching. Int. Electron. J. Math. Educ. **14**(3), 501–512 (2019). https://doi.org/10.29333/iejme/5752
2. Rodríguez, F., Santiago, R.: Gamificación: cómo motivar a tu alumnado y mejorar el clima del aula. Grupo Oceano (2017)

3. Robledo, P., Fidalgo, R., Arias, O., Álvarez, M.L.: Percepción de los estudiantes sobre el desarrollo de competencias a través de diferentes metodologías activas. Revista de Investigacion Educativa **33**(2), 369–383 (2015). https://doi.org/10.6018/rie.33.2.201381

4. Sánchez, C.: Herramientas tecnológicas en la enseñanza de las matemáticas durante la pandemia COVID-19. Hamut'ay **7**(2), 46–57. Author, F.: Article title. Journal 2(5), 99–110 (2016)

Short Paper (AIWA 2023)

Chatbot Feedback on Students' Writing: Typology of Comments and Effectiveness

Besma Allagui[(⊠)] [iD]

General Education Department, Rabdan Academy, Abu Dhabi, UAE
ballagui@ra.ac.ae

Abstract. Providing feedback is time-consuming. A chatbot has the potential to facilitate provision of detailed feedback saving instructors time and energy. However, the effectiveness of chatbot feedback has not been determined. In this study, chatbot end-comments on 28 students' written papers were classified by topic and function. The comments were further evaluated for whether they reflected the five characteristics of effective feedback. Results demonstrated the ability of the chatbot to provide a variety of comments. The characteristics of these comments nevertheless, did not seem to reflect feedback best practices. The study provides recommendations for further chatbot feedback research, and in particular calls for more partnership between artificial intelligence developers and writing researchers.

Keywords: First Keyword · Second Keyword · Third Keyword

1 Introduction

From a social perspective, teacher written feedback is the method that teachers-as-readers use to interact with students. It is also an essential component of the writing process that, if well-understood, helps students to improve their writing skills [1]. It draws students' attention to understand their writing weaknesses and regulate their learning [1, 2]. However, providing feedback on student writing is complex and time consuming. It is stated that teachers spend 15–30 min on a single paper [3]. One way to reduce the burden on teachers is through the use of artificial intelligence (AI). Currently, chatbots, a machine learning and artificial intelligence tool which can interact with a user by asking questions and responding to questions, are becoming popular in the writing classroom that may potentially provide teachers with a tool to produce feedback. Researchers have used chatbots to perform various teaching activities including, delivering writing instructions, scaffolding of argumentative writing, providing a conversational partner [4–6]. These studies have demonstrated the promising effects of chatbot on improving students' writing skills. Although chatbots can support writing instruction, it remains to be seen whether chatbots can effectively assist teachers in the provision of corrective feedback.

Given that chatbots are becoming more technically advanced such as ChatGPT, assessing the types and effectiveness of feedback generated by a chatbot could be a necessary to help instructors provide AI-generated feedback more effectively. Feedback can

O. Gervasi et al. (Eds.): ICCSA 2023 Workshops, LNCS 14112, pp. 377–384, 2023.
https://doi.org/10.1007/978-3-031-37129-5_31

be classified by its focus (local vs global aspects), by its topic (mechanics, organization, content), or by its role (evaluation, suggestion, reader response) [7]. To date, research has not examined specifically, what type of feedback can be produced by a chatbot and if this feedback reflects the characteristics of effective feedback.

According to writing researchers, good feedback practices should include 5 characteristics: (1) Effective feedback should focus on both content and grammar. Research demonstrated that many teachers currently focus on mechanics which results in improving the readability of the paper without elaborating on its content [7]. (2) Effective feedback is both positive and negative. Feedback should include both praise and criticism. Research revealed that providing students with a combination of negative and positive feedback leads to better writing quality [8]. On the flipside, excessively negative feedback can result in feeling less motivated to rewrite [9, 10]. (3) Effective feedback is specific and relevant to the assignment or task at hand. Researchers found that students are appreciative of detailed and specific feedback because it helped them understand the errors that they must avoid [11] (4) Effective feedback is appropriate. Teachers should focus on what the students can do. It is important that feedback is at an appropriate level of challenge so that student can understand it and make use of it [12] (5) Effective feedback engages learners in the writing process. It is important that teachers do not appropriate students' writing by correcting every single mistake but rather by pointing at inconsistencies and giving them responsibility to make the last decision.

Therefore, in this study we aimed to investigate the types of end-comments and the extent to which these comments reflect best feedback practices. End-comments are described as the paragraph at the end of the paper where the teacher gives summary feedback [13]. We focused particularly on these questions:

1. What types of end-comments does the chatbot provide?
2. Do the chatbot end-comments reflect the feedback best practices?

2 Methodology

The Institutional Review Board determined the study to be exempt from full review. The method employed was exploratory and descriptive. We aimed to identify the types of comments generated by a highly advanced chatbot (ChatGPT) and examine whether the generated comments reflect the feedback best practices as determined by the review of the literature. Two instruments were used to examine the types of comments that AI may produce and the extent to which these comments reflect best teacher feedback practices: students' written samples and evaluation rubric. The written samples were selected from an undergraduate General Education course which focuses on writing, reading and critical thinking skills. The topics of the essay varied between crime and punishment, homeland security and disaster management and military. The students were required to choose their own topic and write a 750 argumentative essay in support of their own position while acknowledging the opposition. Argumentative writing was chosen because it is important for college readiness [14].

First, we asked ChatGPT to read each student essay and write an end-comment that should be specific, detailed, balanced, and engaging. The prompt also asked the chatbot to start with a positive evaluation of the entire paper and organization followed with a negative statement on style and correctness before ending with a suggestion for the next paper and offering assistance.

After collecting the end-comments, 2 writing teachers read the papers and scored each comment using a rubric specifically designed to for this study based on a review of the literature to measure the extent to which AI-generated comments can reflect best feedback practices. The rubric was reviewed by experts and the final version included 5 criteria pertaining to good feedback: focus, balance, specificity, appropriateness, and learner engagement. Each criterion was measured on a scale from 1 (Never) to 4 (Always) as follows. The raters were trained in one session on using the rubric:

1. Feedback Focus:

   Always: Feedback consistently focuses on both content and mechanics.
   Sometimes: Feedback occasionally focuses on both content and mechanics.
   Occasionally: Feedback focuses on content, but does not provide information on mechanics.
   Never: Feedback does not mention both content and mechanics.

2. Feedback Balance:

   Always: Feedback is both positive and negative.
   Sometimes: Feedback is sometimes both positive and negative.
   Occasionally: Feedback provides an imbalanced view, either only mentioning the strengths or only focusing on the weaknesses.
   Never: Feedback does not mention both the strengths and weaknesses of the situation.

3. Feedback Specificity:

   Always: Feedback provides specific and concrete examples to support the feedback provided.
   Sometimes: Feedback provides some specific examples, but may also rely on generalizations.
   Occasionally: Feedback does not provide specific examples to support the feedback.
   Never: Feedback is solely based on generalizations and does not provide any specific examples.

4. Feedback Appropriateness:

   Always: Feedback is appropriate and clearly stated.
   Sometimes: Feedback may be appropriate in some instances, but may also be vague.
   Occasionally: Feedback is inappropriate and vague.
   Never: Feedback is not appropriate and not clear.

5. Feedback Engagement:

   Always: Feedback encourages engagement and promotes active reflection and improvement.
   Sometimes: Feedback may encourage engagement, but may also be perceived as passive or disinterested.
   Occasionally: Feedback does not encourage engagement and may be perceived as dismissive or disinterested.

Never: Feedback does not encourage engagement and actively discourages reflection and improvement.

Next, comments were read and analyzed qualitatively using a coding scheme adapted from Smith [13]. It was decided to focus on the topic and function of the comment because it was important to see if the AI tool can diagnose writing issues in different aspects and if it is able to adopt different roles.

Data were analyzed both qualitatively and quantitatively. Qualitative analysis included coding the resulting comments on the basis of topic and function using the coding scheme. Quantitative analysis included descriptive and inferential statistics.

3 Results

The produced essays were generally between 603 and 750 words. Results from the thematic analysis of the produced comments are presented in Table 1:

Table 1. Typology of end-comments produced by Chabot

Type	Sub-type	Frequency	Percentage
Topic	Mechanics	30	17.64
	Organization	56	32.94
	Content	84	49.41
Total		**170**	
Function	Evaluation	64	71.9
	Suggestion	25	28.08
	Reader response	0	0
Total		**89**	

The chabot produced the most comments on content especially with regards to introducing the topic and claim and providing counter-arguments. The chabot also provided more of the comments on organization rather than on mechanics. Below is an example of the produced end-comment:

The essay provides a comprehensive overview of the topic of introducing a tax system in the UAE. The writer has discussed the various reasons why the government should start collecting more taxes and the possible challenges that could arise. The essay also includes alternative opinions on the topic, making it well-rounded. The writing style is clear and concise, and the arguments are well-structured. However, some of the sentences could benefit from a more concise phrasing. Overall, the writing quality is good, and the essay is well-suited for its purpose.

In this example, the chabot focused on the content and structure of the essay, including clear and concise writing, well-structured arguments, and the need for some sentences to be phrased more concisely.

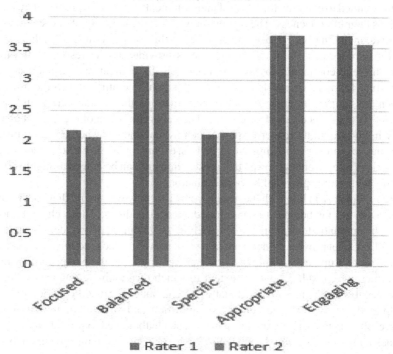

Fig. 1. Human evaluation of the chabot end-comments

The raters' evaluation of the chatbot comments are displayed in Fig. 1:

Figure 1 provides an overview of the ratters' evaluation of the effectiveness of the chatbot comments. Generally, the feedback was found to be appropriate and highly engaging. Raters agreed that the provided comments were balanced including both negative and positive statements. There was also a consensus on the focus and specificity of comments. The comments were general suggestions for improvement rather than detailed feedback (e.g. The language used in the essay can be improved by using more formal and precise language, avoiding repetitions, and using more varied vocabulary).

The interrater agreement for each criterion was measured using Cohen's Kappa. Values ≤ 0 indicate no agreement and 0.01–0.20 indicate none to slight, 0.21–0.40 indicate fair, 0.41– 0.60 indicate moderate, 0.61–0.80 indicate substantial, and 0.81– 1.00 indicate almost perfect agreement. The results from the evaluation of the produced comments shows a good inter-rater agreement level between the raters in their assessment of the effectiveness of the feedback on all five criteria ranging from 0.65 for specific to 0.92 for focused.

4 Discussion

The study aimed to examine the types of end-comments that can be produced by a chabot as well as their effectiveness. The results showed that the majority of end-comments are evaluative, including both praise and criticism. While some comments include suggestions for improvement, none of the comments provided reader response. It was also shown that end-comments focused primarily on the content and to a lesser degree on structure followed by mechanics. While this could be attributed to the differences between the samples in terms of content and structure, the results seem to indicate the ability of AI to produce varied comments. The major limitation of the Chabot appeared mainly in not providing reader response such as reactions of whether the writing was interesting, exciting or confusing. Nevertheless, evaluation of the end-comments against the criteria of effectiveness showed that most comments can be judged as highly effective given the high scores provided by both evaluators.

Our findings are in line with the results from [14] study who found that both ChatGPT and Blender are far behind humans in pedagogical abilities. These chatbots need to learn to be emphatic to maximize their usefulness. In our study, we demonstrated that ChatGPT does not provide reader response which serves as a connection between teacher and student and invites students to view their writing from the perspective of readers [3]. Furthermore, results about the extent to which the chatbot comments reflect best teacher feedback practices revealed that using chatbot can provide generic information to help students improve the content, organization and style of their writing which could result in better writing quality papers. The chatbot need to provide more explicit feedback taking into account the students' experience. However, the agreement between the raters that the chatbot-produced comments are balanced and quite engaging seem promising. Evaluators' positive assessment of chatbot comments may mean that AI can greatly contribute to writing instruction and assessment by providing honest praise. Furthermore, acceptance of AI-produced feedback will eventually lead instructors to adopt the new methodologies in their classrooms for better learning and assessment opportunities. These results are supported by [15] who found a high agreement between chatbot grading and human grading. Our study demonstrated that chatbot has more potential than automated tools for providing feedback which has yielded mixed results [16].

5 Implications, Limitations and Conclusion

The study found that chatbot may not be a very effective way to provide detailed and specific end-comments. Therefore, AI should partner with writing researchers to implement the characteristics of good feedback into their language models. In particular, the chatbot needs to improve its social presence and provide more accurate and specific comments. It would be a great idea if the chabot was more intelligent. Meanwhile, chatbot can still be considered a very useful tool in providing students with directions and timely generic suggestions and supporting teachers in assessing students' writing. Overall, the study has contributed to the body of research related to the social aspects of chatbots by examining its potential as a method of providing feedback. Nevertheless, this study had several limitations. This study is a first step towards examining the effectiveness and typology of chatbot-produced feedback. It suffers from some limitations that should be addressed in future studies. First, the study relied on a small sample of essays on a particular genre. Future studies may include a larger sample written on a variety of genres (narrative, informative, persuasive). Another threat to the generalizability of the current study relates to the prompt. While we asked the chatbot to answer the same question when providing feedback on the students' papers, disclosing more information about each paper may yield different results. Therefore, researchers should continue to explore the effectiveness of chatbot by varying the way the feedback is generated (i.e. reformulating the request). Despite these limitations, the study revealed important features of chatbot-generated end-comments. Improving these features should be a continuous goal for artificial intelligence developers.

References

1. Graham, S., Harris, K.R., Santangelo, T.: based writing practices and the common core: meta-analysis and meta-synthesis. Elem. Sch. J. **115**(4), 498–522 (2015)
2. Black, P., Wiliam, D.: Assessment and classroom learning. Assess. Educ. Princ. Policy Pract. **5**(1), 7–74 (1998)
3. Hyland, K., Hyland, F.: Feedback on second language students' writing. Lang. Teach. **39**(2), 83–101 (2006)
4. Guo, K., Wang, J., Chu, S.K.W.: Using chatbots to scaffold EFL students' argumentative writing. Assess. Writ. **54**, 100666 (2022)
5. Lin, M.P.C., Chang, D.: Enhancing post-secondary writers' writing skills with a chatbot. J. Educ. Technol. Soc. **23**(1), 78–92 (2020)
6. Vázquez-Cano, E., Mengual-Andrés, S., López-Meneses, E.: Chatbot to improve learning punctuation in Spanish and to enhance open and flexible learning environments. Int. J. Educ. Technol. High. Educ. **18**(1), 1–20 (2021). https://doi.org/10.1186/s41239-021-00269-8
7. Chou, C.-Y., Zou, N.-B.: An analysis of internal and external feedback in self-regulated learning activities mediated by self-regulated learning tools and open learner models. Int. J. Educ. Technol. High. Educ. **17**(1), 1–27 (2020). https://doi.org/10.1186/s41239-020-00233-y
8. Wen, Y.: Teacher written feedback on L2 student writings. J. Lang. Teach. Res. **4**(2), 427 (2013)
9. Barkaoui, K.: Teaching writing to second language learners: insights from theory and research. TESL Report. **40**, 14 (2007)
10. Junining, E.: A critique on giving feedback for English as a foreign language (EFL) students' writing. Asian J. Educ. E-Learn. **2**(1) (2014)
11. Zheng, Y., Yu, S.: Student engagement with teacher written corrective feedback in EFL writing: a case study of Chinese lower-proficiency students. Assess. Writ. **37**, 13–24 (2018)
12. Wulandari, Y.: Effective feedback to improve students' writing skills. Educalitra Engl. Educ. Linguist. Lit. J. **1**(1), 10–17 (2022)
13. Smith, S.: The genre of the end comment: conventions in teacher responses to student writing. Coll. Compos. Commun. **48**(2), 249–268 (1997)
14. Tack, A., Piech, C.: The AI teacher test: measuring the pedagogical ability of blender and GPT-3 in educational dialogues. arXiv preprint arXiv:2205.07540 (2022)
15. Ndukwe, I.G., Daniel, B.K., Amadi, C.E.: A machine learning grading system using chatbots. In: Isotani, S., Millán, E., Ogan, A., Hastings, P., McLaren, B., Luckin, R. (eds.) AIED 2019. LNCS (LNAI), Part II, vol. 11626, pp. 365–368. Springer, Cham (2019). https://doi.org/10.1007/978-3-030-23207-8_67

16. Qu, W.: Research on the application of automatic scoring system in college English writing. In: 2016 International Conference on Economics, Social Science, Arts, Education and Management Engineering, pp. 694–698. Atlantis Press, August 2016

Author Index

O. Gervasi et al. (Eds.): ICCSA 2023 Workshops, LNCS 14112, pp. 385–386, 2023.
https://doi.org/10.1007/978-3-031-37129-5

Printed in the United States
by Baker & Taylor Publisher Services